the Islanders *and the* Orb

The History of the
Harris Tweed Industry,
1835 - 1995

the ***Islanders*** *and the* ***Orb***

•

The History of the
Harris Tweed Industry,
1835 - 1995

•

JANET HUNTER

First published in Scotland in 2001
by Acair Ltd, 7 James Street,
Stornoway, Scotland. HS1 2QN

Tel: 01851 70 3020
Fax: 01851 70 3294
E-mail: acair@virginbiz.com
www.acairbooks.com

The publisher is grateful for financial assistance
from the Harris Tweed Authority
towards the publication of this volume.

A CIP catalogue record for this title is available from the British Library.

ISBN:
(pbk) 0 86152 736 4
(hbk) 0 86152 741 0

Cover and book design Margaret Anne MacLeod, Acair Ltd.
Printed by ColourBooks Ltd., Dublin

CONTENTS

CONTENTS

CONTENTS

CONTENTS

Acknowledgements

I am grateful to the following people for interviews granted and for their hospitality:

Ken Bartolomy, Kendibig; the late Charles Brander, Huntly; Bruce Burns, Stornoway; the late Miss Marion Campbell, Plocrapul; Mrs Myra Campbell, Norfolk; Mike Ferris, Stornoway; Cllr. Angus Graham, Back; Ian Lawrence, Mintlaw; Chris and Bill Lawson, Northton; Iain Macaskill, Inverness; Mrs Mary MacDonald, Sgarastamhòr; the late Mrs Kate Macdonald, Northton; Mrs Bella Macdonald, Perth; Miss Nora MacDonald, Drinishader; Iain Maciver, Stornoway; John MacKay, Horgabost; Maureen and Donald John Mackay, Luskentyre; Sheriff Colin Scott MacKenzie, Stornoway; Harris Mackenzie, Stornoway; A. Mackinnon, Tarbert; Garry Maclean, Garynahine; Callum Maclean, Knockaird; Donald MacLeod, Shawbost; Mal MacLeod, Lews Castle College; F. MacLeod, Luskentyre; Mrs Rachel MacLeod, Luskentyre; Kenny MacSween, Strond; Alex Morrison, Knockaird; Donald Morrison, Bragar; Murdo Morrison, Stornoway; Derek Murray, Shawbost; Murdo Murray, Back; Mrs Nancy Robertson, Dunblane; the late Robert Stewart, Stornoway; Frank Thompson, Stornoway.

Past and present members of staff at Acair have provided ongoing advice and support for which I thank them. They are: Joan Morrison, Heather Delday, Norma Macleod and Margaret Anne MacLeod. I am also grateful to very helpful librarians and archivists. They are: Susan Corrigall of the National Register of Archives in Edinburgh, Robert Steward, Highland Regional Archivist, Inverness, David Fowler and the staff at Western Isles Library, Liz Mackie and Linda Masson, Taylor Library, University of Aberdeen.

I am very grateful to my colleagues in the Department of Celtic in the University of Aberdeen: to Professor Donald Meek for his unfailing support and help; to Nancy McGuire, David Findlay and Alasdair Ross for help with indexing, referencing, citations of cases and proof-reading; to James Chalmers, Department of Law, for advice on citation of cases. I am particularly grateful to Professor Colm O Baoill for reading the manuscript at an early stage and correcting numerous inconsistencies and for his meticulous proof-reading.

I am very grateful to those lawyers who generously gave me specialised advice about the Court Cases which form part of the history of the Harris Tweed industry. Sir Charles Fraser gave me a helpful introduction to the complexities of the 'Harris Tweed case'. J. A. McLean of Burness, Edinburgh, kept a watching brief on the manuscript as it evolved and tactfully pointed out potential pitfalls. Judge David Edward guided me through the different stages of the litigation and Trade Mark law and then read the chapter on the litigation. I am most grateful to him for the help so willingly given. John MacAskill, a writer and retired lawyer with an interest in the Harris Tweed industry, kindly read the manuscript and suggested some improvements.

I was very fortunate to be able to draw on the extensive knowledge of the Harris Tweed industry which was generously made available to me by Angus MacLeod, Marybank, Stornoway and by the late James Shaw Grant. James Shaw Grant also read the final manuscript and his approval was very heartening. I have to thank Lady Anne Dunmore for making the Dunmore Family papers available to me. I am also grateful to her for lending the portrait of Catherine, Countess of Dunmore. John Murdo Morrison, Tarbert, kindly devoted his time and energy to tracking down information which I would not have found without his detective skills. He has also supplied a number of photographs for the book. I thank him for his interest and help. The wide knowledge of island history possessed by my brother, Sandy Matheson, Stornoway, provided a constant reference point, for which I thank him.

Members of the Board of Management of the Harris Tweed Authority have been patient and supportive throughout the long gestation of this book. I have to thank Dr. Calum MacLeod, past Chairman of the HTA, who asked me to write the book. I am particularly grateful to Duncan Martin, Chairman of the HTA, and to the late Donald John MacKay, ex-Chief Executive of the HTA, who gave me a great deal of their time and help. I have to thank Mary Macdonald and Calum MacAulay in the HTA Office for dealing patiently with my regular phone calls and queries. I am deeply indebted to Ian Angus Mackenzie, Chief Executive of the HTA, who has patiently advised and encouraged me. I am grateful that he never seemed to lose faith in my ability to finish the work.

Finally, I wish to thank my husband, Graham Hunter, for the legal expertise he provided and for his unfailing support and encouragement throughout the years it has taken to finish the book.

Abbreviations

AC - Appeal Case
C Sess - Court of Session
FTC - Federal Trade Commission
HC - House of Commons
HCA - Harris Crofters' Association
HIDB - Highlands and Islands Development Board
HIE - Highlands and Islands Enterprise
HL - House of Lords
HRA - Highland Regional Archive
HTA - Harris Tweed Association
(Harris Tweed Authority after 1993.)
IHTP - Independent Harris Tweed Producers
NASWM - National Association of Scottish Woollen Manufacturers
OH - Outer House
RPC - Reports of Patent, Design and Trade Mark Cases
RTSA - Retail Trading-Standards Association
SC - Session Cases
SLT - Scots Law Times
TGSI - Transactions of the Gaelic Society of Inverness
TGWU - Transport and General Workers' Union

Preface

It would be reasonable to assume that Mr Henry Lyons, a tailor in the City of London, was slightly apprehensive in the early days of August 1906. He was due to appear at the Thames Police Court on 10th August to answer a charge of fraud, a charge which had been instituted by the Board of Trade. The basis of the charge lay in the wording of the advertisements for Mr Lyons' so-called 'Harris Tweed suits made to order for 32/6d'.

> 'Our Harris Tweed suits cannot be beaten. The ordinary tailor's price is 55s. We have now made arrangements with the Highland peasants ...'[1]

Under cross examination, Mr Lyons admitted that the tweed used in the suits had in fact been produced at his mills in Huddersfield. Even at this dramatic point in the trial, the worst that Mr Lyons might have anticipated was a heavy fine. The magistrate, however, took a very serious view of what he deemed to be a clear case of fraud and accordingly sentenced Mr Lyons to two months imprisonment. Consternation seized the court at the enormity of the sentence. According to the *Daily Mail* reporter, the defendant, Mr Lyons 'fell down in a fit'.[2]

The case of the Board of Trade v. Henry Lyons created a considerable sensation in the national and regional press, including the Highland newspapers, as much for the severity of the sentence as for the fraud perpetrated. The *Daily Mail* of 11th August reported the defendant's dramatic reaction to the sentence. The *Daily News* emphasised the consequences of such fraudulent practices for the crofters of the Hebrides.

> 'A considerable trade is now done in the cloth, the price of Harris Tweed is high and it is difficult to get enough of it ... The matter affected very seriously the trade carried on by the crofters of the outlying islands of Scotland. One of these islands is named Harris, from which the tweed takes its name.'[3]

The eventual fate of Mr Lyons was not as serious as it appeared to be when sentence was passed. The Board of Trade, in instigating the prosecution, had simply been concerned to eradicate the type of fraudulent claims made in Lyons' advertisements. It had not expected the magistrate to impose a prison sentence on the perpetrator. On October 12th of that year the sentence was reduced on appeal to a fine of £20 and costs. [4]

The fraud perpetrated by Henry Lyons was neither the first nor the last example of such practices in the textile trade. Attempts to *pass off* various types of merchandise, usually, but not necessarily, inferior goods as something else, are legion and have given rise to extensive case law on the offence of passing off. One of the earliest recorded examples of legal action against the offence of passing off is interesting in relation to Harris Tweed. The action was decided in England in 1580 during the reign of Queen Elizabeth 1.

> 'An action upon the case was brought in the Common Pleas by a clothier, that whereas he had a great reputation for making of his cloth, and by reason whereof he had great utterance to his great benefit and profit, and that he used to set his mark to the cloth, whereby it should be known to be his cloth, and another clothier perceiving it, used the same mark to his ill-made cloth on purpose to deceive him, it was resolved that an action will lie.' [5]

The foundation of the modern law of passing off was laid in 1872, in a judgement which declared:

> 'A man is not to sell his own goods under the pretence that they are the goods of another man; he cannot be permitted to practise such a deception, nor to use the means which contribute to that end. He cannot therefore be allowed to use names, marks, letters, or other indicia, by which he may induce purchasers to believe that the goods which he is selling are the manufacture of another person.' [6]

The Henry Lyons incident illustrates one of the most frequent threats to the Harris Tweed industry throughout its history. *Passing off*, or imitation of the genuine article by unscrupulous manufacturers outwith the Hebrides, has always been a major threat. When the industry moved out of its first phase as a small cottage industry, a second threat to its security came from those who allowed inferior cloth to be sold as 'Harris Tweed', in order to meet the demand for increased production. If either imitation Harris Tweed, or inferior quality Harris Tweed, had been allowed to flood the textile market, the genuine article would have suffered and a vital source of income for the people of the Outer Hebrides would have been lost. In 1909 the Harris Tweed Association was formed to safeguard the industry, firstly from those who would pass off an imitation product as 'Harris Tweed', and secondly, from those who would erode the standards of production. If either imitation or inferior production had gone unchallenged, the name 'Harris Tweed' would rapidly have had no more relevance to the Island of Harris than Cheddar cheese now has to the Cheddar district of Somerset, or the Witney blanket to the market town of Witney in Oxfordshire. In other words the name 'Harris Tweed' would have become no more than a generic term.

While much of this book deals with the efforts to protect the reputation of Harris Tweed and promote its sale in home and foreign markets, a human interest will be found in the inevitable tensions which arose from time to time between different interest groups within the industry. These conflicts reflect the fact that production of Harris Tweed was a vital and integral part of Island life for over a century. Families and communities prospered in the good years and, equally, they suffered during the lean years. While not quite the Biblical pattern of seven prosperous years followed by seven years of famine, a cyclical pattern of intensive production followed by a few slack years seems to have held sway throughout most of the twentieth century. Each period of slump was followed by new sales records when Harris Tweed reasserted its leading role in the textile world. That pattern seems to have faltered towards the end of the century as slack periods became longer and periods of recovery failed to reach the high points of earlier years.

In 1993 the Harris Tweed industry entered a new phase with the passing of an Act of Parliament which brought into being the Harris Tweed Authority. This new statutory body, which replaced the old Harris Tweed Association set up in 1909, was charged with responsibility for 'promoting and maintaining the authenticity, standard and reputation of Harris Tweed'. The passing of the Act and the creation of the Harris Tweed Authority marked a new relationship between national government, local government and the industry. The statutory role of the Harris Tweed Authority means that it will be in a position to protect the industry in Britain and in wider world markets more effectively than a voluntary association, such as the original Harris Tweed Association, could do.

Not long after it came into being, the Harris Tweed Authority decided that, at this new juncture in the history of the industry, there should be a permanent and comprehensive record made of the history of the industry from its beginnings in the mid-nineteenth century to the passing of the Harris Tweed Act in 1993. This is the remit which this book will strive to fulfil.

Preface

1 Gwatkin, 'Notes on the Historical Development of the Harris Tweed Industry and the Part Played by the Harris Tweed Association Ltd.'
[hereafter: Gwatkin 'The Harris Tweed Industry'], 9, HTA Office Stornoway.

2 *Daily Mail*, 11. 8. 1906.

3 *Daily News*, 1. 8. 1906.

4 Gwatkin, The Harris Tweed Industry, 9.

5 J. Drysdale and M. Silverleaf, *Passing off: law and practice*.

6 *ibid.*, 9.

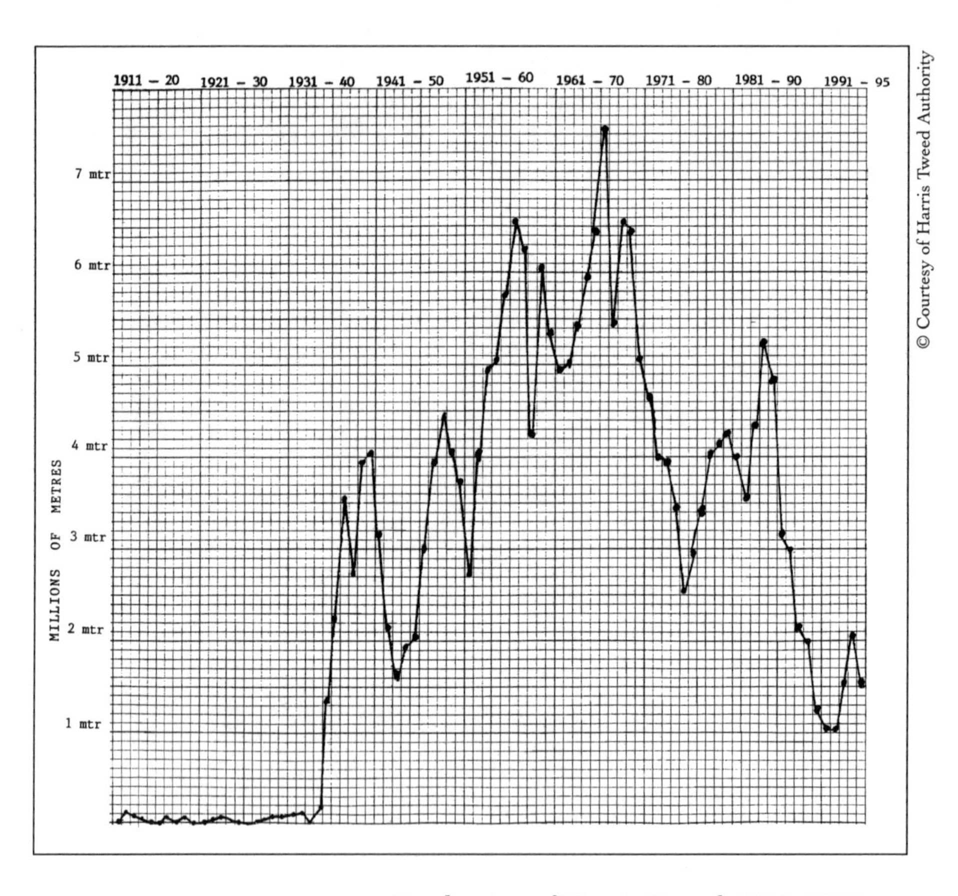

Production of Harris Tweed, 1911-1995.

1

The Historical Background to Harris Tweed

As had been part of the normal way of life in rural communities from time immemorial, the people of the Outer Hebrides wove cloth for the needs of their families from the wool of their own sheep. Perhaps the only exceptional feature about this cloth in the pre-industrial age was that the cloth woven in Harris was noted for the tasteful combination of colours used by these home weavers.

The development of the Harris Tweed industry has to be seen in the context of events elsewhere in Scotland and in the wider world. As the Industrial Revolution spread to the Highlands, the old subsistence lifestyle by which people met all their material needs from the produce of the land and sea, began to change. The events which contributed to these changes also contributed to the introduction of the Harris Tweed industry which, perhaps with the exception of fishing, was to become the economic mainstay of Harris and Lewis, and to a considerably lesser extent, of the rest of the Outer Hebrides.

Until approximately the middle of the 18th century, small tenants had paid their rents in both cash and produce, and this included woven 'plaids'. By the beginning of the nineteenth century, small tenants throughout the Highlands and Islands were being moved off the better land to new townships on the coasts in order to allow the landowners to create sheep farms or make a substantial profit from the booming markets in kelp. Cash rents were demanded for the new crofts and the income to pay the rent was expected to come from employment in one of the ancillary industries on the estate. Of necessity, the traditional subsistence economy gradually gave way to one based on the payment of rents in hard cash.

Harris, which had been part of the estate of MacLeod of Harris and Dunvegan, was among the first of the Hebrides to feel the cold wind of change in the 18th century. The rental for Harris increased by almost 70% between 1735 and 1754 and by a further 50% by 1769. [1] Because the Dunvegan estate was heavily in debt, Harris was sold in 1779 for £15,000 to Captain Alexander MacLeod, a son of Donald MacLeod of Berneray, one of the major tacksmen in Harris. [2] Captain Alexander spent freely in his attempts to develop a fishing industry in

Harris. He also 'established a factory for spinning woollen thread'.[3] Captain Alexander's son, Alexander Hume MacLeod, inherited Harris in 1790 and embarked on a policy of doubling rents and exploiting the profits to be made from kelp, a product much in demand during the wars with France. The small tenants, who made up the seasonal workforce, came to depend on the cash income from kelping to pay the increased rent. The use of kelp as a fertiliser for crops was forbidden. Cultivation of cereal crops declined in favour of the potato which provided a much better return than cereals in the wet and windy climate of the Hebrides. To this day, the lazybeds in which the potatoes were planted can be traced wending their way through the rocks or up the hillsides. Nobody seems to have anticipated that kelp might not always be needed, or that the potato crop might fail. Yet, the harsh lesson of the folly of depending on one industry and one crop to maintain an increasing population was, by the opening of the nineteenth century, just one generation away.

When the kelp boom collapsed at the end of the Napoleonic War in 1815, the workforce on all the kelping estates became redundant. There were few alternative sources of employment. Without a cash income, tenants slipped into arrears of rent and increasing destitution. At the same time, the population of the Hebrides was rising inexorably, possibly because of the better diet afforded by increasing use of the potato, possibly because of the introduction of vaccination against smallpox, or possibly because it had suited landowners to retain a large population to work in the kelp industry. Between 1755 and 1831, the population of Harris rose by 98%, Lewis by 127%, North Uist by 141% and South Uist by 211%, and that increase was in spite of significant emigration over the period.[4]

As kelp went into decline, it was inevitable that proprietors and Factors would seek an alternative source of estate income. Commercial sheep farming, which had been spreading throughout the mainland Highlands from the closing years of the 18th century, now gained pace in the Hebrides. Unfortunately for the tenants of small jointly held farms and for the cottars on the arable machair of the islands, commercial sheep farming was deemed, as it had been in the mainland Highlands, to be incompatible with their continued presence on the land. Commercial sheep farmers could and did pay a good rent. They insisted on the maximum amount of grazing to make their farms commercially viable. The small tenants, who from time immemorial had lived on the good arable land, had served their purpose in the kelp boom. In their increasing poverty after the decline in kelping, they had become a liability to the estate, a liability which had to be removed.

Under Alexander Norman MacLeod, who succeeded his father, Alexander Hume MacLeod, in 1811, the whole of North Harris from Hushinish to Kinlochresort and Cliasmol was cleared for a sheep farm. Horgabost was let as a sheep farm to an Alexander Torrie from Argyll. James Hogg, the Ettrick Shepherd, was interested in taking Luskentyre, which eventually went to Donald Stewart, who was to become one of the most infamous Factors in the history of Harris. In 1818, while Alexander Norman MacLeod was in residence at his house in Rodel, that village was cleared in particularly harsh circumstances.[5] In 1828, 'ten crofts and four half crofts in Scarista Bheag and fourteen crofts in Scarista Mhòr' were cleared.[6] Some of these people went to Cape Breton, others to the Bays on the rocky east coast of Harris, and others cannot now be traced.[7] Despite the income from these sheep farms, Alexander Norman MacLeod was bankrupt by 1830. In 1834, Harris was sold to the Earl of Dunmore. In that year the debts secured on the Harris estate were nearly £27,000 in excess of the price of £60,210 for which it was sold.[8]

A similar pattern of economic decline and change of ownership took place in Lewis, the Uists and Barra. Mrs Mary Stewart-MacKenzie (perhaps better known as Lady Mary Hood, the young widow of Sir Samuel Hood) had inherited Lewis from her late father Lord Seaforth in 1814. Despite Lady Mary's marriage in 1817 to the Hon. James Stewart-MacKenzie of Glasserton, neither she nor her husband could pay off the debts inherited from Lord Seaforth. Lewis was sold to Mr James Matheson of Achany in 1844. In 1838 MacNeill of Barra sold his estate to Lieut.-Colonel John Gordon of Cluny, who in 1839, acquired considerable portions of the Clanranald estates in South Uist and Benbecula. The harsh treatment of tenants on the estates owned by Gordon of Cluny earned this particular landowner the censure of both Sir Edward Pine Coffin and the immigration authorities in Quebec during the Potato Famine of 1846 to 1851. In 1856, Lord MacDonald sold his North Uist estate to a Sir John Powlett Orde, whose successors sold off parts of the North Uist estates over the following fifty years.

Unlike the old hereditary proprietors the new proprietors had money. Ownership of a Highland estate was becoming fashionable and this fashion was endorsed by Queen Victoria's purchase of Balmoral in 1848. The pastimes of hunting and fishing pursued by these proprietors gave rise to the use of the term 'ghillie', the Gaelic word for 'boy', which in itself suggests a condescending and colonialist attitude to the status of those they employed to protect their salmon and deer and to row their boats. In the management of their Highland estates the proprietors did not usually concern themselves with the mundane day-to-day business of collecting rents, selling produce, deciding who should be evicted for falling into arrears of rent, or, as in the example of Sir James Matheson and the Bernera tenants, even which common grazings should be annexed to make way for a deer forest. Responsibility for estate management seems to have been left largely to the Factors or 'chamberlains' as they were then called. For the greater part of the year proprietors were absent from their estates or even did not visit the estate for years on end. It was left to the Factor to be as despotic, or benevolent, as his nature inclined. It is clear from both the oral tradition and a significant range of documentary evidence that in the nineteenth-century Highlands, Factors were generally feared, and in some instances loathed, for the way in which they treated the tenants under their control.

Evidence given to the Napier Commission of 1883 reveals the reputation in Harris of the Factor, Donald Stewart, who set about acquiring all the best farms in Harris for himself and his nephew, Alexander MacRae. [9] John R. MacDonald, *Am Bàillidh Dòmhnallach*, one of Dunmore's Factors in Harris, did not win such public opprobrium as Donald Munro in Lewis, but he too was hated by the Harris tenants for the tyranny and petty spite he exercised in his dealings with them. [10] John Murdoch, the Highland Land Law campaigner described the tenants' 'state of slavish fear' of the Factor in South Uist in the time of Lady Emily Gordon Cathcart, daughter-in-law of Colonel Gordon of Cluny. [11]

Duncan Shaw, who had been appointed estate Factor when the Earl of Dunmore bought Harris, earned adverse publicity in the Scottish press when he called in the army to assist in the clearance of Borve in order to enable Donald Stewart to extend his farm from Luskentyre to Scarista. Giving evidence to the Select Committee on Emigration in 1841, Shaw showed himself as capable as any modern spin-doctor of putting a favourable gloss on his actions.

> ' ... constant disputes occurred between the tenant of the surrounding land and the crofters (the tenant being Donald Stewart of Luskentyre). They were miserably poor; payment of rent except by labour was out of the question; they were much in arrears, even for the price of meal annually imported. The tenant of the large farm refused to renew his lease if Borve were not included in it. The proprietor could not afford to lose so good a tenant ... paying £600 a year. ... Such of them as from age or other infirmities were unfit subjects for emigration were offered better lands elsewhere in Harris ... ' [12]

'Better land elsewhere in Harris' meant land in the Bays district on the east coast where, as anyone who knows the island can testify, a thin layer of acid soil barely covers the rockiest terrain anywhere in the island.

The *Glasgow Chronicle* of July 1839 [13] describes the consequences of the deforcement when the people of Borve tore up the notices to quit and refused to be moved:

> '... five men who had been most active in the illegal proceedings were selected and carried prisoners to Portree. The visit of the military excited the deepest alarm among the poor islanders, who were heard to express in Gaelic their terror that the scene of Glencoe was about to be acted over again.'

Whether or not Alexander, Earl of Dunmore, knew of this incident is now impossible to ascertain. For his Factor, Duncan Shaw, to suggest that the Bays offered better land than Borve was palpably untrue. The fact that the tenants of Borve were in arrears reflects the increasing poverty of the ordinary people in Harris. The harvests of 1836-37 had been particularly bad. Potatoes had failed to such an extent that, with hindsight, those years can be seen as a foretaste of the Potato Famine of 1846-51. Was this then the time at which, according to her son, the Countess of Dunmore started buying tweeds to be sold in London or was it 1844 as tradition maintains, or did this enterprise start in 1851 just after the famine?

Whichever date is correct, it does seem ironic that just as the commercial weaving of tweed was being introduced to the Island of Harris as a cottage industry, the textile industry elsewhere in Scotland had largely abandoned its cottage industry status and become mechanised, albeit in mills which were, at least in their first stages, small family businesses. The textile industry had played a key role in the Scottish Industrial Revolution with the introduction of the flying shuttle to Galashiels in 1788. By 1839, with trivial exceptions, all of the weaving trade in Galashiels was performed in factories and many weavers elsewhere who owned their own looms worked in loom-shops. [14] Broadcloth manufactured in Aberdeenshire and the Borders had established a good reputation in England by the early decades of the 19th century and by 1825 some 24,800 people in Scotland were producing woollen goods to the estimated value of £450,000. [15]

It is claimed that the word 'tweed' came into use by mistake around 1832, when a Borders firm, Messrs William Watson and Son, of Hawick, sent a quantity of 'tweels' to Mr James Locke, one of the earliest London merchants to deal in Scottish tweeds. 'Tweel' is defined in the Concise Scots Dictionary as a local dialect form of 'twill', which is 'a diagonally-ribbed cloth produced by passing the weft threads over one and under two or more warp threads'. Rather than go into the technical differences between tweeds and twills, it should be sufficient to know that not all tweeds are woven like twills, although most tweeds contain an element of twill in their weaving. (Explanation from HTA spokesman) In the invoice the word 'tweel' was written so indistinctly that it was read as 'tweed'. The designation appealed to Mr Locke who recognised the marketing possibility of cashing in on the association between the Scottish Borders, the River Tweed and the popularity of Sir Walter Scott. The Border tweeds were originally produced in the dull colours of drab blue and grey, but in time this fashion palled. Sir Walter Scott, while Sheriff of Selkirkshire, gave a boost to the flagging Borders industry by having a pair of trousers made in a checked plaid thus setting a new and significant fashion. [16]

The story of Sir Walter's boost to the Border tweed industry may be apocryphal, but his role in starting the 19th-century craze for tartan is well-attested and it was this fashion, adopted by the gentry, which was eventually to have a seminal role in the beginnings of the Harris Tweed industry. Thanks to Sir Walter's romanticisation of things Highland and his participation in 1822 in the City of Edinburgh's reception for George 1V, aspiring Scottish gentry became obsessed by the 'tartan cult'. By the early 1840s, landowners were decking out their employees in so-called 'Estate Tweeds' which gave a perceived touch of class to the Estate entourage of those who had no claim to a family tartan. These Estate tweeds, which mimicked the setts of tartan, incidentally provided the stalkers and ghillies with an effective camouflage when out on the hill.

George Murray, 5th Earl of Dunmore, the new proprietor of Harris, had no need to invent a clan tartan for his ghillies. The traditional story about the origin of the Harris Tweed industry claims that in approximately 1840, the Earl of Dunmore ordered tweed to be woven locally in the Murray tartan for his Harris retainers. If this is true, he was surely one of the first to set a fashion which was to be followed over the decade by sundry landowners and tenants and which achieved the Royal seal of approval when Prince Albert himself designed the Balmoral tartan in 1853. According to local tradition that order for Murray tartan tweed made in Harris proved to be such a success that friends of the Dunmore family willingly placed orders for tweeds and thus began the Harris Tweed industry. This is the story as it has been passed down the generations. It will be worth looking at this version in more depth before accepting it completely at its face value.

Whether this version of the story is fact or fiction, there is no doubt that demand for Harris Tweed had become well-established by the 1880s and continued to gain favour with the buying public and the textile merchants of Edinburgh and London as the new century dawned. From its introduction to these national markets demand for the product was based primarily on its reputation as a warm, hard-wearing, yet flexible cloth, more or less impervious to rain. It was particularly suitable for gentlemen engaged in the outdoor sports associated with the Highlands, climbing, hill-walking and of course shooting and fishing, and, as time went on, the market extended to include golfers, riders and cyclists.[17] This established expectation of high quality explains why poorly woven tweed, or tweed containing fibres other than wool, when passed off as Harris Tweed, endangered the reputation of and the market for the genuine article.

The second important selling point for Harris Tweed, a selling point which was promoted enthusiastically by the gentry associated with the early days of the industry, was based on a wish to benefit the 'very poor people of the outlying islands of Scotland', as the *Daily News* reporter at the Henry Lyons trial explained. A strange juxtaposition of romanticised benevolence and hard-headed, some might say hard-hearted, indifference to much that was happening in the Highlands seems to have characterised many of those whose leisure activities made them familiar with the area.

A third incentive to buying Harris Tweed made itself felt in the latter part of the nineteenth century at a time when a number of benevolent agencies had become involved in the marketing of tweed produced on Highland estates. It can scarcely be coincidental that the establishment of agencies such as the Scottish Home Industries Association and the Highland Home Industries and Arts Association, both established in 1889, should have been created relatively soon after the founding in 1884 of Ruskin's Home Arts and Industries Association. Even the similarity of the names points to a link and the stated objectives of the founders of the Highland Home Industries and Arts Association confirm the similarity of the underlying philosophy.

John Ruskin, a 19th-century writer, philosopher and academic, had been publishing essays on ethics, education and philanthropy from 1862. His teaching laid great emphasis on the superiority of the hand-made artefact, particularly that of hand-spun and hand-woven textiles, for which he maintained 'only the well-wisher's custom is asked, not his charity'. [18] Ruskin saw an intrinsic value in a hand-made product which reflected something of the life and soul of the worker. Although his railing against mechanisation was seen by contemporary industrialists as perverse at a time when machine-made products were cheaper and of more consistent quality than their hand-made equivalents, there were some who were persuaded that the hand-made product did have an innate value which made it worth paying more for than for its mass-produced counterpart. By 1884, Ruskin's teaching had been sufficiently accepted to enable him to form 'The Home Arts and Industries Association' which attracted over the ensuing years a significant number of affiliated societies in England and Wales.

These three early reasons for buying Harris Tweed have retained their validity until the end of the twentieth century. Genuine Harris Tweed has always enjoyed a reputation for high quality. The Outer Hebrides are seen as a homeland by many exiles, a Gaelic heartland, a place around which a romantic aura still lingers. The link between the cloth and the Hebrides stirs the imagination of buyers from all parts of the world. The cachet which a craft-made product enjoys over the mass-produced item is something that those wearing Harris Tweed are still at pains to emphasise. Much of the history of the industry throughout the twentieth century is concerned with the battle to safeguard those attributes of Harris Tweed as it took its place in an increasingly competitive textile market.

I met a man in Harris Tweed
As I walked down the Strand;
I turned and followed him like a dog
The breath of hill and sea and bog
That clung about that coat of brown,
And suddenly, in London Town,
I heard again the Gaelic speech,
The scrunch of keel on shingly beach;
The traffic's never-ending roar
Come plangent from a shining shore;
I saw the little lochs where lie
The lilies, white as ivory;
And tumbling down the rocky hills
Came scores of little foaming rills,
I saw the crofter bait his line,
The children herding yellow kine,
The barefoot woman with her creel,
The washing-pot, the spinning wheel,
The mounds thrown up by patient toil
To coax the corn from barren soil.
With buoyant step I went along
Whistling a Hebridean song
That Iain Og of Taransay
Sang one enchanted day.
I was a man renewed indeed
Because I smelt that Harris Tweed
As I went down the Strand.

These lines may not be great poetry but they typify the romantic view of the Hebrides and Harris Tweed.

Reference - The Historical Background to Harris Tweed

1 A. Morrison, 'Harris Estate Papers, 1724-54,' *Transactions of the Gaelic Society of Inverness*, XLV, 36-37.
2 W. C. MacKenzie, *History of the Outer Hebrides*, [hereafter: MacKenzie Outer Hebrides], 485.
3 J. Knox, *Tour through the Highlands of Scotland, and the Hebride Isles*, 158-9, quoted in MacKenzie, *Outer Hebrides*, 485.
4 *Report to the Board of Agriculture for Scotland on Home Industries in the Highlands and Islands in 1914* [hereafter: 'Scott Report, 1914'], 28.
5 Evidence from Donald MacDonald, Grosebay to the Napier Commission, quoted in Lawson, *St. Clement's Church at Rodel* [hereafter: Lawson, '*St Clement's*'], 30.
6 Lawson, *St Clement's*, 31.
7 Lawson, *TheTeampull at Northton and the Church at Scarista*, [hereafter: *Northton and Scarista*], 30.
8 MacKenzie, *Outer Hebrides*, 495.
9 Evidence from John MacLeod (Iain Fìdhleir) to the Napier Commission, quoted in Lawson, *St Clement's*.
10 Lawson, *Harris Families and How to Trace Them*, 12 and 14.
11 Hunter, *For the People's Cause: The Writings of John Murdoch*, 30.
12 Evidence from Duncan Shaw to the Select Committee on Emigration, 1841, quoted in Lawson, *Northton and Scarista*, 33-35.
13 *Glasgow Chronicle*, July 1839, quoted in Lawson, *Northton and Scarista*, 35.
14 N. Murray, *The Scottish Handloom Weavers*, 1790-1850: a social history, 3.
15 D. Bremner, *The Industries of Scotland: their Rise, Progress and Present Condition*, 155.
16 *ibid.*, 156.
17 *The Queen*, June 4th, 1898.
18 Ruskin, *The Works of John Ruskin*, 13 vols.

2

The Dunmore Family and Harris

Much of the writing on the history of Harris Tweed is peppered with references to 'the Earl of Dunmore' as if there had been only one Earl of Dunmore. There were, in fact, four Earls of Dunmore who were proprietors of Harris between 1834 and 1919 when the last part of the Dunmore estate in South Harris was sold to Lord Leverhulme.

Dunmore, a small village in the parish of Airth, in Stirlingshire, was the chief Scottish seat of the Earls of Dunmore. The village of Dunmore stands on the south bank of the Firth of Forth about 8 miles south-east of Stirling. The Earldom of Dunmore was created in 1686 for Lord Charles Murray, younger son of the Marquis of Atholl, as Master of Horse to Queen Mary, wife of James II. The Earldom of Atholl, a district in the north of Perthshire, was held by the Murray family. Thus the Dunmore family was an integral part of the Scottish peerage and the British establishment.

In 1834, George Murray, 5th Earl of Dunmore, bought Harris from the bankrupt proprietor, Alexander Norman MacLeod. This Earl of Dunmore, who was married to Susan, a daughter of the Duke of Hamilton, owned Harris for only two years before his death on 11th November 1836. He was succeeded by his son, Alexander, the 6th Earl (1804-1845), who was thirty-two when he inherited Harris. Alexander's wife was Catherine Herbert, a daughter of the Earl of Pembroke and his Russian wife, Countess Woronzow. [1] It may be that Catherine inherited from her mother the creative talent she was to display in drawing designs for the Embroidery School she set up in Harris in 1849 and in the Dunmore Pottery she established in Stirlingshire. However, Catherine Herbert, Countess of Dunmore, is remembered with affection in Harris for the important role she played in encouraging the Harris Tweed industry and for her restoration of St Clement's church at Rodel.

Tragedy struck the Dunmore family in 1845, when Alexander, the 6th Earl, died aged 41. Catherine, his wife, was left a widow with four young children, Susan, Alexandrina, Constance and an only son, Charles Adolphus, who was only four at the time of his father's death. Catherine's letters to her factor in Harris suggest that she enjoyed coming to the island with her children, but that on various occasions she could not subject them to the arduous journey because one or other of the children had been ill. When she did come, she was anxious that her employees should not be put to too much trouble. Like many visitors since, she went home with fresh eggs wrapped up in her luggage. On one unfortunate occasion the suitcase got lost in transit, no doubt to the detriment of the fresh eggs. On Catherine's death, her daughter replied to a letter of sympathy from the then factor in Harris, urging him to see to the building of roads to the Bays, as that would have been her mother's wish. [2]

Until Charles reached adulthood, his mother seems to have acted as Tutor, that is she made a proprietor's decisions about Harris, on behalf of her son. Whether Alexander, the 6th Earl of Dunmore had begun to promote the making of Harris Tweed just before his death in 1845, and his widow Catherine continued this enterprise on her own, or whether she initiated it at some time between approximately 1840 and 1851, or even as early as 1839, is difficult to decide as there are conflicting versions of the story. However, as her Embroidery School was established there in 1849, it does seem likely that she was actively involved in Harris by that date.

If one were to ask in Harris or Lewis today about the beginnings of the Harris Tweed industry, one would be told with unswerving confidence that in 1844 Lord Dunmore ordered tweed to be woven in the Murray tartan and this tweed was used as a uniform for his keepers and ghillies on the Harris Estate. This traditional version of the story goes on to claim that two sisters from Strond in South Harris, who came to be known as 'the Paisley sisters', were sent to Paisley to learn improved weaving techniques. The Murray tartan Harris Tweed was such a success that Lady Dunmore saw its potential as a source of income for the local people and that is how the industry began.

The site of the Paisley sisters' black house in Strond can still be identified by local people and some versions of the story claim that the sisters came from Pabbay. The story has been repeated in this form in most written accounts of the industry, in official surveys, in advertising material and in books and articles. It has been repeated so often that it has gained a sanctity which one hesitates to question. It is likely that the bones of this version of the story derive largely from an article written in 1895 in *Ealadhna Dùthchasach na h-Alba*, a publication by the Scottish Home Industries Association. It was repeated in its essential details in 1914 in the authoritative Scott *Report on Home Industries in the Highlands and Islands to the Board of Agriculture for Scotland*, thereby gaining credence among social researchers beyond the islands. The story thus existed in the oral tradition in which it continued to accumulate accretions which have seldom been questioned and in various published sources which lent an aura of authority to the oral tradition.

Let us examine what can be firmly established about the Paisley sisters in the first instance. Bill Lawson (a genealogist and local historian based at the *Cò Leis Thu?* genealogy centre in Northton in Harris) has drawn on estate rentals, census returns, parish registers and on the fund of genealogical knowledge still extant in the local oral tradition to produce a comprehensive record of all families in the Western Isles for the last two centuries. Mr Lawson's research shows that the family to which the Paisley sisters belonged - Norman MacLeod, his wife, Christina MacSween, and three daughters, Marion, Christina and Mary, lived in Lingerbay at the time of the 1841 Census. Mary was in Pabbay in 1841, married to an Alexander Morrison. In the 1851 census, the mother and two daughters, Marion and Christina were in Strond, and Mary was still in Pabbay. There is no record of the father, Norman MacLeod, in the census of 1851. He may have died by then, or he may have been away from home at seasonal employment. Mrs Campbell, *Bean Shrannda*, as she was known in Gaelic, the tenant of the tack of Strond and Killegray, on whose land the family were living in 1851, was known to have given small plots to people who had been cleared from other communities in South Harris. These people did not have crofts, simply small potato patches. The 1851 census lists shoemakers and 'weaveresses' among the population of Strond. [3]

Marion (1821-1880) and Christina (1826-1893) would have been very young women of twenty-three and eighteen respectively if, as tradition maintains, Lord Dunmore started the industry in 1844 and arranged for their training at that early stage of the enterprise. Travel to the mainland was not as unthinkable as one might suppose for young Island women, although their ability to communicate in English must be open to question. Within ten years of 1844, large numbers of young women from the Hebrides were moving round the Scottish fishing ports as gutters during the herring boom of the second part of the 19th century. Admittedly the gutters worked in groups with other Gaelic-speaking girls and the need to understand English may not have been too pressing. If the training of the Paisley sisters took place after a first visit of the Countess of Dunmore to Harris in 1851, as another version of the story suggests, they would not have been exceptional in moving temporarily to Paisley, but their ability to speak English would still have been a potential difficulty. Some sources name Alloa rather than Paisley as the centre to which the Paisley sisters were sent for training and this would have been closer to the Dunmore family home in Stirlingshire. Further evidence in support of Alloa comes from an article contributed to an undated brochure published by the Harris Council of Social Services in which the late John MacLean of Leverburgh stated that his grandmother was one of the women sent to Alloa by Lady Dunmore. No more of the career of the Paisley sisters has been documented, although the article in a Scottish Home Industries publication does make an oblique reference without identifying individuals, to training of local people in improved methods of weaving.

There are incidental references to the Countess of Dunmore and Harris Tweed in the evidence given to the Napier Commission in 1884, by Rev Roderick Mackenzie, and by Kenneth Macdonald, Scaristavore, but no dates or specific details are given there. The Rev. Roderick Mackenzie, Free Church minister in Tarbert, told the Napier Commission in 1883 that were it not for the efforts of Mrs Thomas in encouraging the making of webs and stockings, destitution would be of more frequent occurrence than it was. (Mrs 'Captain Thomas', as she was known locally, spent some time in Harris while her husband, Captain Thomas, conducted a survey on behalf of the Admiralty.) Mr MacKenzie went on to claim that the people derived the greater part of their living from these industries as they had been more remunerative than both the land and fishing in the preceding three years. [4] He felt that Harris owed more to Mrs Thomas than to anybody else, but he was corrected, with a degree of asperity, not to say triumph, by the next witness, Kenneth MacDonald, the seventy-year-old Factor for North Harris and tenant of the farm of Scaristavore in South Harris, who said that 'the Countess Dowager was manufacturing webs before Mrs Captain Thomas was known in this part of the world'. [5] Kenneth MacDonald, Coinneach Sgoilear, had been Assistant Factor in 1847 when the whole of Harris belonged to the Dunmores and would have known the facts about the family better than the Free Church minister in Tarbert who, in 1883, was a mere youngster of forty-five.

The earliest published version of the beginnings of Harris Tweed is to be found in the booklet entitled *Ealadhna Dùthchasach na h-Alba,* published by the Scottish Home Industries in 1895. The account of the industry was written by a 'Mrs S. MacDonald' who claimed personal knowledge of the Countess's work in Harris. This is the source used in the Scott *Report to the Board of Agriculture for Scotland on Home Industries in the Highlands and Islands in 1914.*[6]

Because Mrs MacDonald's story in the Scottish Home Industries booklet has been the basis for subsequent versions it is worth quoting the most significant parts of what she wrote.

> 'It was not till the year 1844 that the people of Harris were shown how they might develop powers of earning money and getting a market for their goods by a new manufacture, for it was then that the late Earl of Dunmore (proprietor of the whole of Harris) sent a pattern of the Murray tartan to be copied in 'tweed', when webs of this material were so successfully made that Lord Dunmore not only used it for his keepers, ghillies, and other retainers, but adopted it for his own wear. It was then that his noble wife, Catherine, Countess of Dunmore, began to devote her splendid energies to teaching the people how best to help themselves by disposing of the products of their labour - a lesson much needed at that time of difficulty when the failure of the potato crop was causing great and widespread distress. Lady Dunmore promptly established an extensive connection with leading tradesmen in Edinburgh and London, and hundreds of pounds were paid quarterly or half-yearly to the workers. It was not till the year 1851 that she visited the island, but she afterwards very frequently went there, stimulating the workers by her presence to yet greater efforts in the new industries. Orders increased and prices rose as the cloth improved in texture and pattern and she never wearied in her labours till her death, which lamentable event took place in February 1886. She is gone to the great loss of the people of Harris! The writer can never forget her beautiful countenance, as she smilingly met the workers, who came flocking to Rodil House to receive payment from her own hands, and listened with untiring sympathy as they told her of their various needs and of their love and gratitude. Some ladies, wishing to buy direct, having found that the present writer would forward

the Harris products when applied for, now send orders for the stuffs required ... The people are not making less cloth since they lost their benefactress, but they sell it to less profit; for, when needing the necessaries of life, they will accept low prices from dealers, who, in their turn have to part with the goods at a low rate to the great city dealers, in order to cover their own expenses. This has reduced the price per yard below its true value. From 3s 6d to 3s 9d per yard is not too much to give the workers, for tweeds so durable. This price, even barely allows the workers 6d per day for wages.' [7]

The words 'These industries' refer to the making of tweed, the Embroidery School which has already been mentioned, and the less well-known industry of stocking-making, started in 1857 by the late Countess of Dunmore and Mrs Thomas. In the Embroidery School, local women were taught how to embroider cambric for trousseaux and layettes. Mrs MacDonald tells how Lady Dunmore sent an embroidery teacher to the island, paid her salary and built a house as a workroom and residence for the teacher. Apparently the industry ceased when there was no one 'to trace out the delicate, intricate patterns, which used to be drawn entirely by one honoured hand, without aid from any of the labour-saving appliances of the present day'. [8]

The 'one honoured hand' was, presumably, that of the Countess herself, rather than that of the teacher.

There is much of interest in this story, particularly the statement that Lady Dunmore did not visit Harris until 1851. Mrs MacDonald was writing at that transitional stage in the industry when it was moving from being solely dependent on the patronage of the landed gentry to a closer dependence on the ability of the local merchants to act as intermediaries with merchants in the cities. The identity of 'Mrs S. MacDonald', if it could be ascertained, would help us to assess the reliability of what she said. The polished style points to someone totally fluent in English and with more than an elementary education. The tone and content of the account suggest a person resident in Harris for long enough in the year to be responsible for taking and dispatching orders for tweed. The Scottish Home Industries Association must have been aware of this involvement when they commissioned an account of the industry from Mrs MacDonald. Looking at the Harris census for the relevant period, it is likely that the author of the account was Mrs Sarah MacDonald, wife

Catherine, Dowager Countess of Dunmore, widow of Alexander, 6th Earl of Dunmore.

Charles, 7th Earl
of Dunmore.

Gertrude, Countess of Dunmore,
wife of Charles, 7th Earl of Dunmore.

Amhuinnsuidhe Castle built for Charles, Earl of Dunmore c.1866.
The castle was sold with North Harris Estate to Sir Edward Scott, c.1868.

A typical home of the small tenants who produced Harris Tweed in the Hebrides during the 19th century.

Preparing raw wool,
end of 19th century,
early 20th century.

Carding and spinning by hand.

Allan MacKenzie's water-powered carding mill at Lòn na Fèille, Direcleit, Harris.

of Roderick MacDonald (1824-1909), farmer at Kyles (Caolas) and Northton. Roderick MacDonald married a Sarah Grant (1841-1912) of Grantown-on-Spey, in Forres in 1868. [9] If Mrs Sarah MacDonald was the author of the piece she would have had, as a tacksman's wife, sufficient social status to be present at 'Rodil House' and observe Lady Dunmore in her dealings with the people. She would also have had the opportunity of learning at first hand from her husband about events in Harris before she came there in person in 1868. Some details, such as the picture of the Countess listening sympathetically to the concerns of the workers who came to receive payment for tweeds, are not convincing when we remember that few, if any, of these people could speak enough English to explain their concerns. Was Mrs MacDonald perhaps gilding the lily when she described the reticent people of Harris 'expressing their love and gratitude' to the Countess? And if she gilded one lily did she gild a few others as well?

It is somewhat difficult to reconcile the known facts of the death of the 6th Earl of Dunmore in 1845 and his widow's absence from Harris until 1851 with much expansion of the industry between 1844 and 1851. Any significant income from the making of Harris Tweed is also hard to imagine when one knows the circumstances of the Harris people during the Potato Famine of 1846 till at least 1851.

An application was made in 1847 on behalf of the Countess of Dunmore for Government assistance under the Drainage Act and £500 was granted to provide employment for people so that they could buy meal. By 1850, with the famine still continuing, it is clear that the poorest in the community were suffering extreme deprivation. A detailed account of the situation was published in the *Inverness Advertiser* of 28th May.

> 'Harris, 7th May, 1850. The paupers in Harris are suffering what may be called starvation. The scanty means of the Poors' Board have usually been distributed in meal and though no rule has been observed as to periods and quantities, it may be safely stated that eleven weeks have elapsed since the last distribution took place at which each received three stones (of 14 lbs) of Indian corn meal and they have received 7 lbs each since. .... Receiving nothing from the Highland Relief Fund, and supposed at a distance to be maintained by the Poor Law Board, they would perish but for the charity of their neighbours and what food they can pick up from

> the shores ... their numbers are diminished by uncommonly sudden deaths that give rise to painful suspicions of starvation ... Lady Dunmore is proprietor of the island but is doubtless as ignorant of such proceedings as Her Majesty herself.'[10]

Although the Scottish Home Industries booklet of 1895 provides the earliest published account of how the industry started, an earlier account which seems to contradict Mrs MacDonald's version in the important detail of when the industry started, is to be found in an unpublished family history, provisionally entitled 'Chronicles of the Dunmore branch of the Atholl and Tullibardine Families' compiled by Lord Charles, 7th Earl of Dunmore, the son of Lady Catherine Dunmore. Presumably Lord Charles Dunmore heard the gist of what he wrote from his mother Lady Catherine herself.

> '1839 This year Catherine, Countess of Dunmore initiated an industry on her husband's Estate in the Western Isles that was destined in later years to become famous under the name of 'The Harris Tweed Industry'. The poor people of the island were wont to bring their webs of cloth to the House of Rodel where they were duly inspected, measured and valued according to the degree of excellence in the weaving. As soon as the price per yard had been agreed upon, Lady Dunmore paid ready money for the 'web'. The webs were then stored until the end of the season when a large consignment was despatched to Dunmore House in Stirlingshire from which head depôt the tweeds eventually found their way to the various establishments in Glasgow, Edinburgh, Manchester, Leeds and London besides many private orders being received from sportsmen.'[11]

As far as can be ascertained, any business correspondence belonging to Catherine, Countess of Dunmore, which might have resolved the discrepancy between the dates given by Lord Charles Dunmore and Mrs MacDonald, perished when the repository containing the archives of Messrs Mackenna & Co., the Dunmores' London solicitors, was destroyed in the Second World War blitz.

It is just possible, but hard to believe, that the Countess of Dunmore was actively encouraging weaving in Harris and arranging for webs to be sent to Dunmore without ever having set foot in the island. Was Lord Charles correct in his belief that his mother was arranging for the sale of tweeds as early as 1839, two years before he was born and just three years after his father inherited the estate, and does his statement imply her presence in Harris? If his date is correct, Lady Dunmore may have been trying in a small way as early as 1839, in the aftermath of the less severe famine of 1836-37 (which is seen as a fore-runner of the major famine of 1846 to 1850) to alleviate the suffering of the people, while at much the same time, the estate factors were subjecting small tenants on the west coast of Harris to ruthless clearance in order to increase estate revenue. Or was Mrs MacDonald, writing in 1895, correct in claiming that Lady Dunmore did not come to Harris until 1851 and carried on her late husband's initial enterprise through her Factors? It may even be that the industry did not get off the ground until as late as the mid-1850s.

It seems impossible to establish the facts at this late date, but each version of the story carries slightly different implications for the role of the proprietor in reacting to poverty among the people of Harris. If 1839 or 1844 are correct, the making of tweed apparently did little to relieve distress during the years of the potato famine. Possibly, the market was still limited to the Countess's personal contacts. The application made under the Drainage Act legislation on behalf of the Countess of Dunmore, the apparently inadequate ministrations of the Poor Board and migration in search of work on the mainland seem to have been the means by which people survived during the famine. If Lady Dunmore did not visit Harris until 1851, but relied on her Factor to administer the selection and dispatch of webs on her behalf, did she come as a belated response to reports of destitution on her island estate or did personal circumstances delay her visit until six years after her husband's death? It is this apparent contradiction between what the largely absentee proprietors did on their own initiative and what the Factors did as estate managers in the name of the proprietor which makes generalisations about the role of the Highland landowner fraught with danger of misrepresentation.

It is worth mentioning that Lord Charles, 7th Earl of Dunmore, disposed of the North Harris estate, including the newly built and vastly expensive Amhuinnsuidhe Castle, to Sir Samuel Scott in 1868. There is an unverified story, both in the oral tradition of Harris and tradition within the Dunmore family, that the Scotts acquired the North Harris estate from Lord Charles in lieu of repayment of a debt incurred in the building of Amhuinnsuidhe Castle. Like the Dunmores, the Scotts were generally seen as liberal and benevolent proprietors. The Reports of the Napier Commission of 1883 and the Deer Forest Commission of 1894 show that criticism was confined to the behaviour of the Estate Factors.

Yet another variation on the story of Harris Tweed is given by an Alice Leslie, also writing in *Ealadhna Dùthchasach na h-Alba*. This lady appears to give as much credit to Mrs Thomas for encouraging the making of Harris Tweed as is usually given to Lady Dunmore.

> 'When she (Mrs Thomas) returned to Edinburgh for the winter (of 1857) she sent down better fleeces for them to card, dye, spin and then weave the wool into the far-famed 'Harris Tweed', which, during the process of weaving, acquires the well-known smell of peat which is so much a part of itself, that there has been a 'smelling house' built in Glasgow in order that the imitation tweed may become inoculated with the peat smell. Mrs Thomas then talked of the people among her friends, and by this means got quite a sale for the tweed, she having found that the truck system prevailed in the island to a very great extent; that is to say, if meal was wanted (as it always was in a home), the industry of perhaps months, certainly weeks, in the shape of a roll of tweed, was exchanged for a bag of meal for far below the adequate value, but still so necessary that it must be had at all cost. Then, probably the man who took the tweed for meal would again exchange it for something he required and so on it went, until eventually it found its way to a clothier, then a tailor, and perchance, ultimately to a smart suit in a Highland shooting lodge or Norwegian fishing, or to India or the New World.' [12]

After 30 years of selling tweeds from her home in Edinburgh (i.e. until about 1887), Mrs Thomas moved to London where she opened a depôt at Berners St. After three years during which she acted as a wholesaler for Harris Tweed in London she married again, moved to St Leonards (which St Leonards is not mentioned), and joined the newly formed Scottish Home Industries Association.

There are similarities in the versions of the Harris Tweed story by Alice Leslie and S. MacDonald and one wonders whether there had been a degree of conflation over the years. Certainly the encouragement of home industries was not confined to the work of these two ladies in Harris. Harriet, Duchess of Sutherland, established an Industrial Society at Golspie in 1849. The sale of the work of crofters' wives at an exhibition in 1850 was such a financial success that it led to the beginnings of the Sutherland Home Industries. The knitting of stockings was promoted on Sir Kenneth MacKenzie's estate in Ross-shire, on the MacLeod estate in Skye, and in South Uist on the estate of Lady Gordon-Cathcart, daughter-in law of Col. John Gordon of Cluny. Lady Gordon-Cathcart introduced the making of tweed for sale in London to South Uist in 1877.[13] As Lady Dunmore had done with Harris Tweed, Lady Gordon-Cathcart bought the webs of South Uist tweed from the makers and sent them to Messrs Parfitt of Jermyn St. London. A Mr Blatchley who had been connected with that firm is quoted in the Scott Report of 1914 as saying that while the Uist tweeds were hard-wearing, some pieces had accidental defects and there was considerable waste due to the webs not consisting of multiples of suit lengths.[14] Similar difficulties had been apparent to Lady Dunmore and Mrs Thomas in Harris. They seem to have coped by providing some skilled instruction and by putting aside flawed tweeds for charitable use. Obviously this was not an economically viable solution and could not be used indefinitely in a commercial context.

It is clear from the articles by Mrs MacDonald and Alice Leslie that towards the end of the nineteenth century a number of external problems had arisen for the expanding Harris Tweed industry. The most serious problem was of course production of imitation Harris Tweed by using a 'smelling house' to inject the smell of peat. The tension between the Scottish Home Industries Association and the local merchants can be detected in the criticism of the truck system. These developments mark a new phase as merchants began to take a prominent role in the expansion and protection of the industry. We can thus see the expansion over forty years of the small cottage industry started by the Countess of Dunmore in Harris to a point at which more commercial interests in the form of agencies, merchants and imitators take an interest in selling homespun cloth. Of these homespuns, Harris Tweed was to be the most successful and long-lasting product.

Reference - The Dunmore Family and Harris

1 From correspondence with Lady Anne Dunmore, 5. 8. 1999.

2 Correspondence in Dunmore Family Papers: Rodel Papers, Section II, Bundles 7, 31 & 36. NRA(S) Survey No. 3252.

3 Oral information based on 19th century Census Returns given to the author by B. Lawson of *Cò Leis Thu?* Genealogy Centre, Northton, Harris.

4 *Report of the Commissioners of Inquiry into the Conditions of the Crofters and Cottars in the Highlands and Islands of Scotland*, [hereafter: 'Napier Commission'], pp., 1183-1184, questions 17897 and 17898.

5 *ibid.*, p 1190, question, 17981.

6 *Report to the Board of Agriculture for Scotland on Home Industries in the Highlands and Islands in 1914*, [hereafter: 'Scott Report,'], 33.

7 Scottish Home Industries, *Ealadhna Dùthchasach na h-Alba*, c.1885, [hereafter: 'Scottish Home Industries'], 69-71.

8 *ibid.*, 72.

9 Oral information given to the author by B. Lawson, *Cò Leis Thu?* Genealogy Centre, Northton.

10 *Inverness Advertiser*, 28. 5. 1850.

11 'Chronicles of the Dunmore branch of the Atholl and Tullibardine Families', n.d. Dunmore Papers: Rodel Papers, Section II, Bundles 32 & 33.

12 Scottish Home Industries, 74.

13 Scott Report, 34.

14 *ibid.*

3

The Agencies and the Merchants

A number of parallel developments in the Harris Tweed industry became apparent during the last two decades of the nineteenth century. Firstly, the making of 'Harris Tweed' for sale was no longer confined to Harris. With the encouragement of Lady Gordon-Cathcart, a similar tweed was also being made in South Uist. It had also spread north to Lochs and Uig, those districts of Lewis which lay nearest to the Harris border. Those developments inevitably gave rise to the question as to what could legitimately be described as 'Harris Tweed'. Should the name be reserved for tweed made only in Harris, or could any tweed made in exactly the same way also be described as 'Harris Tweed'? According to a Guide to Stornoway written by Bailie Donald MacIver in 1912, the first web of Harris Tweed to be offered for outside sale from Lewis was made in 1881.[1] Handwoven tweed for sale was also being produced in places such as Sutherland and Shetland where there had been a similar tradition of hand-weaving for domestic consumption, although as far as is known these tweeds did not claim to be 'Harris Tweed'. While Harris weaving was generally acknowledged to have been superior to that of most other districts, particularly in its tasteful design, hand-made tweeds from other places were certainly providing competition in the textile markets of the south.

Another development in the last decades of the nineteenth century was that the promotion for sale of tweeds on behalf of the crofter-weaver was no longer confined to a few members of the Highland land-owning class, acting as patrons. The selling agencies which came into being, such as the Scottish Home Industries Association, Highland Home Industries Association and the Crofters' Agency were, in a sense, an extension of the patronage originally afforded by individual members of the landed gentry, who retained their involvement in the industry by becoming Presidents of those agencies. The actions of the agencies, in providing instructors, setting up local depôts and securing wider markets encouraged a more commercial and professional approach to the production of Harris Tweed than had been possible under the sole patronage of Lady Dunmore or Lady Gordon-Cathcart.

A parallel development from approximately 1880 involved the use of local merchants as middlemen. The Scott Report of 1914 mentions that a 'Mr Norman MacLeod of Tarbert sold tweeds to various wholesale houses in 1879, obtaining prices from 4/- to 6/- a yard'.[2]

The impression formed on reading the Scott Report was that two 'camps' had developed. The 'camp' represented by the agencies, which was led by members of the aristocracy, had grave concerns as to whether the hand-weavers were getting a fair deal when selling their tweeds through the local merchants. On the other hand the merchant-dealers were coming to realise that they had a significant interest and influence in the commercial production of Harris Tweed.

The ethos underlying the formation of the agencies seems to have been that of benevolent gentry helping their Highland tenants to find a source of extra income by forming 'Industrial Societies' and encouraging 'Home Industries'. In the spirit of Ruskin much emphasis was placed on handcrafts. If one considers other aspects of Highland estate policy in the 1880s, it seems that such apparent benevolence was not incompatible with older attitudes such as encouraging emigration, the Killarney and Saltcoats schemes for example, which the Prime Minister, Lord Lothian, saw as preferable to reform of land tenure in that it was a permanent means of eradicating the land agitation of the 1880s at its roots.[3] The most important aspect of the efforts to encourage home industries was that the patrons made an effort to find a market for the goods produced, much as Lady Dunmore, Mrs Thomas and Lady Gordon-Cathcart had done before them. At the suggestion of the Marchioness of Stafford, Sutherland Home Industries led the way in 1887 with an exhibition of work by the tenantry.

An influential agency, the Scottish Home Industries Association, was established in 1889, under the patronage of H. R. H. Princess Louise (a granddaughter of Queen Victoria and later to be Princess Royal) and the presidency of the Countess of Rosebery. The aims of the Association were to find a market for the products of home industries, to improve their quality by providing instruction and to pay a fair price for the labour involved in making the products. Of course tweed-making was only one of these home industries. A depôt for home-made products was established at 14 Lower Grosvenor St. in London. Later that year, another body, the Highland Home Industries and Arts Association was set up covering the counties of Inverness, Ross and

Cromarty, Sutherland, Caithness, Elgin and Banff. Its aims were very much in the tradition of Ruskin's Home Arts and Industries Association of 1884. The objectives of the Highland Association stated,

> 'It may be that the hand cannot compete with the machine when rapidity of production and an immediate profit are aimed at; but there is undoubtedly an appreciation of home-made fabrics; - the revival of such industries would greatly promote thrift and add to the comfort and to the self-respect of the poorer classes of people engaged in agricultural and pastoral occupations, - the artistic faculty of the race would be revived and stimulated - better fabrics - and more comfortable homes would result.' [4]

Various estates followed this example in setting up their own associations to promote home industries, although most did not achieve notable financial success. Lack of working capital and an inadequate financial base were the main problems for all the associations. After quite some debate the Scottish Home Industries Association decided in 1896 to become a limited liability company with the Duchess of Sutherland as president of the Board of Directors. The debate surrounding this decision centred on the wish to provide the weavers with an adequate return for their work in the form of the price paid for their tweeds, while a commercial selling organisation, such as a limited liability company, would have to make a deduction from the retail price of tweed to cover the cost of selling it. [5] From this distance in time, it looks as if there might have been a split in the ranks of the aristocratic patrons over the issue, as Mrs Mary Stewart-Mackenzie of Seaforth then set up another selling agency, the 'Crofters' Agency'. In order to avoid confusion, it is as well to distinguish between this lady who lived at Brahan Castle, Conon Bridge, Ross-shire and her husband's ancestor, also Mary, the widow of Admiral Hood and daughter of Lord Seaforth. The first Mary Stewart-MacKenzie, or Lady Mary Hood as she then was, inherited Lewis from her father in 1814 and sold it to Mr James Matheson of Achany in 1843. The second Mrs Mary Stewart-MacKenzie of Brahan Castle, later Lady Mary, was a staunch patron of the Harris Tweed industry in the early years of the twentieth century. A little girl born to a tweed merchant in Northton, Harris was given a silver christening cup by the second Mary Stewart-

MacKenzie. This child was given the Christian names 'Mary Stewart MacKenzie' in honour of her benefactress.

Although not an agency in the sense of the bodies mentioned above, the Congested Districts Board also played a part in shaping the development of the Harris Tweed industry. Despite the measure of land tenure reform introduced by the 1886 Crofters' Act, the over-riding problem in the Outer Hebrides was still insufficient land available to support the crofter and cottar population. The second phase of the Land Wars which followed the 1886 Act led to incidents in Lewis such as the Park Deer Raid and the Aignish Riot when landless cottars and crofters with less land than they needed, tried to win back from the proprietors ancestral land still being used for sheep farms or deer forests. In 1892 the Government set up the Deer Forest Commission to identify land which might be made available to crofters and cottars. Its report was published in 1895 without recommending 'any solution to the problem of shortage of land'. [6] The Liberal government then fell and a Conservative administration came into power in 1895. In 1897 that Government passed the Congested Districts (Scotland) Act which set up the Congested Districts Board to administer a fund of Government money intended, among other objectives, to develop industries in the congested areas. [7] Under Section 4 of the Act, funds were specifically made available for developing spinning and weaving. In 1911, the Congested Districts Board became the Board of Agriculture for Scotland. From 1897 when it was established, the Congested Districts Board became virtually the Government's agent in encouraging the Harris Tweed industry. For example, the Board provided the large cast iron boilers which solved the problem of dyeing a large enough quantity of wool exactly the same shade at any one time.

In addition to the Scottish Home Industries Association depôts in London and Edinburgh, depôts were set up in Stornoway and Tarbert. In an effort, not wholly successful, to avoid falling into the truck system, (a system whereby workers were paid in goods rather than in cash) for which the merchants had been so roundly criticised by the agencies, the managers of these depôts were instructed to pay for all purchases of tweed in cash, leaving it entirely to the option of the crofter whether they would or would not make purchases of groceries, wool and other commodities which the Association stores offered for sale. If the

Association depôts were dealing in a variety of household goods, it is clear that they must have been in competition with local merchants and were very probably resented for that reason. Mrs Stewart-MacKenzie's Crofters' Agency also bought tweeds for cash in its depôts and limited its advances to wool.[8]

The Scottish Home Industries Association appointed a travelling Inspector with a view to improving the quality of tweeds and in 1898 the Congested Districts Board set up an instruction scheme in Lewis with Sheriff Campbell as chairman of the supervising committee. A Mr Alexander Lamont was appointed to the post of Inspector and his salary was paid by the Board.[9] It was at this point that the problem of small dyeing pots became apparent and the 30 gallon boilers were supplied. The extension of the tweed industry to North Uist was another project taken up by the Congested Districts Board and a grant was made to the Scottish Home Industries Association to open a tweed depôt at Lochmaddy. Shortly afterwards, depôts were opened at Obbe (now Leverburgh) in Harris, Uig in Lewis, Lochboisdale in South Uist, and Creagorry in Benbecula. In 1902 arrangements were made through the Board's committee in Stornoway to advance funds, free of interest, for the purchase of improved looms. The looms cost from £6 to £8 each and payments were arranged for one-third in advance, one third in six months and the final third at the end of a year. Between 1899 and 1911 the number of looms in Lewis increased from 161 to approximately 300.[10]

The local merchants of Lewis and Harris who had started dealing in tweeds were entrepreneurs, pursuing a new business opportunity. As they were engaged in business as individuals, rather than as a body, when they began to act as middlemen in the sale of tweeds, they have not left to posterity the same amount of documentary evidence as was left by the Agencies. From what can now be gleaned from the oral tradition, some merchants did use the truck system and some did not. While the business acumen of these merchants provided a service to the individual weaver by selling his tweeds on a wider market than could be found at home, the merchants themselves did not have the capital to build up a large stock of unsold tweeds, nor to hang on to tweeds until the best price could be obtained. Expansion of this branch of the industry was inhibited by the merchants' own limited capital base. They were dependent on selling to the slowly increasing stream of visitors to the Islands and to their own growing contacts with textile merchants and tailors in the south.

As regards their use of the truck system, the Scott Report quotes evidence given by Millicent, Duchess of Sutherland, to the Departmental Committee on the Truck Acts which testified that at the end of the 19th century,

> 'It was found that some people who dealt at the (Scottish Home Industries) depôt at Tarbert in Harris were so poor that they were often in want of wool or necessaries between the time they began to make a web of cloth and the finishing of it, and it was judged necessary to advance such commodities which comprised wool, dyes, meal and sugar.' [11]

It is easy to understand how in the face of such poverty, weavers could all too readily find themselves beholden to a merchant who was willing to take their tweed for sale and be only too glad to accept meal or household necessities on credit. That they might have been driving a poor bargain probably seemed a lesser evil than having no bargain at all. In 1887 the provisions of the Truck Act of 1881 were extended to include all cases where a dealer bought goods under the value of £5 made from cotton, silk, or cloth from a person working at his or her own home without employing anyone but members of the family. [12]

However, the use of the truck system was not so easily stamped out as instances of its use can be identified well into the 1930s in Harris. [13]

The role of local merchants as middlemen in the sale of Harris Tweed took two different forms. There was the type of business transaction described above whereby a weaver took his cloth to a local merchant to be sold and was paid either in cash or, using the truck system, was given credit, which he then used up in buying goods from the merchant's store. On the other hand, some merchants would buy raw wool from a number of local sources and 'farm' this wool out to be carded, spun and woven by a local weaver. In time, this type of merchant came to be known as a 'Small Producer' or an 'Independent Producer' of Harris Tweed. Eventually, as these independent producers acquired their own sales outlets, this type of transaction developed to the stage whereby the small producer-cum-merchant supplied the weaver with yarn (i.e. wool which had already been carded and spun) and placed with the weaver an order from a southern buyer for a particular length of tweed in a particular pattern. This form of business opened the door to some independent producers supplying weavers with yarn which had been millspun on the mainland, a practice condemned by those, particularly the Harris weavers, who still preferred to use only handspun yarn. The practice of resorting to millspun yarn in order to speed the overall production of tweeds was not confined to independent producers, but came into use among individual weavers themselves, particularly in those areas of Lewis in which commercial weaving had gained ground.

It is clear that as long as carding the raw wool by hand remained the norm there would be an insurmountable restriction on the rate at which tweeds could be produced, a restriction which inevitably limited the number of webs available for sale. Carding the raw wool by hand could take as long as all the other processes put together. This explains the resort to machine-carding as the market for tweed increased. There seems to have been some debate as to the demerits of machine-carding, for example, the claim that it took away something of the character of handwork. [14] As there were no carding mills in the Islands in the late 19th century, the practice of sending raw wool to the mainland to be carded had become established. The strongest objection to machine-carding lay in the fact that it introduced the possibility of the weaver opting to have the wool machine-spun after it had been carded. It was then all too tempting to take advantage of the mill's spinning facilities and receive yarn sent back ready for the loom. The inherent danger of using millspun yarn from a mainland mill was that nobody could guarantee that the yarn received had been made from the wool which had been sent to the mill, or even that the yarn was made from pure virgin wool.

In 1900, in an attempt to prevent the use of millspun yarn becoming prevalent in Harris, Sir Samuel Scott, Proprietor of the North Harris Estate, erected a carding mill at Lòn na Fèille, the old market stance at Direcleit just outside Tarbert on the road to South Harris. This mill would card, but not spin, the wool brought to it by weavers from all over Harris. It was a water-powered mill and in the height of summer there were times when carding was held up by a shortage of water. For example, in the summer of 1911, work was suspended for six weeks due to the drought.

In Stornoway, Aeneas MacKenzie started the Patent Slip Carding Mill in 1903. The mill took its name from its location at the old Slip, which was a significant ship-building and repairing enterprise built by Sir James Matheson. The slipway ran across what is now Shell Street cutting off access to the rest of Newton Street. The Patent Slip Mill was to be the progenitor of S. A. Newall and Sons Ltd. and the old arched gateway off James Street into what was once Newall's yard, still bears the name 'Patent Slip Mill' above the archway. By 1906, another carding and spinning mill was erected on Lewis Street in Stornoway by Kenneth MacKenzie. In 1908 the Patent Slip Mill added spinning facilities. No doubt these last two mills wished to capture for themselves some of the business going to mainland spinners.

The significant contribution of the Harris Tweed industry to the economy of Lewis was increasingly recognised in the early years of the 20th century. According to the estimates of Ex-Provost Donald Smith of Stornoway, Chairman of the local committee of the Congested Districts Board, the value of tweed sales for Lewis in 1903 was £8000, in 1904 it was £15,000 and in 1905, £20,460. [15] Production in Harris increased more slowly in the same period. There were strong suspicions that the increased production of so-called 'Harris Tweed' in Lewis was largely dependent on the use of millspun yarn. [16]

Those merchants who sold only Harris Tweed made from handspun yarn realised that they had to take steps to protect their own business. The method they chose was to require weavers to sign a declaration stating that,

> 'I hereby guarantee that the length of Tweed as described below is entirely handspun, handwoven and home-dyed Harris Tweed.
>
> Signature:............................. Address:............
> Description of the tweed (colour and design)...................... No........'

Unfortunately, this safeguard was only partially satisfactory as instances of false declarations were mentioned and roundly condemned in the Scott Report. [17]

By 1906 the Harris Tweed industry was becoming a victim of its own success as the case of Henry Lyons demonstrates. The Sixth Report of the Congested Districts Board noted in 1903 that the workers could not supply the whole demand for their cloth. [18] If the suspicion that the increased output in Lewis was dependent on an increased use of millspun yarn was correct, there were thus two kinds of handwoven tweed being sold as Harris Tweed, one contained all or part millspun yarn and one all handspun yarn. While the use of millspun yarn, by itself, might simply have been a source of concern to those who continued to use only handspun, the deterioration in weaving associated with the increased output from Lewis brought the reputation of the whole industry into disrepute among London wholesalers, earning the disparaging term, 'Stornoway tweed' for tweeds produced in Lewis. The Scottish Home Industries Association closed its depôts in Lewis because the amount of handspun tweed obtainable did not justify the expense of keeping depôts there. The Crofters' Agency however kept its depôt at Balallan open.

When the price of tweed produced from handspun yarn came to be affected by the bad reputation of tweed produced in Lewis from millspun yarn, the interests of the Scottish Home Industries Association, the Crofters' Agency, the Harris merchants and those merchants in Lewis who dealt only in tweed made from handspun yarn came together. The need for a trade mark and a definition of Harris Tweed had become obvious to everyone involved in the industry.

Reference - The Agencies and the Merchants

1 *Report to the Board of Agriculture for Scotland on Home Industries in the Highlands and Islands in 1914* [hereafter: 'Scott Report,'], 35.
2 *ibid.*
3 Ewen Cameron, *Land for the People? The British Government and the Scottish Highlands*, c. 1880-1925 [hereafter: 'Cameron, *Land for the People?*'], 70.
4 Scott Report, 43.
5 *ibid.*, 45.
6 Cameron, *Land for the People?* 80.
7 *ibid.*, 84.
8 Scott Report, 45.
9 *ibid.*, 46.
10 *ibid.*, 48.
11 *ibid.*, 45.
12 *ibid.*, 37.
13 See Finlay J. MacDonald, *Crowdie and Cream*, 130.
14 Scott Report, 1914, 55.
15 *Sixth Report of the Congested Districts Board*, 33 and *Eighth Report*, 21, quoted in Scott Report, 48.
16 Scott Report, 48 to 49.
17 *ibid.*, 49 & 50.
18 *Sixth Report of the Congested Districts Board*, 33, quoted in Scott Report, 48.

4

Applications for a Trade Mark

Although various people seem to have recognised the need for a trade mark to protect the good name of Harris Tweed at much the same time, it is not entirely clear as to who took the first step on the way to acquiring the trade mark. A group of Harris merchants and Mrs Mary Stewart-MacKenzie of Brahan Castle, who had established the Crofters' Agency, would appear to have made separate applications for a trade mark before 1909. It is worth recording the sequence of events, in so far as they can be ascertained, as there is a strong belief current in Harris to this day that their own merchants 'gave away' the exclusive rights of the people of Harris to the term 'Harris Tweed' by letting the Lewis merchants share it. Interestingly, there does not appear to be the same resentment directed against the Uists, perhaps because the Uists never presented the same level of competition.

Unfortunately, little, if any, of the correspondence relating to applications for a trade mark has survived. McKenna and Co., the solicitors in London who acted both in the formation of the Harris Tweed Association Ltd. and in the application for a trade mark, have no papers relating to the original application. An inspection of the file at the Patent Office revealed no more than the original Statement of Case and regulations. [1] It appears that any documents which did exist were lost during the 1939-45 blitz of London. [2] In attempting to reconstruct what took place, we therefore have to rely on a few papers from the Patent Office, a few papers in the Harris Tweed Association archive lodged with Highland Regional Archives in Nairn, contemporary newspaper reports, the Scott Report of 1914 and the personal recollections of those involved. This is less than satisfactory as there are contradictory statements and some interesting questions remain unanswered.

It seems likely that the Lyons case of 1906 brought concerns over the use of millspun yarn to a head. Also, the passing in 1905 of the Trade Marks Act made provision for the first time for the registration of 'standardisation marks', a term changed in 1938 to 'certification marks'. Because the voluntary declaration as to the type of yarn used had failed to eliminate the covert use of millspun yarn, those Harris merchants who were anxious to protect the industry believed that if a standardisation mark were to be obtained, all tweed offered for sale as Harris Tweed could be inspected and, if passed as genuine Harris Tweed made from handspun yarn, it would then receive a certifying stamp. This system would renew public confidence in the name 'Harris Tweed' and would prevent the practice of passing off tweed made from millspun yarn as genuine Harris Tweed. Some years were to elapse before an accepted system of certification was established.

The *Highland News* of 1st September, 1906, reported a meeting in Stornoway of dealers in home-made tweeds in order to consider what steps were required

> 'for placing the industry in the island on a more satisfactory footing. The meeting was a very harmonious one, and, if the resolutions are honourably carried out, will doubtless result in much good.'[3]

The use of the word 'honourably' seems to imply that the possibility of dishonourable conduct was not too far from somebody's mind! Between 1906 and 1909, three different trade mark applications were lodged. One came from the Harris Tweed Association of Tarbert, that is a group of Harris merchants dealing in tweeds, one from a Mr. Roderick Smith who had been Secretary of that Association, and one from the Scottish Home Industries Association Ltd. None of these applications reached registration, probably because the Board of Trade had to consider whether the term should be confined to Harris or should include Lewis and the neighbouring islands as well. Mr Horridge, K. C. representing the Board of Trade in the Lyons case, had argued in terms of all the Outer Hebrides being included.[4]

We now have to leap forward in time to consider retrospective evidence from one who was part of the group of Harris Tweed merchants in Tarbert in 1908. In the *Stornoway Gazette* of 30th November 1951, Donald M. Morrison of Tarbert publicly refuted a remark made by the Chairman of a meeting held in Tarbert during the General Election campaign of that year. The meeting was held on behalf of Malcolm K. MacMillan, the then Labour candidate. When the discussion turned to the state of the Harris Tweed industry, the Chairman of the meeting articulated the belief of many in the audience, that the people responsible for the present state of the Harris Tweed industry were those who had 'sold their birthright'.[5]

Donald M. Morrison declared in his letter to the Editor of the *Stornoway Gazette* that this statement was 'entirely wrong and without foundation, as the following facts will prove'.

> 'When the proposal to obtain a protecting Trade Mark was initiated in 1906, strong antagonism was shown by some in Harris to the proposal. The same antagonism was experienced by the late Mr. R. F. Matheson, Factor, North Harris Estate, when he suggested to the Harris Tweed dealers of those days that they should approach the Board of Trade for such a Trade Mark in the years 1886 to 1890. The matter was then dropped and not revived again until 1906. When in 1906 renewed steps were taken in the matter and the Board of Trade was approached, the Committee set up for the purpose again met with strong opposition from some of the traders in Harris. Nevertheless the Committee pushed on with the idea until their efforts were crowned with success when the Trade Mark was granted in 1908. It would appear that some people think that the Trade Mark was granted to Lewis only in the year 1934, the fact being that they were granted the Trade Mark at the same time as Harris in 1908.
>
> In the year 1907, I received a letter from the Board of Trade stating that the late Messrs Donald MacIver and Donald MacAulay, merchants of Bayhead Street and Cromwell Street respectively, were claiming that, in the event of Harris being granted a Trade Mark, Lewis also would insist on participating in any benefit accruing from the Mark proposed for Harris. I did, of course, strongly protest, but the Board of Trade refused to listen. The Trade Mark was accordingly granted to Harris, Lewis, North and South Uist and Barra in the year 1908. We in Harris, if we were to have a Trade Mark at all, had to agree to this. The alternative was a refusal by the Board of Trade to consider our application for protection.'[6]

Donald M. Morrison's letter goes on to emphasise how the trade mark had safeguarded the words 'Harris Tweed' from becoming simply a generic term. It says that Millicent, Duchess of Sutherland and the late Lady Seaforth (previously Mrs Mary Stewart-MacKenzie of

Brahan Castle) had paid the £300 expenses incurred in the granting of the trade mark, apart from £30 collected in Harris. It also says that the Lewis merchants Donald MacIver and Donald MacAulay had served on the Harris Tweed Association with Donald Morrison until their deaths. Donald M. Morrison suggested that some of the misunderstanding about the original inclusion of Lewis in the provisions of the trade mark could be explained by the fact that after the deaths of the original Lewis merchants on the Harris Tweed Association there had been no further representation of Lewis interests in the Association until 1934, when application was made for an amended trade mark which would admit the use of millspun yarn. The perception in Harris seems to have been that tweed made in Lewis had not been eligible for the name 'Harris Tweed' until 1934, when the definition of Harris Tweed attached to the trade mark was amended to allow the use of millspun yarn, a change which was not universally popular in Harris. Mr Morrison's letter made it quite clear that the Board of Trade had insisted from the beginning that Lewis and all the other islands in the Outer Hebrides should be granted the trade mark at the same time as Harris. The discrepancy between the dates 1908 and 1909 may be explained by the delay between filing an application and the final registration of the trade mark.

A somewhat oblique report in the *Highland News* of 2nd March 1907 complicates the picture still further. Under the heading, 'The Protection of the Harris Tweed Industry' the *Highland News* reported,

> 'The recent and much-talked of prosecution relating to the selling of millspun tweed described as 'Harris Tweed' has for months occupied the minds of the wholesale and retail houses of Harris Tweeds in London. Many theories have been mentioned, many changes advocated, yet it rested with Mrs Stewart-MacKenzie of Seaforth, (and Brahan Castle) whose interests in the Harris people and those of the neighbouring islands is well known, to bring about the protection which the inhabitants of the Outer Hebrides so much desire by the obtaining for their interests of a trade mark from the Board of Trade.
>
> Much trouble has been encountered, as in the first place, the trade mark was *practically granted* (author's italics) for the tweed exclusively manufactured in Harris, eliminating any tweed made in

neighbouring islands and it is only with the zeal which Mrs MacKenzie of Seaforth exercised and has so far shown her interest in the Hebrides, that the trade mark granted to Harris has been extended to Lewis and North and South Uist.

This result was only attained by Mrs Stewart-MacKenzie of Seaforth, who, with Provost Anderson of Stornoway, waited upon the Registrar of Trade Marks last Saturday (the 23rd inst.) exerting to the utmost the needs and requirements of the people.

In future (presuming no opposition or like branding is registered) all Harris, Lewis and neighbouring islands (known as the Hebrides) tweed of handspun, handwoven home manufacture will be branded 'Harris Long Island Tweed, Handspun, Handwoven'.

The crest of the Right Hon. the Earl of Dunmore will form the centre part of the branding in recognition of the great part his late mother, the Countess of Dunmore exercised in bringing before the public the qualities and propensities of hand-made tweed.'[7]

It would appear from this report that some group, presumably a group of Harris merchants, had, in 1907, 'almost' acquired a trade mark which would have been exclusive to tweed made in Harris. If Mrs Stewart-MacKenzie of the Crofters' Agency had any territorial affiliations, these were surely with Lewis rather than Harris, as she was the wife of a descendant of the MacKenzies of Seaforth. As her colleague in the lobbying of the Board of Trade was Provost Anderson of Stornoway, presumably they were both concerned to protect Lewis interests in the Harris Tweed industry. It is worth noting in the by-going that the crest obtained was not that of the Dunmore family. In the early 1990s, with the help of Anne, Countess of Dunmore, the Dunmore family crest was compared with the Orb mark. They are not the same and the origins of the orb and cross as used in the Harris Tweed trade mark remain obscure.

Despite the suggestion in the *Highland News* that Mrs Stewart-MacKenzie had acquired a trade mark, a report from a fortnight later poses the question as to whether she had actually been granted a trade mark or had simply filed an application for one. On 16th March 1907 the *Highland News* headline was 'Tweed Trade in Conference'. This report said,

'The Duchess of Sutherland, President of the Scottish Home Industries Association, held a conference on Thursday forenoon with the leading Stornoway traders in homespun tweeds. The traders present were:- Messrs Donald MacAulay, Donald MacIver, Alex. MacAulay, Alex. MacIver, and David Tolmie. There were also present Miss Chaplin, Major Matheson, Ex-Provost Smith, Provost Anderson, and Mr Wrigglesworth, Director of Messrs J.G. Hardy Ltd. London. On the motion of Major Matheson, Provost Anderson was called on to preside. After a general discussion of the situation with regards to the tweed industry, and particularly with reference to the *proposed* (author's italics) Trade Mark for Harris homespun tweeds, which has been applied for to the Board of Trade by Mrs Stewart-MacKenzie of Seaforth, the following resolution was adopted, viz.:-

'That in view of the desirability of having one Trade Mark established for the tweed made in the Long Island, or Outer Hebrides, and known as 'Harris Tweed', it is unanimously agreed to unite with the Scottish Home Industries Association in having the proposed Trade Mark passed by the Board of Trade and the meeting expresses the hope that Mrs Mackenzie of Seaforth will also join in this matter.' Her Grace, the Duchess of Sutherland undertook to make representations on the subject to the Board of Trade, and Provost Anderson was asked to correspond with Mrs MacKenzie with a view to obtaining her co-operation.'[8]

Mrs Stewart-MacKenzie was President of the Crofters' Agency. The Duchess of Sutherland was President of the Scottish Home Industries Association. It certainly seems that some powerful lobbying of the Board of Trade was taking place but, so far as can be made out, there seems to have been little substantial difference between the two ladies as to the inclusion of all the islands in the proposed trade mark. Remembering Mrs Stewart-MacKenzie's actions in 1896 in setting up the Crofters' Agency when the Scottish Home Industries decided to become a Limited Company, it may be that there was a personal rivalry between the ladies. Again there may well have been some competition between the two agencies when the Crofters' Agency was first to receive an order from King Edward VII and Queen Alexandra on their visit to Stornoway in 1902. - 'Royal Patronage for Lewis tweeds'. [9] Thanks possibly to a touch of royal diplomacy the Scottish Home Industries Association also received an order which was described in the *Highland News* the following week as 'a consignment of selected Lewis tweeds'. [10] It is also interesting to note that two of the Stornoway traders present at the Duchess of Sutherland's 'Trade Conference' were the men mentioned in Donald M. Morrison's letter, Donald MacIver and Donald MacAulay, the traders who had written to the Board of Trade insisting that Lewis should participate in the benefits of any trade mark granted to Harris.

Whatever rivalries may have been associated with the earlier applications for a trade mark which had been filed between 1906 and 1909, those applications were withdrawn and were superseded by one submitted on 15th December 1909. The critical difference between the earlier applications and that of 1909 lies in the fact that the first applications were applications for ordinary trade marks, not what was, at that time, called a standardisation mark and is now known as a certification mark. [11] The advice from McKenna and Co. in 1909 to apply for a standardisation or certification mark was an inspired stroke well ahead of its time as a standardisation trade mark gave the industry much stronger protection than an ordinary trade mark would have done. [12]

Negotiations between the various interested parties led to the incorporation on 9th December 1909 of the Harris Tweed Association Ltd., a company limited by guarantee with a registered office in London. Over fifty years later when commenting on the fact that the registered office of the HTA Ltd. was in London, John S. Gwatkin of McKenna & Co, the solicitors for the HTA, said, 'the fact that the Company (i.e. the Harris Tweed Association Ltd.) was based in London rather than in the Hebrides suggests that the grant of a certification mark was its principal object'. [13] As it transpired at the time of the litigation involving the HTA in the late 1950s and early 1960s, the fact that the HTA was based in London was to prove to be unfortunate as it gave grounds for much misunderstanding and misrepresentation of its role.

The Articles of Association of the Harris Tweed Association stated:-

> 'The objects for which the Company is established are the protection of the interests of manufacturers and merchants of and dealers in tweed made in the Islands of Harris, Lewis and Uist in Scotland, and to promote the manufacture and sale of such tweed. To protect the trade against offences under the Merchandise Marks Acts and otherwise to prevent the use of false trade marks and descriptions in respect of tweed made in imitation thereof.
>
> And in furtherance of such objects to register a trade mark or trade marks under the powers given by section 62 of the Trade Marks Act, 1905.'

The Articles of Association also provided that the Committee of Management of the Harris Tweed Association should be composed of two members from the Scottish Home Industries Association Ltd., two from the Crofters' Agency and two from the Harris Tweed Association of Tarbert. These people were Millicent, Duchess of Sutherland of Dunrobin Castle, William Harrison, Agricultural Engineer, Leigh, Lancashire, Mary Stewart-MacKenzie of Brahan Castle, Conon Bridge, George Favorke, Accountant, Haywards Heath, Sussex, Norman MacLeod J.P., Merchant, Tarbert, Harris, Donald M. Morrison, Merchant, Tarbert, Harris and Edward Charles Brown, Chartered Accountant, Cannon St. London. Three members, who were required to be one representative of each of the founding bodies, comprised a quorum.

The trade mark was not registered until October 1910. A letter dated 23rd February 1910 from McKenna & Co. in the name of the Harris Tweed Association Ltd. to the Board of Trade made an application, No. 319214 for registration of a Trade Mark under Section 62 of the Trade Marks Act 1905 in Class 34. [14] The letter also states specifically that the earlier applications had been withdrawn. These would include the application made by Mrs Mary Stewart-MacKenzie.

The registered design consisted of a globe surmounted by a cross with the words 'Harris Tweed' in the first line, and, in the second line, the words 'Made in Harris', 'Made in Lewis', or 'Made in Uist', according to the place of manufacture. [15] The original definition of Harris Tweed read as follows:-

"Harris Tweed' means a tweed handspun and hand-woven and dyed by the crofters and cottars in the Outer Hebrides.'

The newly formed Harris Tweed Association appointed three inspectors, one based in Tarbert, one in South Harris, and one in Uist to cover the Uists and Berneray, an island in the Sound of Harris between North Uist and Harris. Stamping of the cloth with the mark began early in 1911, but according to the Appendix to the Scott Report, the Harris Tweed Trade Mark was not adopted in Lewis until April 1912.[16] Strange as it may seem, in light of the quantity of Harris Tweed apparently produced in Lewis, John Gwatkin explained the lack of an inspector based in Lewis as an indication that very little handspun tweed was being produced there at that time.[17] The first few months of 1911 had seen quite a boom in the weaving industry in Lewis. Bailie Donald MacIver estimated the output from Lewis at £60,000 and, even when pressed by Dr Scott to re-examine these figures, he could only reduce them to £50,000. This £50,000 did not take account of makers who were dealing direct with London wholesalers. Writing only three years later, Scott stated that it was alleged that most of this Lewis tweed was being produced from millspun yarn. The only definite data for handspun tweed being made in Lewis came from the Crofters' Agency depôt in Balallan which could account for tweed to the value of £500.[18] The Harris Tweed Association Ltd. saw fit, in November 1911, to bring a case against a tailor who was charged, unsuccessfully as it turned out, with selling tweed made from millspun yarn as genuine Harris Tweed.

The estimated value of tweed stamped in Harris in 1911 was £27,135 compared with £25,842 in 1910. In North Uist (which for stamping purposes included the surrounding islands) the figure for 1911 was £6,579. Apparently South Uist had not been actively involved in tweed production and the estimated output was valued at £907.[19]

Towards the end of 1911 the price of tweed made in Lewis slumped, allegedly through over-production and inferior workmanship. The early months of 1912 saw no improvement. In the spring of 1912, a number of Stornoway merchants opened negotiations with the Harris Tweed Association for the introduction of the trade mark in Lewis on condition that they should have representation on the Management Committee.[20] According to a Special Resolution passed at an Extraordinary General Meeting of the Association held at 28 Budge

Row, London, on 3rd May 1912, and confirmed on 3rd June 1912, the Articles of Association were changed to allow the Committee of Management to consist of eight members. The representatives of the Scottish Home Industries Association and the Crofters' Agency remained as in 1910, but John MacLeod replaced Norman MacLeod J. P. and, with Donald Morrison, represented the Harris Tweed Association of Tarbert on the Harris Tweed Association Ltd. The two new members were Donald MacIver and Malcolm MacDonald as representatives of the Lewis Harris Tweed Association. A representative of each of the four associations formed a quorum which was required to authorise any transaction of business. [21]

From the start, the majority opinion of those involved in the industry favoured a definition covering all the Outer Hebrides. The Board of Trade supported these terms and would have dismissed any attempt to confine the trade mark to Harris. The request from the Lewis merchants for the introduction of the trade mark in Lewis was in essence simply a request for an inspector to be placed in Lewis to stamp tweeds if they conformed to the definition. It is difficult to see how the Association could legally have refused to stamp tweeds simply on the grounds that they had been made in Lewis, when Lewis had been specifically included when the trade mark had been granted. It was also part of the avowed purpose of the Harris Tweed Association to eradicate production of imitation Harris Tweed and encourage the genuine cloth. Had stamping been refused to Lewis tweeds it would have been even more difficult than it turned out to be to wean the industry in Lewis away from millspun yarn. The election of representatives of the industry in Lewis to the Committee of Management was done in accordance with the Articles of Association which made provision for the election of 'other persons interested in promoting the objects of the company'. The decision to admit two representatives of the Lewis Harris Tweed Association was not made solely by the two Harris representatives, but by a unanimous decision of all members of the Committee of Management. The accusation of 'selling the birthright of Harris' arises from a misunderstanding of what actually happened, rather than from any negligence on the part of the individuals involved in the application for a trade mark.

Reference - Applications for a Trade Mark

1 Gwatkin, Preliminary draft of 'Notes on the Historical Development of the Harris Tweed Industry and the Part Played by the Harris Tweed Association Ltd.', (c. 1960) [hereafter: Gwatkin 'Preliminary Notes'], 8. HTA Office, Stornoway.
2 *ibid.*, 17.
3 *Highland News*, 1. 9. 1906.
4 Gwatkin, Notes on the Historical Development of the Harris Tweed Industry and the Part Played by the Harris Tweed Association Ltd., [hereafter: 'The Harris Tweed Industry'], 10-11.
5 *Stornoway Gazette*, 30. 11. 1951.
6 *ibid.*, 30. 11. 1951.
7 *Highland News*, 2. 3. 1907.
8 *ibid.*, 16. 3. 1907.
9 *ibid.*, 20. 9. 1902.
10 *ibid.*, 27. 9. 1902.
11 Gwatkin, 'The Harris Tweed Industry', 11.
12 Information to the author from J. McLean, Burness, HTA Solicitors.
13 Gwatkin, 'The Harris Tweed Industry', 11.
14 McKenna & Co., on behalf of HTA Ltd., to Board of Trade, 23. 2. 1910, HRA/D 190 I [m]).
15 *Report to the Board of Agriculture for Scotland on Home Industries in the Highlands and Islands in 1914* [hereafter: 'Scott Report'], 12.
16 *ibid.*, 183.
17 Gwatkin, 'The Harris Tweed Industry', 12.
18 Scott Report, 183.
19 *ibid.*, 182-183.
20 *ibid.*, 50.
21 Memorandum and Articles of Association of the Harris Tweed Association Ltd., HTA Office, Stornoway.

5

The Trade Mark in Operation: 1911 to 1914

The Harris Tweed Trade Mark was registered in October 1910 and stamping with the Orb Mark started in Harris in early 1911. At the same time, the market for Harris Tweed reached an unprecedented level and every effort, legal and otherwise, was being made throughout Lewis and Harris to meet the demand. It had been the intention of the Harris Tweed Association that the Orb Mark would guarantee any customer that he was buying genuine, good quality, handspun Harris Tweed. The Association, however, was not immediately successful in restricting the use of the term 'Harris Tweed' to the genuine handspun article. Its ability to promote the new trade mark was seriously restricted by its own precarious financial situation. For that part of 1911, when stamping with the trade mark was introduced (at a fee of a halfpenny per yard) the Association's total income was £261. 4s. 2 ½d. Its total expenses were £243. 6s. 1d, leaving a small profit of £17. 18s. 1d. Early in 1912, an inspector was appointed to Lewis at a cost of £53. 11s. 4d, but stamping of tweed in Lewis only brought in £13. 17s. 10d. Thus the full year of 1912 ran at a loss of almost £18 with an income of £276. 19s. against an expenditure of £314. Had it not been for the introduction of stamping in Lewis, the Association would have been able to meet its expenses out of income, but with such a small margin of profit that it could not incur other outlays, such as legal costs or extensive advertising.[1]

Whether or not extensive advertising or frequent prosecutions would have solved the problem of tweed from millspun yarn being passed off as Harris Tweed is now difficult to judge. The use of millspun yarn and the deception of passing off continued to bedevil the industry for many years to come. The underlying problem facing the Harris Tweed Association was that practices which were dictated by the short-term financial interests of weavers and independent producers, or even, as some might have claimed, by sheer economic necessity, were not easily abandoned. Tweed which did not qualify for the trade mark still reached the market as 'Harris Tweed'. One has to sympathise with the ordinary customer who simply wanted a hard-wearing Harris Tweed jacket to wear at weekends or on holiday. He could seek the advice of his tailor or gentleman's outfitter, but it is doubtful whether even these 'experts' were fully aware of the complex situation which surrounded the production of 'Harris Tweed' at the time. Briefly, the production of Harris Tweed by the old cottage method involved carding the wool by hand, spinning this wool into yarn on a domestic spinning-wheel and then weaving the tweed by hand on a domestic loom. As mechanisation was introduced some of these processes came to be done by machine. Machine-carding was the first step and this was commonly used by the end of the 19th century. Machine-spinning of the wool into yarn began on a much more restricted scale at approximately the same time, but the definition of Harris Tweed did not accept machine-spun yarn until 1934. The requirement for hand-weaving has never changed.

Thus in the first decade of the 20th century, three types of tweed had come into being in the Outer Hebrides and all of these were sold as 'Harris Tweed'. These types of tweed were:

(1) a tweed, hand-made in all processes apart from machine-carding;

(2) a tweed, largely produced in Lewis, in which all the yarn was machine-carded, machine-spun and handwoven;

(3) what was known as a '50-50 tweed', i.e. a tweed in which the wool was machine-carded; the wool for the warp was machine-spun, while the wool for woof (or weft) was handspun. The tweed was then handwoven from 50% handspun and 50% machine-spun yarn. This type of 50-50 tweed was mostly made in Lewis.

Only the first type of tweed, that is the tweed made entirely from handspun yarn, qualified for the Orb trade mark and the name 'Harris Tweed'. The Scott Report explained how the other types reached the market as Harris Tweed.

> 'In Lewis there is a type of opinion which professes to prefer machine-spun yarn, according to one point of view, for the warp in order to strengthen it, or, according to another for both warp and woof, but in ordinary trade, tweeds made in Lewis, by either of these

methods, are rarely sold as containing machine-spun yarn, and most of them find their market somewhere or other, as 'Harris Tweed'. It may be calculated that the cost of production of a tweed made altogether of machine-spun yarn, but handwoven and hand-finished, is at present (i.e. 1911-1912) between 1.9d and 1.10d per yard. If it passes as Harris Tweed, there is a profit of 1/- a yard, or nearly £3 on a web. One method is particularly despicable, namely to induce two persons to sign a form of guarantee, which is attached to the web, specifying that it is both handspun and handwoven - in one such case a guarantee was noticed when it was even declared that the wool was hand-carded as well. Assuming - as it is to be feared is too often the case - that these guarantees are attached to webs which are composed of altogether millspun yarn, those who sign such documents lay themselves open to serious consequences.' [2]

While such practices certainly involved flagrant dishonesty, the underlying economic pressure of a declining fishing industry made it very difficult for those Lewis fishermen who had taken up weaving to revert to wholly handspun yarn. The deception lay, not in using millspun yarn, which could certainly produce a good quality tweed, but in 'passing off' tweed made from millspun yarn as Harris Tweed. There is little doubt that the passing off was done with the intention of deceiving the public and cashing in on the reputation of genuine wholly handspun Harris Tweed. The determination of so many producers and weavers to persevere in using millspun yarn probably sprang from a number of reasons. It is possible that one of these reasons was a genuine conviction that millspun yarn produced a better tweed and Scott does argue a strong case for the industry in Lewis specialising in tweed made from millspun yarn, marketed as such, and competing on equal terms with Harris Tweed. However, it is most likely that the strongest reason for using millspun yarn was the economic advantage gained by selling this cloth at a considerable profit as genuine Harris Tweed. When wholesalers and retailers recognised that the name Harris Tweed did not necessarily guarantee good quality cloth, either because of the use of inferior yarn (possibly millspun yarn which was not 100% pure wool) or most probably because of poor weaving, they simply stopped buying it. The inevitable result was a dramatic slump in the market for Harris Tweed towards the end of 1911.

In 1912, a number of Stornoway tweed merchants applied to join the Harris Tweed Association and have an inspector based in Lewis. The Orb stamp would thus be applied to Lewis-made tweed which conformed with the trade mark regulations. While this may have been a wise decision on the part of these merchants, it did bring its own problems. By insisting that tweeds they handled should be made from wholly handspun yarn, they were demanding that Lewis weavers should return to the practices used at the turn of the century, when genuine Harris Tweed was made in Lewis. The Scott Report explains that even if the Stornoway merchants who joined the Harris Tweed Association had succeeded in excluding millspun yarn, by doing so they would have cut off a great part of the trade of the local mills which had by 1910 installed spinning machinery. To prevent this, the owners of these mills would naturally have done all in their power to secure another outlet for machine-spun yarn. Even if the merchants had overcome the opposition of the Stornoway mills, they could not afford to crush them, for local machine-carding would still have been required. [3]

A technical survey of the processes involved in making tweed was undertaken, somewhat belatedly one might feel, in 1912-1913. The conclusion reached was that there was a substantial balance of opinion in favour of handspinning and handweaving. There was, however, a considerable body of opinion which maintained that good quality millspun yarn, particularly for the warp, produced a hard-wearing tweed. [4] The explanation of the difference between the qualities of handspun and millspun yarn given by the experts was as follows:-

> 'The durability of a cloth made of pure wool lies in the amount of twist given to the yarn in spinning. A machine can impart any amount of twist to yarn but, in practice, each additional turn of the machine increases the costs of production, and therefore the tendency is for the manufacturer to diminish the quantity of twist. In hand-spinning, on the contrary, it is convenient for the worker to give a large amount of twist to her yarn. ... It follows that the average handspun thread is likely to be stronger than the average machine-spun thread, through this cause. ... The stress of production which induces manufacturers to diminish the twist in their yarns also leads them to introduce shoddy (reconstituted yarn made from rags) into their cloth. It is practically impossible

for the hand-spinner to use shoddy owing to the severe difficulty in turning it into yarn. ... One reason that shoddy wears so badly is that the fibre of the wool is very short and so the yarn tends to break or fray.'[5]

Those in favour of allowing the use of millspun yarn would say that the problem did not lie so much in the use of millspun yarn per se, as in the temptation to skimp on the degree of twist given to the yarn, and, even more heinous, the introduction of shoddy into the fibre. None of these faults was necessarily inherent to millspun yarn. It was the acceptance of inferior yarn combined with unskilled or careless weaving which resulted in poorly produced tweed which did not live up to expectation. This was the situation which was damaging the reputation of, and the market for, handspun Harris Tweed.

It has been suggested that the Harris Tweed Association's insistence that the term 'Harris Tweed' should be confined to tweed made of handspun yarn was, by 1910, a vain attempt to turn the clock back. By ignoring the reality of the situation in Lewis it was doomed to failure from the start. Although the members of the Association were acting from the best of motives in trying to protect the industry with a trade mark, they had gone down the wrong road, and rather than seeking a remedy for the real ills affecting the industry, such as poor standards of production during a boom in the market, they had created a situation in which deception was almost inevitable.

One important reality which the founders of the Harris Tweed Association and the Board of Trade ignored in 1910 was the different weaving traditions in Lewis and Harris. Traditionally the making of tweed in Harris had been an occupation for women and once it became a commercial enterprise it earned some extra income for the home. It was two women from Harris, the Paisley sisters, who are credited with being the first commercial weavers for the Earl of Dunmore. In Harris, weaving was a cottage industry in the truest sense and a supplement to the family income. In Lewis however, long before commercial weaving entered the picture, weaving for local outlets had been done by men as a specialised activity and was therefore seen as a principal source of income for the weaver. Every township had its tradesman-weaver to whom crofters brought their wool to be turned into cloth.[6]

Shearing the Sheep.

Marion Campbell dyeing wool in an iron boiler.

Marion Campbell washing the dyed wool in the burn.

Calum MacKenzie, Main St. Tarbert, on *Beart mhòr,* early 20th century.

Woman on *Beart mhòr* in corrugated iron weaving shed.

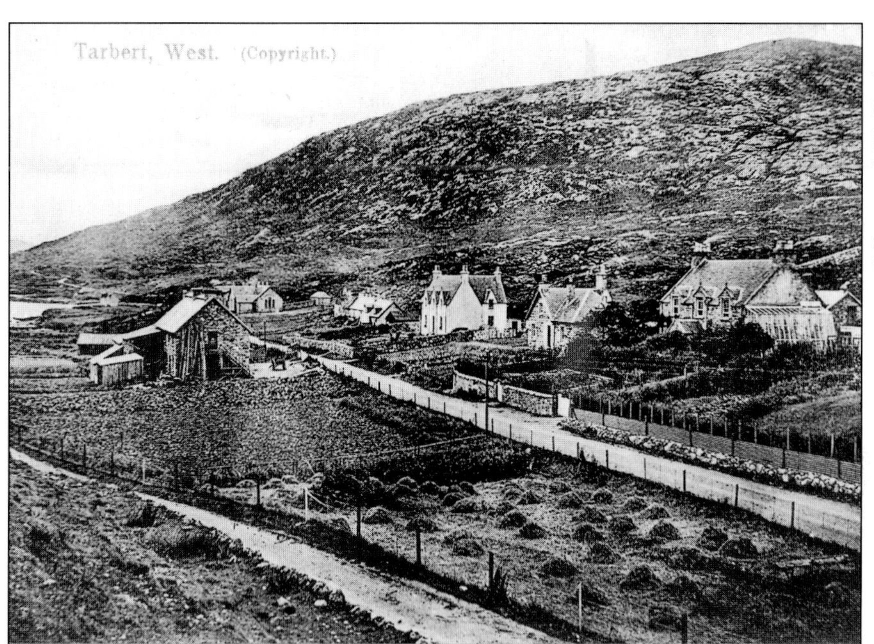

Mill at West Tarbert.
The mill lies to the left of the road going north towards Stornoway.

© Courtesy of J. M. Morrison, Tarbert

Miss Marion Campbell weaving at her old wooden loom the *Beart mhòr*.

Waulking the newly-woven tweed by beating it rhythmically on a board. This finishing process is known in Gaelic as the *luadh*.

Marion Campbell with
a finished Tweed.

By the turn of the century, a number of factors combined to reinforce the predominance of men in weaving in Lewis. The older type of loom used in the islands was known as the *beart bheag*, the little loom, in which the shuttle, made from the shin-bone of a sheep, was thrown by hand. In the 1890s the Congested Districts Board made interest-free loans available for the purchase of a new bigger loom with a flying shuttle, the *beart mhòr*. These new looms, originally imported from Galashiels, had a much greater output per hour than the *beart bheag*, but as they were much heavier to work, they tended to be used by men. According to Angus MacLeod of Marybank, Stornoway, the first *beart mhòr* in Lewis was acquired by James MacKenzie, 4 Gravir, Lochs, about 1895 and a Kenneth Nicolson, a self-taught joiner, made one for himself, after seeing MacKenzie's loom. In 1903, Archibald MacRae, a joiner and turner of 65 Keith St. Stornoway started producing them at approximately £6 to £8 each.[7] By 1911 there were between 250 and 300 of the new looms in Lewis. At the same date Scott reports that nine out of ten weavers in Harris were women.

The other important reality ignored was the fact that Lewis had become inescapably dependent on the use of millspun yarn by 1910 because changing patterns of involvement in the fishing industry had forced men in Lewis to turn to weaving as a principal source of income rather than long-line fishing. As mainland ports with a railway terminus became more attractive landing spots, the cured fish from the islands could no longer compete in price with fresh fish from mainland ports. As one source of income, participation in fishing, diminished another had to be found, and that was increasingly to become participation in the making of tweed. To make a livelihood comparable to what he might have earned as part-owner of a small fishing boat, the weaver had to have a sufficient supply of yarn and it seemed to him that only millspun yarn could give him that. These circumstances combined in the first decade of the 20th century to bring inexperienced weavers into the industry just as the demand for Harris Tweed was increasing.

The increasing demand for Harris Tweed also encouraged some merchants to become middlemen, specialising to a greater or lesser extent in marketing Harris Tweed. As entrepreneurs, these merchants played a considerable role in expanding the market for Harris Tweed. A description of this type of merchant's business relationship with the crofters was given by Mr Calum John MacDonald, a native of Balallan, and a much respected senior inspector with the Harris Tweed Association in the middle decades of the twentieth century. Giving evidence in preparation for the Harris Tweed case of 1964, Mr MacDonald said,

> 'In my young days the practice was for the crofters to process their own wool. They would shear the sheep, wash and dye the wool and thereafter tease the wool by hand, mainly in the wintertime. They would then place the wool into bags marked 'weft' and 'warp'. These bags were then handed to the merchant who had a contract with one of the island mills to convert the dyed and teased wool into yarn. After the first World War there were two spinning mills in Stornoway and another at Tarbert, if I recollect rightly. The merchants would use one or more of these mills for converting the wool into yarn. When we got the yarn back from the merchant, we would send it to a local weaver. After the weaving had been done the cloth came back to us in a greasy state. My mother would then get in some women friends to carry out the waulking process - that is to say the shrinking, washing and cleaning of the cloth. The practice was for the merchant to pay the weaver and then after deducting the costs of carriage, weaving and cleaning, the balance went into my mother's account.'[8]

While Mr MacDonald does not say under what name such tweed was eventually sold, there is no doubt that a significant proportion of tweed made on similar terms was sold as Harris Tweed, both before the introduction of the Orb mark and for many years after 1911. As used by Mr MacDonald the term 'merchant' means the local trader who kept a general store selling all types of goods as well as dealing in tweeds. Over time some of these merchants came to specialise in tweeds. These specialist tweed merchants, or Independent Producers, had no plant of their own, but relied on local or mainland mills for dyeing and spinning, and after some years, for finishing, when hand-finishing went out of fashion. They were essentially entrepreneurs, taking orders for particular patterns of tweed which they then issued with a pattern and the necessary quantity of yarn to a weaver, and finally invoicing and baling the cloth to the customer. Such a complex enterprise was beyond the financial capacity of the average crofter or crofter-weaver. Such entrepreneurs were also known as 'Small Producers' to distinguish them from the large mills.

The emergence of independent producers demonstrates how the industry had changed from the cottage industry established in Harris in the middle of the previous century. When the industry started, the production of the cloth had been the sole preserve of the crofter and his family, but the marketing had, of necessity, been in the hands of charitable agencies, or individuals, with easier access to the market place. The role of these charitable agencies was gradually supplanted by local private enterprise. Where a public body, such as the Scottish Home Industries Association, could not afford to risk its reputation by infringing the law, some individual entrepreneurs could and did take such a risk in claiming that cloth made from millspun yarn was 'Harris Tweed'.

The outbreak of the First World War in 1914 removed the majority of the young men from the islands. People were concerned with much more urgent issues than reforming the Harris Tweed industry. Thus no significant steps were taken to alter the structure and practices of the industry until after the war.

Reference - The Trade Mark in operation: 1911 to 1914

1 *Report to the Board of Agriculture for Scotland on Home Industries in the Highlands and Islands in 1914* [hereafter: 'Scott Report,'], 201-202.
2 *ibid.*, 61.
3 *ibid.*, 63-4.
4 *ibid.*, 138.
5 *ibid.*, 139.
6 Gwatkin, 'The Harris Tweed Industry', 14.
7 *Highland News*, 23. 1. 1904.
8 Gwatkin, 'The Harris Tweed Industry', 20-21.

6

The Leverhulme Era and Afterwards: 1918 to 1928

The impact of the First World War on the Hebrides was particularly severe in terms of the number of men lost. From the middle of the 19th century, island men had traditionally enrolled in the Royal Naval Reservists and in the Militia because the retainer and training bounties provided a welcome supplement to their meagre incomes. Islanders who were already trained soldiers or seamen were among the first to be mobilised on the outbreak of war. They were among the volunteers who took the brunt of the losses sustained in the disastrous early years of the war. Scarred as the islands were by that disproportionate loss of young men, their families could take comfort from the fact that they died in the service of their country. No such comfort was available to anyone when 181 survivors of the war, 174 from Lewis and 7 from Harris, were drowned at the entrance to Stornoway harbour when the *Iolaire* foundered on the Beasts of Holm in the early hours of New Year's Day 1919. The emotional scars of that tragedy were to last for generations. Yet another lasting scar was left on the islands in 1923-24 when many young men and women decided to emigrate to Canada in the hope of finding employment there that they could not find at home. The names *S.S. Metagama, S.S. Marloch* and *S.S. Canada* are etched in Hebridean memory alongside that of the *Iolaire*. It is, perhaps, ironic that once they had created a new life on the other side of the Atlantic, many of those exiles contributed to the increased sales of Harris Tweed in the United States and Canada.

Although the making of tweed had been important to the economy of the Hebrides as the fishing began to decline in the first decade of the twentieth century, it was to become even more important in the difficult years after the First War when the Russian Revolution removed the traditional export markets for herring in eastern Europe. Despite strenuous attempts by the government to expand the home market for herring, attempts which under wartime conditions led to Stornoway Pier and Harbour Commission collecting record dues in 1917, the long-term outlook for herring was never to be so rosy as it had been before the war. When wartime agricultural subsidies were also withdrawn, it must have seemed to islanders that Harris Tweed was the only economic lifeline left.

The purchase of the Island of Lewis by Lord Leverhulme in 1918 may have seemed propitious, until the details of his plans emerged. His implacable opposition to the crofting system came as a harsh blow to all those who had looked forward to the Government fulfilling its promise of making smallholdings available when the war was over. The controversy over the Leverhulme interlude will occupy minds for years to come, not least the controversy surrounding his plans to make Stornoway a major fishing port. With hindsight, and our knowledge of the parlous state of the fishing industry, we can but speculate as to how the islands might have fared had these plans been fulfilled. In the Leverhulme debate, the focus is almost always on his plans for the land and the seas surrounding the Hebrides. When compared with these issues, there is little memory left today of the interest he took in the Harris Tweed industry.

Lord Leverhulme bought Lewis from Major Duncan Matheson in May 1918 for £143,000. In late 1918, he opened negotiations to buy South Harris from Alexander, 8th Earl of Dunmore, great-grandson of the Earl of Dunmore who had bought Harris in 1834, and grandson of Catherine, Countess of Dunmore of Harris Tweed fame. In May 1919, Leverhulme bought most of South Harris and St Kilda for £36,000. The sale of South Harris did not sever the Dunmore interest in the islands as we find Viscount Fincastle, the son of Lord Dunmore, adding his voice to the debate in the 1930s about the amended definition of Harris Tweed and the use of mainland millspun yarn. In October 1919, with his appetite for an island empire apparently still unappeased, Leverhulme bought North Harris from Sir Samuel Scott for £20,000, with Sir Samuel retaining a fifteen year lease on Amhuinnsuidhe Castle. [1]

At the time of Leverhulme's purchase of Lewis and Harris there were, in addition to the independent producers of Harris Tweed who had no spinning capacity of their own, two dominant island mills which were both spinners and producers distributing machine-spun yarn for weaving on commission. Those mills, both in Stornoway, have already been mentioned. They were Kenneth MacKenzie Ltd. of Lewis St, the successor company to the Lewis Wool Mills Company, a carding and spinning mill started in 1906 by Kenneth MacKenzie, and S. A. Newall and Sons Ltd., which had been started about 1906 by S. A. Newall, a farmer and flesher who had at one time been tenant of Aignish Farm. The carding mill started by Aeneas MacKenzie at the Patent Slip in 1903 had added spinning plant in 1908. This mill changed hands when

Aeneas MacKenzie went bankrupt in 1910 and the business was then taken over by a Mr Morrison. [2] In 1918, an associate company of S.A. Newall and Sons Ltd. bought the Patent Slip mill, although it seems that neither carding nor spinning had been carried on there for some years before Newalls took it over. [3]

According to Nigel Nicolson, Lord Leverhulme seems to have realised that the image of Harris Tweed as a cottage industry was one of its most important selling points, especially in the United States and in the luxury end of the market. He also recognised that the practice of sending yarn out to weavers in the rural townships of the island provided a remunerative source of employment in districts which had little, if any, alternative source of income. [4] Despite those apparent concessions to tradition, Leverhulme's subsequent actions call into question his real understanding of the industry. Within less than a year of buying Lewis, Leverhulme began his programme of imposing on the tweed industry the efficiency of production which was the hallmark of all his other business ventures. He consulted with experts, as was his wont, and came to the conclusion that millspun yarn was indistinguishable from handspun and that hand-spinning was a waste of time. 'As much as £4 a week could be earned by a good weaver, but only 12/- a week by a good spinner'.[5] His convictions about the industry were articulated in a speech to the Philosophical Institute of Edinburgh on 4th November, 1919, when he declared:

> 'all the labour available in Lewis and Harris can be concentrated on handloom weaving, undiluted by time spent on the starvation earnings to be made by handspinning.' [6]

This statement was tantamount to dismissing as an irrelevance the legal definition of Harris Tweed, with its requirement for handspun yarn.

As part of his plan to modernise the production of tweed, Leverhulme acquired, in March 1919, a controlling interest in Kenneth MacKenzie Ltd. He purchased two-thirds of the firm's Ordinary shares and the remainder four years later. [7] Kenneth MacKenzie remained as Chairman and Managing Director of the company with his fellow Directors being Sir Herbert Morgan, Mr Frank Clarke and Mr Alexander J. MacKenzie, a son of Kenneth MacKenzie. [8] Both father and son were later to become Provosts of Stornoway. Sir Herbert

Morgan and Frank Clarke were also Directors of Leverhulme's fishing-related companies, the Stornoway Fish Products & Ice Co. Ltd. and Lewis Island Preserved Specialities Co. Ltd. Frank Clarke was Leverhulme's English agent. [9] Herbert Morgan seems to have been Leverhulme's right hand man who, in addition to undertaking a variety of business responsibilities on Leverhulme's behalf, attended to details as diverse as researching the correct style of address for royalty or recommending a hosier who could supply white shirts and underwear for his employer. [10] Leverhulme also tried to buy S. A. Newall & Sons, but the owner was unwilling to sell.

The innovations introduced to Kenneth MacKenzie Ltd. as a result of Leverhulme's purchase of a controlling interest in the company are described in a promotional feature published in the *Overseas Daily Mail* of 29th November, 1919. This article, written by a Walter Wilson, is of particular interest in that it is the first known occasion on which a producer from Lewis explicitly admits that his tweed was made from millspun yarn. [11]

> 'Though since the introduction of millspun yarn the production of Harris Tweeds has been greatly accelerated, it has at no time been equal to the demand. The three sets of carding engines and 1,200 spindles introduced by Mr MacKenzie ten years ago are now totally inadequate to meet requirements and another important step forward has been taken.'

The 'important step forward' refers to the conversion of the original firm into a new 'company with a share capital of £50,000 with the object of further developing the industry'. [12] The original spinning capacity of about 3,000 lbs per week, described as being 'inadequate to meet requirements' was about to be doubled to '6,000 lbs per week by the installation of two additional 300-spindle mules, run by a private electricity plant'. [13]

The *Overseas Daily Mail* feature continued:

> 'At the outset the Company propose to erect a large mill in close proximity to the centre of Stornoway. The main idea is to produce yarn in greater quantities for the hand-loom weavers; no weaving

will be carried on at the mill, but it is hoped when the machinery is running that sufficient yarn will be made to keep the weavers regularly employed.' [14]

Hand-spinning had persisted to a greater extent in Harris than in Lewis, until after the First War, partly through the lack of readily available millspun yarn in the remoter districts. However, by 1920, Kenneth MacKenzie Ltd., with its increased spinning capacity, 'was sending three times more yarn from the Stornoway mill to Harris than to Lewis'. [15] The next step to increase the use of millspun yarn was the setting up of a carding and spinning mill at Tarbert, the Harris Handwoven Tweed Co. Ltd., a MacKenzie subsidiary. In 1922, another carding and spinning mill was ready at Geocrab on the Bays side of Harris. It is said that the inspiration for the Geocrab mill lay in the pity Leverhulme felt on seeing a woman from the Bays walking across the moor carrying a heavy load of wool to be carded in Tarbert. His pity however seems to have been somewhat misplaced as the people of the Bays refused to use the spinning facilities at Geocrab. Preferring to use handspun yarn, and knowing that the introduction of millspun would sound the death-knell for the traditional skill of hand-spinning, they argued their point of view at meeting after meeting until a 'sudden slump in the whole industry, which rendered almost unsaleable the thousands of yards of finished tweed that had accumulated in the mills at Geocrab, Tarbert and Stornoway'. [16] The files in Unilever House contain a comment on Geocrab from Lord Leverhulme to a Mrs C. MacSween of Scalpay, dated 2nd June 1924, in which he wrote, 'I went to great personal expense to put a spinning-mill at Geocrab so that the crofters' own wool could be spun on the island and to ensure its quality, but I have never been asked for one single pound to be spun'. [17]

With the expertise in promotion and distribution gained from his experience as a successful manufacturer of soap, it is not surprising that Leverhulme turned his attention to advertising the tweed made for his mills. Kenneth MacKenzie Ltd. started advertising much more extensively than ever before. They advertised in trade journals and, in conjunction with large departmental stores, promoted Harris Tweed garments in the national press. [18] The feature in the *Overseas Daily Mail* provides an interesting example of this promotional campaign for tweeds which were made from millspun yarn.

> 'Harris Tweeds have now reached a high standard of excellence, and in designing, dyeing and manufacture the cloths being put on the market by Kenneth Mackenzie Ltd. have no superior. The company has built up a large connection in all parts of the country ... Agencies have now been established throughout the world by Kenneth Mackenzie Ltd. for the sale of the Harris Tweeds, and they are receiving orders from unexpected quarters. The cloths are finding their way in increasing quantities to Iceland and Scandinavia, to Australia and New Zealand, to Canada and America and South Africa.' [19]

Leverhulme was also responsible for the greatly extended use of the Domestic Hattersley Loom which differed from the large wooden *beart mhòr* in that it was worked by the feet and the shuttle was thrown automatically across the web. The Hattersley loom was introduced to assist ex-service men who had lost a hand. Ludicrous as it may seem to the modern weaver, the question arose, in all seriousness, as to whether the use of the Hattersley did actually constitute 'hand-weaving'. Two important advantages of the Hattersley loom were that it increased a weaver's rate of production and wove more intricate patterns. The conditions under which the new looms were made available were described in Kenneth MacKenzie's promotional feature in the *Overseas Daily Mail* :

> 'At present the looms in use are antiquated and entail a considerable amount of labour to work them. Messrs Kenneth MacKenzie Ltd. propose to give weavers the opportunity of showing their skill on one of the latest hand-looms on the market ... and the output will be much larger than now made by the use of the present looms. The only stipulation will be that as the looms are the property of the Company, they must be used exclusively for its work.' [20]

While this was a sound commercial move in that it ensured an outlet for MacKenzie's yarn, by creating a class of tied weaver, it contained the seeds of a potentially serious problem for the craft status of the industry. This questionable alteration in the status of the weaver was compounded by another Leverhulme-inspired innovation. In his speech to the Philosophical Institute of Edinburgh on 4th November, 1919, already mentioned, Leverhulme had gone on to say:

> 'My intention is to erect at convenient centres in Lewis and Harris small power-driven dyeing, carding and spinning industries to prepare the crofters' wool for the hand-loom weavers to work into cloth, in or near their own homes.'[21]

The words 'in or near their own homes' referred to the establishment of weaving sheds containing four to six looms in Ness, Barvas and Carloway.[22] These sheds were to be heated by peat stoves in which the smoke from the peat was to go straight up the chimney but 'it wouldn't be a bad thing if a little smoke is allowed to escape into the shed for advertising purposes'.[23] At about the same time the mill-owning producers are believed to have introduced Hattersley looms into part of their premises and employed weavers there.[24] In moving the weaver away from his own croft into a mini-factory, Leverhulme was setting a dangerous precedent. Had this trend continued, a growing section of the industry would have become wholly factory-based. If a factory in Lewis, or Harris, could produce 'Harris Tweed' it would only have been a matter of time before a factory on the mainland, in England or even in Japan, would have claimed the right to do the same. Any hope of protecting the craft status of the industry and thus the income of crofter-weavers would have been sacrificed in the interests of the profits of the mill-owning producers.

All this discussion of Leverhulme's contribution to the development of the Harris Tweed industry ignores the fundamental fact that the tweed produced at this time by Kenneth Mackenzie Ltd. would not have conformed to the Harris Tweed Association's definition of Harris Tweed and would almost certainly have been rejected by the buying public if it had been known that it was made from millspun yarn. The fact that there could be any doubt in contemporary minds about that point is a measure of the extent to which the use of millspun yarn had, by the 1920s, crept in without the knowledge of the buying public. It would be difficult to demonstrate now how the independent producers described their product, as what they described as 'Harris Tweed' may or may not have been what it claimed to be. With the large mill-owning producers the evidence is there to be judged on its merits.

It is interesting to examine the way in which the feature writer in the *Overseas Daily Mail* handled the issue of whether or not the tweed being produced from what was clearly millspun yarn was actually sold as 'Harris Tweed' or 'Lewis Tweed'. On first reading the article, as the ordinary uninformed reader would have done, the impression given is that the writer is describing only Harris Tweed. The article ignores the spinning mill of Mr Aeneas MacKenzie and also the existence of the Newall firm, all of which suggests that it was editorially inspired. It said that Harris Tweeds had reached a high standard of excellence, and in designing, dyeing and manufacture, the cloths being put on the market by Kenneth Mackenzie Ltd. had no superior. 'One strong point in favour of the Lewis and Harris Tweeds is that they are made of pure Scotch wool. Being handwoven, shoddy cannot enter into their composition'. For some months the demand had exceeded the supply. In a final paragraph entitled 'The Genuine Article' the writer pointed out that the success of Lewis and Harris Tweeds had brought many imitations, about which a word of warning should be uttered. Knowing that it had not been possible to meet all demands for Harris and Lewis tweeds, certain producers beyond the Scottish borders had devoted a number of their looms to the production of cloths which at first sight possessed the appearance of the original fabrics. The article ended by declaring that the imitations had not the slightest connection with the Hebrides, and that it was misleading to describe them as 'Harris Tweeds'. In the opinion of John S. Gwatkin of McKenna and Co., all this suggests that MacKenzie's were in 1919 a little uncertain as to whether their millspun product could properly be described as Harris Tweed, and they therefore used the term 'Lewis and Harris Tweeds'. [25]

The final point made in the *Overseas Daily Mail* article was a plea to purchasers to ensure that the tweed they were buying had been supplied by Kenneth Mackenzie Ltd.

> 'In this matter purchasers can render a useful service by communicating with Messrs. Kenneth Mackenzie Limited, Stornoway, or when buying, obtain a guarantee from retailers that the article sold as Harris Tweed has been supplied by the company. Every yard of the genuine material is guaranteed handwoven, and that is the best warranty that can be given, because no machine-woven tweeds can provide the same wearing qualities and characteristics.' [26]

The emphasis on the best source of the 'genuine material' surely indicates that the author's information and inspiration came directly from none other than Messrs Kenneth MacKenzie Ltd. Somewhat in contradiction of the impression given by the ambiguously worded article in the *Overseas Daily Mail*, we learn from evidence given in the Harris Tweed case that Lord Leverhulme hit on the idea of marketing some of the millspun tweed produced by the Lewis and Harris Handwoven Tweed Company (his mill in Tarbert, Harris) and possibly some of the millspun tweed produced by Kenneth Mackenzie Ltd., under the name 'Macloom Tweed', an idea which Lord Hunter commended. [27]

Colonel Macarthur, Chairman of the Harris Tweed Association in 1962 and senior partner of the firm Stewart, Rule and Co., had been in practice as a solicitor in Stornoway in 1924 when Lord Leverhulme gave up his development schemes in Lewis. At that time he acted for the MacKenzie family in buying back from Lord Leverhulme his whole shareholding in Kenneth MacKenzie Ltd. [28] In 1961, when John Gwatkin was preparing his briefing papers on the history of the Harris Tweed Industry, Colonel Macarthur told him that he remembered Lord Leverhulme's preference for the name 'Macloom' for tweed produced from millspun yarn. [29]

In a brochure for S. A. Newall and Sons entitled *The Story of Lewis and Harris Homespuns*, written circa 1922 by F. J. Newall, one can detect an ambiguity similar to that found in MacKenzie's promotional article in the *Overseas Daily Mail*. The brochure gives a fairly accurate history of the industry and describes in detail the original processes involved in making Harris Tweed, including hand-carding, which, by the time the brochure was written, had largely been abandoned. The only forms of spinning mentioned are those done by the distaff and whorl or by the spinning-wheel, and this by one of the major island producers of millspun yarn! The writer takes refuge in quoting from an article in the *Transactions of the Gaelic Society of Inverness* in which the traditional method of hand-finishing is described and scrupulously avoids any undesirable reference to mill processes. While the term 'Harris Tweed' is not used in the main text of the brochure, the 'unsolicited' testimonials at the foot of each page refer frequently to Harris Tweed, as do the order forms at the back. Near the end of the brochure is a 'poem' composed by F. J. N. entitled 'A Muse on Harris Tweed'. The final line of each verse has a variation on the merits of 'Harris Tweed'. The question which cannot now be answered with any certainty is were S. A. Newall and Sons advertising in this brochure only the genuine handspun article bought in by them from weavers in Harris, or were they promoting tweed made from their own millspun yarn at the same time, hoping that the customer would not ask about the difference between Lewis and Harris Tweeds?

It may be that the apparent confusion between the genuine handspun product and the millspun product which occurred in advertising material put out in the early 1920s by MacKenzies and Newalls, was simply a felicitous ambiguity on the part of a feature writer struggling with the complexities of definitions, or it may be that a deliberate attempt at disguising the difference between the two types of tweed was being made. Putting the best complexion possible on the matter, it may simply be that these firms were advertising only that small section of their business which was based on the sale of the genuine article bought by the mills from weavers who used only handspun yarn.

Nonetheless, to the uninformed buying public, any tweed produced in the islands tended to be thought of as Harris Tweed, sometimes, as has been suggested, because of deliberate attempts by producers to deceive, sometimes by subtle attempts to confuse. The difficulty for the Harris Tweed Association in knowing exactly what was going on was compounded by the fact that, as the stamping records of the Harris Tweed Association show, both Newalls and MacKenzies certainly did have a policy of buying in as much as they could of the genuine handspun tweed, produced mainly in Harris. Thus the mill-owners were advertising and selling both their own tweed made from millspun yarn and genuine Harris Tweed made from handspun yarn. The scope for confusion between the two types of tweed was perhaps quite convenient for anyone who wished to take advantage of it. These somewhat dubious practices continued throughout the remainder of the decade until the Harris Tweed Association received an injection of new blood in 1928.

The question remains as to who were the economic realists, Leverhulme who had no time for handspun yarn, the independent producers, Newalls and MacKenzies who were all using considerable quantities of millspun yarn, or the Harris Tweed Association and those relatively few weavers and producers in Harris who continued to use only handspun yarn? Could the industry have provided employment for as many people as it did or met the market demand for tweed using only handspun yarn? Was the tweed produced from millspun yarn in any significant way inferior to tweed made from handspun yarn? Could a hand-spinner ever expect to receive a living wage commensurate with the time involved in the task?

Before attempting to answer these questions, it should be remembered that after the First War a new and less elite market for Harris Tweed had emerged. That market was no longer composed of the benevolently-minded friends of Lady Dunmore or the Duchess of Sutherland. The customers of the post-war years were not simply the aristocracy and minor aristocracy who bought their clothes from a bespoke tailor and spent their autumns on the Highland grouse moors, but the reasonably affluent middle classes, teachers, doctors, lawyers and businessmen who at weekends became golfers, hillwalkers or anglers, and bought their clothes ready-made from a multiple store. This ordinary man or woman wanted a serviceable garment with good wearing qualities, not a luxury item. Yet if the hand-spinner were to receive a living wage, the cost of handspun tweed had to be at the luxury end of the market. It could be argued that to cater for the new and less exclusive mass market, the Harris Tweed industry had to accept more cost-efficient methods of production. In responding to market forces, the majority of the industry was, consciously or unconsciously, evolving with the times. The process of legitimising that evolution was to occupy the years between 1928 and 1934.

Reference - The Leverhulme Era and Afterwards: 1918 to 1928

1 Nigel Nicolson, *Lord of the Isles: Lord Leverhulme in the Hebrides* [hereafter: Nicolson, *Lord of the Isles*], 122.
2 Gwatkin, Notes on the Historical Development of the Harris Tweed Industry and the Part Played by the Harris Tweed Association Ltd., [hereafter: Gwatkin,'The Harris Tweed Industry'], 19.
3 *ibid.*, 19-20.
4 Nicolson, *Lord of the Isles*, 23.
5 *ibid.*, 119-120.
6 Quoted in Nicolson, *Lord of the Isles*, 120.
7 Nicolson, *Lord of the Isles*, 121.
8 *Overseas Daily Mail*, 29. 11. 1919.
9 Nicolson, *Lord of the Isles*, 49.
10 *ibid.*, 96.
11 Gwatkin, 'The Harris Tweed Industry', 27.
12 *Overseas Daily Mail*, 29. 11. 1919.
13 Nicolson, *Lord of the Isles*, 121.
14 *Overseas Daily Mail*, 29. 11. 1919.
15 Nicolson, *Lord of the Isles*, 220.
16 *ibid.*, 221.
17 *ibid.*, 220 & 252.
18 Gwatkin, 'The Harris Tweed Industry', 26.
19 *Overseas Daily Mail*, 29. 11. 1919.
20 *ibid.*
21 Quoted in Nicolson, *Lord of the Isles*, 120.
22 Gwatkin, 'The Harris Tweed Industry', 26; and Nicolson, *Lord of the Isles*, 120.
23 Nicolson, *Lord of the Isles*, 120.
24 Gwatkin, 'The Harris Tweed Industry', 26.
25 *ibid.*, 28-9.
26 *Overseas Daily Mail*, 29. 11. 1919.
27 *Argyllshire Weavers Ltd. and Others v. Macaulay (A.) (Tweeds) Ltd., and Others*, [1964] RPC No. 16, 477 [hereafter: 'Harris Tweed Case 1964,'], at 508.
28 *ibid.*, 509.
29 Gwatkin, 'The Harris Tweed Industry' 30.

7

Towards an Amended Definition: 1928 to 1934

Although the crucial debate over an amended definition of Harris Tweed took place over sixty years ago, there are still many who either remember the personalities involved, or know of them at one remove. For those whose memories of the time are vague or non-existent, the story will be enriched by an understanding of the different personalities and bodies who played a part, for better or worse, in amending the definition of Harris Tweed.

The issues

It is worth reiterating that the 1909 definition of Harris Tweed stipulated that it had to be made from handspun yarn. Thus tweed made from millspun yarn should not have been sold under the name 'Harris Tweed'. While the use of millspun yarn was seldom mentioned explicitly in advertising material, its use seems to have been common knowledge to everyone involved in the industry, but not to the buying public at large. There is no suggestion that genuine handspun Harris Tweed was not being produced after the First War. It was, but the quantity of cloth made in accordance with the definition was only a fraction of the output of cloth made from millspun yarn which was being passed off as 'Harris Tweed'.

It is a measure of the extent to which the use of millspun yarn had become accepted in Lewis that the issue uppermost in people's minds was not whether or not millspun yarn should be allowed in a product to be sold as 'Harris Tweed', but whether the yarn used should be confined to yarn produced by the local mills or whether mainland millspun yarn could also be used. It was generally assumed by most Lewis producers that the product would be called 'Harris Tweed' whether local or mainland millspun yarn was used. There seems to have been little realisation that opening the door to mainland producers threatened the native industry on a much wider front than the use of yarn spun in the local mills would have done.

Millspun yarn was imported to the islands from mainland spinning mills, such as Hunters of Brora, Holm Mills of Inverness, Black of

Wick, and from mills further afield such as Laidlaws of Keith, Huntly Woollen Mills, Smiths of Peterhead, Macnaughtons of Pitlochry and Macnabs of Slateford, Edinburgh, all of whom were probably using Scottish wool, and from Lumbs of Elland, Yorkshire, whose wool was not necessarily even Scottish wool. To a greater or lesser extent, mainland millspun yarn had been in use since the beginning of the industry in Lewis. However, the demand for Harris Tweed after the First World War caused a significant increase in the use of mainland millspun yarn. Some of this yarn arrived already dyed and some of it came as hanks of white yarn which were then dyed in the yarn (rather than in the wool) on the crofts. Although most of the mills mentioned probably did supply a good quality yarn, the possibility of inferior yarn, adulterated with shoddy, finding its way into a cloth subsequently passed off as 'Harris Tweed' posed a very real danger to the good reputation of the genuine material.

The importing of mainland millspun yarn by merchants and independent producers, who had no spinning capacity of their own, has frequently been justified by the claim that the local spinning mills either could not meet the needs of the independent sector of the industry because they did not have the spinning capacity to cope with increased demand, or would not readily meet the demands of this sector because they saw it as a source of competition to their own production of the cloth they sold as 'Harris Tweed'. The perception in the independent sector of the industry seems to have been that the local spinning mills deliberately set out to eliminate competition from the independent producers and merchants by charging them more for their yarn, thereby reducing the profit that an independent producer could make on a web, or that the local mills were deliberately slow in fulfilling an order for yarn, thereby making it difficult for an independent producer to meet the deadline for an order. These charges against the local mills were to fester away for many years, causing suspicion and antipathy between the independent producers and their rivals, the large producers, i.e. the local mill-owners.

By the late 1920s, as well as using imported yarn, many producers had started sending webs of tweed to the mainland to be finished by specialist finishing firms, because there was no finishing plant in the islands and hand-finishing was going out of fashion. The result was that all processes in the production of this so-called 'Harris Tweed', were becoming mainland-based, except that of hand-weaving in the islands. Mainland spinning mills inevitably recognised an opportunity to expand their own business by taking over all processes in the production of what they chose to call 'Harris Tweed' except hand-weaving which they had done on commission in the islands. An ingenious example of the sort of subterfuge adopted by a mainland firm to meet the minimum requirement of hand-weaving in the islands may be seen in the instance of A. & J. Macnaughton of Pitlochry. This firm went to the trouble of sending their mainland millspun yarn to Harris to be woven on four looms in a loom-shed beside Tarbert pier. The webs were then shipped back to Pitlochry to be finished. Commenting on this practice in the Harris Tweed case of 1964, Lord Hunter said:

> 'So far as I can see the only sensible object of the *modus operandi* described must have been to obtain by that method the selling advantages attaching to the use, legitimate or illegitimate, of the name 'Harris Tweed'. Otherwise one cannot imagine any mainland spinner shipping his yarn all the way from Pitlochry to Tarbert, taking it into a shed at the end of the pier there, having it woven in the shed and then immediately shipping it in the greasy state all the way back to Pitlochry for finishing.' [1]

Whatever accusations might have been levelled at the local spinning mills in Stornoway and Tarbert over the use of millspun yarn, they were at least providing employment within the islands. When a mainland firm indulged in practices such as those of A. & J. Macnaughton, the greater share of the value of processing and all the profits went into mainland pockets. At the same time, the people producing genuine Harris Tweed made from handspun yarn were finding it increasingly difficult to compete in price with the imitation 'Harris Tweed' produced from mainland millspun yarn.

It may astonish the reader to learn that 'Harris Tweed', made from shoddy or even from cotton, was being produced in the 1920s as far away as Japan and America. In other words, the term 'Harris Tweed' was quickly becoming so debased that it was almost a generic term, i.e. the words 'Harris Tweed' were simply coming to mean 'a type of tweed similar to that produced in Harris in the mid-19th century'. The work that it had supplied to the people of the Outer Hebrides could thus be done by anyone anywhere in the world. If we remember that the original purpose of the Countess of Dunmore in encouraging the commercial production of tweed in the mid-19th century had been to give the people of Harris a means of supplementing their incomes, we can appreciate how far the industry had moved away from that original aspiration. By the end of the 1920s Harris Tweed was in imminent danger of having as little connection with the Outer Hebrides as cheddar cheese now has with the Cheddar Gorge. By the late 1920s, it was obvious to all concerned that steps had to be taken quickly to resolve the problems surrounding the definition of 'Harris Tweed'.

The participants in the debate

The various bodies and personalities involved in the negotiations to amend the definition of Harris Tweed reflect a fascinating cross-section of island and national life. Besides the Harris Tweed Association who were the custodians of the Orb Trade Mark and the Board of Trade to whom application to amend the definition had to be made, there were the various producers, such as the local mill-owners, independent producers and merchants based in the islands and mill-owning producers operating from the mainland; there were public figures who came to the defence of the industry in Parliament and in the pages of the *Stornoway Gazette*; perhaps most fascinating of all was the strong voice of the Church participating in the debate on behalf of the crofter-weavers.

The Harris Tweed Association

The role and responsibilities of the Harris Tweed Association in the industry have frequently been misunderstood. The original Memorandum and Articles of Association stated that:

> 'The objects for which the Company is established are the protection of the interests of manufacturers and merchants of, and dealers in, tweed made in the Islands of Harris, Lewis and Uist ... and to promote the manufacture and sale of such tweed. To protect the trade against offences under the Merchandise Marks Acts and otherwise to prevent the use of false trade marks and descriptions in respect of tweed made in imitation thereof. And in furtherance of such objects:- to register a trade mark or

trade marks under the powers given by section 62 of the Trade Marks Act, 1905.' [2]

The Articles of Association empowered the Committee of Management to fill any vacancy with a person nominated by whichever body had nominated his predecessor, e.g. the Crofters' Agency, the Scottish Home Industries Association, the Harris Tweed Association of Tarbert or the Lewis Harris Tweed Association. By a Special Resolution passed on 10th February 1932, the Association revoked the old provision that two members were to be elected from these bodies. This clause was changed to give the Committee of Management power to appoint any person, either to fill a casual vacancy or to make an addition to the Committee, that person to hold office only until the next Ordinary General Meeting and then to be eligible for re-election. [3] Although the Association was often misrepresented as being concerned primarily with the interests of the Stornoway mill-owners, this was not actually the case. The Association regarded itself as the proprietor of the certification mark, acting in the capacity of a custodian or trustee of that mark, in the interests of all sections of the Harris Tweed industry. [4] Its members were chosen from people who did not have a personal financial involvement in the industry.

The absence of accountability in the constitution of the Harris Tweed Association was questioned when a comprehensive survey of the industry was undertaken in the *Lewis Association Report of 1943.*

'The present constitution of the Harris Tweed Association calls for comment. Power is vested in a 'Committee of Management' and apart from this committee the Association has few, if any members ... This system, whereby the absolute control of large sums of money (the proceeds from stamping fees) derived from a particular industry, and to a large extent the welfare of the industry itself, is vested in a committee which is responsible to no one and which co-opts whomsoever it will to fill its ranks, has obvious defects and undesirable potentialities. It is, indeed, a matter of no small credit to the individuals concerned that the system has worked so well and that an Association so constituted should have done such good work.' [5]

It may well be asked why the Harris Tweed Association, as proprietor of the certification trade mark, had not acted to prevent producers passing off as 'Harris Tweed' a cloth which did not conform to the definition. The Association seems to have been in a state of suspended animation for at least fifteen years before 1928. Its members had aged, with some of the founding members of 1909 still serving. [6] The members of the Association were also widely dispersed from one another in Harris, Lewis and London. Many island weavers who were making genuine tweed which was entitled to the Orb stamp did not always bother to apply for it and the income from stamping fees 'seldom exceeded £100 and was often less. On such a small income the H. T. A. could do little in the way of advertising or protecting the name 'Harris Tweed' under the Merchandise Marks Act'. [7]

The Committee of Management of the Harris Tweed Association in the late 1920s comprised Lady Seaforth (formerly Mrs Mary Stewart-Mackenzie) as Chairman, William Harrison, John MacLeod, Donald Morrison, John Morrison, Francis Wigglesworth, George Ellis and John Mackenzie. [8] Lady Seaforth died in 1933 and was succeeded as Chairman by Francis Wigglesworth. In 1932 Colonel Neil Macarthur was elected to the Committee of Management. In 1933, Mr W. H. Martin took over as Secretary of the Harris Tweed Association from Mr Edward Brown who had been the first Secretary to the Association in 1909. McKenna & Co., at that time of Basinghall St London, had acted for the Association in registering the Trade Mark in 1909, and continued until the 1960s as legal advisers to the Association.

By the more stringent standards of the late twentieth century, there would certainly appear to have been a conflict of interest in the appointment of Colonel Macarthur to the HTA Board of Management. A solicitor in Lochmaddy, then Stornoway and by 1926 in Inverness, Colonel Macarthur became a Director of Kenneth Mackenzie Ltd. in 1929 as the representative of a Mackenzie family trust. [9] Conflict of interest is particularly evident in light of the friction which was to take place within a very short time of his appointment between the HTA and Kenneth Mackenzie Ltd. over the use of millspun yarn. It would scarcely be surprising if the Directors of S. A. Newall & Sons Ltd., Mackenzie's main competitors at the time, were less than happy with the appointment. Whether any consideration was given in 1932 to the likelihood of a conflict of interest is now difficult to ascertain. None of those involved in the appointment are still alive. Those who remember Colonel Macarthur in the 1950s speak of his integrity, his discretion and his intimate knowledge of both the Harris Tweed industry and the islands. It seems probable that when the appointment was mooted, members of the Board of Management saw in Colonel Macarthur an able man whose legal skills would be of use to the Board. At a time when conflict of interest was scarcely recognised as an issue to be considered, Board members would in all probability have been only too pleased to have his services. Certainly, by the time of his retirement as Chairman of the HTA, it was generally acknowledged, even by those who may have perceived a conflict of interest, that Colonel Macarthur had given many years of valuable service to the HTA.

Two new appointments made to the Committee of Management of the Harris Tweed Association in 1928 seem to have been the catalyst which stirred the Association into long overdue activity. George Ellis was a cloth merchant in London selling many other tweeds in addition to Harris Tweed. He was known to Lady Seaforth through her connection with the Crofters' Agency of which he was soon to become Managing Director. Francis Wigglesworth of John G. Hardy and Co. was also a cloth merchant in London. Both these men were in due course to become Chairmen of the Harris Tweed Association.

The addition of George Ellis and Francis Wigglesworth to the Committee of Management seems to have encouraged the Association to assert its authority within the industry. Its first action was to threaten S. A. Newall & Sons and Kenneth Mackenzie Ltd. (the firm had been bought back by the Mackenzie family from Leverhulme when he gave up his schemes in Lewis) with proceedings under the Merchandise Marks Act unless they desisted from selling tweed made from millspun yarn as Harris Tweed. [10] Colonel Macarthur, by then in practice in Inverness, advised Mackenzies and Newalls that they should consider applying to the Board of Trade to have the 1909 definition altered to bring it 'in line with the general practice then prevailing in the Island'. [11] Colonel Macarthur seemed to imply that the 'general practice then prevailing in the Island' was the use of millspun yarn. The possibility of the Stornoway mills making application to the Board of Trade to have the definition altered, and the blatant infringement of the Trade Mark which was taking place, persuaded the HTA that negotiations to find a more realistic definition of Harris Tweed were now needed. The difficulty was going to be to find a definition that would be acceptable to a number of diverse interests.

The local mills

The local mills had two separate areas of activity. One was as suppliers of yarn to any independent producer or crofter who wished to buy millspun yarn. A second activity was as producers of tweed, i.e. they acted as 'converters' turning their own millspun yarn into tweed, which they marketed either under a brand name such as 'MacLoom', 'Lewis Tweed' or 'Harris Tweed'. It was in their capacity as producers of tweed that they were in competition with the independent producers and crofters. The longest established of these local mills were S. A. Newall and Son and Kenneth Mackenzie Ltd., both in Stornoway. In addition to these firms there was what had been the Lewis and Harris Handwoven Tweed Co. Ltd. set up in Tarbert as a subsidiary of Kenneth Mackenzie Ltd. in Lord Leverhulme's day. This mill in Harris had been taken over after Lord Leverhulme's death by a Mr Norman Robertson who had been Lord Leverhulme's factor in Harris. Thereafter the name was changed to the Harris Handwoven Tweed Company Ltd. [12]

The incorporation in 1930 of a new tweed manufacturer, James Macdonald & Co. Ltd. brought to the island scene a new mill and an interesting character who was subsequently to play a controversial role in the industry. Reviewing James Macdonald's activities over the years from the start of his involvement in 1930 until the Harris Tweed case of 1964, Lord Hunter commented:

> 'For the next 30 odd years Mr James Macdonald moves through the story rather like a chameleon, and it is no exaggeration to say that at one time or another he has been on almost every possible side in the controversies of the period.' [13]

James Macdonald, a crofter's son of 1 Habost, Lochs, started life as a fisherman. He served in the navy during the first World War, rising to the rank of Petty Officer. In the 1920s he responded to an advertisement by J. & J. Tod, wholesale provision merchants of Leith, for a commission agent to work in Stornoway. He began his work for Tod's using a bicycle to get around his island customers, but soon graduated to using a car.

When the firm opened a warehouse on the corner of Francis Street and Kenneth Street in Stornoway, James Macdonald set up business as an independent producer of Harris Tweed at the back of the premises. [14]

The late 1920s were a boom period for Harris Tweed and James Macdonald must have seen the commercial advantage of increasing his own involvement in the industry. By 1930, he had worked up a considerable business of his own as an independent producer using mainland millspun yarn. In 1930, together with his employer, Gilbert Archer of J. & J. Tod, he set up a mill in the disused canning factory, a relic on Cannery Rd. from the Leverhulme era, under the name James Macdonald & Co. Ltd. Until the amendment of the certification mark, James Macdonald & Co. Ltd. imported substantial quantities of mainland spun yarn, with a poundage running into six figures in 1932 and 1933. [15] In 1933, carding, spinning and finishing plant were installed in the mill, thus making James Macdonald & Co. Ltd. the first 'vertical' mill (i.e. a mill capable of handling all processes in one unit) on the island.

Despite his initial dependence on importing mainland millspun yarn, it would seem, from his own admission, that James McDonald was aware, perhaps as early as 1931, of the threat posed to the industry in the islands by an involvement with mainland spinners. Equally it might be alleged that he saw the possibility of good business as a spinning mill if some means of restricting yarn to solely island production could be achieved. He took a leading part in bringing about a revision of the definition attaching to the certification trade mark regulations. Defending his early use of imported millspun yarn and confessing to the error of his former ways in a letter to the *Stornoway Gazette* in April 1934, James Macdonald said,

> 'I am further accused of building up my business on imported yarn. I do not dispute the fact that the beginning of my Harris Tweed business was built on imported yarn, but that is no argument in the present question. I soon realised the detrimental effect imported yarn had on my business and consequently made every effort to provide my own good quality.' [16]

What has puzzled islanders ever since is why, within 12 years of stoutly campaigning for an amended definition by which all processes of production would be confined to the islands, James Macdonald abandoned his declared conviction and in 1946 set up a firm in Oban which was to challenge the validity of the definition he helped to devise in 1934 by selling as 'Harris Tweed', tweed made from mainland-spun yarn.

Independent producers

Because most of the independent producers were operating on a relatively small scale compared to the mills, we do not have the same amount of documentary evidence as to their existence or business practices. Certainly many island families seem to have been engaged in the industry at one level or another at some point in time. It would thus be impossible to record them all by name and only those most prominently involved in the debate over the definition will be mentioned. It would also be rash to assume that all independent producers and merchants operated in the same way, or that they were all necessarily engaged in passing off cloth made from millspun yarn as 'Harris Tweed'. What can be gathered now about a rather secretive section of the industry is that practices varied between producers, and that the activities of any one producer varied from time to time. The distinction between the general use of millspun yarn in the industry in Lewis and the predominant use of handspun yarn in Harris must also be remembered.

One example of the working methods of an independent producer was described in 1961 by Mr Calum John MacDonald, who was at the time a senior inspector with the Harris Tweed Association. He had been employed in 1928 as a pattern designer by an independent producer, Kenneth Macleod, trading as Malcolm Macleod, of Balallan in the parish of Lochs in Lewis. Giving evidence in 1964, Mr Macdonald said that the use of imported millspun yarn in Balallan in the late 1920s 'was connected with the appearance of a large multiple, namely Montague Burton, as a purchaser of tweed in about 1929'. [17]

Mr Macdonald described how the pattern for the tweed and the necessary yarn were issued to a local weaver and the finished tweed was invoiced and baled by the independent producer to the customer. [18] He also said that mainland finishing was used when ten or more pieces were ordered. Over time, the traditional method of hand-finishing by waulking became less readily available and the rougher finish produced by hand-waulking became generally less acceptable to wholesale customers who wanted a smooth and consistent feel to the tweed they were going to sell. The increased use of mainland finishing seems to have arisen in the mid-1920s. From the evidence presented in the 1964 case Lord Hunter concluded that:

> ' ... it was probable that some finishing was being done on the mainland during the Leverhulme period ... Although there was, at this time, no finishing plant on the Islands, the weight of the evidence suggests that the larger producers and perhaps the mills, did not use mainland finishing on a large scale until the mid-1920s, and many of the small producers, particularly outside the Stornoway area, could probably still rely on hand-finishing for some years after that. Paisley finishers such as Seedhills, Fultons and McHardies, from the mid-1920s, at times did a good deal of finishing of tweeds sent to them by producers in the Outer Hebrides and Seedhills had started doing some finishing for Kenneth Mackenzie's during the early 1920s. Newalls apparently came to Seedhills rather later, though there is evidence of some finishing having been done for Newalls by Huntly Woollen Mills beginning as early as November 1920 ... ' [19]

The type of business described in Balallan was probably more or less typical of the businesses of other independent producers throughout Lewis. The essential difference between the independent producers and the mill-owning producers was the fact that independent producers and individual crofters did not have spinning facilities and, if they did not use handspun yarn, they had to buy their yarn from a local or mainland spinning mill.

A number of independent producers came to the fore in Stornoway in the late 1920s, among them one or two of particular interest because of the part they were to play in the debate over an amended definition of Harris Tweed. Among these was Maclennan & Maclennan, a firm established in 1929 by Colin Orrock, whose father had been factor to Lord Leverhulme. Maclennan & Maclennan had its own registered trade mark, CEEMO. The firm produced two different types of handwoven tweed. One type contained a large percentage of camel hair and lambswool in the yarn and was sold as Camlan. Another tweed made from a softer imported English millspun yarn suitable for ladies' wear was sold as either CEEMO Homespuns or sometimes as CEEMO Harris Tweed. [20]

Another firm on the scene in the late 1920s was Smiths of Peterhead. This firm was not an independent producer in the same sense as those just described, but it was to play an important part in the industry after 1934. Smiths of Peterhead had an associate company, Alexander's Kirkburn Mills, which for a long time had been buying webs of Harris Tweed from crofters and selling these throughout the trade. Smith's Mill had been one of the many suppliers of millspun yarn to the islands for quite some time. About 1930-31 this mill began 'converting' their yarn into 'Harris Tweed' by the expedient of sending yarn to weavers in Lewis, principally in Leurbost. The greasy tweed was shipped back to Peterhead for finishing, a system of operating which caused some qualms of conscience among the firm's sales staff who knew that this was not the same cloth as they had been selling as 'Harris Tweed' for their associate company Alexander's Kirkburn Mills. [21]

One of the most prominent of the independent producers was David Tolmie who was chairman of the Lewis Harris Tweed Association when the amended definition was being debated. From his firm's headed notepaper, it appears that the first David Tolmie started as an independent producer as early as 1871. His son, also David, expanded the business on his return to Stornoway from Jamaica about 1928. The history of this firm as recounted by a descendant of the first David Tolmie was as follows. The original David Tolmie had come to Stornoway from Inverness in the last quarter of the 19th century as a commission agent, taking orders for a whole variety of goods, sugar, flour, tea, etc., and was paid a commission on those orders. At first he operated from premises on Cromwell St. in what was then known as Pringle's Close. In the course of his work as a commission agent he accepted bolts of tweed from merchants ordering for village stores. About 1900, David Tolmie started selling these bolts of tweed to contacts he had made in London through the provisions side of his business. This first David Tolmie took pride in having suggested to his friend, Kenneth Mackenzie, that he would be wiser to start a spinning mill on some spare ground on Lewis Street, rather than the roller skating rink that Kenneth Mackenzie had first envisaged.

Under the chairmanship of the second David Tolmie, the Lewis Harris Tweed Association seems to have rallied together all those in the industry who were opposed to the exclusion of imported millspun yarn. In a submission to the Board of Trade in September 1933, the secretary of the Lewis Harris Tweed Association claimed to be 'representing 80% of the manufacturers and merchants engaged in the trade in Lewis'. This Association was one of the main protagonists in the dispute with the HTA over the form an amended definition should take.

A meeting of the Lewis Harris Tweed Association was held on 12th September 1933 to consider the proposed amendment to the definition of Harris Tweed which had been submitted to the Board of Trade by the Harris Tweed Association. With the exception of Rev. Murdoch MacRae who was at the LHTA meeting to represent the views of crofter-weavers in his parish, and P. Skinner, company secretary of Kenneth Mackenzie Ltd., most of those present were producers or merchants of Harris Tweed.

The proposals for amendment submitted by the Harris Tweed Association to the Board of Trade, and which the LHTA met to consider, fell into two parts: (1) the proposed new definition of Harris Tweed and (2) the wording to go on the label issued with 'Orb stamped' tweed which was identified as 'Condition (c) part 2'. The Harris Tweed Association had proposed that the amended definition should be as follows:

> "Harris Tweed' means a Tweed made from pure virgin wool produced in Scotland, spun, and woven and finished in the Islands of Lewis, Harris, Uist, Barra and their several purtenances and all known as the Outer Hebrides.'
>
> 'Proposed Condition (c) Part 2. Wherever the Harris Tweed Trade Mark is used there shall be added in legible characters to the Harris Tweed Trade Mark the words 'Made in Harris', or 'Made in Lewis' or 'Made in Uist' or 'Made in Barra' as the case may be, and for the purpose of distinction there shall also be added the words 'Handwoven Handspun' (in the case of Tweeds made entirely from handspun yarn) and the words 'Handwoven Millspun' (in the case of Tweeds containing any portion of millspun yarn.'[22]

(In passing, it is interesting to note that the new HTA definition simply says 'woven' rather than 'handwoven' a strange omission, in light of the later insistence on 'handwoven'!)

A number of features in the new definition and the conditions proposed for the label by the Harris Tweed Association were not acceptable to the members of the Lewis Harris Tweed Association.

'After considerable discussion and consideration' the meeting agreed unanimously that their secretary should inform the Board of Trade that while the Lewis Harris Tweed Association agreed that

> 'an alteration to the existing Trade Mark was urgently required to protect the industry in the Western Isles, the Amendments proposed by the Harris Tweed Association Ltd. should not be granted and that the following Amendments on the trade mark should be made:-
>
> '(1) Definition. Harris Tweed means a Tweed made from 100% pure virgin wool produced in the Western Isles or Highlands of Scotland dyed with fast vegetable dyes, spun and hand warped and which is hand woven by the Crofters and Cottars or their families in the Islands of Lewis, Harris, Uist and Barra and their several purtenances and all known as the Outer Hebrides.
>
> (2) Proposed Condition (c) Part 2 Wherever the Harris Tweed Trade Mark is used there shall be added in legible characters to the Harris Tweed Trade Mark the words 'Made in Harris' or 'Made in Lewis' or 'Made in Uist' or 'Made in Barra' as the case may be, and for the purpose of distinction there shall also be added the words 'Handwoven Handspun' in the case of Tweeds made entirely from handspun yarn.' [23]

The covering letter from the Lewis Harris Tweed Association to the Board of Trade made a number of further points in support of its stance, points which go a long way to explaining the attitudes of its members. These were:

> 'That the majority of the Members of the Harris Tweed Association Ltd. of London, the Owners of the present Mark, are not directly connected with the industry in the Islands. That for a considerable number of years until June 1933, Lewis had no Representative on the Association; that on 7th June 1933 a Lewis Representative was appointed, but that this Representative is a Director of one of the three Mills in Stornoway engaged in the spinning of yarn and who are themselves manufacturers and finishers of Harris Tweed.

That in all negotiations leading up to the present proposed Amendments of the Mark no Representative of Lewis was present nor was any Meeting with the Members of the London Association held in Lewis.

That Harris Tweed has been handwoven from imported yarn for the past thirty years and that the use of such yarn has in no way been detrimental to the industry. On the contrary, it is clear that during this period the trade has undergone a very considerable expansion and that imported yarn is used by 50% of the workers.

That the definition proposed by the London Association which limits the use of the Mark to Tweed handwoven from yarn spun and tweed finished in Lewis would be fatal to the livelihood of thousands of workers engaged in the industry.

That this proposal would limit the yarn to be used to that produced by the three Mills above referred to carrying on business in Stornoway and that it has been and can be proved beyond all doubt that the spinning capacity of the said Mills is totally inadequate to meet the demands of the trade in addition to their own requirements under normal conditions, and further that it can be proved by this Association that the existing stamp has in fact been used on tweed manufactured from imported yarn.

Further the three Mills referred to are the only manufacturers who own finishing plants. Such plants have only been introduced in the current year and it is submitted that the requirements of the trade today require a finish which cannot be given by the old methods used throughout the islands and that the finishing should be done in the same way as it is at present and as was done by the Mills referred to prior to the installation of their own plants.

That the signature of over 4,000 weavers, warpers and others actually engaged in the making of Harris Tweed can be produced in support of the submission by this Association that the definition of Harris Tweed should be in accordance with that stated above.

The Meeting was emphatically of the opinion that the words 'Handwoven Millspun' should not on any account be permitted to be used on the proposed Mark. It is submitted that the words 'Handwoven Handspun' make a sufficiently clear distinction from tweed made in the ordinary way. In any event it is submitted that 'Handwoven Handspun' tweed is commercially non-existent and that all parties engaged in the trade, including buyers and others, are fully aware that practically the whole output of tweed is made from millspun yarn and that the use of these words would quite necessarily cause a very considerable loss to the trade.

The meeting was unanimously of the opinion that the greatest and only real need of the Harris Tweed trade was protection against sale of tweed manufactured by machinery outside the Hebrides and sold as Harris Tweed and that the Amendment of the Regulations as set forth above would give the manufacturers all the protection they require and would also give a guarantee to buyers that the tweed was actually handwoven in the Islands.' [24]

A number of points in this statement call for further comment and clarification. The use of the term 'Harris Tweed Association of London' seems to have been chosen in order to lend weight to the claim of the Lewis Harris Tweed Association to be considered the authentic voice of the industry in Lewis and to invalidate any claim of the existing Harris Tweed Association that they were the guardians of the industry as a whole. The representative for Lewis referred to was Colonel Neil Macarthur, a Director of Kenneth Mackenzie Ltd. [25] which suggests that the Lewis Harris Tweed Association realised the potential conflict of interest posed by Colonel Macarthur's dual role! The statement that in all the negotiations 'no Representative of Lewis was present nor was any meeting with Members of the Harris Tweed Association of London held in Lewis' reflects concern about the decision of a meeting held in Tarbert at which Mr Wigglesworth of the existing Harris Tweed Association had reached an agreement with the people of Harris as to the form of the proposed amendment to the definition, the form which the Lewis Harris Tweed Association found unacceptable.

Apart from the very carefully worded definition proposed by the Lewis Harris Tweed Association, perhaps the most interesting paragraph above is that which objects to the inclusion of the description of tweed as being 'Handwoven Millspun', especially the view that the use of these words would 'quite necessarily cause a very considerable loss to the trade'. The implication seems to be that the Lewis Harris Tweed Association felt that the public had to be protected from knowing that millspun yarn was being used!

The proposed new definitions and conditions of labelling are worthy of close examination. The proposed Harris Tweed Association definition said quite unequivocally 'a Tweed made from pure virgin wool produced in Scotland, spun, woven and finished in the Islands of Lewis, Harris, Uist and Barra etc', without specifying whether the yarn was spun by hand or machine, thereby leaving the way open for either type of yarn to be used, as long as it was spun in the Outer Hebrides. However, the wording of the new Harris Tweed Association label, 'Handwoven, Handspun,' or 'Handwoven, Millspun', a formula drawn up in agreement with the Harris producers, would have made the use of millspun yarn in some tweeds quite clear to the purchaser.

The Lewis Harris Tweed Association definition is subtly different. It said, 'Harris Tweed means a tweed made from 100% pure virgin wool produced in the Western Isles or Highlands of Scotland dyed with fast vegetable dyes, spun and hand warped and which is hand woven by the Crofters and Cottars or their families in the Islands of Lewis, Harris Uist and Barra, etc.' The use of the words 'and which' suggest that weaving is the only process which must be done in the Outer Hebrides, and all other processes could, arguably, be done in the 'Western Isles or in the Highlands of Scotland'. Certainly that is the interpretation which must be made once it becomes clear from the context of the petition to the Board of Trade that the intention was to leave the door open to the continuing use of mainland spun yarn. The '100% pure', the 'fast vegetable dyes' and the 'hand warped' seem like window dressing to impress, if not to distract from the intention to allow the use of mainland millspun yarn.

With such widely differing opinions as to the way in which the Harris Tweed industry would be best equipped to adapt to the demands of an increasingly commercial and aggressive marketplace, it is not surprising that the pages of the *Stornoway Gazette* were at times monopolised by those who wished to participate in the debate. The 'Letters to the Editor' in 1933-34 were of such interest as to merit a chapter to themselves.

Reference - Towards an Amended Definition: 1928 to 1934

1 *Argyllshire Weavers Ltd. and Others v. Macaulay (A.) (Tweeds) Ltd., and Others* [1964] RPC No. 16, 477 [hereafter: 'Harris Tweed Case 1964'), at 511.
2 Memorandum and Articles of Association of the Harris Tweed Association Ltd. [hereafter: Memorandum and Articles of Association], Clause 3.
3 *ibid.*, Clause 22, and also 14 to 15.
4 Gwatkin, Notes on the Historical Development of the Harris Tweed Industry and the Part Played by the Harris Tweed Association Ltd., [hereafter: Gwatkin, 'The Harris Tweed Industry'], 44.
5 Lewis Association *Report, No. 2, The Harris Tweed Industry* [hereafter: 'Lewis Association Report'], 46.
6 'Harris Tweed Case' [1964] RPC No. 16, 477, at 510; also Memorandum and Articles of Association, 13.
7 Gwatkin, 'The Harris Tweed Industry', 31.
8 Memorandum and Articles of Association, (1932) 13.
9 'Harris Tweed Case' [1964] RPC 16, 477, at 518.
10 Gwatkin, 'The Harris Tweed Industry', 31.
11 'Harris Tweed Case' [1964] RPC 16 , 477, at 518.
12 *ibid.*, 509.
13 *ibid.*, 510.
14 Angus MacLeod, 'Community Talk: Notes on the Harris Tweed Industry', 1993.
15 Gwatkin, 'The Harris Tweed Industry', 32.
16 *Stornoway Gazette*, 27. 4. 1934.
17 'Harris Tweed Case' [1964] RPC No. 16, 477 at 515.
18 Gwatkin, 'The Harris Tweed Industry', 21.
19 'Harris Tweed Case' [1964] RPC No. 16, 477, at 505 .
20 *ibid.*, 511-512.
21 'Harris Tweed Case' [1964] RPC No. 16 , 477, at 512-13.
22 Excerpt from Minute of the Lewis Harris Tweed Association, 12. 9. 1933. HTA Office, Stornoway.
23 *ibid.*
24 *ibid.*
25 'Harris Tweed Case' {1964] RPC No.16, 477 at 518.

8

An Amended Definition Achieved

No doubt there are those who deplore some of the more interminable controversies which, from time to time, fill the letters page of the *Stornoway Gazette*. Equally, there is no doubt that, in retrospect, such letters convey a flavour of the dominant concerns and personalities of the day. There is also no doubt that the acrimony caused by the eventual decision to exclude mainland millspun yarn from the definition of Harris Tweed has lingered in some minds to this day. Rightly or wrongly, the exclusion of mainland millspun yarn is seen as having contributed to the dominance of the local mills and the demise of the independent producers and individual crofter-weavers as a significant part of the Harris Tweed industry.

The public debate over an amended definition of Harris Tweed reached the pages of the local and national press in 1933. One of the first and most telling letters came on 8th December 1933 when the *Stornoway Gazette* published a letter from Viscount Fincastle, great-grandson of Catherine, Countess of Dunmore, in which he spelled out the danger of using imported yarn.

> 'A vast quantity of Harris Tweed is being sold at prices which the Outer Islands cannot compete with: and the problem of meeting this competition is complicated by the fact that a great deal of the tweed produced in Lewis and Harris does not come within the conditions governing the existing Trade Mark, inasmuch as it is not entirely hand-made. In addition to this there is a general neglect of the use of the stamp in the case of the tweeds which do comply.
>
> It may be said, therefore that the bulk of the tweed which comes from the Outer Islands bears no stamp or mark of origin to distinguish it from tweeds which have been produced outside the Highland area or, what is worse, from tweeds manufactured abroad and imported into this country. In fact, the term 'Harris Tweed' has almost become a generic one - the industry, so far as the Outer Islands are concerned, is likely to become extinct.' [1]

The *Scottish Daily Express* carried a news item on 20th December describing how the smell of peat smoke was sprayed onto imitation Harris Tweed - a sensational heading and a shocking revelation.

> 'Peat Smell in Tweed - for 2d. Imitation beats their last defence. 'Harris Tweed even to the smell of the peats - For many years the unique hairiness and toughness of Harris Tweed has made it a favourite with sportsmen and women - its colour and general appearance, but not the smell of peat infused through every fibre of it. Until the latest Lancashire invention! For twopence a yard extra you can now buy our 'Harris Tweeds' from Midland looms sprayed with a synthetic essence which exactly copies the smell of peat smoke.' [2]

By spring 1934 the dispute between those for and against the use of mainland millspun yarn, had become intense. A letter in March to the *Stornoway Gazette* from T. B. Wilson Ramsay, M.P. for the Western Isles, echoed the warnings of Viscount Fincastle in greater detail:

> 'Researches into the problem go to show that a tweed passed off as Harris Tweed is being made extensively in America, Japan, the continent of Europe and on the mainland of both England and Scotland with disastrous consequences. The Board of Trade ... tell me that a Bill is going to be introduced in Parliament ... to set up a Tribunal to deal with trade problems like that of Harris Tweed. This Tribunal may deal the death-blow to the industry in the Long Island. For these foreign and mainland firms can call as witnesses before the Tribunal those weavers who use 'imported yarn' or send their tweed outside the Hebrides to be 'finished'. The evidence of these weavers would go to prove that the manufacture of Harris Tweed ... has now become a generic term and need not be manufactured in the Long Island at all.' [3]

On 30th March, a correspondent under the nom de plume of *Siarach* ('West-Sider' or one who lives on the west side of Lewis) took issue in the *Gazette* with the M.P., accusing him of 'completely delivering the crofter-weavers into the hands of their mill-owning competitors'. *Siarach* argued that the danger to the livelihood of the crofter weaver lay in excluding the use of mainland millspun yarn.

'The present position of the mills in Stornoway ... are purely private companies run by private individuals ... They will be selling Harris Tweed against the crofters, so it will be to their advantage to keep the crofter-producer waiting for his yarn. ...' [4]

The Rev. Murdoch Macrae, Kinloch, sent copies of correspondence between himself and Wilson Ramsay M.P. to the *Gazette* which published the letters on 6th April. Mr Macrae, acting as spokesman for the Lewis crofter-weavers, suggested that an inquiry by the Board of Trade would reveal that the crofter was suffering as much, if not more, from the unfair competition of the local mills as mass producers of Harris Tweed than from external competition. It becomes apparent from Mr Macrae's letter that there had been a split in the unanimous opposition to excluding mainland yarn expressed at the meeting in September 1933 of the Lewis Harris Tweed Association. Mr Macrae wrote to Wilson Ramsay:

'I quite agree with you when you say that the importation of yarn must cease, that in fact is one of the stipulations in our suggested trade mark, 'millspun in the Outer Hebrides', but when the spinning is to be done by the existing mills which are themselves mass producers of Harris Tweed, the situation becomes a serious one, and is fraught with dangerous possibilities for the crofters. ... The granting of a trade mark which will confine the spinning of yarn to the existing mills will give those mills a monopoly, which no doubt they desire, but which will be disastrous for the crofter.

The only solution ... is to have a plant established in the Islands which can cope with the crofters' demand for yarn. ... Furthermore, there is already operating in Harris a mill which confines its operations to the spinning of the crofters' yarn. This mill-owner must find this work to be an economic proposition. ... I agree with you that the finishing process outside the Island should cease.' [5]

Mr Macrae had suggested in this letter that 'the local mills should give the wool to the crofters to be dyed by hand', and that tweeds should be finished by hand 'thus providing employment for many men and women'. In making such an unrealistic suggestion, Mr Macrae seems to be unaware of the extent to which the production of tweed, even by the individual crofter-weaver, had become a commercialised process in which consistent quality, economies of scale and production costs were of crucial importance. He was taken to task by James Macdonald, of Messrs James Macdonald & Co. Ltd., in a letter to Stornoway Town Council which he copied to the Editor of the *Stornoway Gazette*.

> 'The Rev. Mr Macrae ... suggests that all wool should be dyed by the crofter, with vegetable dye, I presume. I wonder if he realises that there is not sufficient vegetable dye material available in the island to supply the industry, even in its present state, for six months.' [6]

In another letter to the *Gazette* of the same date, James Macdonald attacked Mr Macrae in even more explicit terms than in his letter to the Town Council. In his letter to the Editor he said:

> 'On reading the reply of the Rev. Mr Macrae, Kinloch, to Mr Wilson Ramsay, M.P., I was greatly surprised to note his vindictive attitude towards the Stornoway wool mills. If Mr Macrae was as fair as I would expect a gentleman of his calling to be, he would at least give them credit for their good deeds. Is he not aware that the three local mills pay approximately £1000 per week in wages, of which 75% goes to the country weavers?
>
> I would suggest to the Rev. Mr Macrae that he leave our business alone and pay attention to his own Book, which does not warrant him figuring in trade disputes. Lord Fincastle ... and the other members of the Harris Tweed Association, Ltd. can be entrusted with the interests of the crofters in the industry, as they have been in the past, without being dictated to by a minister whom we would not expect to know warp from weft.' [7]

While this letter does not advance the debate, it does provide an interesting perspective on James Macdonald. *Siarach* returned to the attack in that same issue of the *Gazette*. Condemning the proposal for hand-dyeing, *Siarach* wrote, somewhat more temperately than James Macdonald:

'I am very doubtful, however if the industry can be carried on today as Mr Macrae suggests. In the hand-dyeing (I notice he does not say vegetable dyeing) it would be a great lottery what colour would come out of the pot, and this would never do. A stamp based on this would soon be discredited. Anyone who has any experience of the trade knows that even hand-finishing can make a great difference to a pattern. Crofters have no experience of dyeing except the old 'vegetable dyeing' and everyone knows that practically no one does this today and everyone knows what a gamble it was.' [8]

Siarach certainly seems to have had an intimate knowledge born of experience in the industry. He gave his proposals for a stamp as being:

'(a) the wool shall be only Highland wool. (No one proposes that the wool should be limited to Lewis and Harris.)
(b) the yarn should be fast dyed.
(c) The yarn shall be spun in the Highlands of Scotland.
(d) The quality and cut of the yarn would be fixed (inferior yarn can be made and has been made in the Hebrides as well as on the Mainland; we must guard against it).
(e) Cloth shall be 28 in. and weight 11 oz. (more or less).
(f) THE TWEED SHALL BE HANDWOVEN BY THE CROFTERS IN LEWIS AND HARRIS AND NOT MILL-WOVEN.

... This is the clause that must be insisted on. I hope that such a stamp would satisfy Mr Macrae.' [9]

The mill-owners' contribution to the debate came on 13th April in a long and detailed letter from P. Skinner, Secretary of Kenneth Mackenzie Ltd. Mr Skinner's interpretation of Mr Macrae's position and the detailed case made in defence of the mill owners are of particular interest in understanding the complexities of the issues.

'With regard to Mr Macrae's letter, ... We are afraid that Mr Macrae is not sufficiently wordly minded to gauge the intricacies of this complicated situation and that, instead of voicing the sentiments of the crofters whom he supposedly represents, he has become merely the mouthpiece of a particular interest. - (i.e. of independent producers) When we entered the Harris Tweed industry as spinners of yarn some twenty-six years ago we built up a sound business by manufacturing a good quality yarn, giving at the same time an expeditious service. ... We have not, however, made any attempt to cater for the supply of cheap (and necessarily lower quality) yarn demanded by some of the Island merchants, who, perforce, have had to obtain supplies from Yorkshire or the mainland. Tweeds made from these yarns definitely entered into direct competition with those of the crofters who made their own tweeds; ... The introduction of imported yarn in bulk inevitably led to intensive price cutting, which resulted in the slump after the War. When the demand for our yarn was thus curtailed, in order to keep our employees (both in the town and in the country) in employment, we were obliged to convert our production of yarns into tweeds and organise a selling Department for their disposal. ... there were others in the industry who ... exploited the market with ever cheapening tweed made from lower quality yarns, and eventually robbed the crofter of the market for his tweeds. ... To instance this, we may state that the last price we paid for a crofter's tweed was 3/- per yard, while it is common knowledge that some merchants in the Island are selling tweeds in London as low as 2/4 for perfect pieces. ... One is apt to forget that in place of a small straggling and intermittent occupation supported by the sentimental interest of a limited market, we have today an organised and flourishing industry in our midst which of late years has risen to be the major industry in the Islands. ...' [10]

The indefatigable *Siarach* was back the following week pouring scorn on the mill-owners in general and on 'P. W. Cumming Skinner's' knowledge of the industry in particular. (This ironic use of the full name of a man who was generally known as 'Pat Skinner' has an element of sarcasm which suited *Siarach's* purpose!) In doing so he managed to hit one or two nails on the head. His letter said:

'It must be obvious to everyone now, that the attempt to discredit tweed made from the yarn spun in mainland mills is a ramp on the part of the Island mill-owners. The letter subscribed by a certain

Mr. P. W. Cumming Skinner on behalf of Messrs Kenneth Mackenzie, Ltd. displays, on his part, a profound ignorance of the history of the tweed trade, which is not surprising in view of his short experience of it, and the ingenuousness of his whole outburst verges on the pathetic, especially when he suggests (he does not say it directly) that yarn was imported from the mainland because it was poorer and cheaper than Messrs Kenneth Mackenzie's. What an absurdity! Yarn spun by Highland mills was used in Lewis for the manufacture of Harris Tweed long years before Messrs Kenneth Mackenzie entered the trade ... and it was on this yarn that the foundations of the Harris Tweed trade was laid. ...

The position of Mr James Macdonald would be comical if it were not so serious for the crofters. This gentleman has built up a business on yarn from mainland mills, now, having within the last six months gotten himself a mill in Stornoway, he wants the Board of Trade to give a stamp which will apply only to yarns spun in mills, like his, on the Long Island, which is the same as declaring that what he has sold for years as 'real Harris Tweed' was not entitled to this description. ... It is quite true that the Stornoway mills do employ considerable labour ... but that is no reason why they should have a monopoly of the trade for themselves. The letter of Messrs Kenneth Mackenzie Ltd. where they claim to be something like a philanthropic institution for the crofters makes some strange reading. ... I trust my letters have not been in such bad taste as this Mr P. W. Skinner's impudent attack on the Rev. Murdoch Macrae, but I am sure the reverend gentleman is well able to defend himself.' [11]

Siarach's reprimand to P. W. Cumming Skinner seems to imply that due to the Rev. Murdoch Macrae's calling as a minister nobody dare disagree with him. If so, this is perhaps an intriguing insight into island attitudes to the clergy, even when they engaged in matters of worldly rather than spiritual concern.

In the same issue, a letter from a 'A Crofter's Son' provides an insight into the real economics of weaving. Challenging James Macdonald's claim that the local mills paid £1000 per week in wages of which 75% went to country weavers, 'A Crofter's Son' wrote:

'The weaver's wage is 1s per weaver's yard (*'slat dùbailt'*), which works out at less than 5 pence farthing per lineal yard. If we allow 3 farthings per lineal yard for other expenses, weaving costs less than 6d per yard. According to Mr Macdonald's approximate figures of £1000 per week this means that the three mill-owners in Lewis produce over two million and eighty thousand, (2,080,000) yards of Harris Tweed per annum. He also refers to 'his own Book, which does not warrant him figuring in trade disputes'. Does he by any chance mean the crofter's own book, in which he keeps record of what he does with his wool? According to our book, it rots in the barn for want of a purchaser, and it will not pay us to make it into Harris Tweed, unless we get at least 3s. 9d. per lineal yard for it.' [12]

Undoubtedly the most important letter of the week was the Rev. Murdoch Macrae's reply to Mr Skinner of Kenneth Mackenzie Ltd. As *Siarach* had predicted, Mr Macrae was well able to defend himself. Referring to the claim that he was the mouthpiece of local merchants rather than the crofters of his district, Mr Macrae used the rhetorical skills of an experienced preacher to berate Mr Skinner for making 'this unworthy and grossly untrue statement without producing a shred of evidence to substantiate it'.

After lengthy excoriation of Mr Skinner and the firm he represented, Mr Macrae spelt out the specific details of the crofters' complaints against the mill-owners.

'Mr Skinner boldly claims that his firm, as manufacturers and spinners of good quality yarn, gave what he called 'an expeditious service' to the crofters. Is Mr Skinner aware of ... the dissatisfaction, which was general throughout the Parish with the manner in which the Lewis Wool Mills served the crofters? The complaints were loud and general, and were made not by one or two merchants, but by the entire crofting community. Is Mr Skinner aware of the fact that at a public meeting of crofters held in Balallan a representative of his firm was asked to explain why crofters' wool from the Parish lay untouched in the Lewis Mills for periods of twelve to eighteen months? Mr Skinner, as a recent addition to the firm, must surely be ignorant of such matters of fact in the history of his firm, or else he would not have the audacity to come forward and claim that they had given an 'expeditious service' to the crofters. ...' [13]

This letter went on to dismiss Mr Skinner's explanation of why the Stornoway mills started converting their yarn into tweed and ended with a rebuke for James Macdonald:

> 'Mr Skinner goes on to say that the 'introduction of imported yarn in bulk' led to the demand for their yarn being curtailed, and that in consequence they were obliged to convert their production of yarn into tweeds and organise a selling department for their disposal. I would say that the importation of yarn in bulk is partly explained by the very fact that Mr Skinner's firm was so busily engaged in making and selling tweeds that they could not serve the crofters with the yarn they required. The crofter was compelled to resort to the use of imported yarn because the local mills could not provide, to use Mr Skinner's phrase, 'an expeditious service'.
>
> Mr Macdonald's letter is scarcely worth referring to. It does not contain one constructive suggestion but it can be fairly described as a truthful revelation of Mr Macdonald's mentality and culture. ...' [14]

James Macdonald's capacity for personal animosity and the gratuitous insult was demonstrated in a petty rejoinder to Mr Macrae the following week. One sentence only, but a sentence which betrays the chip on his shoulder:

> 'I did not intend to make any reference to the Rev. Mr Macrae's letter which appeared in the last issue of your valuable paper, but I wish to say that if his letter is that of a cultured gentleman and the fruit of a University and Divinity training, then I prefer to be content with my elementary education.' [15]

Although the debate in the press appeared to have reached stalemate by the end of April 1934, considerable progress was being achieved behind the scenes. W. H. Martin, Secretary of the Harris Tweed Association, had been in regular correspondence with the Registrar of Trade Marks and the Comptroller-General at the Patent Office from mid-1933 on the question of an amended definition of Harris Tweed. The Board of Trade had decided to communicate the HTA proposals to the 'various persons' who had made representations to the Board on the matter.

Representations had been received by the Board of Trade from interested parties in Lewis and Harris, including: John Macarthur, J.P., Schoolhouse, Balallan, J. MacAulay, Grimshader, M. MacKinnon, 64 Balallan, Donald Macdonald, Secretary of the Harris Tweed Association, Tarbert, Donald G. Mackenzie, The Lewis and Harris Tweed Industries Ltd., 18 Golden Square, London, Rev. Murdoch Macrae, Free Church Manse, Kinloch, A. Macdonald, Secretary of the Lewis Harris Tweed Association, 22 New St., Stornoway. (27 New St. in other correspondence.) Representations from parties on the mainland included, among others, Campbell, Smith, Mathieson & Oliphant, (Edinburgh solicitors) on behalf of A. & J. Macnab Ltd. of Slateford Edinburgh, A. & J. Macnaughton of Pitlochry and James McLardie & Sons, Meikleriggs Works, Paisley. [16]

By December 1933 the members of the Harris Tweed Association were becoming impatient at the lack of response from the Board of Trade and instructed the Secretary, W. H. Martin, to write the Comptroller to say that they were being subjected to great pressure by various persons who were interested in the Harris Tweed industry to get a move on. They feared that questions might be raised in the House unless a satisfactory reply was given that definite progress was being made. [17]

In January 1934, the Comptroller replied saying that because of the conflicting views expressed to the Board of Trade by the various interests concerned, and because of the possibility of a Bill providing for the definition of Trade Terms being submitted to Parliament, a decision on the amendment should be deferred. The Comptroller went on to suggest that 'important sections of the interests concerned were not represented in the Harris Tweed Association and that it might be advisable to include representatives of other sections of the industry'. [18] Unsurprisingly, Mr Martin replied in the strongest terms, refuting any suggestion that the Committee of Management was at all unrepresentative. The Committee consisted of six members, two representing Harris, one representing Lewis, and three members from London, two of whom were engaged in dealing with genuine Harris Tweeds and the other a well-known businessman who had been associated with the Association since its inception. Asking somewhat querulously what other sections of the industry should be represented on the Committee, he went on to explain that mainland interests, from whom the opposition presumably emanated, had no right to use the name 'Harris Tweed' on their cloth. [19]

He might also have made the point that the HTA did not claim to represent 'sectional' interests within the industry.

Whether Mr Martin and his Committee of Management were being deliberately disingenuous or whether they genuinely believed that the Committee was truly representative of all legitimate island interests is difficult to assess. They may have decided that crofters and independent producers who used mainland-spun yarn were of necessity debarred from contributing to the debate on an amended definition. Certainly, the presence of Colonel Macarthur, a Director of Kenneth Mackenzie Ltd., as the Lewis representative on the Harris Tweed Association, gave excellent ammunition to those who saw him and the Association as representing a sectional interest (i.e. the mills) and in no way as spokesmen for the ordinary weaver or independent producer. Despite the apparent indignation of the Committee of Management of the Harris Tweed Association at the accusation that they were not representative of all the interests involved in the debate, they seem to have taken the warning to heart, as consultation with those interests took place over the ensuing months. This vital rapprochement led to much more cordial communications between all parties by June when a plethora of letters was dispatched in all directions.

A meeting of the 'Crofters and Cottars of Lewis and Harris' was held in Tarbert on 2nd May at which the Rev. Murdoch Macrae as Secretary promised to inform the Registrar at the Patent Office that the meeting had unanimously agreed on a definition which would cover all the interests of the crofters and cottars of Lewis and Harris.

It was also agreed that the meeting should send a deputation to London to meet with the Harris Tweed Association on the 1st of June. The deputation consisted of Rev. Malcolm MacIver, Free Church Manse, Lochs, Rev. Murdoch Macrae, Free Church Manse, Kinloch, and the Rev. Norman MacLeod, The Manse, Miavaig, Uig.

At this meeting in London, the members of the Committee of Management of the Harris Tweed Association and the deputation from the 'Crofters and Cottars of Lewis and Harris' agreed on a new definition of the Harris Tweed Trade Mark and regulations on the wording of the label. Firstly, the new definition read as follows:

> 'Harris Tweed means a tweed made from pure virgin wool produced in Scotland, spun, dyed and finished in the Outer Hebrides and handwoven by the islanders at their own homes in the Islands of Lewis, Harris, Uist and Barra and their several purtenences and all known as the Outer Hebrides.'

This definition differed to some extent from the definition agreed at the meeting of 2nd May in Tarbert, but 'the Rev. Murdoch Macrae, stated that as Secretary of the Tarbert meeting he would withdraw the definition put forward as a result of that meeting'. [20]

Secondly the regulations governing the wording of the label stated:

> 'Wherever the Harris Tweed Trade Mark is used there shall be added in legible characters to the Harris Tweed Trade Mark the words 'Made in Harris' or 'Made in Lewis' or 'Made in Uist' or 'Made in Barra' as the case may be, and for the purpose of distinction there shall also be added the word 'handspun' in the case of tweeds made entirely from handspun yarn.' [21]

Mr Martin concluded that letter with a formal request to the Board of Trade to substitute this new definition for that submitted on 30th June 1933. The success in arriving at an agreed definition represented a measure of compromise by the HTA in the omission from the label of the words 'Handwoven Millspun' and a much greater compromise on the part of those who had been determined to allow the continued importation of mainland millspun yarn. While confining all processes of production to the islands was crucial at the time, the words 'handwoven at their own homes' were to be of equal importance in due course!

Somewhat prematurely, in view of the fact that total agreement had not been reached in the Islands, and the Board of Trade had still to be satisfied that there was general acceptance of the new definition and regulations, T. B. Wilson Ramsay hailed Friday 1st June 1934 as 'a red letter day in the history of the industry'. Writing to S. A. Newall, he explained that under the Merchandise Act of 1887, protection under trade descriptions law required that there should be, alongside the trade description, an equally conspicuous statement declaring the name of the place in which the goods were produced. Only if these conditions were fulfilled on the label of Harris Tweed would it be protected from imitation by cloth manufacturers outwith the Islands. [22] Mr Ramsay might have more usefully sent this explanation of the reason for the wording of the label to Mr Allan MacLeod of 41 North Shawbost to lay before a meeting of weavers from the West Coast District of Lewis, including Galson to Ness, and the east of Uig, on 19th June in Shawbost Schoolhouse. That meeting found the new definition to be:

> 'entirely satisfactory and the best means of protecting the Harris Tweed Industry from rich vested interests on the Mainland and abroad and sufficient to meet present day demands.'

They strongly recommended, however that the specific district of origin such as 'Made in Lewis', 'Made in Harris' etc. be omitted from the Mark and 'Made in the Outer Hebrides' substituted instead. [23]

Siarach, who would have had the news of this decision on the local grapevine within hours, wrote to the Editor of the *Stornoway Gazette* lamenting that, after all that had been written about the mills by many crofter correspondents, they would rue the day when the crofters were so completely brought into the power of the mill-owners and would have to pay the price demanded by the mills for spinning yarn, a price which was already much higher than the mainland mills charged. He ended his letter with a resonantly defiant declaration, reminiscent of the Book of Lamentations.

> 'My allies against the mills have gone over to the enemy, but I have still sufficient faith in the rightness of our cause and in the injustice of the mill-owners' cause to write a final warning under the name of *Siarach.*' [24]

The letter from Allan MacLeod on behalf of the West Side weavers was one of a number of responses to attempts by the HTA to reassure the Patent Office that there was general support for the new definition. Mr W. H. Martin had assured the Patent Office that he did not anticipate opposition from the Lewis Harris Tweed Association, except for importers of mainland spun yarn, nor from Harris, although its representatives, D. M. Morrison and John Mackenzie, who had been party to the definition submitted the previous year, had been unable to attend the meeting in London on 1st June. He had also had a positive response from all the mill-owners, including James Macdonald who had wired the HTA Office in London on 8th June saying,

> 'Definition splendid cannot be improved to suit all parties.'[25]

Mr Martin was wrong in his assessment of the mood of the Lewis Harris Tweed Association. On 13th June, this body rejected the new definition by seven votes to four, the seven who rejected the definition all being importers of yarn. One of the members of the Lewis Harris Tweed Association who had voted to reject the new definition, Kenneth MacLeod, Harris Tweed Merchant, Shawbost, later changed his mind and wrote to Mr Martin as Secretary of the HTA, stating that he wished to change his allegiance. The letter states:

> 'On Wednesday the 13th inst. I supported the decision of the Lewis Harris Tweed Association to include the use of Imported Yarn in the Suggested New Definition for the amended Harris Tweed Trade Mark, but since then I have decided to support the definition adopted by the Harris Tweed Association at the recent meeting in London as I deem it necessary for the welfare of the Industry to confine each process of manufacture entirely to the Outer Hebrides.'[26]

The most significant negotiations taking place in the weeks following the meeting of 1st June in London were concerned with establishing an agreement with the mills which would ensure that the crofters and independent producers would be assured of a ready and adequate supply of local yarn at a fair price. The Rev. Murdoch Macrae wrote in detail to both Wilson Ramsay, M.P., and to S. A. Newall, Managing Director of the Patent Slip Mill, on these points. Having examined invoices for yarn and the Shipping Manifestos in the offices of the Pier and Harbour Commission for the year 1932, which he admitted was a peak year, Mr Macrae estimated that 600,000 lbs. of yarn would be required from the local mills to meet the expected demand. As the mills were primarily manufacturers of Harris Tweed, he feared that it would be in their own interests to wipe out their competitors to secure a monopoly in the manufacture of tweeds in addition to the monopoly they had already achieved in the supplying of yarn. He posed a number of questions:

'(1) **Quantity** - Are the mills prepared to supply, say 600,000 lbs. of yarn over and above spinning facilities being provided for the crofter?
(2) **Quality** - How are we to determine that we are given the quality stipulated by the definition?
(3) **Price** - Now this is where they can do the damage to their competitors, by fixing a price which will make it impossible for any other manufacturer to compete with them.
Some agreement must be arrived at on these points.

Then take Spinning for the Crofter. My crofters here at Balallan can get their wool spun, and well spun, on the mainland at present, and for the past number of years, for 4 ½d per lb. The price in Stornoway was 9d and no discount, at Tarbert 8d and 10% discount. ... Now take a consignment of 500 lbs. of wool which is not an extra big consignment. My crofter at Balallan would pay £11-11/- (eleven guineas) more to get 500 lbs. of wool spun in Stornoway than he pays at present, i.e. the charges are practically 100% more. ... I have been in touch with the Mill-owners constantly since coming back from London. ... some progress has been made towards drawing up an agreement on all these matters except the cost of spinning, which I am afraid is going to end in a deadlock.

If we are to be in the hands of the Mills for our future supplies, we must have ample security that our supplies will be forthcoming in time. Take for instance the time now given by firms for repeat orders. It is around six weeks. If the man who gets word to repeat an order in six weeks cannot get his yarn within five weeks, how can he get the order filled? If he cannot, the custom will go to some person who can be relied upon to fill the order in time, and naturally the only people who can do this will be the Mills.

Then another question which is going to be a matter of serious controversy unless something is done is the representation of these parts on the Harris Tweed Association. Agitation is springing up. The argument is why is this new mark to be given to the Harris Tweed Association in London, who have no outstanding connection with the

Outer Isles, and I think that unless the membership of the Association is increased from the Islands, the Board of Trade will be asked to give the new Mark to an Association set up on the Islands.'[27]

On 21st June Mr Macrae had written in much the same terms to Mr Newall of S. A. Newall & Sons. In this letter he was confirming, in writing, a verbal agreement made between himself and Mr Newall at a meeting which would seem to have involved the mills in general.

The confirmation was given at Mr Newall's request. The main points of the letter were as follows.

'I am sending you as requested the proposals we agreed upon at the meeting last Wednesday.

(1) **Supply of Yarn**. The figures as per shipping Manifesto for 1932 were 520,000 lbs. The mills agreed to supply with their present machinery 600,000 lbs. per year-apart from the production for their own consumption and apart from the Crofters' Spinning, and if the demand warranted such procedure, the mills were fully prepared to extend their producing capacity and to cope with such rising demand.

(2) **Quality**. This of course is defined in the Definition but the mills were prepared to have their yarn subjected to any test which might be imposed by the buyer, i.e. the buyer was free to test the quality of the yarns supplied.

(3) **Price**. The mills were prepared to quote a price which will reasonably compare with the prices on the mainland.

The question of the cost of spinning was left undecided as the mill-owners agreed to go into the matter and see if some reduction in the price was possible. ... The question of prices in the future was considered and it was suggested that a Joint Board to consider all such matters as prices, rates of wages, and also to adjust any differences which might arise and to remove any grievances which might lead to harm in the Industry. It was agreed that such a Joint Board was necessary and should be set up.

Credit. This is a question which I never raised. It was raised by the importers. I assumed (that with) ... a reliable customer, the

Stornoway mills would give him as good terms as he could get anywhere, but if a bad customer they would have perfect liberty ... to refuse credit. ... It was further agreed with regard to the spinning of Crofters' wool that no wool should be at the mill for more than one month.

It was also agreed in view of the shortness of time given for repeat orders, that the trade should demand a minimum of 8 weeks' notice. This would enable the mills to make reasonably sure of delivering the yarn to their customers in time. ... I think this covers all that we agreed upon. ... I am sending a report of our meeting last Wednesday to Mr Morrison, Tarbert, for his use at the meeting of workers to be held in Tarbert next Wednesday. ... I am sure they will agree to support the Definition.' [28]

There is a great deal of information in these two letters about the terms on which the Islanders based their decision to support the amended definition or otherwise. In light of the subsequent reversion to the illegal use of mainland wool, the defence of those involved would be that the mills did not fulfil their side of the agreement, and that charge was being levelled as late as the last decade of the 20th century. The mills would, of course, maintain that changing circumstances made it impossible for them to keep the price of yarn at a level acceptable to the crofters and that unreasonable demands were being made.

It is also clear from these letters why the Rev. Murdoch Macrae was held in such high esteem by the generations of Islanders who were aware of his role as a doughty champion of the crofters. What is of interest to the observer is the changing attitudes of the Islanders in the period after the First War, their rejection of the 'benevolent paternalism' of the original founders of the Harris Tweed Association and their sturdy independence of mind. All of these qualities are evident between the lines of Mr Macrae's letter.

An undertaking from S. A. Newall and Son was issued on 20th June with the reference 'SAN / DM'. It was headed 'Patent Slip Wool Mills Ltd., Stornoway, Scotland'. It gave an undertaking to supply yarn in the following terms.

'We guarantee that this company will produce for sale to workers and others in Lewis and Harris at a moderate and reasonable price not less than 200,000 lbs. (Two hundred thousand pounds) of yarn per annum; and will, should the demand for yarn require it, be prepared to increase production to yield a further supply of 200,000 lbs. (Two hundred thousand pounds) for sale.' [29]

There may have been similar undertakings issued by the other two spinning mills in Stornoway, but if there were, no record of these has been found. From the undertaking to supply 200,000 lbs. per annum, it would appear that this is one third of Mr Macrae's estimated requirement of 600,000 lbs. of yarn per annum, which would thereby imply that the mill-owners had come to an agreement to split the estimated requirement into one third each.

Having considered the application from the Harris Tweed Association and the representations made to them, both orally and in writing by other interested parties, an order was issued by the Board of Trade on 18th September, sanctioning the following amended definition and regulations as from 19th November 1934:

'Harris Tweed means a tweed made from pure virgin wool produced in Scotland, spun, dyed and finished in the Outer Hebrides and handwoven by the islanders at their own homes in the Islands of Lewis, Harris, Uist and Barra and their several purtenences and all known as the Outer Hebrides.'

The regulations governing the wording of the label stated:

'Wherever the Harris Tweed Trade Mark is used there shall be added in legible characters to the Harris Tweed Trade Mark the words 'Made in Harris' or 'Made in Lewis' or 'Made in Uist' or 'Made in Barra' as the case may be, and for the purpose of distinction there shall also be added the word 'handspun' in the case of tweeds made entirely from handspun yarn.' [30]

Reference - An Amended Definition Achieved

1 *Stornoway Gazette*, 8. 12. 1933.
2 *Scottish Daily Express*, 20. 12. 1933.
3 *Stornoway Gazette*, 16. 3. 1934.
4 *ibid.*, 30. 3. 1934.
5 *ibid.*, 6. 4. 1934.
6 *ibid.*, 13. 4. 1934.
7 *ibid.*
8 *ibid.*
9 *ibid.*
10 *ibid.*
11 *ibid.*, 20. 4. 1934.
12 *ibid.*
13 *ibid.*
14 *ibid.*
15 *ibid.*, 27. 4. 1934.
16 Representations from 'interested parties' to the Board of Trade in 1933. HRA/D 190/ 1(ff).
17 W. H. Martin to Comptroller, Industrial Property Department, Board of Trade, 7. 12. 1933. HTA Office, Stornoway.
18 Copy letter from Comptroller, Industrial Property Department, Board of Trade to W. H. Martin, 25. 1. 1934. HRA/D190 / 1 (ff).
19 W. H. Martin to Comptroller, Industrial Property Department, Board of Trade, 31. 1. 1934. HRA/D190 /1 (ff).
20 W. H. Martin to Comptroller, Industrial Property Department, Board of Trade, 8. 6. 1934. HTA Office, Stornoway.
21 W. H. Martin to the Registrar, Patent Office, Trade Marks Branch, 4. 6. 1934. HRA/D190 /1 (ff).
22 T. B. Wilson Ramsay, M.P. to S. A. Newall and Sons Ltd., 4. 6. 1934. HRA/ D190/ 1 (ff).
23 Allan MacLeod, 41 North Shawbost to W. H. Martin, 20. 6. 1934. HRA/D190/1 (ff).
24 *Stornoway Gazette*, 15. 6. 1934.
25 W. H. Martin to Comptroller, Industrial Property Department, Board of Trade, 8. 6. 1934. HRA /D190 / 1 (ff).
26 Kenneth MacLeod, Shawbost to W. H. Martin, 20. 4. 1934. Copy letter in HTA Office, Stornoway.
27 Rev. Murdoch Macrae to T. B. Wilson Ramsay, M. P., 9. 7. 1934. HRA /D190/ 1 (ff).
28 Rev. Murdoch Macrae to S. A. Newall, 21. 6. 1934. HRA/D190/ O/57/ 1961
29 Undertaking in 1934 re supply of yarn for sale, signed: S. A. Newall, Managing Director, Patent Slip Woollen Mills Ltd. HRA /D190 / O/57 / 1961.
30 W. H. Martin to Registrar, Patent Office, Trade Marks Branch, 4. 6. 1934. HRA/D190 /1 (ff).

9

The Embargo Case: 1938 to 1942

When the amended definition which confined all processes of manufacture of Harris Tweed to the Outer Hebrides came into effect in November 1934, one of the immediate results was that production of Orb-stamped tweed increased from 95,241 yards in 1934 to 1,485,246 yards in 1935 and this output continued to increase each year with only one minor pause until the outbreak of the Second World War. [1] The result was a significant increase in stamping fees for the Harris Tweed Association. Nonetheless, the intransigence of those who had lost out in the debate over the terms of the amended definition posed a problem as a number of Lewis producers continued to use imported mainland yarn. Those producers who had gone over to locally produced yarn feared, rightly or wrongly, that the cheaper 'Harris Tweed', produced from imported mainland yarn would eventually reduce the market for Orb-stamped tweed. Within less than four years the industry was plunged into a bitter public dispute which led to the Stornoway dockers imposing an embargo on all imported yarn. The Embargo Case is now but a hazy memory. Although it is emblazoned in the chronologies of the history of the Harris Tweed industry, the words 'the Embargo Case', convey little useful information to most people today. It was alleged at the time that the dispute was caused by an 'unholy alliance' between the mill-owners and officials of the Transport and General Workers' Union in a conspiracy to damage the business of those independent producers who continued to import mainland-spun yarn.

In the immediate aftermath of the amended definition a number of significant changes took place in the islands. A. & J. Macnaughton closed down their weaving sheds on Tarbert pier. As the definition stipulated that tweed had to be woven at the home of the crofter, the Stornoway mills removed all looms from their premises apart from those used for pattern weaving. Concentrations of looms in producers' premises in other parts of the island were dispersed. Power-looming of imitation Harris Tweed in the Borders and Yorkshire stopped. [2] The plan to set up a mill in Lewis which would confine itself to carding, dyeing and spinning yarn for the crofter-weaver and independent producer, came to nothing. James Macdonald & Co. Ltd.

was already what is called a 'vertical mill', i.e. it had installed plant which covered all the processes involved in the production of yarn and the finishing of woven tweeds. Kenneth Mackenzie Ltd. and S. A. Newall & Son followed this example. S. A. Newall & Son, in conjunction with Kenneth MacLeod, an independent producer in Shawbost, set up the Lewis and Harris Dyeing and Finishing Co. Ltd. in Newall's premises. [3] Kenneth Mackenzie Ltd. arranged for their dyeing and finishing to be done through an associated company, Kemp and Co. (Stornoway) Ltd., an off-shoot of Kemp Blair & Co. of Galashiels. This company was originally owned jointly by Mackenzie and Kemp Blair & Co., but eventually became a subsidiary company of Kenneth Mackenzie Ltd. The original Chairman and Managing Director of this company was a Mr Kemp Colledge of Galashiels who was also for some years Managing Director of the Harris Handwoven Tweed Co. Ltd. of Tarbert which became a subsidiary company of Kenneth Mackenzie Ltd. Until Kemp & Co. (Stornoway) was operational, Kenneth Mackenzie Ltd. made use of dyeing and finishing facilities at James Macdonald & Co. Ltd. and Newalls. [4]

A new mill, Messrs Thomas Smith and Co.(Stornoway) was set up by the Peterhead firm which had been sending its own millspun yarn to weavers in Lochs and taking the greasy tweeds back to Peterhead for finishing before 1934. A. P. C. Lawrence came to Stornoway as Managing Director of this new mill. The two mills in Harris, that is the mills at Tarbert and Geocrab, continued their production of millspun yarn as before. The Rev. Murdoch Macrae became a member of the Harris Tweed Association.

While these developments in the islands pointed to better employment prospects through increased production of tweed eligible for the Orb stamp, external competitors turned their attention to ever more sophisticated methods of passing off their own products as 'Harris Tweed'. The Harris Tweed Association used the increased revenues from stamping fees to mount a much wider-ranging publicity campaign than they had been able to do hitherto, in order to make the Orb mark familiar to wholesale and retail buyers and to the ordinary individual buying a garment made from Harris Tweed. Nonetheless, eternal vigilance by the Harris Tweed Association, coupled with the threat of legal action when cases of passing off could be identified, became a way of life for the Association and its legal advisers, Messrs McKenna & Co.

One of the developments which was to be highly significant to the industry was the formation in December 1934 of a branch of the woollen section of the Transport and General Workers' Union.

A series of meetings under the auspices of the Transport and General Workers' Union was held in Stornoway and other parts of Lewis which resulted in 'almost five hundred weavers and crofters becoming members of the Union'. John Buchan, the Union organiser for the TGWU, said that the conditions now operating in the production of handwoven Harris Tweed had removed the old argument that the employers could not pay higher wages because of competition from the mainland of Scotland and England and foreign countries like Japan. Provided that the cut-throat competition of rival manufacturers and merchants in the Outer Hebrides ceased, then, and not until then, would Harris Tweeds come into their own again. ... Now that the Union was firmly established in the Outer Hebrides, the immediate tasks were to persuade the employers to form an Association to meet the Union representatives to discuss and decide on

'(1) a standard wage for weavers to operate in all parts of the Outer Hebrides ... ;

(2) to stamp out, once and for all, the vicious and degrading system of barter.' [5]

Mr Buchan's pinpointing of so-called 'cut-throat competition' from rival manufacturers in the Hebrides was indicative, even in 1934, of his attitude to any obstacle to improving the wages of his union members. He seems to have thought only in terms of organised industry as he knew it in the south, with no appreciation of the long-standing tradition of the independent crofter-weaver or small producer operating on his own behalf. How could he understand the antipathy and suspicion felt by the rural producers towards the mill-owning interests in Stornoway? How could he understand that, in the islands, the rift between town and country was as wide as that between employer and labour? Later in the dispute, a sardonic reference by the local union representative, William Mackenzie, to the mill-owners as 'the big guns up the hill' encapsulates the antipathy with which the mill-owners were regarded by many employees and many rural weavers. It would appear that Mr Buchan had been given to understand by the mill-owners that the independent producers were destabilising wage agreements made between the Union and the mill-owning employers because, it was alleged, that, by using imported mainland, millspun yarn, the independent producers were able to undercut the selling price of tweed commissioned from weavers by the mills.

According to the report in the *Stornoway Gazette*, some 500 weavers had joined the TGWU in 1934, but Mr Angus MacLeod of Marybank, says that in the late 1930s while the mill-workers were members of the TGWU, weavers were not unionised for some years. In 1943 because wages were so low that weavers were about to go on strike, Donald Mackay, a County Councillor, of 11 Kershader, Lochs, took the initiative in forming an independent weavers' union, which later joined the TGWU. [6]

The first efforts at unionisation of the mill-workers resulted in the formation of the Harris Tweed Trade Wages and Conditions Advisory Council, Employers' Committee, which, for the first couple of years, was a joint committee composed of both independent and mill-owning employers, including A. J. Mackenzie and P. W. Cumming Skinner, Company Secretary of Kenneth Mackenzie Ltd., S. A. Newall and R. Pringle of S. A. Newall & Sons, James Macdonald, A. P. C. Lawrence of Thomas Smith and Co. and David Tolmie, an independent producer, and the Union representatives. [7]

Something of a storm in a teacup blew up in early March 1936 when negotiations between the Employers' Committee and Union representatives over spinners' wages and a closed shop ran into difficulties. Somehow, news of the stalemate in the negotiations leaked out and the mill-workers decided to take unofficial action. Willie Mackenzie, the local union representative, sent a telegram to John Buchan the TGWU organiser in Glasgow saying:

'ALL MILLS CLOSED. LABOUR WITHDRAWN FROM MIDNIGHT'

In consternation at this 'bolt from the blue' and the effect that unofficial action would have on negotiations with the employers, John Buchan wrote in haste to his Area Secretary in Transport House absolving himself from any responsibility in the matter. His concern was that the workers had put themselves entirely in the wrong and damaged the prestige of the TGWU. Mr Buchan, who was inclined to blame the employers for leaking the information, surmised in a letter to the Area Secretary that having learned the attitude of the employers during the day on Saturday, the mill workers had held a meeting on the Saturday night and resolved 'to have a go at the bosses'. [8] As it happened the strike was over within a couple of days. It is very likely that in blaming 'the bosses' for leaking the information John Buchan was seriously underestimating the speed and efficiency of the local grapevine. Yet the incident was a foretaste of the militancy which was to come.

The important aspect of this preliminary skirmishing between Union and mill-owners lies in the way the employers from the beginning laid the blame for their refusal to consider a wage increase on the alleged 'cut-throat competition of independent producers of cloth', a phrase which is an interesting echo of John Buchan's own words in his recruitment campaign of December 1934. This reason for refusing a wage increase was given by the mill-owners, time and again over the next few years and was to play a fundamental part in the Embargo case.

Whether the mill-owners were justified in leading the Union to believe that 'cut-throat competition' from independent producers under-cutting the selling price of tweed on the basis of cheaper mainland-spun yarn was a genuine stumbling-block to improving wage rates, was questioned in the course of the Embargo case. Estimates at the time put the proportion of unstamped tweed made from imported yarn at around 10% of the total output. There were strong inferences locally that the allegations were a useful ploy by the mill-owners to enlist the Union's strength in getting rid once and for all of the independent producers who were using imported yarn. This was the basis of the so-called 'conspiracy' allegations.

It is worth clarifying the situation regarding the use by some independent producers of mainland-spun yarn at this point. Despite the amended definition of Harris Tweed which specified the exclusive use of island-spun yarn for the Orb-stamped article, the importation to the islands of mainland yarn was not an illegal activity per se, nor was its use in the manufacture of tweed illegal. Only if that tweed was then passed off as genuine 'Harris Tweed' was an offence committed. Surprisingly, there still seemed to be some ambivalence as to whether a weaver using mainland yarn for tweeds woven and finished in the islands could legitimately describe and sell this product simply as 'Harris Tweed', but without the official Orb stamp and label. Although it was accepted that the Orb mark was the property of the Harris Tweed Association, the question arose, 'Were the words 'Harris' and 'Tweed' also its exclusive property?' It was to become clear in due course, that the Orb Certification Mark did not give the HTA an exclusive property in the words 'Harris Tweed'. While there might seem to be a fair measure of sophistry in claiming that there was such a thing as 'unstamped Harris Tweed' made from mainland yarn, thus denying the definition of Harris Tweed as being a product made completely in the Outer Hebrides, that claim gained ground. When the Embargo case finally went on Appeal to the House of Lords, the Lord Chancellor, Lord Simon, stated that, in his judgement, the words 'Harris Tweed' could legitimately be used on unstamped tweed made from mainland yarn, as long as it had been woven in the islands. He said:

> 'Cloth made out of mainland yarn could not carry the 'Stamp', though it could be sold as 'Harris Tweed', having been woven in the island.' [9]

This judgement by Lord Simon was to be used as justification for yet another attempt by mainland firms to break into the island industry in the 1950s. It was also to cause great difficulty for manufacturers of Orb-stamped tweed in foreign markets, particularly in the United States. Not until Lord Hunter's decision in the Harris Tweed case of 1964 was this differentiation between unstamped Harris Tweed and the Orb-stamped article laid to rest.

Certainly tweed made from mainland-spun yarn was not eligible for stamping with the Orb mark, nor for displaying the Harris Tweed label, but many potential customers were quite happy to buy tweed without the stamp and they provided a ready market for tweed made from mainland-spun yarn. The danger seen by the mill-owners and those island producers who used locally-spun yarn was, of course, that sales of unstamped, cheaper 'Harris Tweed' made from imported yarn would eventually outstrip sales of Orb-stamped Harris Tweed.

Although the striking mill-workers were persuaded to go back to work by the next day, Tuesday 31st March, the Union representatives turned their minds almost immediately to some other way in which they could put an end to the importation of mainland-spun yarn. The next suggestion was that the dockers, who were also members of the TGWU, should be involved in the dispute. On this proposal, the advice of John Veitch, TGWU Area Organiser was,

> ' ... The position simply is that if the members are depending upon the dockers helping them ... we would require to receive the Executive's consent and ... plenary powers to withdraw the dockers to assist them in their trouble. These facts must be made clear to them.' [10]

A wage increase was eventually negotiated for the year June 1936 to June 1937 and having won a temporary respite in Lewis, John Buchan turned his attention to organising the workers at Tarbert and Geocrab.

A human touch in the midst of the political manoeuvring can be seen in a warm and humorous paragraph at the end of a letter full of instructions as to how to proceed with setting up a branch of the Union at the mills in Harris.

> 'It was most kind and thoughtful of you to send us a box of kippers. They are delicious as only Stornoway kippers can be. When the box arrived, Ingles claimed possession of it and deals them out as his special property. We are all looking forward to your visit to Galashiels later in the year and Ingles threatens to have a 'strike' at the school so that he can be available to show you round the Borders. I am glad to report that we are all well and we hope that this finds you, Mrs Mackenzie and the baby also in good health.' [11]

A measure of the dissent and concern surrounding the industry in 1936 is reflected in a statement issued by the Harris Tweed Association, to counter a campaign for a revised definition which would allow the use of imported mainland-spun yarn in the production of Orb-stamped Harris Tweed.

> 'The only substantial criticism of the definition that has been offered is that by excluding the use of imported yarn, an undue advantage has been given to the owners of the local mills who are also largely interested in the marketing of tweeds. ... the exclusion

of imported yarn was decided on as otherwise the claim to have the industry treated as a purely Hebridean industry would have been frustrated. ... It is deliberate misrepresentation to state that the mills are cheating the crofters of their livelihood. The greater portion of the yarn produced in the spinning mills in Stornoway during 1935 was delivered to meet the requirements of independent weavers. ... the independent weaver today is assured of adequate supplies of yarn at a fair price. ... It remains for the producers and distributors to evolve a scheme of price control which will give a fair return to all concerned. This is not a matter for the Harris Tweed Association. If low prices are obtaining, it is entirely the fault of the producing and distributing interests who can take the remedy into their own hands by mutually agreeing not to dispose of their products below a certain fixed price.' [12]

Here the issues inherent to the subsequent Embargo case are being articulated by the HTA as early as 1936. If, as was alleged, independent producers using imported yarn were under-cutting the price of tweed made from island-spun yarn, and thereby preventing the mill-owners from consenting to an acceptable wage increase for local mill-workers, it is not difficult to understand the divisions and resentments which fuelled the controversy.

The HTA's advice to all producers to get together and agree a price structure presumed sufficient good will between the antagonists to allow reasonable discussion to take place and, even more importantly, the will to adhere to an agreement if such could be reached. Far from being willing to come to an agreement on pricing, the Wages and Conditions Advisory Committee (which had originally included mill-owners and some importers) split in 1936. In January 1937, the independent producers using imported yarn formed their own association which they called 'The Harris Tweed Yarn Purchasers Association'.

The whole sequence of events leading up to the imposition of the embargo did not become clear until the case was heard before Lord Jamieson in the Court of Session in November 1938. It is important to emphasise that the Embargo case was a civil case and that none of the parties concerned was in any sense guilty of criminal actions. They were the unfortunate representatives of conflicting business interests. Some of them were young married men with small children and as the

Embargo case dragged on from Appeal court to Appeal court for close on four years, the strain inflicted on them and their families must have been quite horrendous. One of the sad ironies of the situation was that at the end of the day, the intervention of the Second World War did more to put a temporary halt to the dispute than the final judgement in the House of Lords.

While the evidence presented in the Embargo case in 1938 recreates a vanished era in island life, only those parts of the evidence which clarify the sequence of events will be mentioned here. As in any other legal dispute, each side put their own gloss on events.

According to evidence on behalf of the union representatives, John Buchan and John Veitch, an agreement on wage rates was reached in mid-1936 with the employers in the Wages and Conditions Advisory Committee. That agreement was to continue from year to year unless two months notice to alter was given before June 1937. In early 1937, the union representative asked for a 10% wage increase and 100% union membership. This request was not accepted by the Wages and Conditions Advisory Committee, allegedly because of competition from those producers who were undercutting the price of tweed. The explanation given was that several of the independent producers, taking advantage of the market for Harris Tweed created by the Harris Tweed Association's advertising campaign, had indulged in a policy of undercutting, by purchasing yarn from the mainland at a price of about 2/2d per pound as against the 2/6d per pound for island-spun yarn. This policy of undercutting constituted a serious threat to the wage rates of the Trade Union members, particularly the rate paid to spinners in the island mills. [13]

Late in 1937 and early in 1938, a number of meetings took place in an attempt to establish a minimum selling price for tweed and to agree to halt the importation of yarn. When all attempts to reach an agreement broke down in January 1938, Mr Skinner, Secretary of Kenneth Mackenzie Ltd., as representative of the employers' Wages and Conditions Advisory Committee, informed Mr Veitch of the Transport and General Workers' Union that not only would the request for a 10% wage increase be refused, but a decrease in wages would become necessary. Until then Mr Veitch had been restrained from taking direct action by the mill-owners' policy of 'persuasion' towards the importers. On learning that a decrease in wages was proposed, Mr Veitch instructed William Mackenzie, the local union representative, to call on the dockers to impose the embargo on consignments to or from nine importers. Thus, according to the Transport and General Workers' Union, the embargo had been imposed as part of a trade dispute and in defence of the interests of the members of their Union.[14] In other words, the TGWU denied any allegation that the embargo was part of a conspiracy between the mill-owners and themselves to damage the business of the producers importing mainland yarn.

The composition of the Employers' Wages Advisory Committee which had been negotiating with the Union was significant in light of these allegations of a conspiracy between the mill-owners and the Union to damage the importers' business. At first the Wages Advisory Committee had consisted of all employers, including independent producers who were importers of yarn, but later it had come to represent the mill-owners only. In January 1937 an association of independent producers, the Lewis Harris Tweed Yarn Purchasers' Association, had been formed with Mr David Tolmie as Chairman. Under cross-examination by Counsel, as to the composition of the Employers Wages Advisory Committee, Mr Skinner, Secretary of that Committee, said:

> 'after the one day strike in 1936, an informal meeting had been held in the Waverley Hotel attended by the mill-owners and a majority of the merchants in Mr Tolmie's group. At that meeting the responsibility for making negotiations with the Union was thrown onto the shoulders of the mill-owners. ... Mr Skinner added that as the negotiations with Mr Buchan and Mr Veitch representing the Union were very often a great strain, and not altogether pleasant, Mr Tolmie and the other employers outside the mills preferred to abstain from taking part in them. ... They said they were quite satisfied to abide by the agreement we would make with the Trade Union.'[15]

> 'Counsel then asked Mr Skinner to confirm that the only body which has been acting in the negotiations with the Trade union had been the four mill-owners. Mr Skinner agreed saying: 'The four mill-owners as representing the employers'.'[16]

Giving evidence in his capacity as Chairman of the Lewis Harris Tweed Yarn Purchasers' Association, Mr David Tolmie, an independent producer in favour of imported yarn, made some important points which had not come out in Mr Skinner's evidence. Mr Tolmie said:

> 'To begin with a body was formed under the name of the Lewis Harris Tweed Association with the object of obtaining an amendment of the Trade Mark definition ... At that stage there was a distinct stipulation that the mill-owners did not want to interfere with the use of mainland yarn and that stipulation was recorded in the Minutes of the Lewis Harris Tweed Association. When the amendment in the definition was granted, it was also understood that the mill-owners would make no discrimination against the other firms in the industry. Prior to the granting of the amendment, certain guarantees had been drafted regarding the price at which the island mills would supply yarn, the quality of the yarn they would supply, and the conditions on which they would supply it. (It was) understood that these guarantees were to be embodied in the Trade Mark to protect the interests of those who were not mill-owners, but when the Mark was granted the guarantees were not included. Since the amendment of the Trade Mark, the mills had not observed the spirit of the proposed guarantee, instead they had given a very inefficient service in every direction. Deliveries of yarn were most unsatisfactory, the price of their yarn was consistently higher than the price of mainland-spun yarn; the matching of patterns by the island mills was inefficient and there had been continual friction between them and the independent merchants. Early in 1937 an association of Harris Tweed merchants outside the mill group was formed under the name of the Harris Tweed Yarn Purchasers Association of which he was appointed Chairman and Mr Angus MacLeod, Kenneth St, Stornoway, secretary. ... The Yarn Purchasers frequently met with the Lewis Harris Tweed Employers' Advisory Committee, which body represented the mill-owners, in an effort to come to an agreement about the price of yarn and the selling price of tweed.'[17]

A series of crucial meetings took place between November 1937 and January 1938 at which various versions of a draft agreement on a minimum selling price were discussed. David Tolmie told the court about a meeting of the Yarn Purchasers Association in December when twelve out of fourteen members signed, before Bailie John Kennedy J. P., a draft agreement prepared by Mr Skinner on behalf of the Employers' Advisory Committee. That draft contained nothing making it compulsory to purchase only island-spun yarn. At a meeting of this group later in December, a second draft which had been prepared by Mr Williamson, solicitor on behalf of the Employers' Advisory Committee, was presented to the meeting. This second draft contained a clause making the use of island-spun yarn compulsory. The omission of such a clause from the previous draft was the chief point in which the mill-owners considered that the first draft had been 'lacking in effectiveness'. As Chairman of the Yarn Purchasers' Association, David Tolmie had asked his own solicitor to prepare an alternative draft. By the end of the meeting a modified version combining the two drafts and accepting the clause on island-spun yarn was agreed. David Tolmie had informed the members present that it was likely that an embargo on mainland-spun yarn would be used as a lever to compel acceptance of the mill-owners' terms.[18]

One of the questions which was never satisfactorily resolved was the basis on which the list of embargoed producers was compiled. The list certainly did not cover all those importing mainland-spun yarn and at least one of those subjected to the embargo had never used any other than island-spun yarn. The evidence from the independent producers whose yarn was embargoed adds another dimension to the sorry tale.

> 'Mr Murdo Campbell, Coll, Back stated in evidence that an embargo had been placed on the shipment of his finished tweeds although they were made from island-spun yarn and bore the Harris Tweed Association's stamp and he had never imported a yard of mainland-spun yarn in his life. On the 21st of January he sent a consignment of tweeds to be finished and stamped by Messrs James Macdonald and on the 24th he learned from a lad belonging to the village that they had not been shipped. At the time he knew nothing of the embargo and had not been informed of it by anyone. ... He then went to see Mr James Macdonald ... Mr Macdonald advised him to see Mr Mackenzie, (the local Union representative) but not to mention his name as he wanted 'to keep out of this trouble'. When he went to see Mr Mackenzie he was informed that the list of names came from Mr Veitch. Witness asked Mr Mackenzie to telegraph Mr Veitch, but Mr Mackenzie did not think it would be

any use and advised him instead to see Mr Skinner. ... On the following day witness came to town with his father and saw Mr Mackenzie again. In the course of the conversation Mr Mackenzie remarked to witness's father that Mr Skinner had been to Glasgow but to 'keep that quiet'. Witness that day called on Mr Skinner who took a note of his name and address.' [19]

The sort of 'run around' meted out to Mr Campbell may indicate that nobody knew exactly what was going on or who had final responsibility for deciding whose goods ought to be embargoed.

Evidence of the attitude of the mills to producers who were not within a 'price agreement' was given by another independent producer, James Borland.

'Mr Borland ... said that he had been carrying on the firm of Stuart and Stuart since April 1935. ... He began by getting all his yarn from the island mills. This went on until early in October 1936. At that time he had substantial orders for between 12,000 and 15,000 yards of tweed. He went to several of the Island spinning mills in turn but every one refused to execute his orders for yarn although he offered to pay cash. They would not give any reasons. ... Ultimately he had to return the orders. He was however held down to make 20 pieces according to contract. 'I more or less had to beg the yarn for that from two or three firms on the island. I got it some eight weeks after I needed it. ... I was forced to seek supplies elsewhere and as a consequence I began to take supplies of yarn from the Mainland'. ... On another occasion witness said he received an order for 4000 yards of stamped Harris Tweed. He approached Messrs S. A. Newall & Sons to secure yarn. He saw their production manager and he was able to get some from stock, but the manager refused to spin the remainder for him because it needed special spinning. He went to another firm but the managing director, although he accepted his order at 2.10d per lb., said he would not spin it unless he was in the 'price ring' agreement. 'I decided that I could not join the agreement and so, next day he handed me back my order'. He said that that was the first time he got a hint that the powers of the Union could be used to help the spinners enforce this price ring.' [20]

It becomes apparent from evidence given by Mr Skinner, Secretary of Kenneth Mackenzie Ltd., that the 'price ring' mentioned by Mr Borland refers to an agreement, in the first instance a 'gentleman's agreement', between a number of producers, some of these being independent producers and others being mill-owning producers, on a minimum selling price for tweed. Mr Skinner said in reply that the position they had put in front of Mr Borland was that he would not be eligible for the reduced price of yarn which the spinners were prepared to make available to those who agreed with them on minimum prices. It had been agreed to charge a lower price than production costs would justify to those who signed the agreement to maintain tweed prices. [21] This policy was, no doubt, one of the ways in which the mill-owners hoped to 'persuade' those outside the agreement on minimum prices to conform.

Events gathered momentum towards the end of 1937 when James Macdonald broke the 'gentleman's agreement' on a minimum selling price, thereby making a formally signed agreement necessary. Under cross-examination, Mr Skinner said that James Macdonald had intimated that he could not remain a member of the Employers' Advisory Committee because he was not satisfied with the progress made in obtaining a price agreement. Asked whether Mr Macdonald himself had engaged in price-cutting, Mr Skinner said that James Macdonald & Co. Ltd. had sold a large consignment of old stock to a London firm at a cheap rate, as was within their rights.

James Macdonald's breakaway from the Employers' Wages Advisory Committee seems to have alarmed the Union representative, Mr Veitch. Fearing that the Wages Advisory Committee with which he had to negotiate was about to fall apart, Mr Veitch had paid Mr Macdonald a long visit in November. Mr Veitch came back from this meeting very impressed with James Macdonald's view of the industry and fully persuaded that direct action would have to be taken to stop the importation of yarn. [22]

The final meeting which precipitated the embargo took place in the Masonic Hall in Stornoway on 7th January 1938. It was a joint meeting of the Yarn Purchasers' Association and the Employers' Wages Advisory Committee and was chaired by the Rev. Murdoch Macrae, Kinloch. Giving evidence, Mr Macrae said:

> 'I had pled with members present to come to some agreement with regard to a minimum price. We tried to go through the draft agreement clause by clause, but I found that certain of the petitioners in this action were not prepared to agree to a minimum price nor to stop the importation of yarn. These were the two stumbling blocks. ... Due to my conversations with Mr Buchan and my conversation with Mr Veitch in October 1937, in which he told me in the clearest possible terms that unless the employers in the industry were prepared to arrive at some agreement on these matters, the Union would be compelled to take direct action. ... I was afraid that the importation of yarn and the natural increase in the importation of yarn would bring us back to the position we had been in 1930.' [23]

The meeting lasted for five hours and Mr Macrae found it impossible to keep order with 'half a dozen people speaking at once.' No agreement had been reached and clearly all attempts at achieving a voluntary agreement had failed. Within a fortnight of Mr Skinner conveying this information to Mr Veitch the embargo was imposed.

The nine producers whose yarn was subject to the embargo applied to the Court of Session and were granted an *interim interdict* (a temporary order to stop the embargo) by Lord Jamieson in January 1938. He renewed the interim interdict in March 1938. However the embargoed producers were then asked by Lord Jamieson to provide a proof before answer, which was simply a court hearing in which they, as the petitioners, would provide proof of their complaint against the representatives of the TGWU to enable the judge to give a final decision on whether the embargo was lawful or not.

In essence, the complaint by these producers alleged that the Union officials, John Veitch and William Mackenzie and certain rival traders, (i.e. the mill-owners) had conspired to injure their trade. The court was required (a) to establish whether or not there had been a conspiracy between the Trade Union officials and the mill-owners to put the importers of mainland yarn out of business by use of the embargo and if so, (b) to prevent any further use of the embargo.

The evidence in the case [24] brought by the producers against the TGWU representatives Veitch and Mackenzie, was heard by Lord Jamieson, in the Court of Session in November and December 1938. In his judgement which was issued in March 1939, Lord Jamieson dismissed the producers' plea. The nine producers then appealed against Lord Jamieson's decision and the case was considered again before the Second Division of the Court of Session in November and December 1939. This appeal was dismissed by a majority of three out of the four presiding Law Lords in March 1940. The producers appealed yet again, this time to the House of Lords, and this final appeal was dismissed in 1941. The courts were concerned with points of law, not the moral rights of any of the parties in the dispute, and, on points of law, the case for the nine producers failed.

One could be forgiven for asking how these relatively small independent island producers importing mainland-spun yarn could afford to pay for the services of solicitors and Counsel over the three years spent in taking their case on appeal to the Inner House of the Court of Session and then to the House of Lords and thereafter pay the costs which went against them at the end of the day. Not until the Harris Tweed case in 1964 did it become public knowledge that financial support for the independent producers (i.e. the importers) in the Embargo case came from A. & J. Macnaughton, Pitlochry and Laidlaws of Keith, both of whom were exporters of mainland-spun yarn to the islands, and both of whom were to play a significant part in the conflict over unstamped Harris Tweed in the 1950s. This financial support for independent producers in the islands from mainland spinners makes it clear that there were much larger issues at stake for the mainland spinners than simply the financial well-being of a few island producers. [25]

Reference - The Embargo Case: 1938 to 1942

1 HTA stamping records. HTA Office, Stornoway.
2 *Argyllshire Weavers Ltd. and Others v. Macaulay (A.) (Tweeds) Ltd., and Others* [1964] RPC No. 16, 477 [hereafter: 'Harris Tweed Case 1964], at 527.
3 Angus MacLeod, 'Community Talk: Notes on the Harris Tweed Industry'.
4 Harris Tweed Case [1964] RPC 16, 477, at 525.
5 *Stornoway Gazette*, 28. 12. 1934.
6 Angus MacLeod, 'Community Talk: Notes on the Harris Tweed Industry'.
7 Report of Meeting of Joint Committee of Harris Tweed Trade Wages and Conditions Advisory Council. HTA Office Stornoway. Also in *Stornoway Gazette*, 25. 11. 1938.
8 John Buchan to John Veitch, 30. 3. 1936. HTA Office, Stornoway.
9 *Crofter Hand Woven Harris Tweed Co. Ltd. v. John Veitch and Another*, [1942] Session Cases (House of Lords.) No. 1, at 4. Also *Crofter Hand Woven Harris Tweed Co. Ltd. v. John Veitch and Another*, 1942, Appeal Court, 435, at 437. This case is colloquially known in the Islands as 'The Embargo Case' hence: [hereafter: 'Embargo Case'].
10 John Veitch to John Buchan, 2. 4. 1936. HTA Office, Stornoway.
11 John Buchan to Willie Mackenzie, 24. 6. 1936. HTA Office, Stornoway.
12 *Stornoway Gazette*, 24. 7. 1936
13 *ibid.*, 18. 11. 1938.
14 *ibid.*, 25. 11 1938.
15 *ibid.*, 2. 12. 1938.
16 *ibid.*
17 *ibid.*, 25. 11. 1938
18 *ibid.*
19 *ibid.*
20 *ibid.*
21 *ibid.*, 2. 12. 1938.
22 *ibid.*
23 *ibid.*
24 'Embargo Case', 1940 SC No.13, at 141; Also 1942 SC (H.L.) No.1. at 1.
25 'Harris Tweed Case' [1964] RPC No. 16, 477, at 536.

10

During the Second World War

If those involved in the Embargo case were hoping that the Appeal courts would resolve the controversy over imported yarn, they would have been disappointed with the final judgement. Neither side came out as a clear winner. The argument over imported yarn broke out again in 1943 when the *Lewis Association Report on the Harris Tweed Industry* recommended that if the local mills failed to provide a satisfactory service to independent producers they should be allowed to import mainland yarn. The restrictions imposed on textile production as a result of the war seem to have exacerbated the grievances between the two sides of the industry, mill-owners and independent producers, employers and employees.

Despite these internal problems and controversies, sales of Harris Tweed increased after the amended definition until the first year of the war. Harris Tweed was 'much the largest revenue producer of the three island industries of agriculture, fishing and tweed'. [1] Stamping figures show a steady increase, with close to 3 million yards being stamped in 1938, close on 4 million yards in 1939 and over four million yards in 1940. Throughout the war, production of tweed dropped back by approximately one million yards each year from 1941, reaching a low point of under two million yards in 1944.

The absence of approximately 60% of male weavers [2] and many young women on war service clearly had its effect on the level of production. War-time rationing of wool and restrictions on other materials posed insurmountable difficulties for those still in the industry. From 1941 a license from the Board of Trade was needed to buy a new loom. The Board was especially anxious not to increase the number of looms in the islands in view of the short supply of wool and the danger of reducing the income of the average weaver if too many new weavers came into the industry. In certain special cases of disabled ex-servicemen it was possible to get the support of the Ministry of Labour for permits under the rehabilitation scheme. [3]

The 1942 Concentration of Industry Orders led to the closure for a period of Thomas Smith's dyeing and finishing plant, the work of which was transferred to Kemp & Co. Substantial portions of the spinning capacity of Newalls and Mackenzies were also closed down. [4] Yarn supplies to independent producers and crofter-weavers were liable to be delayed by several months and this, of course, involved loss of income and markets. Lack of knowledge, or misunderstandings of the regulations on getting coupons for all tweed sold, whether or not the coupons were needed to buy further supplies of yarn, resulted in a number of weavers being prosecuted and fined sums between £2 and £25. [5] Price controls, fixed by the Board of Trade in 1942, restricted the maximum selling price of tweed to 5/6d per yard for handwoven and 9/- per yard for handspun-handwoven tweed. This made it difficult for the independent producer to make any worthwhile profit. [6]

Weavers who received yarn to be woven for the Stornoway mills were particularly badly affected by a disproportionate increase in the costs they had to meet in comparison to the wage rate paid per yard. The weaver was responsible for paying the cost of transporting yarn from the mill to his home and for returning the greasy tweed to the mill. Unlike the weaver's wage, carriage costs had increased by almost 100%. The existing wage rate at the time was 1/3d per eight-foot yard, a halfpenny per shot for extra shots, a penny for extra shuttles (but only above two) and nothing for beaming and tying-in, changing of reeds or changing of healds. Discontent among the weavers increased as it became clear that they were receiving a raw deal. Although the agreement reached between the Hebridean Spinners' Association (the mill-owners) and the Transport and General Workers' Union in 1935 had covered both mill employees and weavers, by the 1940s the weavers began to feel that the TGWU were neglecting their interests. Support for the Union from weavers gradually declined and war service removed the last of the active membership. Nonetheless, the TGWU continued to negotiate agreements affecting the weavers, the last agreement being in June 1942. [7]

This dissatisfaction among weavers with the TGWU came to a head in January 1943. At a mass meeting in the Masonic Hall in Stornoway, a new Union, the Harris Tweed Weavers' Union, was formed with some 556 members. Angus MacLeod records in his manuscript history of the industry, that among those elected to represent the weavers at that meeting were Councillor Donald MacKay, 11 Kershader as Chairman and Mr D. Thomson, 24 Coll as Secretary. The demands submitted from the new Weavers' Union to the employers were:

1. Payment at the rate of 2/- per eight feet yard, for plain tweeds, eighteen shots per inch and one shuttle.
2. For each additional shot, over eighteen to the inch, one penny per shot.
3. For patterns requiring more than one shuttle, a penny for each additional shuttle.
4. Beaming and tying-in 2/6d per tweed.
5. Changing of reeds, 1/- per change.
6. Changing of healds, i.e. changing healds from twill to herringbone, etc. payment of 1/- per change.
7. The transport of tweeds to and from weavers' premises should be at the carrier's rather than at the weaver's risk. [8]

On receiving these demands, the Hebridean Spinners' Association replied that it was not competent for them to negotiate independently with the new Harris Tweed Weavers' Union, despite its numerical strength, during the tenure of a pre-existing agreement with the Transport and General Workers' Union. Needless to say, the leaders of the new Union were less than satisfied with this response. They gave the employers twenty-one days notice that they would cease work on 5th March 1943 if an amicable agreement had not been reached by then. When it became clear that the situation had reached deadlock, Ernest Bevin, Minister of Labour and National Service, appointed a Committee of Investigation into the causes of the dispute.

Meeting with all parties, in camera on 19th April, the Committee of Investigation quickly established that the immediate issue was the refusal by the Hebridean Spinners' Association to recognise and negotiate with the new Weavers' Union. The employers stated that if the weavers who had formed the new union became members of the TGWU and resumed work, negotiations between themselves and the TGWU could be opened immediately. The Executive Committee of the Harris Tweed Weavers' Union was concerned that the TGWU had neglected the weavers' interests in the past. They were also anxious to protect the autonomy of their new union. They argued that as the Harris Tweed weaving industry was both localised and specialised, a national union did not have the expertise needed to protect the particular interests of the weavers. Harking back to the Embargo case, the Weavers' Union voiced their suspicion that the TGWU was more interested in the large producers than in the small independent producers whom the new Harris Tweed Weavers' Union wished to encourage. Arbitration by the Committee of Investigation finally produced an agreement between the TGWU and the Harris Tweed Weavers' Union to form a new Harris Tweed Weavers' Branch of the Transport and General Workers' Union. Copies of an agreement in the following terms were issued to all parties concerned:

> ' ... as the Harris Tweed weaving industry has very special features, this should be recognised by the creation of a Harris Tweed Weavers' Branch of the Transport and General Workers' Union, ... as part of the Union rules, the members of the Branch would have the right to elect their own Branch officials and members of the Branch Committee who would be responsible for the direction of their own local affairs. Furthermore, in connection with any proposed revision of the Agreement between the Union and the Hebridean Spinners' Association, representatives of the Branch would have the right to attend with the official from the Area Office of the Union at any meeting with the Association; ... no Agreement could be reached between the Union and the Association without the consent of the Branch.' [9]

This statement resolved the immediate difficulty. Work was resumed and negotiations opened between the Hebridean Spinners' Association, the independent producers and the TGWU including three local representatives of the weavers.

In retrospect, it is perhaps difficult to comprehend the optimism as to the outcome of the war among those who formed the Lewis Association in January 1943. Certainly the members of the Association could have had little idea of the time-scale involved before their plans could be realised. The purpose of the Association was 'to survey and study the social and economic needs of the Island of Lewis, and to draw up progressive plans for development'. Committees were established to investigate economic and social questions roughly along the lines of a Royal Commission. People with specialist knowledge were invited to participate in the various discussions which contributed to the series of reports eventually published.

It is made clear in the Foreword to *Report No. 2,* that the section entitled 'The Harris Tweed Industry' was the result of the most difficult investigation the Association had yet made.

> '... on one major and two minor points it was impossible to reach unanimity.' [10]

The Association thus decided to publish both the report accepted by the majority and a report putting forward the view of the minority. The divergence of views was over the importation of mainland yarn. Clearly memories of the mass emigration after the First World War prompted the declaration that it was the Government's responsibility to find employment for hundreds of ex-servicemen and women soon to be returning to the island. It also seems that members of the Association were well aware of the widespread local perception that the mill-owners had a strong hold over the independent producers and crofter-weavers in the supply of yarn from the local mills. One of the preliminary statements declares that 'the industry must be maintained as far as possible in the hands of the crofters'. [11]

Fifty years after its publication, the *Report* is of interest for the detail of its debate as well as for its recommendations. However, as it pays no attention to the state of the industry in Harris, the *Report* cannot be taken as a fully representative picture of the industry at the time. A few fundamental tenets, indicative of the contemporary situation in Lewis, were stated at the outset. 'The people of Lewis must make the first and greatest contribution to the prosperity of the industry by setting aside motives of personal or sectional advantage and curb the temptation to snatch ready profits at the expense of the industry's good name and future stability' [12] and 'the interests of the customer should come first'. [13]

The need for a Minority Report was caused by a tied vote on a motion dealing with relations between the Hebridean Spinners' Association (the mill-owners) and the independent producers. The majority recommendation was passed on the casting vote of the Chairman. After considering and rejecting a series of proposed solutions to the problem of guaranteeing an equitable supply of yarn for the small independent producers, the Majority Report came out in favour of allowing yarn to be imported if the mills failed to meet the reasonable demands of the independent producers. No thought seems to have been given to what would constitute reasonable demands. The recommendation was that:

> 'the onus be placed on the Hebridean Spinners and the Harris Tweed Association to devise a system acceptable to the other sections of the trade, which will give the independent producers a guarantee of adequate supplies of yarn, of the same quality as the spinners produce for their own use, at a cost comparable to that ruling for similar yarns on the mainland, and on reasonable delivery terms; and that failing agreement on such a system, the Trade Mark be amended to permit of the use of mainland yarn of specified quality, and of Scottish manufacture.' [14]

As representatives of the mill-owners, Mr Pringle of Newalls and Mr Kenneth Mackenzie moved that the resolution be deleted from the *Report*. The vote was tied and the chairman gave his casting vote for the recommendation. Such was the controversy in the meeting over this result, which was even contrary to the expressed opinion of a meeting of independent producers, that it was agreed to have a *Minority Report* prepared and issued with the *Majority Report*. The *Minority Report* contained a detailed argument demolishing the reasoning and contentions behind the majority recommendation. It also questioned the competence of a decision taken by a bare majority of the 19 people present at the meeting when the Association comprised some 135 ordinary members.

The mill-owners were unwilling to accept responsibility for devising a system which they believed could be rejected whenever it suited the independent producers. [15] The distrust felt by the mill-owners for the independent producers, a distrust which, needless to say, was reciprocated, is quite clear in the *Minority Report*. The nub of the controversy was whether, after 1934, the mills had provided the independent producers with sufficient yarn on acceptable terms.

The independent producers argued that (1) the Harris Tweed industry had originally been the crofters' industry; that (2) the trade mark had been introduced to protect that crofter industry from competitors; that (3) the amended definition of 1934 had protected the industry from outside competition but had failed to protect the crofter from the mills as the only suppliers of yarn and as manufacturers of tweed; that (4) instead, the mills had been protected from outside competition at the crofters' expense; that (5) the mills had a monopoly of the production and distribution of yarn and being themselves the largest users of yarn they had both the incentive and opportunity to keep independent producers short of yarn and stifle competition; that (6) an undertaking by the mill-owners to meet the need for yarn from the independent producers had not been honoured and thus the independent producer should be allowed to buy his yarn from other sources and secure the Trade Mark for the tweed so produced. The independent producers also based their argument on the contention that the existing supply of yarn was unequal to the demand and that this situation would be exacerbated under post-war conditions.

Only one written memorandum in support of the case for the 'spinners' (i.e. the mill-owners) was submitted to the Association. This memorandum does not present a reasoned argument, but is a series of somewhat idiosyncratic declamations in the form of answers to a question:

> '(Q) Does the Harris Tweed industry belong to the crofters in the Outer Hebrides?
>
> (A) No. It is as well to explode this fallacy once and for all.
> The Harris Tweed industry belongs to:
> Firstly the members of the Transport and General Workers' Union (Mill-workers' and Weavers' Branches).
> Secondly to all people who have invested capital in its development.
> Thirdly, any person or persons who wishes to become engaged in it as producers in the future.' [16]

As the *Report* points out, these statements did not invalidate the independent producers' claims to engage in the industry free from restrictions which acted to the advantage of another section of the industry.

The *Minority Report* presented a more reasoned case for the spinning mills than the only memorandum submitted on behalf of the mills. It defined the scope of the term 'Independent Producer' more rigorously than was done in the *Majority Report*.

'In the report and in this document, the term 'Independent Producer' covers all makers of Harris Tweed who do not spin their own yarn. Into this category fall:

(a) the genuine Independent Producer of Harris Tweed under the Trade Mark.
(b) War time Speculators operating under the Trade Mark.
(c) Independent Producers who are yarn importers and therefore do not qualify for the Trade Mark.' [17]

The *Minority Report* then examined the contentions made on behalf of the independent producers.

'The argument ... seems to be:
(a) That there is a chronic shortage of yarn.
(b) That this due to the deliberate exercise of their will by the spinners.
(c) That the plant in the island is now and will be forever insufficient to supply all the looms working in the Island with the yarn they require.

These arguments are not founded on fact. There is admittedly a shortage of yarn at the moment which is felt by the mill-owners and independent producers alike, but this is due entirely to war time rationing and restrictions. ... The Government, besides rationing wool to the spinners has placed severe restrictions on the volume of labour and machinery which may be employed. The yarn shortage is further aggravated by the entry of many new independent producers into the industry during this period of restrictions. Before the war the position was entirely different and the spinners often had to canvas for yarn orders to keep their plants going. ... Two out of the four mills started as spinners only and were forced into the tweed manufacturing side of the industry by the necessity of finding a stable outlet for their yarn. ... It is in spinning machinery that the bulk of their capital is invested. Since the looms are the property of the weavers, it is open to anyone to start a tweed business without investing capital in productive machinery and the majority of the independent producers in Lewis can leave the industry at any time without sacrificing capital. It is far otherwise with the spinner whose capital is invested in expensive machinery for which he must always find employment.' [18]

The reasons given for rejecting the recommendation to allow importation of mainland yarn were the stated opposition of the Harris Tweed Association, [19] of independent producers, [20] the opposition of the spinners themselves and the effect the proposal would have on employment in the spinning mills. The solution to the problem of yarn supplies suggested in the *Minority Report* was that the Association of Independent Producers should set up a yarn merchant's business which would have considerable bargaining powers as against the individual mills and could incorporate technical facilities of benefit to its customers, particularly to the crofter-weaver.

One reason for the mill-owners' attitude to independent producers was exemplified during the debate by James Macdonald who had objected to the term 'Small Producer' being used to cover every producer apart from the mills, many of these producers being, as he said, 'by no means small'.

> 'James Macdonald suggested that the term should be 'speculators.' They were in the trade today and out of it tomorrow. They were quite different from people who had a stake in the industry and could not clear out of it when the market went against them. ... Mr Macdonald told of a man who got some coupons for yarn. He bought the yarn, handed it to a weaver and did nothing himself except pack the finished tweed in canvas and send it away, yet he had £26 profit. 'Can you term that anything else but a speculator?' he asked. 'They can run out of the industry tomorrow and crack their fingers at those who have been spending thousands of pounds in building it up.' [21]

This was rich criticism, from a man whose own first foothold in the industry had been of a similar type. The Hebridean Spinners' Association had a strong, if perhaps somewhat intemperate, voice in the Lewis Association, in the person of James Macdonald. The independent producers and crofter-weavers had a persuasive voice in the person of Stephen MacLean. Stephen MacLean was not an active participant in the debate on the Harris Tweed industry, as at the time he was seriously ill in his home in Stornoway and died soon after the *Report* was issued, but through his personal friendship with a number of members of the Executive Committee of the Association he was able to persuade them, from his sickbed, that the small independent producers (of whom his own father was one) should not be left totally dependent on the local mills for their supplies of yarn. In the Harris Tweed case of 1964, Lord Hunter described Stephen MacLean's contribution to the debate:

> 'The small independent producers were fairly strongly represented, having as their leading spokesman the late Mr Stephen MacLean, a local solicitor who was the son of Mr Murdo MacLean of the Crofter Handwoven Tweed Company. ... Mr Stephen MacLean, as one would expect, made full use of what had been said *obiter dicta* in the Embargo Case. ... The *Majority* and *Minority* Reports, read as a whole, ... show to what extent self-interest still operated in the Islands, and also establish that the continued use of some mainland yarn was well-known.' [22]

An *obiter dicta* is a comment made by a judge which carries weight and may be of persuasive value. Although it does not bear directly on the case in hand, it may be acted on and, in due course, acquire substantial authority. In the instance quoted above it refers to Lord Simon's statement in the Embargo case which said that although cloth made out of mainland yarn did not qualify for the stamp it could be sold as 'Harris Tweed' having been woven in the Islands. It was a remark which was to be used to justify numerous attempts to break into the Island industry for years to come.

We are left to ponder why the members of the Lewis Association saw fit to throw into question the hard-won definition of Harris Tweed, established in 1934, by even considering the admission of mainland-spun yarn. Had the mills really drifted away from the 'gentleman's agreement' to produce adequate supplies of yarn after 1934? They would deny that they had. Early in 1937, they had bought wool when the price was high and were left trying to sell their yarn in competition with mainland spinners when the price of wool dropped, thereby tempting some independent producers to take advantage of the lower price of mainland spun yarn. [23] The newest mill, Thomas Smith & Co., had not been party to any 'gentleman's agreement' as they came to Lewis after the amended definition had been accepted.

In defence of the Lewis Association, James Shaw Grant, who was Secretary of that Association when the *Report* was compiled, made the following points.

'The Association's decision was taken by the narrowest of majorities - the Chairman's casting vote. It was taken during the War when conditions in the industry were unusual, to say the least, and it did not reject the 1934 definition. It merely suggested that, if the spinners failed to produce a satisfactory system for ensuring a fair distribution of yarn, the Board of Trade should, as a last resort, be asked what its attitude would be towards an alteration of the definition.

At the same time, the Association urged that the Board of Trade should incorporate the words 'Harris Tweed' in the definition, which would have given the industry the protection it finally won through the Hunter judgement. It asked for standards of quality to be introduced for the different weights of Harris Tweed - an issue the HTA had subsequently to face up to. It also raised, for the first time, the issue of teaching textile technology in a local college and re-structuring of the HTA to make it a more representative body.' [24]

A copy of both *Reports* was sent as a matter of courtesy to the TGWU. The Union's comments on a section in the *Majority Report* entitled 'The Effects of the 1934 Revision' are of particular interest. This section of the *Majority Report* explicitly attributes almost 'all the dissatisfaction in the industry to the effects of the amended definition'. The TGWU totally disagreed with this statement. Taking the amended definition of Harris tweed clause by clause, the TGWU response asserts (a) that the amended definition returned to the crofter a home market for all his wool; (b) that by confining dyeing and finishing to the Outer Hebrides, employment, which had previously gone to the mainland, had been returned to the islands; and (c) that by insisting on tweed being handwoven by the crofter at his own home, the situation of the crofter had been greatly improved in comparison with his situation before 1934. It is at this juncture that the TGWU writer provides us with information which is not recorded quite so explicitly elsewhere. The Area Secretary of the TGWU started by reviewing the history of the industry:

'Before 1935 the position with reference to payment for weaving was indeed a scandal. Several traders in tweed were also merchants, and did not pay cash on the return of a Tweed. The unfortunate Crofter-Weaver had to accept provisions in payment, and any complaints as to this method were dealt with by the Trader stopping the supply of yarn to the weaver concerned, a very serious penalty indeed, considering the fact that several traders owned the looms the weavers were working and charged a rental for same, sometimes as high as half the recognised charge for weaving. Needless to state, complaints were few, but reports came to us and unfortunately, we could only raise the matter in a general way, owing to the fact that no weaving would be obtained if names were mentioned. Probably, several of the Traders referred to are classified under the term of 'Small Producers' ... we prefer the term 'Trader' because these people do nothing for or in the industry. Neither do they take the risk of investing their money in the industry. All they do is grumble about the price they have to pay for wool, weaving and finishing, and sit back and collect the profits obtained from other people's labour. Several of them, not content with the profits made from stamped tweed, and regardless of the fact that they were diverting a considerable amount of work from the island continued, after the new definition was operating, to obtain supplies of yarn from the mainland and return the woven tweed there for finishing. ... Is it from this source that the alleged dissatisfaction springs? Because, if so, they neither toil, nor yet do they spin, but creep into the industry at busy periods, collect their profits from the results of other people's planning and labour, and, having no stake in the industry to lose, they simply vanish during lean times. No right thinking person would pay any attention to their complaints except perhaps to inform them that if their complaints are as stated, they were only being treated as they justly deserved.' [25]

This is eloquent and highly emotive language in defence of the spinning mills, reminiscent of parts of the debate within the Lewis Association. An equally eloquent argument has been advanced for the independent producer by Angus MacLeod of Marybank. Angus MacLeod spent a lifetime in the industry as an independent producer and was never afraid to voice his beliefs or sign his name to them in the 'Letters' page of the *Stornoway Gazette*. What he says is contrary to the accepted wisdom of his day, some would say even contrary to the verdict of history, nonetheless, there is a body of opinion which will say that he is right and the received wisdom is wrong. Angus MacLeod wrote in 1995,

'Undoubtedly the registering of the 'Orb mark' in 1911 was a good thing. When it was originally registered the Harris Tweed industry was a crofter cottage industry. The development of the industry in the first twenty years after registration of the 'Orb' was largely, and increasingly, based on mainland yarn. The question now is whether that fact should have been acknowledged when the definition was amended in 1934. It was quite natural for the local spinners to argue against mainland yarn. It was also quite natural for those producers who were using mainland yarn to be sceptical about the spinners' motives.

With hindsight one asks whether the situation was handled correctly. It is never right to be restrictive in industry and the amended definition was restrictive. Again, it is never right to create a monopoly, particularly at the expense of others. The amended definition created a yarn spinning monopoly when it confined 'Orb' marked tweed to that made from yarn spun in the Outer Hebrides. I feel that a lot of scaremongering was done in connection with the practice of importing mainland yarn. I feel that if mainland yarn had been allowed, the eventual situation would not have been any worse than it became, probably a lot better. As long as qualification for the Orb mark was conditional on weaving being carried out in the homes of the Island crofters in the traditional way, that condition would have protected the cloth.

There was another weakness in the course that was followed in 1934 and that was in registering the Orb and not the words 'Harris Tweed'. As a result, the argument arose as to what was 'Harris Tweed'. Certainly cloth qualifying for the Orb mark is Harris Tweed, but there was ambiguity in the law as to whether unstamped cloth made from mainland yarn was or was not Harris Tweed. If the situation as it stood in 1933 had been fully acknowledged and mainland yarn accepted as the fact that it was, then there would have been no ambiguity as to what could correctly be called 'Harris Tweed'. If mainland yarn had been accepted in 1934, weavers in the Outer Hebrides would have been a lot busier and, furthermore, a lot of bad blood in the industry could have been avoided. The Embargo case of 1938 would not have been necessary, nor would the Harris Tweed case of 1964. The judgement in 1964 simply confirmed and tightened the monopoly of the Stornoway spinners and the spinners did not use their privileged position wisely. The time soon came when small producers could not buy a pound of yarn from the Hebridean spinners at a price that enabled them to manufacture cloth at the same price as the spinners charged for their own tweed. Despite the fact that advertising and the public perception of Harris Tweed had been based on the crofter cottage industry, that side of the industry, which should have been encouraged, was discouraged and eventually killed off.' [26]

In stating his perspective of the issues, a perspective in which he would not be alone, Angus MacLeod makes no claim to being an expert in trade mark law. As it transpired in the 1950s, the whole problem of what was, or was not, entitled to be called 'Harris Tweed' was to be the subject of bitter controversy.

If one examines the controversy within the Lewis Association, it is clear that even in 1944, views similar to those expressed much later by Angus MacLeod were current in the industry at that time. Accepting very similar arguments from the independent producers of the day, members of the Association declared their wish to protect the crofter-weaver, to whom it was acknowledged 'the industry belonged'. It may be that the lack of a reasoned written memorandum from the mill-owners in the preliminary debate allowed the manufacturers case to go by default, or it may be that the recommendation to allow importation of mainland yarn on license was partially inspired by a wish to demonstrate that members voting for it were not in the pocket of one overly forceful mill-owner on the Executive Committee. Nonetheless, it seems in hindsight that the Association let its heart rule its head. In failing to distinguish between crofter-weavers, independent producers, and 'speculators', groups which were by no means synonymous, and in supporting the importation of mainland yarn, the Lewis Association unwittingly encouraged a new and determined breed of mainland 'speculator' to break into the industry, something that none of the members voting for the majority recommendation would have seen as in any way desirable at the time.

Reference - During the Second World War

1 Lewis Association *Report, No. 2, The Harris Tweed Industry* (1944) [hereafter: 'Lewis Association Report, Majority Report/Minority Report'], 41, para. 4.

2 Department of Labour and National Service: Report of Committee of Investigation on the Causes of the Dispute Involving Weavers in the Harris Tweed Industry in the Island of Lewis, 18. 5. 1943. [hereafter: 'Report on Weavers' Dispute]. Typescript in Western Isles Library, Stornoway.

3 *Stornoway Gazette,* 3. 5. 1944.

4 *Argyllshire Weavers Ltd. and Others v. Macaulay (A.) (Tweeds) Ltd., and Others,* [1964] RPC No. 16, 477 [hereafter: 'Harris Tweed Case 1964'] at 538.

5 *Stornoway Gazette,* 10. 9. 1943.

6 *ibid.,* 19. 2. 1943.

7 'Report on Weavers' Dispute'.

8 *ibid.*

9 *ibid.*

10 Lewis Association Report, Foreward, vii.

11 *ibid.,* 43, para. 13.

12 *ibid.,* 43, para. 10.

13 *ibid.,* 43, para. 11.

14 *ibid.,* 70, para. 10 (Recommendations of the Majority Report).

15 *ibid.,* 78, (Minority Report) see e.g. para. 17.

16 *ibid.,* 53, para. 40.

17 *ibid.,* 71-72, (Minority Report).

18 *ibid.,* 73-74, (Minority Report).

19 *ibid.,* 59-60, para. 60.

20 *ibid.,* 60, para. 61.

21 *Stornoway Gazette,* 27. 4. 1944.

22 'Harris Tweed Case' [1964] RPC 16 , 477, at 538.

23 *Stornoway Gazette,* 2. 12. 1938.

24 James Shaw Grant to the author, 8th July, 1999.

25 T.B. Meikle, Area Secretary, TGWU, Transport House, Glasgow to James Shaw Grant, The Lewis Association, 22. 12. 1944. HTA Office, Stornoway.

26 Angus MacLeod, Marybank, Stornoway, to the author, 10. 7. 1995.

11

Post War: *The Report on the Crofter Woollen Industry*

The initiative taken by the Lewis Association in conducting its own survey of the economic situation in the Island of Lewis was but one manifestation of the widespread concern felt at the economic decline in and depopulation of the Highlands and Islands during the 1930s. Before the war, in an effort to identify measures which would improve economic conditions in the Highlands and Islands, the Government had set up a Highlands Sub-Committee of the Scottish National Development Council under the Chairmanship of Major Edward Hilleary. During the war, Tom Johnston, Secretary of State for Scotland in the war-time coalition Government, kept Highland issues high on his agenda. Commissioning a radical review of the crofter woollen industry by a Committee of the Scottish Council on Industry was part of this pattern of keeping a finger on the pulse of the Highlands and Islands. Important as it was at the time, most of what is contained in the *Report on the Crofter Woollen Industry* has now been superseded by changes in the Highland economy, but it is salutary to note how long it took before some of the recommendations made in this report were put into effect.

The Scottish Council on Industry was representative of the Local Authority Associations, the Chambers of Commerce, the Trade Union Congress, the Development Council and the Banks in Scotland. Although the *Report* was not published until 1946, evidence was collected during the war from a wide spectrum of bodies and individuals in the Highlands and Islands, at much the same time as the Lewis Association was conducting its own surveys. A list of the individuals and bodies from whom evidence was taken is given at the beginning of the *Report on the Crofter Woollen Industry*. Because the list includes people on both sides of the controversy over imported mainland yarn, it is not surprising that many of the opinions expressed in the *Report on the Crofter Woollen Industry* are similar to those to be found in the *Lewis Association Report on the Harris Tweed Industry*.

The scope of the *Report of the Committee on the Crofter Woollen Industry*, was similar to that of the *1914 Scott Report* to the Board of Agriculture on

Home Industries in the Highlands and Islands of Scotland. The *Report on the Crofter Woollen Industry* provided detailed information on the state of the woollen industry in the Highlands and Islands in the 1940s and examined thoroughly the options for post-war development of all forms of the woollen industry, including Harris Tweed. The views expressed on the controversies and problems in the Harris Tweed industry were influential at the time, and are worth pondering on even today.

The terms of reference given to the Committee on the Crofter Woollen Industry were:

> 'To enquire into the present position of all branches of the woollen industry in the Highlands and Islands with reference to wool production and manufacture both of factory and home-made origin and to make recommendations upon:
>
> 1. Adoption of distinctive trade marks and certificates of quality for genuine and factory products;
> 2. Methods of obtaining and preparing yarn for the crofting communities by the establishment of small scale carding and spinning mills;
> 3. Improvement in design and technique in the industry;
> 4. The system of marketing;
> 5. The possibility of other lines of manufacture.' [1]

The report opened with emphatic advice that Harris Tweed should retain its image as a quality product aimed at a high class market. It went on to discuss what the members of the Committee believed had been the economic importance of millspun yarn in establishing a larger commercial market for Harris Tweed in the early decades of the twentieth century. [2] Significantly, the *Report* accepted that this 'was done by appropriating the goodwill of handspun'.[3] As the investigating Committee of the Scottish Council on Industry had no exact data on the relative proportions of handspun to millspun yarn used in the early years of the twentieth century, the increase in the number of looms in Lewis (from 55 in 1899, to 161 in 1906, and 250-300 in 1911) was taken as indirect evidence for increased production of tweed made from millspun yarn imported from the Scottish mainland. [4] The apparent assumption in the report that all millspun yarn came from the mainland was wrong. The report makes no mention of the fact that Kenneth Mackenzie had started a spinning and carding mill in Stornoway in 1906 and the Patent Slip Mill had added spinning plant in 1908, thus ensuring a supply of local millspun yarn, which, of course, was not at that time a legitimate component of Harris Tweed! Because the claim that the origins of a larger commercial market for Harris Tweed had been based on imported millspun yarn was employed during the fifties, by mainland producers attempting to break into the Island industry, it is worth examining what the *Report* actually said.

> 'About the beginning of the present century the demand for Harris Tweed began to outrun hand-spinning capacity. ... It is clear from the number of weavers that a new stage in the development of the industry had then been reached. Substantial quantities of yarn were being obtained from the Scottish mainland ... and this yarn was being converted into tweed on the island looms and marketed as Harris.' [5]

The *Report* went on to describe how application was made for a Trade Mark to protect the old handspun industry, and quoted the definition of 1911, which stipulated that only handspun yarn was to be used. It continued:

> 'The attempt to secure (by the Trade Mark of 1911) the name of Harris for the original handmade article was a failure. The (Harris Tweed) Association was not strong enough to defend its position. An industry grew up in the Hebrides based on the use of imported millspun yarn which was woven in the islands, and the article produced by these methods was sold as 'Harris Tweed'. ... It is proper to emphasise this development, for while Harris Tweed is certainly the 'birthright' of the Harris producer in an obvious sense, there was created subsequently a new type of industry, with new and greater commercial possibilities. This industry belonged to Lewis as well as to Harris and was at first based on millspun yarn.' [6]

The figures given for the increase in the number of looms derive from the *Scott Report* of 1914,[7] but the positive view of imported millspun yarn adopted by the Committee came, not from the *Scott Report* of 1914, but from the lobbying of the independent producers of the 1940s. The Scottish Council on Industry Committee failed to recognise the implications of its own admission'[8] that the new commercial industry which grew up in Lewis did so by 'appropriating the goodwill of the handspun article'. It ignored, or failed to appreciate, that the marketing of millspun Lewis tweed as 'Harris Tweed' was, to quote the opinion of Lord Hunter in 1964, a fraudulent trade deliberately deceiving the customer into thinking that what he was buying was actually the traditional handspun article.

Whatever the reason for doing so, the Committee paid little heed to those sections of the *Scott Report* which make it clear that the rapid growth of the industry based on millspun yarn, whether imported or from Island mills, caused a serious problem in 1912-13, by destroying the reputation and economic viability of handspun Harris Tweed.[9] Scott said that the large gain made from the misdescription of tweed made from millspun yarn and sold as 'Harris Tweed', 'wrecked the system'.

> 'The spinning machines in Stornoway and on the mainland supplied the demand for yarn; but more weavers were required and the combination of machine-spun yarn with bad weaving seriously injured the sale of tweeds. Among the wholesale merchants in London, the deterioration in quality has given rise to a new trade term, namely 'Stornoway tweeds' which covers all those produced in Lewis.'[10]

Moving on to the mid-1930s, by which time Island millspun yarn had been accepted under the amended definition of 1934, the *Report on the Crofter Woollen Industry* identified a problem inherent to that new definition, namely that 'an article associated by sentiment and advertising with handicraft, has nevertheless an important element of machine-work in its make-up'.[11] In identifying the vital significance of the customer's perception of what is or is not 'genuine Harris Tweed', the report showed a measure of insight which was at odds with the inconsistency in its inference that the Lewis industry based on millspun yarn at the beginning of the century was legitimate. In passing, it is of interest to note that the *Report* gave an estimated increase in imports of mainland yarn from 60,000 lbs. in 1937 to 400,000 lbs immediately before the Second World War. [12]

The existence in 1934 of a 'gentleman's agreement' by the mill-owners to supply independent producers with yarn was seen as unsatisfactory. [13] The report then described the creation of a 'vicious circle' whereby the independent producer, dissatisfied for whatever reason with the service of the Island mills, resorted to mainland yarn, whereupon 'the local mills felt under less obligation to render him satisfactory service'. [14] This 'vicious circle', coupled with an unsympathetic attitude by the mill-owners towards the independent producers, was seen as lying at the root of the problem of Island yarn supplies, rather than a lack of local spinning capacity, a topic fiercely debated in the *Majority* and *Minority Reports on the Harris Tweed Industry* in the *Lewis Association Report*. Despite apparently accepting the argument advanced by the independent producers as to the important contribution that mainland millspun yarn had made to the early development of the industry, and, despite acknowledging that its admission would remove the monopoly of the local mills, thereby solving the problems of the independent producer, the Committee on the Crofter Woollen Industry did not advocate the admission of mainland yarn, principally because 'the Board of Trade would regard it as weakening the legal position of the existing Trade Mark'. The Board of Trade was, of course, one of the most influential bodies giving evidence to the Committee, and it seems to have been supportive of the amended definition of Harris Tweed in 1946. Yet, throughout the next decade, the ambivalent attitude of the Board of Trade was to be crucial in the controversy over the use of imported mainland yarn.

In an attempt to solve the problem caused by the use of imported yarn, the Committee on the Crofter Woollen Industry suggested an additional Certification Trade Mark, to be applied to all island-produced textiles, including Harris Tweed. This 'Hebridean Mark', granted to a properly constituted body, other than the Harris Tweed Association, would apply both to Orb-stamped Harris Tweed made from Island yarn and to tweed made from mainland yarn, thus allowing the production of a greater variety of textiles in the Islands. [15] It was thought that the proposed 'Hebridean Mark' would also help to counteract the monopoly of the local spinning mills by supplying a measure of competition to the Orb Mark.

In responding to the report, the Harris Tweed Association expressed grave reservations as to the wisdom of introducing a Hebridean Certification Mark for Island producers of textiles who did not use island-spun yarn. The Harris Tweed Association said:

> 'We feel that such a Trade Mark would be confusing to the buying public and would detract from the present Harris Tweed Trade Mark. ... We feel that we should be guilty of sacrificing the birthright of the Outer Hebrides if we consented to this suggestion.' [16]

The request from Harris that a clearer distinction should be made between 'handspun' and 'millspun' by adding, where appropriate, the word 'millspun' to the label supplied with the tweed, was dismissed by the Committee, because it would 'prejudice the customer against millspun as having less handwork in its manufacture'. [17] However, in order to help the handspun industry (which was based predominantly in Harris) it was tentatively suggested that the definition in the Trade Mark should be amended 'to allow tweed, where the warp was millspun, but the weft handspun, to be ranked as handspun'. [18] Again, this suggestion was ruled out as it was thought that the Board of Trade would regard the application of the handspun cachet to tweed of mixed yarn types as misleading. [19] This type of tweed, in which the weft was handspun and the warp millspun, came to be popularly known as '50-50 tweed'. The Harris Tweed Association had first become aware of its existence during the Second World War and approached the Board of Trade about stamping '50-50 tweed'. At that time, the Board of Trade did not consider that an amendment to the Regulations for stamping would be required. The Association therefore authorised that such tweed should be stamped with the words 'Handspun weft'. [20] Thereafter the Government included tweed in which the weft was handspun and the warp millspun as a category for which the controlled price fell between wholly handspun and wholly millspun tweed. [21]

Digressing for a moment from the *Report on the Crofter Woollen Industry* to follow the history of 50-50 tweed, the subsequent use of the 'Handspun weft' stamp was eventually stopped in Harris because it was feared that there was some abuse of it. According to a local stamper, he suspected that he was being asked to stamp as 'Handspun weft', cloth that was entirely made from millspun yarn. As a result, the Harris Tweed Association dropped the use of the stamp for handspun weft for a number of years. On 9th January 1961, the Harris Tweed Association approached the Board of Trade again on the subject of tweed in which the weft was handspun and the warp millspun. On 29th March 1961, the Board of Trade approved an amendment to the Regulations governing the use of the Harris Tweed Trade Mark. The words to be added to the Regulations were:

> "handspun' in the case of Tweeds made entirely from handspun yarn, or the words 'handspun weft' in the case of Tweeds made as to the weft entirely from handspun yarn.' [22]

When the *Report on the Crofter Woollen Industry* came to consider the Harris Tweed Association, the comments in the *Lewis Association Report* on the HTA were repeated. The complaint that the Harris Tweed Association was 'an English Company with its registered office in London', a charge levelled at the HTA by the Lewis Harris Tweed Association during the 1934 controversy over the amended definition, was also repeated. It is perhaps indicative of changing attitudes in Scotland to the traditional paternalism of English-domiciled gentry that this charge of 'Englishness' should be made in 1946. Quoting from the comments on the Harris Tweed Association in the *Lewis Association Report*, the *Report on the Crofter Woollen Industry* recommended that the Harris Tweed Association should be restructured to become 'more representative of, and accountable to, the Islanders', either by alteration of the Articles of Association or by liquidation and re-formation as a Scottish company, 'representative of the Island Local Authorities, the mills, weavers and independent producers or their respective Associations'. [23] Needless to say, the Harris Tweed Association was 'not impressed by the proposal for a new elected body to administer the Trade Mark'. It refuted the charge that it was an 'English Association' as the Management Committee were all Scots and, with the exception of the Chairman, were all resident in Scotland, four out of the seven members being resident in the Outer Isles. It had been a 'mere matter of convenience' that the Association was registered in London 'because the law agents employed in the formation of the Company had been in London'. [24]

In a final section entitled 'A General Policy for Highland Woollen Industries', the *Report on the Crofter Woollen Industry* put forward a number of suggestions, among which were recommendations for 'technical education for those employed in the woollen industry and a general all-Highland system of quality control by an agency operating under the Secretary for State for Scotland'. [25] To the recommendation on technical education, the Harris Tweed Association replied:

> 'We welcome the fact that Inverness County Council has appointed a whole-time instructor whose function it is to train and advise on the technicalities of weaving, dyeing, designing and hand-spinning.' [26]

This instructor, Mr Hegarty from Barra, went round from village school to village school with a miniature demonstration loom. He is still spoken of with respect and affection in Harris today. On the question of quality control, by November 1945, the Association had drawn up and submitted to the Board of Trade a standard of quality for Harris Tweed which required that:

> 'tweeds presented for stamping must contain no less than 18 picks and 18 ends to the square inch of finished tweed. The application for this amendment to the Regulations governing the use of the Trade Mark was granted as from 19th June 1946.' [27]

The need for a stipulated number of picks (or threads to use a layman's language) per square inch, was explained graphically by an Island weaver, who said, 'some tweed was so loosely woven that you could spit peas through it'. Somewhat disdainfully, a Press Statement from the Harris Tweed Association explained:

> 'In recent war years there has been a tendency in some quarters to exploit the demand for Harris Tweed by putting on the market Cloth of an inferior quality which, while complying with the terms of the definition, was deficient in some of the essential characteristics of the standard cloth.' [28]

One of the most important recommendations in the *Report on the Crofter Woollen Industry* stated that legislation on the lines of the Merchandise Marks (Trade Descriptions) Bill of 1934 would be of great value to crofter industries. [29] The discussion on this recommendation [30] explains that while the Trade Marks Act of 1938 gave protection to Certification Marks, it did not give an exclusive right to any accompanying descriptive words. For example, while the Harris Tweed Association had the exclusive use of its Trade Mark, known as 'the Orb Mark', the Association did not have the exclusive use of the accompanying descriptive words 'Harris Tweed'. Although some years were to pass before the right to the words 'Harris Tweed' were to become a real source of contention, the *Report on the Crofter Woollen Industry*, published in 1946, continued almost prophetically:

> 'The rightness or otherwise of 'descriptions' in this sense, whether they are included in a Certification Trade Mark or not, is a question which has to be settled by the interested parties in the Courts; and the decision of the Court will turn on the accepted meaning of a description in the trades concerned. If those who genuinely are entitled to the use of a Trade description are insufficiently organised, or not vigilant enough in the early stages of the abuse of the description, it is clear that they will be in danger of losing the right to the description.' [31]

Four key phrases, in this paragraph , 'in the Courts', 'meaning of a description', 'not vigilant enough' and 'danger of losing the right to the description', provide a brief summary of what was to happen during the decade which lay ahead, when a group of independent producers of unstamped Harris Tweed challenged the exclusive right of the Harris Tweed Association to the term 'Harris Tweed' in the United States and Britain. The recommendations for some sort of compromise between the opposing parties in The *Lewis Association Report on the Harris Tweed Industry* and the *Report on the Crofter Woollen Industry* could perhaps be seen as straws in the wind before the storm which lay ahead for the Harris Tweed Association and the Island mill-owners.

Reference - Post War: *The Report on the Crofter Woollen Industry*

1 Scottish Council on Industry, *Report of the Committee on the Crofter Woollen Industry* [hereafter: '*Report on the Crofter Woollen Industry*'] 3.
2 *ibid.*, 14.
3 *ibid.*, 26.
4 *ibid.*, 13.
5 *ibid.*
6 *ibid.*, 14.
7 *Report to the Board of Agriculture for Scotland on Home Industries in the Highlands and Islands* (1914). [hereafter: 'Scott Report'], 48.
8 '*Report on the Crofter Woollen Industry,*' 26.
9 Scott Report, 29.
10 *ibid.*, 61-2.
11 '*Report on the Crofter Woollen Industry,*' 15.
12 *ibid.*, 18.
13 *ibid.*, 20.
14 *ibid.*, 21.
15 *ibid.*, 25.
16 Press Statement by the Harris Tweed Association, Edinburgh, 26. 3. 1946. HTA Office, Stornoway.
17 '*Report on the Crofter Woollen Industry,*' 26.
18 *ibid.*
19 *ibid.*, 26-27.
20 Transcripts of evidence in *Argyllshire Weavers Ltd. and Others v. A. MacAulay (Tweeds) Ltd. and Others* (1964) Court of Session, Outer House: Vol. 1, 4707-08: Evidence of Colonel Macarthur. HRA/D190/1a (xxxv).
21 Statutory Rules & Orders 1947/2639. Copy in HTA Office Stornoway.
The selling price of 50-50 tweed set under Statutory Rules and Orders, 1947, No. 2639. Goods and Services (Price Control) Apparel and Textiles.
The General Apparel and Textile (Manufacturers Maximum Prices and Charges) Order, 1947, Part II of the First Schedule: Sub-paragraph (5) of paragraph 1 was amended to read: (5): 'In respect of goods being tweed (including Harris Tweed) handwoven in the Outer Hebrides and being tweed:- sub-section (ii) made from yarn spun in the Outer Hebrides of which not less than 50 per cent was handspun, to which the certification trade mark has been applied, together with the words 'handspun weft', the sum of 10s 5d per yard.'
22 Transcripts of evidence in *Argyllshire Weavers Ltd. and Others v. A. MacAulay (Tweeds) Ltd. and Others* (1964) Court of Session Outer House: Vol. 1, 4710: Evidence of Colonel Macarthur. HRA/D190/1a (xxxv).
23 '*Report on the Crofter Woollen Industry*', 29.

24 Press Statement issued by the Harris Tweed Association, Edinburgh, 26. 3. 1946. HTA Office, Stornoway.

25 *Report on the Crofter Woollen Industry*, 47-53.

26 Press Statement issued by the Harris Tweed Association, Edinburgh, 26. 3. 1946. HTA Office, Stornoway.

27 H. L. Saunders, Controller Industrial Property Department, Board of Trade, to the Harris Tweed Association, as Registered Proprietors of the Trade Mark No. 319214, re amendment to the Regulations governing the use of the Trade Mark: 'The Board of Trade hereby sanction ... the amplification of the first paragraph headed "Conditions in regard to use of the Trade Mark" by the addition of the words, "and shall not affix the Trade Mark" to any Tweed which contains less than 18 picks and 18 ends per square inch of "finished tweed"'. 27. 5. 1946. HTA Office, Stornoway: File entitled 're: The Merchandise Acts, 1887-1953. Case to Advise'.

28 Press Statement issued by the Harris Tweed Association, Edinburgh, 26. 3. 1946. HTA Office, Stornoway.

29 '*Report on the Crofter Woollen Industry*,' 61.

30 *ibid.*, 53.

31 *ibid.*

Scouring raw wool in the mill.

Filling the dye vat.

© Courtesy of J. L. Rodger for HTA

Colour-blending the dyed and un-dyed wool.

© Courtesy of J. L. Rodger for HTA

-ding the wool.

Spinning the yarn on a spinning frame.

n for the warp
l weft, bagged
d labelled to go
t to weavers in
eir own homes.

Neil MacLean, a weaver in Sandwick, Stornoway, at his Hattersley Domestic handloom.

Milling a length of tweed, one of many finishing processes.

Cathella MacRae stamping the finished tweed with the Harris Tweed Trade Mark.

© Courtesy of J. L. Rodger for HTA

Bales of Tweed on Stornoway pier being shipped on the Loch Dunvegan to markets all over the world.

© Courtesy of J. L. Rodger for HTA

Harris Tweed on sale.

12

Scottish Crofter Weavers and James Macdonald of Oban

The Committee on the Crofter Woollen Industry was fully justified in its warning that vigilance would be required if the industry wished to avoid losing the right to the description of Harris Tweed as a product exclusive to the Outer Hebrides. The particular circumstances affecting the industry throughout the war had given rise to a variety of threats to the Orb trade mark, some threatening, temporarily, the reputation for quality associated with the name 'Harris Tweed', others more fundamentally, threatening the right to the term 'Harris Tweed'.

Restrictions on textile production, both during and immediately after the war, had inflated demand for any kind of material, including Harris Tweed. This artificial demand brought its own problems for the industry, among them a black market in Harris Tweed. In 1947, the Government removed wartime restrictions on the national wool clip and wool was then sold at auction. Naturally wool prices shot up, soaring from 1s 4 ½d to 3s 2d per pound. However, controls on the selling price of cloth had not been removed at the same time, and it quickly became uneconomic for weavers and independent producers to buy yarn at vastly inflated prices, when a commensurate increase could not be asked for the finished tweed. The need for vigilance in protecting the Trade Mark and the reputation of Harris Tweed in these circumstances becomes abundantly clear from a report in the *Daily Record* entitled 'Black Market in Tweed may Grow':

> 'The black market in Harris Tweed may be intensified by the recent removal of wool controls - unless the Board of Trade quickly aids crofter-weavers by raising the controlled price for finished cloth. ... The flourishing tweed black market is centred in London. Reputable trading organisations describe the bulk of the cloth finding its way there as 'shoddy stuff' which should never have been made at all.' [1]

As the *Daily Record* pointed out, the contrast between the inflated purchasing price of yarn and the permitted maximum selling price of tweed was liable to provide a further incentive to unscrupulous producers or individual weavers to use inferior, and therefore cheaper, yarn in the production of a cloth they then sold as 'Harris Tweed'.

The primary meaning of the word 'shoddy' is 'fibre made from old cloth'. The secondary meaning is 'inferior, trashy or counterfeit'. As used in the *Daily Record* report 'shoddy' may have had either or both meanings. Certainly rumour had it that tweed actually made from shoddy was known. Even if the *Daily Record* report exaggerates the quantity of 'shoddy cloth' reaching the market, a number of weavers in the Islands, and possibly woollen manufacturers elsewhere in Britain, would seem to have been producing vastly inferior tweed, or even 'tweed' made from shoddy, and passing this off as 'Harris Tweed' before wool controls were removed in December 1947. If shoddy was being used for weaving so-called 'Harris Tweed', the shoddy certainly came from spinners outwith the Islands taking advantage of the high price of woollen yarn to sell cheaper shoddy yarn to anyone who would buy it. The great difficulty for the Harris Tweed Association in such circumstances was in identifying the culprits and bringing an action against them.

The extreme example of shoddy being passed-off as 'Harris Tweed' illustrates why the Harris Tweed Association constantly advised the customer that the only absolute guarantee that material was genuine Harris Tweed was the presence of the Orb mark stamped on the cloth. Certainly, the presence of the Orb mark guaranteed, and still guarantees, that material is genuine Harris Tweed, but it is possible for tweed without the Orb mark to be genuine Harris Tweed, as long as it has been made strictly in accordance with the definition of Harris Tweed, even although it has not been presented for stamping. For instance, an island weaver could conceivably produce a length of tweed using the wool of his own sheep, dye and card the raw wool and spin it into yarn totally by hand, weave the tweed in his own home and finish the tweed by the old hand-finishing process. If a passing tourist then came and bought that tweed directly from the weaver, he, or she, would certainly be buying genuine, handspun, handwoven, Harris Tweed. If that tweed had been presented for stamping, it would have qualified for the Orb stamp. The constant problem for the Harris Tweed Association was to determine whether all the unstamped 'Harris Tweed' being offered for sale had actually been made according to the definition, or whether any number of modifications had been introduced in the course of production, even to the extent of weaving from shoddy yarn. Experience had proved to the Harris Tweed Association that most unstamped tweed had been subject to some degree of divergence from the definition accompanying the trade mark.

The Harris Tweed industry, as an overseas exporter, had been given a relatively protected position by receiving under wartime regulations an allocation of wool specifically and solely for the production of Harris Tweed. This special status of the industry provided a happy hunting ground for those who were inclined to put their own quick profits before the longer-term well-being of the industry. While any protection from the stringencies of war-time control of wool might have seemed beneficial to the industry, there was to be a sting in the tail associated with official protection which turned out to be less than beneficial in the longer term.

For some years before the war, the island wool clip had been insufficient to meet the yarn requirements of the Stornoway mills and therefore, in keeping with the clause of the 1934 definition which specified 'pure virgin Scottish wool', quantities of raw Scottish wool had been imported from the mainland by the island mills to make up the shortfall in the island clip. When war broke out rationing of wool was introduced throughout Britain, with the exception of the wool clip in the Hebrides and Northern Isles, which were exempt from the controls imposed on the clip elsewhere in Britain. According to Mr James Barr, who had been Wool Control Rationing Officer for Scotland from 1939 to 1945, a specific allocation of Scottish wool was set aside to be converted into yarn for Harris Tweed. This official protection carried a sting in the tail which is all the more surprising as it involved practices which were in direct contravention of the amended definition of Harris Tweed. Mr Barr described the special arrangements made to protect the Harris Tweed industry.

> 'In each successive rationing period of four months a very large weight of wool was set aside to be converted into yarn for the Harris Tweed trade. The bulk of this wool was, of course, allocated to the Stornoway Spinners, but a substantial weight went to Spinners on the Mainland, (including Spinners in England) who were known to have been in the habit of producing yarn for Harris Tweed weavers; and these spinners were directed to convert this wool into yarn for Weavers in the Outer Hebrides and to use it for

no other purpose. The allocations of wool to Mainland Spinners for the production of Harris Tweed were based on their average annual output of yarn for this purpose during the three years immediately preceding the war. Provision was also made by Wool Control for the supply of additional quantities of mainland-spun yarn to Harris Tweed makers who required weights in excess of their normal needs for the production of Harris Tweed for export. The average weight of mainland wool allotted to the Stornoway mills during the years 1939 to 1949 was 2,835,000 lbs. Mainland Spinners during the same period converted approximately 371,000 lbs annually into yarn for the Harris Tweed trade.' [2]

This startling information was provided in 1953 to Mr John Simpson, Managing Director of an Aberdeen firm, Scottish Crofter Weavers, by Mr Barr, who was in 1953 Secretary of the National Association of Scottish Woollen Manufacturers, a group which by the 1950s was very antagonistic towards the Harris Tweed Association. In 1953, Mr Simpson was gathering evidence in support of his claim that production of unstamped Harris Tweed made from mainland-spun yarn was of long standing as an alternative type of Harris Tweed to 'Orb-stamped' tweed. Mr Barr appears to have furnished Mr Simpson with the information he wanted. It would seem from his letter that Wool Control officials had accepted throughout the war a type of non-stamped 'Harris Tweed' made from mainland-spun yarn. How they could have ignored the fact that the definition of Harris Tweed required that it should be made from Island-spun yarn, and most certainly not from English yarn, is difficult to explain! It may be that Government officials, concerned with exports which would bring in much-needed dollars, were not disposed to concern themselves with the niceties of the difference between Harris Tweed which met the requirements of the 1934 definition and 'Harris Tweed' which claimed to be equally genuine, as long as both sold in the United States. It is also possible that the Board of Trade was not inclined at this time to enter into the dispute as to whether or not there was such a thing as legitimate 'unstamped Harris Tweed', made from mainland yarn. Nonetheless, because tweed woven from mainland and even English-spun yarn was accepted, if only by default, at an official level as 'Harris Tweed', it became much more difficult for the Harris Tweed Association to eradicate the practice after the war.

As early as 1937, the Harris Tweed Association had been confronted with the dilemma as to how it could best protect the trade mark. In that year it sought advice from Counsel on the advisability of prosecuting a weaver for selling as 'Harris Tweed' tweed made from mainland-spun yarn. No doubt the proposed prosecution was seen as an early warning to others engaged in the same practice. The advice of Counsel in 1937 emphasised the difficulties of bringing a successful prosecution against the weaver and pointed out that failure in such a prosecution might undo much of the good that had already been done by advertising Orb-stamped Harris Tweed. To be successful, the Harris Tweed Association would have to establish in court that the weaver was guilty of using a 'false trade description' in offering his tweed for sale as 'Harris Tweed'. Evidence would have to be provided from wholesale and retail cloth merchants that they would not consider tweed made from mainland-spun yarn to be Harris Tweed. [3] Anticipating the contradictory evidence which would certainly be led by the defence to prove that the weaver was not using a false trade description, Colonel Macarthur, a member of the HTA, had articulated, in 1937, his own concerns about the risk of taking legal action:

> 'I have no doubt that plenty of evidence would be produced that there is still a lot of mainland-spun yarn going into Lewis and that there is a substantial quantity of cloth made from that yarn sold as 'Harris Tweed'.' [4]

Colonel Macarthur was well aware that, given the opportunity, the non-Orb producers who were using mainland yarn would combine to present a strong case for recognition of an alternative type of Harris Tweed made from mainland yarn. In view of such discouraging advice from learned Counsel on the possible danger of taking legal action to halt the abuse, it is hardly surprising that the HTA modified its initial tactics in dealing with yet another major threat to the trade mark which came to its attention in 1944.

This threat came from the Aberdeen firm, Scottish Crofter Weavers Ltd. whose Managing Director, John Simpson, has already been mentioned as being in correspondence with Mr Barr of the National Association of Scottish Woollen Manufacturers. As a firm of the same name was, with other mainland producers, to play a significant part in the escalating challenge to the definition of Harris Tweed from 1955 until the controversy came to a head in the Harris Tweed case of 1964, it is as well to avoid confusion and refer to this firm which had been incorporated in 1937, as 'the original Scottish Crofters Weavers Ltd.' to distinguish it from the firm of the same name which was incorporated in 1955 when the original Scottish Crofter Weavers Ltd. went into voluntary liquidation. [5] References in this chapter will be to the original Scottish Crofter Weavers Ltd., not to its successor of the same name.

Scottish Crofter Weavers Ltd. did not manufacture cloth themselves. The various materials sold by the company were made elsewhere and were then returned to the warehouse in Constitution St., Aberdeen, for distribution. Tweed woven in Lewis was eventually the largest part of Scottish Crofter Weavers' business. A small proportion of this Lewis-woven tweed qualified for the Orb-stamp, but the larger proportion was made from mainland-spun yarn sent to Lewis for weaving and then returned to be finished on the mainland. Scottish Crofter Weavers purchased its yarn from Laidlaws of Keith, Hunters of Brora, Smiths of Peterhead and, significantly, from Lumbs of Elland in Yorkshire who were the company's largest yarn suppliers. Scottish Crofter Weavers Ltd. was also Lumbs of Elland's largest customers for 'Harris-type' yarn. The name 'Hebratex' was registered by the company (and retained in 1955 by the second Scottish Crofter Weavers). Their Lewis-woven tweed, other than the Orb-stamped tweed, was sold as 'Hebratex Harris Tweed', 'Hebratex Harris Handwoven' and 'Light Hebratex Harris Handwoven'. Giving evidence in the 1964 Harris Tweed case, Mr Charles Brown of Burnett and Reid, the company's solicitors, testified that the tweed was stamped at intervals with the words 'Hebratex Fabric', 'Harris Tweed' and 'Handwoven in Lewis'. [6]

In May 1944, Mr W. H. Martin, Secretary of the Harris Tweed Association, received a letter from the Board of Trade containing allegations made to the Board by the Local Price Regulation Committee in Glasgow. The letter from the Board of Trade stated:

> 'The allegations emanated originally from the Local Price Regulation Committee, Aberdeen and are contained in a letter to the Committee in Glasgow, dated February 19th, as follows:-

'According to our information, which seems to be reliable, the enclosed piece of tweed which bears the stamp 'handwoven Harris Tweed Woven in Lewis' came from Yorkshire yarn. This yarn was purchased by Scottish Crofter Weavers, 162 Constitution St. Aberdeen, who then sent it to Smith's Kirkburn Mills, Peterhead, who did the weaving. Thereafter it came back to Aberdeen and was sent on to Paisley to be 'finished'. When that had been done it returned once again to Scottish Crofter Weavers in Aberdeen who applied the 'Hand Woven Harris Tweed' stamp.

On the face of it, this appears to be a flagrant case of a false trade description under the Merchandise Act of 1887. Since the war, however, it has rather become the practice for the Board of Trade not to intervene in matters of this kind, but to rely on the trade association concerned to take the question up in cases where the Act appears to have been contravened. In the present connection as you know, the position is complicated by the existence of the Certification Trade Mark, which was agreed upon after so much controversy, and if the case were brought into Court, the defence would undoubtedly try to show that Harris Tweed is a generic term which might do a good deal of harm to the reputation of Harris Tweed as now established. It would be very desirable, I think, therefore, that the case should be dealt with, if possible, without bringing it to Court. On the other hand the misrepresentation appears to be so flagrant that it can scarcely be passed over.' [7]

This letter reveals the disinclination of the Board of Trade to stand four square in support of the Harris Tweed Association taking decisive action in what the Board itself admitted to be a 'flagrant case of false trade description'. If the tweed in question could be shown to have been woven at Kirkburn Mills, Peterhead, it would have been woven on a power loom, not on a hand-loom. Powered weaving was accepted by all sections of the industry to be a very serious breach of the definition of Harris Tweed and the Board of Trade ought to have recognised the grave implications of such a breach. The breach was particularly serious as it involved a product which formed part of Britain's exports to the United States, where Harris Tweed enjoyed a reduced tariff precisely because it was considered to be the handwoven product of a cottage industry, something which power-loomed tweed certainly was not.

In this particular incident, correspondence flowed to and fro, for over a year, between Mr Simpson as Managing Director of Scottish Crofter Weavers, Messrs Burnett and Reid on his behalf, and McKenna & Co., solicitors for the HTA, with Mr Simpson denying that he had sold power-loomed cloth as 'Hand Woven Harris Tweed' and McKenna & Co. warning Mr Simpson of the possible consequences of false trade description. By the end of 1944, having received little satisfaction from Mr Simpson or Burnett and Reid, his legal representatives, McKenna & Co. asked the Board of Trade to comment on the decision of the Harris Tweed Association to institute proceedings against Scottish Crofter Weavers. The Board of Trade, while 'seeing no objection' to the Association taking legal action, reiterated the earlier warning on the danger of seeking a Court ruling which stated that the description of 'Harris Tweed' could not properly be applied to any cloth which did not conform to the 1934 definition incorporated in the Regulations governing the use of the 'Orb Mark'. [8] McKenna & Co. replied to the Board of Trade requesting the name of the person who had purchased the tweed in question from Scottish Crofter Weavers, so that the necessary prosecutions might be brought, because the Harris Tweed Association felt that 'if they did not deal promptly with the matter, the words 'Harris Tweed' might lose the meaning which they then had with the trade and the public'. [9] The proposed proceedings by the HTA came to naught when the spokesman for the Board of Trade replied:

> 'I am to express the regret of the Board that enquiries have failed to establish any definite evidence of the source from which this piece of tweed was obtained, and there appears to be no likelihood of the necessary information becoming available. In these circumstances, it is assumed that prosecution is not practicable. I am to add that the Board are informed by the Scottish Home Department, with which they have been in communication in an attempt to elicit the above mentioned evidence, that the papers have been referred to the Lord Advocate, and that his view is that the evidence was insufficient for a prosecution, and, moreover that it would be unwise to put in issue the meaning of 'Harris Tweed' without careful consideration.' [10]

With this advice from the Board of Trade, the Harris Tweed Association found itself in an impossible situation. It is difficult to understand why the Board of Trade did not accept that the sooner an abuse was tackled and the legal status of the amended definition confirmed, the easier it would be thereafter to protect the Orb trade mark to which the Board itself had given its approval in 1934. Instead of supporting the Harris Tweed Association in tackling breaches of the definition of Harris Tweed at an early opportunity, the Board of Trade appears to have gambled on the remote chance that the problem would eventually disappear of its own accord.

As Mr Simpson had died some years before the 1964 Harris Tweed case was heard, it was not possible to elicit from him evidence which would cast further light on this incident or his reference to 'a complainant in Lewis'. However, it did emerge from the evidence of Mr Brown of Burnett and Reid that Mr Simpson had some years earlier, knowingly dispatched as 'Hebratex Harris Tweed', cloth which had been power-loomed because of his inability to meet an order with handwoven tweed.

In the 1950s, Mr Simpson waged an increasingly determined campaign against the right of the Harris Tweed Association to the exclusive use of the name 'Harris Tweed'. He tried to recruit to his campaign a number of mainland firms who might have had an interest in breaking into the island industry. He was successful with two firms who were already supplying mainland-spun yarn to island weavers. The most surprising development in this campaign against the Orb trade mark occurred when one of the leading Stornoway manufacturers of Orb-stamped Harris Tweed experienced a sudden conversion to a belief in the legitimacy of 'unstamped Harris Tweed'.

In 1946, James Macdonald, founder and Managing Director of the firm James Macdonald & Co. Ltd., gave up his position in the company, left Stornoway and went to live in Oban where he formed a new company called Macdonald's Tweeds Ltd. The new firm was incorporated on 12th September 1946 and the shares in the company were all held by James Macdonald and his family. It should be remembered that James Macdonald was the man who took part in the debate leading up to the amended definition of 1934 and defended this definition strongly, both at the time and later in the *Lewis Association Report on the Harris Tweed Industry*. He was outspoken in his condemnation of independent producers who had no stake in the industry and made quick profits on the basis of imported yarn.

There was, and still is, a strong belief in Lewis that James Macdonald and the Archer family (owners of J. & J. Tod Wholesalers and of James Macdonald & Co. Ltd.) fell out in 1946, although this was denied by a later Managing Director of the Stornoway firm. Whatever the reason for the move to Oban, James Macdonald's subsequent actions were in direct contradiction to his statement in the *Stornoway Gazette* when he said:

> 'I soon realised the detrimental effect imported yarn had on my business and consequently made every effort to provide my own good quality yarn.' [11]

It was James Macdonald's apparent predilection for changing his stance, not to say his coat, as it suited him, that led Lord Hunter to describe him as:

> 'moving through the story rather like a chameleon, at one time or another on almost every possible side in the controversies of that period.' [12]

By the early 1950s, Macdonald's Tweeds Ltd. came to the attention of the Harris Tweed Association as yet another mainland firm engaging in passing-off as 'Harris Tweed' a cloth which did not conform to the amended definition of 1934. If individual instances of passing-off gave the Harris Tweed Association cause for concern, that concern was as nothing when compared to the effect of the united challenge to the Orb trade mark which was about to come from a group of mainland producers which included Scottish Crofter Weavers and one of James Macdonald's companies. As this challenge involved canvassing support for recognition of 'unstamped Harris Tweed' among official bodies in the United States and Britain, it will be necessary to examine the legal status of the Harris Tweed trade mark in Britain and America.

Reference - Scottish Crofter Weavers and James Macdonald of Oban

1 *Daily Record*, 11. 12. 1947.

2 James Barr, Secretary of the National Association of Scottish Woollen Manufacturers, to J. Simpson, Scottish Crofter Weavers, Aberdeen, 17. 7. 1953, HRA/D/190/ 1(o) Section G.

3 Opinion of John C. Maude, 20. 4. 1937. HRA/D 190/1(o).

4 Col. Macarthur's views quoted by John Maude in his Opinion of 20. 4. 1937. HRA/D 190/1(o).

5 *Argyllshire Weavers Ltd. and Others v. Macaulay (A.) (Tweeds) Ltd., and Others* [1964] RPC No. 16, 477 [hereafter: 'Harris Tweed Case 1964'], at 531.

6 *ibid.*, 531-532.

7 E. Sutton, Industries and Manufacture Department, Board of Trade to W. H. Martin, HTA. 11. 5. 1944. HRA/D190/1(o).

8 *ibid.*, 20. 11. 1944. HRA/D190/1(o).

9 McKenna & Co. to Board of Trade, 28. 11. 1944. HRA/D190/1(o).

10 Board of Trade to McKenna & Co. 12. 2. 1945. HRA/D190/ 1 (o).

11 *Stornoway Gazette*, 27. 4. 1934.

12 'Harris Tweed Case' [1964] RPC No. 16, 477, at 510.

13

The Retail Trading-Standards Association and the Board of Trade

Scottish Crofter Weavers, under the management of John Simpson, seems to have been the first of the mainland firms producing unstamped Harris Tweed to seek support from official bodies in a serious challenge to the Orb trade mark. Simpson's campaign to have unstamped Harris Tweed recognised as a valid alternative to Orb-stamped Harris Tweed gained momentum in 1953. He enlisted support from the National Association of Woollen Manufacturers, from the Secretary of the Retail Trading Standards Association, (RTSA) from Members of Parliament and even caused the Board of Trade to revise its attitude to the Harris Tweed trade mark. The conflict between the HTA and producers of unstamped Harris Tweed came into the open in the American market when producers of unstamped Harris Tweed realised that their exports to the United States and Canada were being impounded by Customs officials there who refused entry to tweed which did not bear the Orb stamp.

The Harris Tweed trade mark, or the Orb mark, as it was colloquially called, had been registered to the HTA Ltd. at the United States Patent Office on 10th December 1912. The amended definition of 1934 was widely publicised in the United States and the United States Federal Trade Commission took action whenever instances of breaching the trade mark were brought before them by issuing an order to 'cease and desist'. The Harris Tweed trade mark registered in Britain was a certification trade mark, which meant that the goods were certified by the proprietor of the mark (e.g. the HTA Ltd.) in respect of geographical origin, material, mode of manufacture, quality, or other characteristics. The definition of Harris Tweed certified the place of origin as being any one of the islands in the Outer Hebrides; the material was certified to be pure virgin Scottish wool; the mode of manufacture specified that all the processes of production were to be performed in the Outer Hebrides and the tweed had to be handwoven at the islanders' homes. Until the Lanham Act in 1946, there was no provision in the United States for registration of certification marks, i.e. marks which signify two things:- (1) that the product has a certain origin and characteristics and (2) that the proprietor of the trade mark has certified that the product does indeed have the requisite origin and / or characteristics. When the Lanham Act was passed, the HTA made application to register a certification mark and this was eventually granted in July 1950. The delay was caused by a dispute as to whether or not a disclaimer of the words 'Harris Tweed' was necessary with a certification mark. [1]

The phrase 'a disclaimer' to the exclusive use of the words 'Harris Tweed' is more readily understood if the term 'Hoover Vacuum Cleaner' is substituted for the term 'Harris Tweed'. If someone wanted to register the words 'Hoover Vacuum Cleaner', they would be required to disclaim an exclusive right to the words 'vacuum cleaner' and each of these words separately, as it would be unreasonable to insist that nobody else could use the words 'vacuum' or 'cleaner' or the words 'vacuum cleaner' together, as there are many makes of vacuum cleaner. Similarly, it would be unreasonable to claim the exclusive right to the word 'tweed' as there are many tweeds, e.g. Donegal tweed. The questions which caused considerable controversy were (1) whether there could be such a product as 'Harris Tweed' which did not carry the Orb trade mark and (2) could Harris Tweed which did not conform to the definition be legally called 'Harris Tweed'? The answer to the first question was that of course there could be Harris Tweed which did not carry the Orb trade mark and the HTA did not dispute that, although its advertising in the States did at times give the impression that unless the tweed was stamped with the Orb it could not be genuine Harris Tweed. To be fair, it had been the Association's experience that, in the majority of cases, tweed which did not carry the Orb trade mark was not in fact genuine Harris Tweed, as it had been made from mainland-spun yarn. On the second question, the HTA had always maintained that tweed which did not conform to the definition ought not to be called 'Harris Tweed'.

By July 1950, registration of a Certification Mark for Harris Tweed in the United States was achieved with a disclaimer only of the exclusive use of the word 'tweed'. There was no request at that time for a disclaimer of the words 'Harris Tweed'. Stanley Brown, the agent for the HTA in the United States, duly registered the Harris Tweed trade mark with the Commissioner of United States Customs. Customs officers were thereafter requested to prohibit the importation of tweed which infringed the mark of the HTA. This meant that if tweed was exported to the United States claiming to be 'Harris Tweed', but without the Orb stamp, it was denied entry. Exports of tweed to Canadian markets were subject to similar controls.

By early 1953, mainland producers who had been sending yarn to the islands for the production of unstamped Harris Tweed, became aware that United States Customs had stopped admitting Harris Tweed unless it bore the Orb stamp. Two mainland suppliers of yarn for the production of unstamped Harris Tweed, A. & J. Macnaughton and Laidlaws, sought the help of the National Association of Scottish Woollen Manufacturers through its Secretary James Barr. S. G. Laidlaw wrote to James Barr on 27th March 1953 saying:

> 'We have been approached by Macnaughtons of Pitlochry with a view to us joining them in a protest against the registration in the United States of the Harris Tweed (Orb) trade mark and the term 'Harris Tweed'. As you know we, like Macnaughtons, conduct a fair amount of business in the Hebrides supplying weaving firms with yarn. The resultant cloth does not comply with the requirements stipulated under the Orb trade mark, but it can still be called Harris Tweed. ... some action should be taken to safeguard the interests of those who manufacture non Orb-stamped cloth. ... Can your Association use its machinery to protect its members, of whom we are one and Macnaughtons another?' [2]

James Barr replied to S. G. Laidlaw suggesting that both firms should contact John Simpson of Scottish Crofter Weavers, who had already started to challenge the registrations of the Harris Tweed trade mark in North America. Mr Barr informed Mr Laidlaw that:

> 'The matter was brought to our notice some time ago by Scottish Crofter Weavers, Ltd., 162 Constitution St Aberdeen, who are actively engaged in objecting to these North American registrations. At the moment efforts are being made through the Board of Trade to break the monopoly of the use of the word 'Harris' which the HTA Ltd. appear to have secured through their registrations of the word in North America. It is not yet known whether the Board of Trade will be prepared to take any steps in the matter or whether they can, in fact, do anything to rectify the position. ... ' [3]

In a campaign such as this, Macnaughtons and Laidlaws were aware of the need for them to maintain a low profile lest they precipitate another embargo on mainland yarn. The Harris Tweed archives contain an unsigned copy of a letter to John Simpson, dated 31. 3. 53, which says:

> ' ... we have had experience of the expense of such action in the Harris Embargo case of pre-war which went against us in the House of Lords. You will probably agree that Laidlaw and ourselves must be wary of publicity as the Embargo might well be brought back in the event of our being too closely identified in a battle with the HTA.' [4]

Hoping to avoid 'the heavy expense' of going to court over the matter, Directors of Scottish Crofter Weavers met with John McLeod, MP for Ross and Cromarty, who advised them to complain to the Board of Trade. In addition to Laidlaws and Macnaughtons, John Simpson sought help from Maclennan & Maclennan, Clansman Tweed Co., both in Stornoway, T. M. Hunter of Brora, and Samuel Lumb, Elland, none of whom joined his campaign, so far as is known. He also asked James Barr of the NASWM if he could suggest any other 'independents'. [5]

In early 1954, John Simpson of Scottish Crofter Weavers made a brief attempt to set up business in Lewis and began negotiations with the Hebridean Spinners to supply yarn for production of Orb-stamped tweed. He thus felt that it was his duty to inform the HTA that, as a member of the National Association of Woollen Manufacturers, he was party to an action being taken in Canada to have the registration of the Harris Tweed trade mark annulled in that country. [6]

It seems likely that the lobbying by the National Association of Scottish Woollen Manufacturers and John Simpson began to have an effect on the Board of Trade by the end of 1953. In December 1953, the Board of Trade complained to the HTA that an advertisement for handwoven Harris Tweed included the words 'Registered Trade Mark granted by the Board of Trade to the HTA', the letter of complaint said:

> 'The Board of Trade does not grant certification marks. ... the Board of Trade merely approves regulations governing their use.' [7]

The HTA apologised and explained that the wording had been used for many years and that this was the first time any objection had been raised. The Association offered to use the wording 'Applied in accordance with regulations approved by the Board of Trade' in future advertising. [8]

The National Association of Woollen Manufacturers, acting on behalf of John Simpson as a member of that Association, found an effective lobbyist in Commander C. E. M. Donaldson, M. P. for Roxburgh, Selkirk and Peebles, a constituency in which production of woollen cloth was a prime industry. In late 1954, Commander Donaldson presented Peter Thorneycroft, M. P., President of the Board of Trade, with a file which included copies of the correspondence between James Barr, Secretary of the NASWM, Scottish Crofter Weavers and the Board of Trade on the dispute over the registration of the Harris Tweed trade mark in North America and 'the essential excerpts' from the 1946 Report on the Crofter Woollen Industry. The accompanying letter from Commander Donaldson described the dispute over unstamped Harris Tweed from the perspective of producers of 'Hebridean crofter woven tweed which for one reason or another is not entitled to carry the 'Orb' mark', i.e. producers using mainland-spun yarn. Commander Donaldson maintained that there was no evidence to show that 'Harris Tweed crofter-woven in the Islands but not carrying the 'Orb' mark could be discredited as spurious'. He was concerned that exclusion of non-Orb-stamped tweed from the American market 'would not only work to the detriment of the remaining independent crofter weavers, but also have a marked and serious effect on our export trade which adds a considerable percentage of dollar earnings to our national economy'. [9]

Although the Thorneycroft family had a long link with the estate of Eishken, in South Lochs in Lewis, there is no evidence to suggest whether Peter Thorneycroft had any personal knowledge of the Harris Tweed industry, nor what his attitude to the dispute may have been. The HTA did not realise at the time that a climate of opinion was secretly being created which portrayed the HTA as a private monopolist seeking to protect its own profits, rather than as a disinterested body protecting the name 'Harris Tweed'. Yet events in 1955 and 1956 were to show how necessary it was for the HTA to publicise the risks associated with buying cloth which its makers called 'unstamped Harris Tweed'.

In 1955, the number and range of complaints to the HTA about so-called 'Harris Tweed' reached an alarming level. There seemed to be a sudden increase in the amount of sub-standard material reaching the retail market as 'Harris Tweed'. Of the many complaints which found their way to the HTA, perhaps the most poignant relates to the purchase of a suit in 1954. A bank clerk wrote to the HTA in early 1956:

> 'Dear Sirs
> During Oct. 1954, I purchased a Harris Tweed suit from Hepworths of Leeds, after being assured by the salesman that it was a very hardwearing material, especially as I am a clerk, and the fronts of my suits get a lot of hard wear rubbing on the desks and ledgers.
>
> After only 8 months wear I discovered that the coat cuffs and trouser turn-ups were fraying very badly. I took the matter up with Hepworths, and they argued that the suit had had very hard wear. In the first place I contend that was not possible in my job, and secondly even if it had been used by someone who had a manual job, 8 months was a ridiculous time to have from a new suit. The outcome was they gave me a small piece of material and £1 (one pound) in cash to cover the cost of repairs to the suit.
>
> Now the suit is completely worn out after 18 months use and to my mind this is not a reasonable span of life under normal wearing conditions. I would point out that the suit was not worn at all during the summer.
>
> I bought the suit after hearing such glowing reports of the wearing qualities of Harris Tweed from friends. Since then however I have seen that the genuine Harris Tweed bears the 'Orb' trade-mark, whilst the label on my suit merely says 'Harris Tweed. Handwoven in the Outer Hebrides'.
>
> I raised this point with Hepworths, but they said that the reason theirs did not bear the 'Orb' trade mark is because they buy in bulk quantity. Now the whole point of my letter is this - I consider that this method of doing business is, to say the least, misleading and I would like to know if it is in the public interest to sell what must be an inferior quality material under the same name as the genuine article. At the moment, I feel very strongly about this and certainly should think twice before recommending Harris Tweed to my friends.' [10]

'Unstamped Harris Tweed' was attractive to large multiple chain stores like Hepworths because it was relatively cheap and enabled the company to undercut the price of coats and suits made from Orb-stamped Harris Tweed. The extraordinarily low price of 'Harris Tweed' jackets being sold by Selfridges in 1955 had caused John Gwatkin of McKenna & Co. to ask Roger Diplock, Secretary of the RTSA to contact Selfridges to enquire where the tweed (which was unstamped) had come from. [11] In retrospect, this request to Mr Diplock as Secretary of the RTSA was tantamount to John Gwatkin putting his head into the lion's mouth. Roger Diplock simply replied that the Northern Clothing Company Ltd. who had supplied the tweed to Selfridges had bought it in Stornoway, 'from a man with the not unlikely name of McPherson'. [12] To Mr Diplock, even to John Gwatkin, and obviously to the Northern Trading Company, the name 'McPherson' may well have sounded quite a common name for a Stornoway merchant. To anyone who knows Stornoway, 'McPherson' was an easily identified name simply because it was quite an uncommon name!

Other multiple tailors besides Hepworths were having to placate irate customers with replacement trousers for their so-called 'Harris Tweed' suits. A Mr Mennell complained to Town Tailors that the turn-ups of his trousers became frayed, followed by the seat of the trousers wearing out within approximately six weeks. [13] It transpired that Town Tailors had been supplied with tweed by Argyllshire Weavers Ltd., one of James Macdonald's companies. Another complaint came from an agent who had seen in Marshall and Snelgroves 'Harris Tweed' coats made from what he could see was an 'inferior type of yarn', which 'looked as if it had been made in the West Riding of Yorkshire'. The coats were selling at 8 guineas each. [14]

Because this incident with Marshall and Snelgroves was the catalyst which precipitated the public row between the RTSA and the HTA, it is worth examining the correspondence in some detail. W. H. Martin, Secretary of the HTA, dispatched a standard letter to Marshall and Snelgroves which quoted the definition of Harris Tweed and continued:

> 'I should of course, make it clear that a trader is not compelled to use my Association's mark and I am quite certain that a House of your reputation would not sell, as being made from Harris Tweed, a garment which did not come up to that description. On

> the other hand, I do receive a number of enquiries from time to time from members of the public enquiring whether a garment sold as being made of Harris Tweed, but not bearing my Association's mark is the genuine article or not. ... While it is naturally a commercial matter for you, you may think that there is some advantage in purchasing Harris Tweed garments which bear my Association's Trade Mark, for, in such event, no query such as the present one would arise.' [15]

Despite a placatory reply to the HTA, Marshall and Snelgroves had sent a copy of Mr Martin's letter to the Retail Trading-Standards Association. The apparently courteous letter from Mr Martin incurred the wrath of Roger Diplock of the RTSA. In high indignation, Roger Diplock sent a copy of the letter to Mr Gwatkin of McKenna & Co. saying :

> 'I enclose a copy of a letter which the Secretary of the HTA Ltd. wrote to our members - Marshall and Snelgrove ... I am sure that when you read this letter you will share my view that it is a most improper letter to have written and that it is couched in terms which can only be taken to infer that no cloth coming out of the Hebrides is a Harris Tweed unless it bears the Ball and Sceptre label. You may recollect that I jokingly referred to the propaganda of the HTA when we lunched together at the Club, but I had no idea at all that this sort of correspondence was being sent from London Wall. ... As you yourself well know, I have on numerous occasions instructed enquirers that the description Harris Tweed could be given to any woollen cloth, hand woven in the Outer Hebrides. ... I think you will agree that the HTA seems to have gone well beyond proper bounds in the action which it has recently been taking - so much so that I feel we must make some quite clear statement in a forthcoming *Bulletin* so that our members know full well that it is possible to buy good quality Harris Tweed which does not bear the Certification Mark of the HTA. ... I shall be glad to talk the whole thing over with you before we publish any statement.' [16]

Neither John Gwatkin nor the HTA had been aware that Roger Diplock had been telling members of the RTSA that any woollen cloth handwoven in the Outer Hebrides could be called 'Harris Tweed'. Mr Diplock sent a copy of the proposed insertion in the RTSA *Bulletin* to John Gwatkin. Although the statement was, in John Gwatkin's view, 'in some respects wholly inaccurate', Roger Diplock was adamant that he intended to put it in the RTSA *Bulletin*. The HTA office-bearers and John Gwatkin then attended a meeting with Mr Diplock to discuss the proposed statement. It is not difficult to imagine their shock when they found the 27-year-old son of James Macdonald from Oban present at the meeting. This young man had been invited to the meeting to testify that for about three years his firm had been selling between ¾ and 1¼ million yards per year of 'Harris Tweed' made from mainland-spun yarn, handwoven in Uist, to Marshall and Snelgrove, Hepworths and Great Universal Stores (all members of the Debenham Group and of the Retail Trading-Standards Association). [17]

Following the meeting, George Ellis, Chairman of the HTA, wrote to Sebastian Earl, Chairman of the RTSA, suggesting that Roger Diplock might have been exceeding his duties in so categorically opposing another Association. Mr Ellis asked for Mr Diplock's statement to be delayed until a meeting could be arranged between Mr Earl and Col. Macarthur who 'knew more about the history of Harris Tweed than any other member of the Association'. Despite this request, the RTSA *Bulletin* containing Mr Diplock's statement about unstamped Harris Tweed went to press before a reply was received from Mr Earl.

The statement in the *Bulletin* declared that in the view of the RTSA, tweeds not marked with the Orb Certification mark could be called 'Harris Tweed' even though they had not been manufactured from yarn spun in the Outer Hebrides. The RTSA based this recommendation on the following evidence:

(a) Trade practice dating from the pre-war period.
(b) The views of the Report on the Crofter Woollen Industry, 1946.
(c) The views expressed by the Parliamentary Secretary, Board of Trade in a letter dated 21st December 1954. (Parts of this letter had been quoted in the meeting with Roger Diplock, but the HTA representatives had not been shown the letter.)
(d) Judgement by the Lord Chancellor, Lord Simon, in an action appealed before the House of Lords in 1941.

The *Bulletin* statement finished by informing its members, that, as the HTA disagreed with the RTSA, it was seeking Counsel's Opinion, and had already been guided by an opinion of Queen's Counsel. [18]

It was inevitable that American papers would pick up the damaging story. Under the heading 'Harris Tweed Tag Subject of High Controversy in UK' the *Daily News Record* of 26th March gave an account of the dispute between the RTSA and the HTA.

> '**LONDON**:- A controversy is currently being waged here on the correct designation of cloth having the right to the Harris Tweed label. ... the Retail Trading-Standards Association, an organisation supported by the country's leading retailers, had issued a ruling that tweeds, other than those manufactured from yarns spun in the Outer Hebrides, may have the right to be called 'Harris Tweed.' ... For many years such tweeds formed an integral part of the pre-war production of Harris Tweed. ... In reply, the HTA states: 'The seven elements in the approved definition have been reduced by the RTSA to four and, of these four elements, two, - relating to the use of virgin wool not necessarily produced in Scotland and mainland spun yarn - are completely at variance with the definition propounded by the HTA for more than 20 years and generally accepted by the trade and public. ... The real truth of the matter is that the HTA's policy of advertising the origins and qualities of Harris Tweed has been so consistently successful that in recent years demand has outstripped output. As a result, for some time past certain firms, wishing to reap the benefit of this advertising, but unable to obtain sufficient tweed bearing the well-known certification mark, have turned to purchasing tweed not complying with the accepted definition. The Association is firmly of the opinion that such tweed does not merit the description of Harris Tweed.' [19]

A brief postcript may be added to what was surely a bad year for the HTA, if a good one for those challenging the Orb stamp. George Ellis, Chairman of the HTA wrote to the *Stornoway Gazette* in December analysing the problems as he saw them. An excerpt from his letter gives the substance of his view.

'Without this industry the Outer Hebrides would be a very depressed area today ... Success constantly begets opportunism, and Harris Tweed is no exception. The ever-increasing flow of yarn into the islands for hand-weaving is of grave concern. This tweed ... is often far short of the quality of the complete Island product and does not stand up to hard wear. Thereby the reputation of Harris Tweed is gravely damaged. Many complaints by dissatisfied buyers have been examined and in practically every instance it has been found that the tweed was unstamped. It cannot be gainsaid that the tweed lives by its reputation and once lost, no amount of publicity will readily recoup it. ... The only process ... carried out in the Islands is the weaving. ... the weaving is only a masquerade to the filching of the good name - HARRIS TWEED. Without that the cloth would not sell. ... In the event of a slump this tweed would quickly disappear without any loss to the owners - and only the weavers who did the weaving would be workless. They have no stake in the industry and no interest in it beyond the use of the name as a selling power. ... The Retail Trading-Standards Association ... has recently changed its view ... This is a direct attack on the Island industry largely sponsored, no doubt, by those very manufacturers who use mainland yarn. ... '[20]

Bad as the year 1956 had been, worse was still to come for the HTA as the decade drew to a close.

Reference - The Retail Trading-Standards Association and the Board of Trade

1 Re. Application for registration of Certification Trade Mark in USA by HTA Ltd, 20. 5. 1948. HRA/D190 1n (ii).
2 S.G. Laidlaw to James Barr, 27. 3. 1953. HRA/D190/ 1 (o) Sect. G.
3 James Barr, Secretary of the National Association of Scottish Woollen Manufacturers (NASWM) to Messrs Robert Laidlaw & Sons Ltd. 30. 3. 1953. HRA/D190/ 1 (o).
4 Letter (unsigned) to John Simpson, 31. 3. 1953. HRA/D190 1 (o) Section G.
5 John Simpson to James Barr, 9. 7. 1953. HRA/D190/1 (o) Section G.
6 Charles G. Brown to Col. Macarthur, 14. 1. 1954. HTA Office, Stornoway.
7 F. Bradley, Industries and Manufactures Department Board of Trade, to HTA, 29. 12. 1953. HRA/D190/ 1(o).
8 W. H. Martin, Secretary HTA to Board of Trade, 11. 1. 1954. HRA/D190/ 1(o).
9 C. E. M. Donaldson, MP to The Rt. Hon. Peter Thorneycroft, MP, 18. 11. 1954. HTA Office, Stornoway.
10 David Milton to HTA, 14. 3. 1956. HTA Office, Stornoway.
11 McKenna & Co. to Roger Diplock, 28. 2. 1955. HTA Office, Stornoway.
12 R. Diplock to J. Gwatkin, 17. 3. 1956. HTA Office, Stornoway.
13 A. Mennell to HTA, 8. 6. 1955. HTA Office, Stornoway.
14 H. Raynor to HTA, 23. 11. 1955. HTA Office, Stornoway.
15 W. H. Martin to Messrs Marshall and Snelgrove, 28. 12. 1955. HTA Office, Stornoway.
16 Roger Diplock to John Gwatkin, 18. 1. 1956. HTA Office, Stornoway.
17 George Ellis, Chairman of the HTA to Sebastian Earl, Chairman of the RTSA, 18. 2. 1956. HTA Office, Stornoway.
18 Gwatkin, Notes on the Historical Development of the Harris Tweed Industry and the Part Played by the Harris Tweed Association Ltd. [hereafter: 'Gwatkin, The Harris Tweed Industry'], 72. See also RTSA *Bulletin* 115, February 1956
19 *Daily News Record*, 26. 3. 1956.
20 *Stornoway Gazette*, 7. 12. 1956. George Ellis, HTA Chairman, to the Editor.

14

Independent Harris Tweed Producers Ltd.

Exclusion of unstamped Harris Tweed from the American market seems to have been the catalyst which led to three mainland producers making common cause against the HTA in the formation of a group calling itself Independent Harris Tweed Producers Ltd. (IHTP Ltd.). It is important to state quite clearly at the outset that, although there were many independent producers of unstamped Harris Tweed, both within the islands and on the mainland, in the end of the day only three mainland producers, Argyllshire Weavers Ltd., A. & J. Macnaughton of Pitlochry and Laidlaws of Keith were involved in the legal challenge to the Orb trade mark. Despite being invited to join in a campaign against the Orb trade mark, independent producers of unstamped Harris Tweed in the islands chose not to ally themselves with the mainland group who eventually came together in 1958 as Independent Harris Tweed Producers Ltd. (IHTP).

Although exclusion of unstamped Harris Tweed from the American market in 1953 was the catalyst which eventually united the mainland producers against the Orb, a slump in the textile market in the early 1950s provided the motivation for their insistence that the unstamped tweed made from mainland-spun yarn was entitled to be called 'Harris Tweed'. The situation was later described by R. A Laidlaw of Laidlaws of Keith as follows:

> 'The position was that it was practically impossible to sell a cloth unless it was called 'Harris Tweed'. ... No real business could be done unless the cloth could be termed 'Harris Tweed'.' [1]

Perhaps the earliest overt indication of the challenge from these producers to Orb-stamped Harris Tweed can be pinpointed to 1952, when James Macdonald set up a second family company, Argyllshire Weavers Ltd. in Oban, as a marketing company for Macdonalds Tweeds Ltd. and a little later set up weaving sheds in South Uist. In November 1951, he received a letter from the Secretary of the HTA enquiring about 'Harris Tweed' labels he was allegedly supplying to customers. The letter 'caused a certain amount of commotion' in the mill in Oban.[2] The details of the commotion are not recorded, but by 3rd December 1951, it had abated sufficiently for James Macdonald to regain his habitual sangfroid. His letter assured Mr Martin that:

> 'You can take my word for it, as you used to do, that since we came to Oban we have not sold, invoiced or confirmed any of our handwoven tweeds as Harris Tweed ... '[3]

The letter ended with an announcement of his decision to begin production of unstamped Harris Tweed made in weaving sheds in Lochboisdale, South Uist.[4]

The HTA eventually sent an emissary to investigate what was going on in Lochboisdale. It transpired that in March 1952, James Macdonald had opened a weaving depôt with 14 looms in Lochboisdale and, slightly later, a larger depôt in Eochar with 32 looms and an additional shed with 32 looms in May 1954. The emissary came back with a very poor opinion of the South Uist weavers who were simply 'peddling away' on looms which the foremen tuned and maintained. Apart from the weaving, all other processes of production, such as spinning the yarn and finishing the greasy tweeds, were carried out on the mainland. This was a 'factory' situation very similar to that which A. & J. Macnaughton had organised on Tarbert Pier prior to the 1934 amendment of the definition. The wool used by the weavers in South Uist was not always of Scottish origin and much of the profit was located on the mainland. The looms belonged to Macdonalds Tweeds Ltd. and each weaver produced two tweeds per week. Because of the inexperience of the South Uist weavers, warping and beaming were generally done by power in Oban, and the weft yarn was dispatched wound on to the bobbins, practices quite foreign to normal production of Harris Tweed. By 1954, James Macdonald was sending yarn to Lewis to be woven on commission, and even then some of the warping and beaming were done by power in Oban.[5]

Wisely, in view of his significant departure from the definition of Harris Tweed, and despite his claim to the HTA that he was within his right in producing 'unstamped Harris Tweed', none of this cloth was invoiced to buyers as 'Harris Tweed'. When asked in the course of giving evidence for the Harris Tweed case, why the tweed sold by his companies was invoiced simply as 'Handwoven Tweed', James Macdonald replied:

> 'Well it is a very difficult question for me to answer to be quite honest with you. I suppose the correct answer would be that the less you put on paper the easier it is to keep out of trouble.' [6]

This reply speaks for itself. Some moments later, he explained his caution by saying:

> 'Well, there is the HTA, for instance. They were watching me like a cat watching a mouse. Everything I did they were just dropping on me.' [7]

By the simple expedient of supplying 'Harris Tweed' labels on request (that is at one stage removed from the bulk sale) he ensured that the final customer was informed that the garment he had bought was made from Harris Tweed. This practice was designed to make it as difficult as possible for the HTA to prove a case against the company. The wording on the labels was cleverly designed to deceive the unwary customer. Only an expert would notice a sophisticated ambiguity such as 100% Pure Virgin Wool Made in Scotland; which might have been true if 'made' meant 'spun', but was open to misconstruction in a case where the origin of the wool was of the essence. [8] The surprising thing about this anonymous invoicing was that traders were prepared to accept, 'with such credulity and starry-eyed trust', assurances from Macdonald's Tweeds Ltd. and Argyllshire Weavers Ltd. that they were actually receiving 'Harris Tweed'. In time, of course, this duplicity led to complaints about garments which did not live up to the expectations of Harris Tweed and to queries from reputable traders and official bodies wanting to establish the definition of 'Harris Tweed' beyond any doubt, a matter which eventually had to be resolved in court.

The importance attributed to the original Scottish Crofter Weavers in the Harris Tweed case was based on its alleged role as 'the bridge' which provided unbroken continuity in the production of 'unstamped Harris Tweed' made from mainland-spun yarn, in other words, as proof that unstamped Harris Tweed had a long unbroken pedigree. [9] The post-war history of the original Scottish Crofter Weavers is relatively brief, but important because of the campaign by its Managing Director, John Simpson, to unite the opposition to the Orb manufacturers. Mr Simpson seems to have shared the view of the island independent producers who supported the importation of mainland-spun yarn and mainland finishing, i. e. that as long as tweed was woven at the weaver's home in the Outer Hebrides from pure Scottish virgin wool, all other processes could legitimately be carried out on the mainland and the end product could claim to be 'traditional' unstamped Harris Tweed. [10] Needless to say, the HTA did not agree with this view and exerted continual pressure on Mr Simpson over his use of the name 'Harris Tweed' on his cloth.

Quite a number of informative letters from Mr Simpson to his Lewis manager, from his company solicitor, Mr Charles Brown, and to other correspondents, survive in the archives of the HTA. Most of the yarn used for production of Scottish Crofter Weavers' 'Hebratex Harris Tweed' was purchased from Lumbs of Elland in Yorkshire. Mr Simpson seems to have 'thought it desirable to check up with Lumbs on the question of the Scottish wool content in all the Hebridean yarn supplied to them'. He told his Lewis manager, John Mackenzie of Arnol, that Lumbs confirmed that they supplied him with 100% Scottish virgin wool.

> 'Any supposition to the contrary may arise from the fact their yarn is possibly finer and more even than that produced by the Stornoway spinning mills or by Brora, and this is due to the higher proportion of Scottish Cheviot wool which Lumbs use combined with a lower percentage of Blackfaced.' [11]

Mr P. Lumb, of Lumbs of Elland, contradicted this in his evidence during the Harris Tweed case:

> '**Question**: So far as the content of your yarn is concerned, I understand that it was always 100% virgin wool?
> **Answer**: Correct.
>
> **Question**: But your recollection is that Scottish Crofter Weavers asked you to make it 100% Scottish virgin wool and ... it was indicated to them, that you could not do this?
> **Answer**: It was not that they always asked us to make it from 100% Scottish wool or that it was being asked for every year, but at certain periods Scottish Crofter Weavers were always having to fight a battle against the Orb stamp, and there were certain times they asked us if we would make it from 100% Scottish wool.' [12]

Writing to John Mackenzie, Mr Simpson expressed the hope that he could 'establish once and for all' that the unstamped tweed produced by Scottish Crofter Weavers was 'no less genuine than the Orb stuff'. He declared that his firm were:

> 'carrying out the spirit of the original regulations to a higher degree in handling our complete work through stores and looms sited actually at the crofts. We have a very good point here in our favour, as this weaving which is going on around the town of Stornoway is thoroughly unsound having in view the objects of the Board of Trade in granting the Orb mark which aimed at maintaining occupation not at mills or looms at Stornoway but at the crofts.' [13]

The 'thoroughly unsound' weaving 'going on around the town of Stornoway' was a reference to 'colonies' of sheds used by individual weavers in Stornoway. The 'weavers' colonies' at Cannery Road and Westview Terrace were the town equivalents of the weaving sheds on the crofts and had to be situated no more than half a mile from the weaver's home. They were built on ground belonging to Stornoway Trust, not to the mills, and were used by weavers who lived in Council houses in which weaving was not allowed. Those weavers worked as independent self-employed weavers working for any or all of the mills, not as employees of one particular mill. Acceptance of tweed woven in these 'colonies' as Harris Tweed involved a very liberal interpretation of the words in the definition 'at the islanders own homes'. The practice was to be criticised by Lord Hunter in the Harris Tweed case. [14] Before a formal Distribution Centre for the allocation of weaving was introduced, there were allegations by rural weavers that, because of their relative proximity to the mills, 'colony weavers' were called on to do urgent weaving and thereby had an unfair advantage over weavers at a distance from town.

In July 1953, John Simpson wrote John Mackenzie about plans for taking premises in Stornoway or in North Uist to provide Scottish Crofter Weavers with island-spun yarn. That letter is full of interesting detail about the period:

> 'We have been approached to take an interest in the Stormgard mill ... at Bells Rd. which contains two and a half spinning units. ... I heard a rumour ... that Smiths were interested in a part of this

building for use as a Dyeing House ... there is a very strong desire on the part of the HTA interests to get us into the Hebrides as we are now apparently the only firm who are in a position to dispute the HTA monopoly. We have a Court Case pending in Canada, aiming at securing annulment of the words 'Harris Tweed' which the HTA have been able to secure by registration both in Canada and USA and which debars ourselves and any other manufacturer from selling our Harris Tweed in these Dollar Markets. The HTA want to consolidate their position, and while we have a certain amount of sympathy with their aims, we cannot be expected to agree to a monopoly which would push us out of the Hebridean industry ... P. S. Do you know anything about the mill in North Uist which I hear is likely to be on the market? ... I understand that this venture was initiated by Sir Douglas Hamilton MP for Inverness ... I rather imagine myself if he is getting out it is because of his inability to make a success of the venture. ... .' [15]

The mill in North Uist was a spinning mill established in 1947 by Hamilton Estates in the hope of encouraging the making of tweed in that island. Weaving was not taken up to any large extent and by the mid-1950s most of the yarn produced was sent up to Lewis. [16] The action in the Exchequer Court in Canada was taken in conjunction with similar action in Belgium and with action over a long period in the United States.

The 1953 venture into island production was not Mr Simpson's first attempt to find premises in the Outer Hebrides. About 1942 Scottish Crofter Weavers had considered taking over the mill at Tarbert and John Simpson had taken Mr Lumb of Ellands up to Harris to advise him on its suitability. During the war he had also considered the premises vacated on Lewis St. by Kenneth Mackenzie Ltd. when that firm moved to Seaforth Road. The plans for Tarbert fell through, allegedly because of the capital cost involved, and nothing came of the plan in 1953 to set up a production unit in Stornoway. [17]

Instead of opening his own production unit as planned, John Simpson began to explore the viability of dispensing with mainland yarn and buying all his yarn from the Stornoway mills. Production by Scottish Crofter Weavers of tweed which qualified for the Orb-stamp continued for less than two years. In early 1955, after much acrimony over discounts from the Stornoway spinners, the experiment was deemed to be a complete failure.

Whether disillusionment with the service and terms offered by the Stornoway mills was a factor in John Simpson's attitude to the Orb manufacturers, or whether he had been sceptical from the beginning about going over to entirely Orb-stamped production cannot now be ascertained. Giving evidence in the Harris Tweed case, Colonel Macarthur said that Mr Simpson had 'not been very enthusiastic' about going over to island-spun yarn, but that Mr Brown, Company Secretary, and Mr Duguid, a Director and considerable shareholder in the company, had been prepared to give it a trial. [18] Sadly John Simpson developed a terminal illness in 1954. The original Scottish Crofter Weavers went into voluntary liquidation in 1955.

On 30th December 1955, a new company was incorporated under the same name. In the Harris Tweed case it was said by Lord Hunter that the new Scottish Crofter Weavers Ltd. became an associate company of Laidlaws of Keith, who bought the assets of the original company from the liquidator. [19] However, in 1959 the then Chairman of Scottish Crofters Weavers, James Irvine-Fortescue, stated that:

> 'Scottish Crofter Weavers Ltd. is not a subsidiary company of Robert Laidlaw & Sons. I am Chairman of Scottish Crofter Weavers but I do not have a single share or any interest whatever in Robert Laidlaw & Sons. The only connection is that Scottish Crofter Weavers buy all their yarn from Laidlaws.' [20]

From 1958, this new Scottish Crofter Weavers Ltd. was one of the three member companies of the IHTP Ltd. The new company continued using yarn from Lumbs of Elland for a short time and thereafter bought its yarn from Laidlaws of Keith. As with yarn from Lumbs of Elland, the wool content of Laidlaw's yarn contained a substantial proportion of non-Scottish wool, including Colonial and Dominion wool. Weaving was still done on commission in Lewis and the greasy tweeds were returned to the mainland for finishing. The product was sold as 'Hebratex Handwoven Harris Tweed' or as 'Hebratex Handwoven Tweed'. Lord Hunter made the point that one of the potential dangers of mainland production of Harris Tweed was exemplified by the fact that a bunch of samples which contained a 'power-loomed pattern which could not physically have been produced on a hand-loom' had been supplied to a prospective agent by the new Scottish Crofter Weavers Ltd. [21]

The third firm of mainland producers which was to be actively involved in the challenge to the Orb stamp and the subsequent litigation was A. & J. Macnaughton Ltd. of Pitlochry. This firm had maintained a weaving shed on Tarbert pier from 1927 till 1934. They had given up these operations in 1934 when the amended definition confined all processes to the Islands. It appears that, despite having an allocation from the Wool Control Board for their Hebridean trade during the war, Macnaughtons had ceased supplying yarn to the Hebrides about 1941 and had not resumed this line of business until 1947. [22] Their sales in the immediate post-war period had been small and spasmodic and by the early 1950s had fallen away almost completely.

In 1951 or early 1952, Mr Blair Macnaughton, a director of the firm, paid a visit to the Hebrides hoping to revive sales of yarn to weavers there. The results of this visit were disappointing, as the weavers were not interested at that time. Then Macnaughtons decided 'to try and revive the old method of sending yarn ... by having it handwoven in the Islands'. [23] The 'old method' was the operation on Tarbert pier, by which mainland-spun yarn was woven in the islands and the greasy tweeds returned to the mainland for finishing, a method which Lord Hunter described as 'having all the appearances of a subterfuge to obtain by that method the selling advantages attaching to the use, legitimate or illegitimate, of the name 'Harris Tweed'.' [24]

At the beginning of their operations in Lewis, in 1953-54, A. & J. Macnaughton Ltd. sent their own Pitlochry-spun yarn to Crofter Handwoven Tweed Co., one of the firms which had been involved in the Embargo case of 1938. The tweed made from this yarn was handwoven in Lewis and returned to Pitlochry for finishing. Crofter Handwoven Tweed went out of business soon after the link with Macnaughtons started and from 1955 the firm had its own agent in Lewis, Ian Montgomery of Airidhbhruaich. The yarn supplied was made from a mixture of Scottish, English and sometimes Welsh wool. Some of the yarn was stake-warped in Airidhbhruaich, but most of it was power-warped in Pitlochry. [25]

Ian Montgomery testified that some sixty to seventy weavers were employed by him, mostly in the Lochs area. They were paid on a piece rate basis at the Union rate and produced, on average, at least one tweed per week. [26] The annual production of Macnaughton's Lewis-made tweed rose from about 5,000 yards in 1953-54 to 258,000 yards in 1959, a significant increase in anyone's terms. According to the evidence of Mr Blair Macnaughton and his accountant, Mr Morrison, this tweed was sold as 'Genuine Harris Tweed'.[27] Lord Hunter's opinion of this second *modus operandi* was that while it was less blatant than the methods adopted at Tarbert between 1927 and 1934, and less blatant than the methods adopted in South Uist by Argyllshire Weavers Ltd. and Macdonald's Tweeds, it was still:

> 'a device to enable the company to attach the name 'Harris Tweed' to its product. Without the use made of that name and the selling points which it conveyed to the mind of the ultimate purchaser ... the product would not have sold.'[28]

Some independent producers in the islands continued to use mainland-spun yarn and others used it from time to time. Among the most prominent of these local producers using mainland-spun yarn was Clansman Tweed Co. Ltd., a company set up at 9 Kenneth St., Stornoway, c. 1950 by Dr David Tolmie, a nephew of the David Tolmie who had been active in the Lewis HTA of the early 1930s and a grandson of the first David Tolmie who had come to Stornoway as a commission agent. This third generation David Tolmie, who had been a doctor in New York, served as a volunteer during the war and then set up a medical practice in Stornoway after the war. Dr Tolmie appointed a manager, William MacAinsh, to run the tweed business. The company continued the tradition established by Dr Tolmie's grandfather of acting as an independent producer, that is having tweeds woven locally on commission. Yarn supplies were purchased from Paton and Baldwins of Alloa, Clackmannanshire. This was stated quite clearly in a circular issued by Clansman Tweed Co. Ltd. in 1951. Indeed, it was the wording of this circular which occasioned a letter from McKenna & Co. on behalf of the HTA. In addition to stating that the yarn used was supplied by Paton and Baldwins, the Clansman circular proclaimed that the company was:

> 'engaged solely in the production of superior quality handwoven Harris Tweeds.'[29]

On behalf of the HTA, McKenna & Co. wrote to Clansman quoting the definition of Harris Tweed and pointed out that the company was not entitled to call its product 'Harris Tweed' if it did not conform to the 1934 definition. Campbell Smith Mathison & Oliphant, solicitors for Clansman, replied maintaining that the firm was quite within its rights to sell their cloth made from mainland yarn as 'Harris Tweed', and any attempted prosecution under the Merchandise Marks Act would be unlikely to succeed. [30]

Incidentally, confirmation of the destruction of McKenna's files in the blitz was given in the course of this correspondence. F. A. S. Gwatkin (father of John Gwatkin), of McKenna & Co. wrote to W. H. Martin, Secretary of the HTA saying:

> 'My records before 1940 were destroyed by enemy action. I have however asked the Solicitors for a copy of Mr Maude's Opinion of 1937.' [31]

The correspondence over the Clansman incident petered out with Mr Gwatkin eventually asking W. H. Martin whether the Association had come across any further advertisements in which Clansman Tweed Co. Ltd. described their product as 'Harris Tweed'. Clansman continued to import mainland yarn for some years before attempting in the late 1950s to go over to Orb production. It is perhaps indicative of the impact of the HTA's advertising of the Orb Mark that in 1952 Clansman lost a customer who stopped buying tweed from the company when he discovered that it did not qualify for the Orb stamp. [32]

Maclennan and Maclennan also continued to use mainland yarn, much of it of non-Scottish origin. The firm changed hands a number of times during the period 1950 to 1961. Their cloth was sold as CEEMO, and usually included the words 'Harris Tweed'. [33] In 1957, Maclennan and Maclennan were taken over by a Yorkshire company and had their finishing done in England by Holroyds of Leeds. Between 1959 and 1960 they decided that part of their production should qualify for the Orb stamp, probably in response to the increasingly effective advertising campaign by the HTA. Maclennan and Maclennan's promotional literature bore such legends as 'Harris Tweed An Island Handicraft'. Describing this company's descent into the 'grosser forms of imitation', [34] Lord Hunter said:

> 'To describe Maclennan and Maclennan's non-Orb product during the last four years of their operations prior to 1961 as an Island handicraft was in my opinion a mis-use of language.' [35]

Maclennan and Maclennan changed hands yet again in 1961 and began to produce a different cloth which was not sold as Harris Tweed.

If we take the total production of cloth sold as Harris Tweed, whether stamped or unstamped, as 'the total', then, in the mid-1950s, the production of Orb-stamped Harris Tweed by the Stornoway mills accounted for approximately 56% of the total. Independent producers in the islands using island-spun yarn in the production of Orb-stamped Harris Tweed accounted for approximately 28% of the total. The output from these first two sources can be judged from the stamping figures kept by the HTA. Turning to unstamped Harris Tweed, the output of tweed woven in the islands for mainland producers from mainland-spun yarn is more difficult to estimate, but it was thought to account for approximately 7% of the total . Production of unstamped tweed woven in South Uist by James Macdonald's companies was estimated to be another 7%. The output of unstamped Harris Tweed by independent island producers using mainland-spun yarn seems to have been as low as 2% of the total. [36] It seems that the policy of pressure and persuasion applied by the HTA, combined with a general easing of yarn supplies from 1948, had been effective in encouraging most local importers of yarn to switch over to island-spun yarn and island finishing, thereby enabling their tweed to qualify for the Orb stamp. [37]

Production of unstamped Harris Tweed at 16% of the total output may not seem unduly significant, but the rate at which it was increasing did give cause for concern. In time unstamped Harris Tweed could have dominated the market. Again, on those occasions when unstamped Harris Tweed turned out to be an inferior product, it damaged the good name of Orb-stamped Harris Tweed. The only recourse available to the HTA was diligent advertising of Orb-stamped Harris Tweed, combined with the threat of legal action against manufacturers describing their cloth as Harris Tweed in breach of the definition. Yet it was these efforts to promote the security guaranteed to the customer by buying Orb-stamped Harris Tweed and to discourage production of unstamped Harris Tweed which brought the HTA into conflict with the mainland firms who eventually formed IHTP Ltd. in 1958.

Reference - Independent Harris Tweed Producers Ltd.

1 *Argyllshire Weavers Ltd. and others v. Macaulay (A.) (Tweeds) Ltd., and Others* [1964] RPC No. 16, 477 [hereafter: 'Harris Tweed Case'], at 551.
2 *ibid.*, 545.
3 James Macdonald to W. H. Martin, 3. 12. 1951. HTA Office, Stornoway.
4 *ibid.*
5 'Harris Tweed Case' [1964] RPC No. 16, 477, at 543.
6 *ibid.*
7 *ibid.*
8 *ibid.*, 545-547.
9 *ibid.*, 534-535.
10 *ibid.*, 533.
11 John Simpson to John Mackenzie, 21. 5. 1952. HRA/D190 1(o).
12 'Harris Tweed Case' [1964] RPC No. 16, 477, at 535.
13 John Simpson to John Mackenzie, 21. 5. 1952. HRA/D190 1(o).
14 'Harris Tweed Case' [1964] RPC No. 16, 477, at 567-568.
15 John Simpson to John Mackenzie, 18. 7. 1953. HRA/D190/1(0).
16 Moisley, H.A. , 'Harris Tweed: A Growing Industry'[hereafter: 'Moisley, 'Harris Tweed'], 367.
17 Transcripts of evidence in *Argyllshire Weavers Ltd. and Others v. A. Macaulay (Tweeds) Ltd. and Others* (1964) CSess OH: [hereafter: 'Transcripts of Evidence in "Harris Tweed Case"'], Vol. 1, 4747: Evidence from Col. Neil Macarthur. HRA/D190/1a (xxxv).
18 *ibid.*, 4750 and 4753.
19 'Harris Tweed Case' [1964] RPC No. 16, 477, at 541.
20 James Irvine-Fortescue to Edwin Stevens, 5. 1. 1959. HRA/D190/ O/ 57/1961.
21 'Harris Tweed Case' [1964] RPC No. 16, 477, at 551.
22 *ibid.*, 549.
23 *ibid.*
24 *ibid.*, 511.
25 *ibid.*, 549.
26 Transcripts of Evidence in 'Harris Tweed Case', CSess OH: Vol. 1, 1697: Evidence of Ian Montgomery. HRA/D190/1a (xxxv).
27 'Harris Tweed Case' [1964] RPC No. 16, 477, at 550.
28 *ibid.*
29 McKenna & Co. to Clansman Tweed Co. Ltd, 17. 9. 1951. HRA/D190/ 1 (o).
30 Campbell, Smith, Mathieson & Oliphant to McKenna & Co. 21. 11. 1951 HRA/D190/ 1(o).
31 F. A. S. Gwatkin to W. H. Martin, 23. 11. 1951. HRA/D190/ 1 (o).
32 'Harris Tweed Case' [1964] RPC No. 16, 477, at 542.

33 *ibid.*, 541.
34 *ibid.*
35 *ibid.*
36 Moisley, Harris Tweed, 364.
37 'Harris Tweed Case' [1964] RPC No. 16, 477, at 540.

15

A Challenge to the Orb from the IHTP

The difficulties which the Harris Tweed Association experienced in the late 1950s and early 1960s in the House of Commons, with the Board of Trade, with the Retail Trading-Standards Association (RTSA) and with the Federal Trades Commission (FTC) in the United States were simply the public manifestations of a campaign which was being conducted in secret by those mainland producers who were determined to have their tweed, made from mainland-spun yarn, accepted as a legitimate alternative to Orb-stamped Harris Tweed. When the facts behind the formation of the group which called itself Independent Harris Tweed Producers Ltd. (IHTP) eventually came to light during the Harris Tweed case, it became clear that the formation of the IHTP was but the culmination of a lengthy struggle by the mainland producers opposed to the Orb trade mark. We have to follow the campaign waged by those mainland producers and then the actions which led to the formation of the IHTP in 1958. The challenge to the Orb in Britain in the late 1950s was closely paralleled in the United States. Although brief reference to events in the United States must be made from time to time in this chapter, in order to simplify a complicated story, those events in the United States will be described in more detail in the next chapter.

Contention over whether the Board of Trade had 'authorised', 'approved' or merely accepted the definition of Harris Tweed used in association with the Orb mark was renewed in early 1958 when Roger Diplock of the RTSA responded to a complaint that advertisments in the United States claimed that the term 'Harris Tweed' had been 'defined by the British Government Board of Trade' and that 'the Harris Tweed Association was established by Special Charter of the British Board of Trade'. [1] These clearly inaccurate claims had been made by Stanley Brown, the HTA agent in New York. The matter was duly raised in the House of Commons when Commander C. E. M. Donaldson M.P., (who had asked a similar question on behalf of John Simpson and the NASWM in 1954) asked the President of the Board of Trade to what extent his Department had been involved-by special charter or otherwise - in the creation of the Harris Tweed Association. The President Sir David Eccles replied that the Harris Tweed Association had never had a special Board of Trade charter and that the advertisement was therefore incorrect. Commander Donaldson then asked to what extent, in agreeing to the registration of the certification mark of the Harris Tweed Association, the President of the Board of Trade had authorised any particular definition of Harris Tweed as the only description of that material which could be permitted in Britain. Sir David replied that the Board's approval of the regulations did not signify that the definition of Harris Tweed in the regulations was the only definition of Harris Tweed. That definition was only relevant *to the use of the trade mark.* [2]

Commander Donaldson then asked what assistance was given to those who produced Harris Tweed of equal quality to Orb-marked tweed, but who, because they were not members of the Harris Tweed Association Ltd., had their goods proscribed from entry into the United States. Sir David replied that the Board of Trade's services were open to any maker of Harris Tweed, 'whether from the islands or not'! Malcolm MacMillan, M.P. for the Western Isles, intervened to ask whether the President was satisfied that there was adequate protection afforded to the Orb mark from illegal use by persons producing and selling imitations of the cloth, and obvious pirating and competition from Galashiels to Japan. In reply to the question from Malcolm MacMillan, Sir David Eccles, President of the Board of Trade, informed the House of Commons, that

> 'The description 'Harris Tweed' is very like that of Bath buns. It covers the manufacture of articles not all made in the place to which the name refers.' [3]

This preposterous statement was tantamount to saying that the term 'Harris Tweed' was as meaningless as 'cheddar cheese'. Whether Sir David Eccles actually realised the full implications of his foolish, or flippant comparison of Harris Tweed to Bath buns, or whether it reflects what he genuinely believed is impossible to know. [4]

The reaction in the Islands to Sir David Eccles' remark was one of anger and consternation. Three Stornoway Town Councillors, Burgh Treasurer Albert Nicol, Bailie Ann Urquhart and Councillor John MacLeod, called for a special meeting of the Council to consider this apparent reversal of the long-established policy of the Board of Trade, especially in view of the very serious state of the Harris Tweed industry at the time. [5] In May, the Board of Trade was disposed to give a more considered response when Malcolm MacMillan M.P. was informed by a spokesman for the President that

> 'Tweed, marked with the Orb mark and the words 'Harris Tweed', is unmistakably 'Harris Tweed'. Whether anything else is 'Harris Tweed' or not is a matter for the Courts. My own opinion, however, would be that tweed produced in England could not legitimately be described as 'Harris Tweed'.' [6]

In October 1958, Roger Diplock of the RTSA complained again about advertisements for Harris Tweed because they contained what he called 'knocking copy', i.e. copy which implied that Harris Tweed which did not bear the Orb stamp was spurious. Mr Diplock conceded that the Harris Tweed Association was entitled to its view that only 'Orb-marked' tweed was genuine 'despite the annual production of over one and a half million yards of 'Harris Tweed' made by non-Orb producers'. However, he threatened that the RTSA would take legal action against the Harris Tweed Association and its advertising agents, Dorland Advertising Ltd., 'if members of the RTSA continued to suffer damage as a result of any future advertisements in similar vein'. [7]

Unfortunately for Mr Diplock, Roy Hale of Dorlands Advertising was not at all intimidated by such threats. Then, resorting to 'reason' rather than bluster, Mr Diplock chose a revealing analogy to illustrate what he saw as the perversity of the Harris Tweed Association in continuing to advertise the Orb stamp as the guarantee of genuine Harris Tweed:

> 'May I re-emphasise that the Harris Tweed Association is perfectly entitled to hold the view that nothing but 'Orb-marked' Harris Tweed is genuine Harris Tweed. The fact of the matter remains, however, that this view is not supported by any sound legal opinion whatsoever and therefore neither the Harris Tweed Association Ltd. nor its Advertising Agency is entitled to indulge in 'knocking copy' in order to make its opinion known to the public. If I may put to you an example of an exactly similar way of thinking, I am quite entitled to hold the personal view that all

Socialist Members of Parliament are, *ipso facto,* traitors to their country. This personal opinion, however does not in any way entitle me to hire newspaper space in order to make these views known to the public as a whole.' [8]

There can be little doubt that the advertising campaign mounted by the Harris Tweed Association on behalf of Orb-stamped tweed was effective. The RTSA received frequent enquiries from retailers who wanted to know whether tweed which did not bear the Orb mark could be genuine 'Harris Tweed'. No doubt these queries were a source of constant exasperation to Roger Diplock. While it is easy to understand why the producers of unstamped Harris Tweed were determined to win the argument with the Harris Tweed Association - they knew that winning the argument could be measured in terms of hard cash - it is less easy to understand the tenacity with which Roger Diplock made their cause a personal crusade.

Over time, misconceptions as to the function of the HTA such as were revealed in the House of Commons, and the concerted efforts to undermine its position, succeeded in portraying it as a private English company, based in London, and closely related to the interests of the Stornoway mill-owners, who were frequently referred to as if they and the Harris Tweed Association were one body. This fabrication fed on the near-universal propensity to favour the 'under-dog'. As the misconception, not to say misrepresentation, gained currency, the mainland producers were cast in the role of gallant little Scottish entrepreneurs whose legitimate business ventures were being frustrated by unscrupulous vested interests emanating from London. Such a misconception may go some way to explaining the wild allegations about the Harris Tweed Association made by Francis Noel-Baker, Labour M.P. for Swindon, in a Private Member's motion asking for a Royal Commission to inquire into the state of the advertising industry in November 1958.

Having decried a number of shady advertisements such as offers of memory-training courses, Mr Noel-Baker turned his attention to the Harris Tweed Association and its advertising campaign. In a remarkably ill-informed and inaccurate diatribe he said of the most recent advertisement for Orb-stamped Harris Tweed:

> 'Then appears a trade mark designed to look like something official. It has an Orb with a crown on top. I have seen the advertisement for many years and I was under the impression that if the tweed coat I bought did not bear the sign it would not be genuine. That is the object of the advertisement which has been devised by the people making this Harris Tweed. Their firm is simply a private independent firm, the Harris Tweed Association Ltd., which competes with other people who make equally genuine tweed. The wording of the advertisement is such that the firm cannot be got at under the existing law. Dorland Advertising Ltd., which prepared the copy, must know it is a swindle. ... Will the Minister tell us what he is going to do about this racket and what advice he intends to give to Dorland Advertising Ltd. about the kind of copy it is producing for its clients?' [9]

Mr Jo Grimond, M.P. for Orkney and Shetland, intervened to object to the use of the word 'racketeers', as he believed that the Association was 'a fairly old-established firm and a respectable undertaking'.

Mr Noel-Baker returned to his theme:

> 'If he (Jo Grimond) knows better than I do, I shall be very glad to have a talk with him later and to withdraw the word 'racketeers'. But from looking very carefully at the advertising copy, and at what is said by the British Retail Trading-Standards Association, I believe that the firm is engaged in a deliberate swindle which is intended to deceive the public.' [10]

Malcolm Macmillan, M.P. asked for a retraction of the 'innuendoes and smears' contained in Francis Noel-Baker's 'outrageously inaccurate statements' in the House of Commons. The spokesman for the Board of Trade said that both he and the President of the Board of Trade 'deplored the use of words such as 'racket' and 'patently dishonest'.' [11]

At the request of George Ellis, Chairman of the HTA, a meeting was arranged with Mr Noel-Baker by Malcolm MacMillan, M.P. Mr Diplock turned up at the meeting, presumably by invitation, and continued his own attack on the Association. In a letter to Malcolm MacMillan after the meeting he mentions the 'indignation his Association' felt over the advertising technique of the HTA. With what can only be seen as heavy irony, or mock humility, he went on to make the common mistake of thinking that Broad Scots was the mother tongue of the Islanders, a mistake which never fails to irritate the Gael.

> 'As a mere Southerner I stand aghast at the extent to which the real business of selling Harris Tweed seems to be given second place to the 'feudin' and 'fightin' (sic) and I really would like to see a reasonable compromise which recognises the long existence of Harris Tweed made from mainland-spun yarn.' [12]

Mr Diplock remained impervious to the explanation that in the years preceding the amended definition of 1934, a widespread use of mainland yarn and a general deterioration of standards had led to 'Harris Tweed' wholly made in Yorkshire, Canada and Japan appearing on the market. John Gwatkin of McKenna & Co. told Roger Diplock that if the only means of achieving an end to the controversy was to allow the term 'Harris Tweed' to become the property of mainland producers, he saw no hope of a compromise. In a sentence which presaged Lord Hunter's judgement of 1964, he pointed out to Roger Diplock that, 'Misdescription does not become any less misleading over a period of years'.

In addition to attacking the Orb mark in his role as spokesman for the RTSA, Roger Diplock appears to have taken an active role in advising the mainland producers to unite against the HTA. He admitted that he 'probably said to Blair Macnaughton 'if you people don't get together you will be picked off like sitting ducks'.' By 'you people' he was apparently referring to Macnaughtons of Pitlochry, Scottish Crofter Weavers of Aberdeen, Macdonalds Tweeds, Argyllshire Weavers of Oban and Maclennan and Maclennan of Stornoway. [13] The planning of the new group which was to become the Independent HarrisTweed Producers Ltd. (IHTP) involved a great deal of consultation during 1957 and 1958. In December 1957, Roger Diplock consulted Blair Macnaughton about the wording of a new definition of Harris Tweed, saying:

'One point seems rather important - should we say that the yarns are made from one-hundred per cent new Scottish wool? Personally, I think we should.' [14]

The wording of a suitable definition proved to be so controversial that, after a meeting of producers of unstamped Harris Tweed in January 1958, Maclennan and Maclennan, whose spinning and finishing were done in England, fell out of the group. Thereafter application was made by the remaining members of the group for registration of a company which was to be called Independent Harris Tweed Producers Ltd. The first definition of Harris Tweed adopted in the Memorandum and Articles of Association of this group was:

'Harris Tweed means cloth made from pure virgin wool, dyed and spun in the Outer Hebrides or elsewhere in Scotland, hand-woven by the Islanders in the Outer Hebrides and finished in the Outer Hebrides or elsewhere in Scotland.' [15]

While it was astute of the IHTP to recognise the protection given to potential purchasers by a specific definition of the product, their original definition was to be altered a few months later when the deficiencies of its wording became apparent. In Autumn 1958, Mr Diplock and Mr Blair Macnaughton paid a fruitless visit to the Hebrides in the hope of persuading a number of producers in the Islands to endorse a definition of Harris Tweed which would be acceptable to the members of the IHTP. The visit from these representatives of the mainland producers took place at a time when the market for tweed was at a particularly low ebb. (Sales of Orb-stamped tweed dropped by almost 2 million yards in 1958.) Earlier in the year, some 40 mill employees in Stornoway had been paid off as redundant and 170 employees were on short time, working only three days a week. Weavers in the rural areas of Lewis were also seriously affected with the worst hit being those who worked for only one or two mills. Tweed merchants were also said to be suffering from a shortage of money. [16] It may be that the IHTP felt that this was an opportune moment to recruit island weavers and advance their own market position. Local memories of Mr Diplock on that occasion recall a somewhat irascible man who would brook no argument with his own entrenched opinions.

On 12th November 1958, the Scottish press gave prominent headlines to the formation of Independent Harris Tweed Producers Ltd. The group comprised Argyllshire Weavers of Oban, A. & J. Macnaughton of Pitlochry and Scottish Crofter Weavers Ltd. of Aberdeen. The subscribers of the new company, which was limited by guarantee and did not have a share capital, were D. A. Macdonald, (Argyllshire Weavers Ltd.), Blair C. MacNaughton and J. R. Morrsion, (A. & J. Macnaughton, Ltd.) J. W. Irvine Fortescue and S. G. Laidlaw (Scottish Crofter Weavers), James Macdonald and J. M. Macdonald (Macdonald's Tweeds Ltd.) The reason given for the formation of the new firm was to compete with 'the Orb monopoly' which had affected their trade with the American market. Another aim of the group was 'to broaden the scope of what could be termed Harris Tweed'. The definition of Harris Tweed was still the 'cloth made from pure virgin wool, dyed and spun in the Outer Hebrides, or elsewhere in Scotland' version from the company's memorandum. [17]

That same week Mr Blair Macnaughton wrote to the Editor of the *Stornoway Gazette* explaining more fully the reasons for the launch of the new company. According to this letter, the foremost objects of the company were 'the development and protection of the industry of hand-weaving in the Outer Hebrides and the promotion of the sales of Harris Tweed in all markets'. Quoting the definition from the company's Memorandum, Mr Macnaughton continued:

> 'This definition debars no section of the Harris Tweed industry provided the cloth is hand-woven in the Outer Hebrides from Scottish-spun yarn containing 100% pure virgin wool and finished in Scotland. It is expected that membership of the new Company will shortly be opened to all producers, Orb or non-Orb, conforming to this definition.'

He blamed 'the bombshell' which had hit the non-Orb producers in January 1957, when they found their tweed debarred by US Customs from the American market by a strict interpretation of the 'monopoly' of Harris Tweed which the Harris Tweed Association had achieved by their registration of the Orb stamp in the USA in March 1950. This had resulted in any cloth calling itself 'Harris Tweed' which did not originate from Hebridean-spun yarn being held up at the port of entry until the words 'Harris Tweed' were removed. Customers who had bought this non-Orb tweed cancelled orders when they were only permitted to designate the cloth as 'handwoven tweeds'. He claimed that crofter-weavers in the Lochs, Coll and Balallan areas of Lewis had thus suffered a considerable loss of revenue. The current series of advertisements by the HTA had 'confused the public into the belief that if a handwoven Harris Tweed did not bear the Orb stamp it must be a spurious article'.

The *Bulletin* of the RTSA welcomed the formation of the new company and supported the IHTP definition as 'broadly covering the factual and proper definition of Harris Tweed'. The *Bulletin* also informed its readers that 'the registration of the new company would not have been effected without careful consideration by the Board of Trade of the complex problems involved'! [18] This statement about the IHTP definition was, of course, seriously misleading. The boast about the 'careful consideration' given to it by the Board of Trade was somewhat ironic, given Mr Diplock's reaction to Stanley Brown's unfortunate references to the Board of Trade advertisement for the Orb mark in the United States!

The leader in the *Stornoway Gazette* of 21st November was less than welcoming to the new company. It said:

> 'The formation of Independent Harris Tweed Producers Ltd. is of the greatest importance to the Western Isles. The Harris Tweed industry is our main industry - at the moment it is almost our only industry - and anything which affects it affects everyone, whether directly engaged in it or not. ... Mr Blair Macnaughton gives as the foremost object of the new company 'the development and protection of the industry of hand-weaving in the Outer Hebrides', The same object is featured prominently in the Articles of Association of the company. It is no discourtesy, however, to the three very reputable firms involved to write that off as so much window-dressing. The primary purpose of the new registration is to further the business interests of the three companies concerned. Any benefit which may accrue to the weavers of the Hebrides will be purely secondary and incidental. This is business and no purpose is served by giving it the colour of altruism. ... Is there anything in the new set-up which would prevent any of the firms using the new trade mark - the three originals, or any who accept the invitation to

join them ... from applying it to tweed for the American market, while at the same time producing a 'Bath bun' 'Harris Tweed' on power looms for sale in the home or other markets? It is most unlikely that the three firms presently concerned would stoop to such a practice, but they have issued an invitation to others to join them, and we are familiar these days with the take-over bid and the acquisition of small family firms of high repute by multiple concerns so large that it is difficult to locate a conscience. The point which concerns the weavers in the Western Isles is not the use to which the three firms intend to put the trade mark today, but the use that may be made of it in ten years hence by someone else, in the absence of proper safeguards. ... With two trade marks to confuse the consumer, protection by advertising becomes so much less effective. Besides, if the Board of Trade is prepared to register two trade marks and two definitions why not ten? Is there anything to stop the Border mills from registering a trade mark for 'Harris Tweed' which has never been nearer the Hebrides than Gala Water and if the Borders can have one, why not Yorkshire?

The Orb trade mark says 'pure virgin Scottish wool'. The new trade mark says 'pure virgin wool'. Can we have another trade mark which is silent altogether about the raw material? The Retail Trading-Standards Association has made itself very busy in this matter ... Can the Association give any assurance that the new definition does not open a door for other definitions which fail to reserve even weaving for the Hebrides? ... The RTSA has carried on a vigorous campaign against the Orb trade mark. Can we take it that the Association will now give the same support to the Orb mark as it gives to the new one? It can hardly do less, if its interest is the maintenance of standards, because any tweed which qualifies for the Orb must also qualify for the definition which the Association approves. ... The new trade mark does not necessarily prove a desire by the mainland mills to help the island weaver, but it does very definitely prove that the mainland mills need the island weavers to help them.' [19]

Now that the participants in the IHTP are largely forgotten it is of interest to note that members of the original Council of IHTP were:

'Mr George Chalmers, Argyllshire Weavers, Ltd., Oban
Mr James William Irvine-Fortescue, C.A. Scottish Crofter Weavers Ltd., Aberdeen
Mr Stuart Graham Laidlaw, Scottish Crofter Weavers Ltd., Aberdeen
Mr Donald Alister Macdonald, Argyllshire Weavers Ltd., Oban
Mr Blair Charles McNaughton, A. & J. McNaughton, Pitlochry, and Mr John Robertson Morrison, A. & J. McNaughton, Pitlochry.' [20]

In a memorandum reacting to the formation of the IHTP, the HTA made the telling point that far from harming the independent producers on the mainland, the advertising campaign of the HTA had created the very market on which the IHTP sought to impinge. The HTA also pointed out that the Arms of IHTP as shown in *The Scotsman* of 12th November 1958 were in fact Arms granted to an individual director of Argyllshire Weavers Ltd. and his heirs and that the assignation of the Arms to Argyllshire Weavers was ineffective. Therefore the Arms could not, in accordance with the Law of Heraldry, be used by Independent Harris Tweed Producers Ltd. [21]

The group emblem or 'Arms' of the IHTP were to be the source of some embarrassment to them in January 1959. The emblem was actually a heraldic shield device which Argyllshire Weavers Ltd. had registered as a trade mark in respect of articles of clothing on 1st April 1953. It so happened that this device had a remarkable similarity to the arms of the Chief of Clan Donald. That fact became known to Sir Thomas Innes of Learney, the Lord Lyon King of Arms, in January 1959. Members of the IHTP were invited to 'discuss the matter with the Lord Lyon'. [22] The result of this discussion was that IHTP had to find a new device which they took care to ensure met with the Lord Lyon's approval before adopting it. When IHTP presented a petition for adoption of their new emblem, the Lord Lyon decided that the Harris Tweed Association should be given an opportunity to oppose the Grant of Arms if it so wished. As the Harris Tweed Association was a company registered in England, there was some doubt as to its standing in the proceedings, but it decided to put in an Answer drafted by Scottish Counsel in which it was pointed out that the IHTP definition of Harris Tweed allowed the use of any kind of wool and the majority of the processes to be carried out on the mainland. The HTA asked the Lyon Court to refuse the IHTP Petition. [23]

At some point in the negotiations over a new emblem, the IHTP filed a Memorial in which they tried to justify the absence of any requirement for the use of pure Scottish wool, which ended with the words:

> 'In short, so far from merit attaching to the sole use of Scottish grown wool, the reverse is the case.' [24]

Apparently, the Lord Lyon did not take kindly to the proposal to use non-Scottish wool in the making of Harris Tweed. As a result of his objections, IHTP adopted, by Special Resolution passed on 29th January 1959, an amended definition which required that the wool used should be of Scottish origin. (The fact that some members of the IHTP had been using non-Scottish wool was proved during the Harris Tweed case and this may explain why their prices for tweed were lower than those of the Orb producers. [25] On being advised of the amended definition, the Lord Lyon decided to issue a decision in favour of IHTP. In the meantime, the Harris Tweed Association had asked the Lord Lyon to receive a delegation which arrived on the afternoon of the day on which the decision had been issued. The Lord Lyon was taken aback to learn from the delegation that the Harris Tweed Association had not received a copy of the Memorial filed by the IHTP and obviously could not, at such short notice, answer the points made in that Memorial. The Lord Lyon then instructed his clerk to tell IHTP not to publish the decision which he had already given. He promised the Harris Tweed Association that he would give them time to answer the points in the IHTP Memorial. However, a few days later, the Lord Lyon changed his mind, and before the Harris Tweed Association had submitted a new memorandum dealing with points made in the IHTP Memorial, the Lord Lyon announced that his decision as already issued should stand. [26]

The Lord Lyon's response to the petition by Independent Harris Tweed Producers Ltd. to be 'created an incorporation noble by a Grant of Arms' is a long but interesting document which reveals that his opinions were largely coloured by the IHTP reference to Lord Simon's *obiter dicta* in the Embargo Case. The Lord Lyon believed that as the IHTP had amended its original definition to make wool of Scottish origin a requirement for their Harris Tweed, this amendment 'removed a salient and major objection to which the Harris Tweed Association rightly drew attention and that the differences between the two incorporations are now reduced to processing, including spinning and dyeing, which the respondents (HTA) maintain should only be done in the islands, whilst the petitioners (IHTP) say it can, and if a large enough output is to be obtained, must in part take place on the mainland, if the number of weavers in the Outer Hebrides is to be maintained and increased and unemployment there prevented.' [27]

Although he went on to discuss the importance for local industry and 'the business-value of local names and indeed of the property in such names and descriptions, e.g. chateau wine', the Lord Lyon's emphasis was on the 'Scottishness' of the product and the protection afforded to the economic and employment interests in both the Hebrides and Scotland. He decided that the IHTP were 'suitable subjects to receive Letters Patent of Arms ... with a MacLeod bull's head in chief ... ' [28] The Lord Lyon's decision continued:

'This bull's head with certain other additaments became the crest of the House of MacLeod of Harris, alternatively styled MacLeod of MacLeod and has thus a connection with the island giving the name to Harris Tweed, but the incident connected with the bull took place upon the mainland in Glenelg, so it is altogether historically a suitable device to be associated with the production of Harris Tweed in the Hebrides, whilst not devoid of some connection with the Highland mainland at Glenelg. In the circumstances, and combined with the symbols of weaving, it appears to me that the arms which came under discussion are appropriate and that the petitioners are of a status as appropriate as many who ordinarily get arms, and that in making this grant the interests in protection and promotion on an extensive scale of the weaving of Harris Tweed as produce of Scotland should be of a wide-spread economic value and in no way incompatible with the promotion of a purely island-processed Harris Tweed by the Harris Tweed Association for a market which wishes that special variety of Scottish cloth.' [29]

On 16th July 1959, Independent Harris Tweed Producers Ltd. applied for two trade marks which were duly advertised in the *Trade Marks Journal* of November 18th 1959. The marks consisted of the Shield device granted by the Lord Lyon with the words 'Independent Harris Tweed Producers Ltd.' in a circle round the shield. A joint Notice of Opposition to these Applications was filed on 18th January 1960 by fourteen Hebridean producers, Kemp and Co. (Stornoway) Ltd. (a finishing company), Stornoway Town Council, the Transport and General Workers' Union, the Harris Tweed Association, the Shetland Woollen Industries Association and the Donegal Handwoven Tweed Association Ltd. In a deposition of evidence prepared for the Harris Tweed case of 1964, and in a paragraph marked in the margin 'For Cross-examination only', Alasdair MacLeod, Town Clerk of Stornoway, who had recently become a member of the Harris Tweed Association stated:

> 'The Town Council decided to join in the opposition to the application. We had hoped to obtain the support of the Lewis Rural District Council, but I regret to say that when the matter came before them, that Council decided not to support the (Harris Tweed) Association by nine votes to six. I subsequently learned that several of the councillors present were weavers and had been doing work for the Shield producers.' [30]

The Island producers who jointly opposed the IHTP application were James Macdonald Ltd. of Seaforth Rd., Stornoway (the company founded by James Macdonald continued under new management on his departure for Oban), Kenneth MacKenzie Ltd., Sandwick Rd., Stornoway, S. A. Newall and Sons Ltd., James St., Stornoway, Harris Handwoven Tweed Co. Ltd., Tarbert, Isle of Harris, Stephen Burns Ltd., 26 Newton St., Stornoway, A. MacAulay (Tweeds) Ltd., 27 North Beach St., Stornoway, Macleod's Tweed Co. Ltd., 60 North Shawbost, Isle of Lewis, Angus Macleod, Park House Marybank, Stornoway, John Macleod & Co., 23 Shawbost, Isle of Lewis, Kenneth MacLeod (Shawbost) Ltd., Isle of Lewis, Alexander Morrison, Glenside, Gravir, Isle of Lewis, Angus Nicolson, 39 Inaclete Rd., Stornoway, Seaforth Harris Tweeds Ltd., 81, Seaforth Rd, Stornoway, David Tolmie and Co. Ltd., 7 Francis St, Stornoway. [31]

The joint Notice of Opposition to the IHTP application outlined the processes involved in the production of Orb-stamped Harris Tweed and contrasted those with the processes used by IHTP. The public perception of Harris Tweed as a product entirely made in the Outer Hebrides was emphasised and the prominence given to the words 'Harris Tweed' in the IHTP trade marks condemned as being both unlawful and misleading to the buying public.[32] In the first part of 1960, Independent Harris Tweed Producers ran an advertising campaign showing the new label which had the trade mark in the form applied for in the centre, and above it the words 'Genuine Harris Tweed', at the side the words '100% Scottish Pure Wool' and at the bottom 'Handwoven by Islanders in the Outer Hebrides', and thereunder 'Label issued by authority of Independent Harris Tweed Producers Ltd.'. This last statement was to be of considerable importance in the subsequent legal action against the IHTP because labels on tweed jackets allegedly passed-off by Hepworths as being made from 'Harris Tweed' had been issued by the authority of IHTP. The wording of one advertisement by IHTP advised the potential customer to:

> 'Look for this label in the shops NOW! It is your guarantee of genuine Harris Tweed. You will find it only on authentic Harris Tweed garments. Made by independent producers, these lovely tweeds are handwoven in the Outer Hebrides.'[33]

At no time did the members of IHTP reveal that their tweed was in any way different from Orb-stamped tweed.

While the launch and subsequent actions of Independent Harris Tweed Weavers Ltd. were probably the major topics of domestic concern for the Harris Tweed Association and the Orb producers between 1958 and 1960, a wage agreement operative from June 1959 between the Harris Tweed Weavers' Section of the Transport and General Workers' Union, the Hebridean Spinners Association and the Hebridean Producers Association was probably of more immediate concern to individual weavers. The weavers coming within the scope of the agreement were required to be members of the TGWU and engaged exclusively in the weaving of tweed which complied with the definition of Harris Tweed 'approved by the Board of Trade in the regulations governing the use of the Orb trade mark'. [34] It seems that in March 1960 at least two of the spinning mills asked weavers on their books to sign an undertaking that they would weave only island-spun yarn. The IHTP learned of this and their company Secretary wrote weavers suggesting that it was not in their interests to sign such an undertaking. Lest a weaver had already signed the undertaking, a form of revocation was included with the letter. [35]

A surprising item of news broke on 21st December 1959 when it became known that James Macdonald had disposed of the shareholding in his companies to Grampian Holdings Ltd. [36] A circular letter to shareholders announced that Grampian Holdings Ltd. had bought out Macdonald's Tweeds Ltd., which included both Argyllshire Weavers Ltd. and Macdonalds of Oban, for £500,000, £355,000 in cash and £145,000 in shares. [37] Lord Hunter commented on this transaction in his judgement in the Harris Tweed case in 1964 saying, 'One feels the timing was again exact'. [38]

After prolonged consideration as to how best to challenge the actions of Independent Harris Tweed Producers Ltd. and have the meaning of the term 'Harris Tweed' decided in a court of law, an action of passing-off was raised by the Orb producers in the High Court of Justice, Chancery Division on 6th July 1960. The plaintiffs, (i.e. the Orb producers making the complaint) were A. MacAulay (Tweeds) Ltd., James Macdonald Ltd., Kenneth MacKenzie Ltd., Kenneth MacLeod (Shawbost) Ltd. and S.A. Newall & Sons on behalf of themselves and all other makers of 'Harris Tweed' in the Outer Hebrides. The action was raised against Hepworths Ltd., Independent Harris Tweed Producers Ltd., Argyllshire Weavers Ltd., A. & J. Macnaughton Ltd. and Scottish Crofter Weavers Ltd.

At last the struggle between the Orb producers and Independent Harris Tweed Producers Ltd. had come into court. The legal proceedings in Britain were to be extremely complicated and extremely lengthy. However, while the IHTP challenge to the Orb had been gaining momentum in Britain, a closely related struggle between the Orb-producers and IHTP had been taking place in the United States. As some of the evidence connected with the legal challenge in the United States was relevant to the final decision in the Harris Tweed case of 1964, it will be necessary to trace events in America after 1956.

Reference - A Challenge to the Orb from the IHTP

1 *Daily News Record*, 8.10 1957.
2 See also C. E. M. Donaldson to Peter Thorneycroft in Chapter 13 'The RTSA and the Board of Trade' :- 'From the information supplied to me, and as far as is known by the National Association of Scottish Woollen Manufacturers, the Board of Trade has never defined or approved any definition of "Harris Tweed" other than that which sets out the minimum specification of "Harris Tweed" entitled to carry the "Orb" mark.' C. E. M. Donaldson, M.P. to The Rt. Hon. Peter Thorneycroft, M.P., President Board of Trade, 18. 11. 1954. HTA Office, Stornoway.
3 Hansard HC, 27 February, 1958, col. 519.
4 *ibid*.
5 *The Bulletin*, 3. 3. 1958.
6 Quoted in John S. Gwatkin, 'Notes on the Historical Development of the Harris Tweed Industry and the Part Played by the Harris Tweed Association Ltd. [hereafter: Gwatkin, 'The Harris Tweed Industry'], 80.
7 Roger Diplock, RTSA, to Roy Hale, Dorland Advertising Ltd., 15. 10. 1958. HRA/D190/ 1x(viii).
8 *ibid*., 22. 10. 1958.
9 Hansard HC, 21. 11. 1958 (Advertising Industry), 1524-1526.
10 *ibid*.
11 *Stornoway Gazette*, 9. 12. 1958.
12 Roger Diplock, RTSA to Malcolm MacMillan M.P., 1. 12. 1958. HTA Office, Stornoway.
13 *Argyllshire Weavers Ltd.and Others v. Macaulay (A.) (Tweeds) Ltd., and others* [1964] RPC No. 16, 477 [hereafter: 'Harris Tweed Case'], at 562.
14 *ibid*., 563.
15 *ibid*.
16 *Stornoway Gazette*, 28. 2. 1958.
17 *Scotsman*, 12. 11. 1958.
18 *Stornoway Gazette*, 14. 11. 1958.
19 *ibid*., 21. 11. 1958.
20 Memorandum regarding the Harris Tweed Association Ltd. HRA /D190/ lx(viii).
21 *ibid*.
22 *Scotsman*, 18. 11. 1958.
23 Gwatkin, c.1960, 'The Harris Tweed Controversy [hereafter: Gwatkin, 'Harris Tweed Controversy'], 49.
24 *ibid*., 50.
25 'Harris Tweed Case' [1964] RPC No. 16, 477, at 564.
26 Gwatkin, Harris Tweed Controversy, 50-51.

27 Copy of The Lord Lyon's response to IHTP petition. HRA/D190/ lx (viii).

28 'The whole device comprised a MacLeod bull's head in chief with a silver shuttle on Azure in Base and a fesse fretty', in the Judgement of Mr Justice Cross in the High Court of Chancery Division, 1. 2. 1961, in the case of A. Macaulay (Tweeds) Ltd. & Ors v. Independent Harris Tweed Producers Ltd., 5.

29 Copy of The Lord Lyon's response to IHTP Petition. HRA/ D190/ lx (viii).

30 Industry, Trade and Public Proofs, in *Argyllshire Weavers Ltd. and Others v. A. MacAulay (Tweeds) Ltd. and Others* (1964) Court of Session, Outer House: p.10, Proof from Alasdair MacLeod. HRA/D190/ lu (ii).

31 Notice of Opposition to Application for Registration of Trade Marks. HRA/D190 Iv [iv].

32 *ibid.*

33 Gwatkin, 'The Harris Tweed Industry', 96.

34 The agreed basis of all weaving was to be 2 shuttles and 18 shots per inch for standard weight 10-11 oz tweeds. The rates were: All weaves - 2 shuttles, 3/3d per weavers yard; 3 & 4 shuttles 3/4d; 5 & 6 - 3/5d; 2d per weaver's yard for every shot in excess of 18 per inch; 2/6d per tweed for beaming with tying-in and all other operations being the weaver's responsibility; 6d for every additional 12 threads or part thereof over 648 . It was agreed to adopt a standard output of 60 weaver's yards per week for 45 hours. Memorandum of Agreement between Hebridean Spinners Advisory Committee, Hebridean Producers Association, Other Producers and Transport and General Workers' Union, Harris Tweed Weavers' Section. HRA/D190/1V [iii).

35 Copy letter from E. T. Stevens, Secretary Independent Harris Tweed Weavers Ltd. HTA Office, Stornoway.

36 'Harris Tweed Case' [1964] RPC No. 16, 477, at 564.

37 Gwatkin, 'The Harris Tweed Industry', 94.

38 'Harris Tweed Case' [1964] RPC No. 16 , 477, at 564.

16

The Problems for the Orb in the USA

To follow the parallel campaign waged by mainland producers against the Orb mark in the United States, we have to go back to 1956 when American papers publicised the dispute between the RTSA and the HTA over the RTSA's advice to its members that tweed made from mainland-spun yarn was entitled to be called 'Harris Tweed'. This incident, which the *Daily News Record* of 26th March 1956 had headlined as 'Harris Tweed tag subject of high controversy in U. K.', [1] in all probability alerted officials of the Federal Trades Commission to the controversy. Eventually direct action emanating from Britain forced the FTC to scrutinise registration of the Orb mark in the United States. The controversy over what was or was not entitled to be called 'Harris Tweed' seems to have been relatively dormant for the best part of 1957, when, most unfortunately for the Harris Tweed Association, Stanley Brown, agent for the HTA in New York, unwittingly made a mistake which played right into the hands of the producers of unstamped Harris Tweed.

The crisis broke in London on 5th December 1957, when a copy of an advertisement inserted in the *Daily News Record* by Stanley Brown landed on the desk of Roger Diplock of the RTSA. The context in which the advertisements were placed was a significant achievement for the Harris Tweed Association in the United States. The aftermath to that achievement became a major source of embarrassment. Stanley Brown made a number of exaggerated claims about the status of the definition of Harris Tweed and of the Harris Tweed Association in his advertising copy. These claims were to provide valuable ammunition to the RTSA in London in their campaign against the HTA and to cause difficulties with the Federal Trade Commission in the United States.

In 1957 the US Government was under pressure from American wool growers to reduce the tariff quotas for woollen and worsted goods imported into the USA. The changed tariff decreed that in any one year, imports of woollen goods beyond 5% of the average annual production of similar goods in the United States, would be subject to an increased import duty. During the early part of 1957 there had been a rush by foreign manufacturers to get their woollen goods into the

United States before the date by which the quota, and therefore the higher tariff, came into effect. The Harris Tweed industry simply could not organise its production in such a way as to compete in this rush to beat the quota deadline. [2] Various manufacturers, such as Avoca Handwoven Irish Tweeds and the HTA, filed statements in support of their particular interests with the Interdepartmental Committee for Reciprocity Information. Japanese manufacturers asked for the quota to be increased to 6%, Avoca Handwoven Irish Tweeds and the HTA asked for exemption from duty for handwoven fabrics.

Because it was impossible for the Harris Tweed industry to cram its total production into the first three or four months of the year in order to beat the deadline when a higher tariff rate would come into effect, the HTA sent a member of its executive committee, the Rev. Murdoch Macrae, to put its case to a committee of the US Federal Trades Commission in Washington. Mr Macrae attended a meeting on 10th December 1957, to suggest to the FTC committee that, because Harris Tweed was a home industry making a single width cloth, it should be exempted from the higher tariff. Despite all the difficulties surrounding the meeting, that request was ultimately granted.

Some weeks before the meeting, Stanley Brown, the HTA agent in New York, had decided to insert two full page advertisements for Harris Tweed in the *Daily News Record*, the leading textile newspaper in New York. The first advertisement appeared on 8th October and the second on 12th November 1957. The copy in both advertisements contained serious inaccuracies: that on 8th October read:

> 'The term 'Harris Tweed' has been defined by the British Government Board of Trade ... ' ... 'The Harris Tweed Association ... is established by Special Charter of the British Board of Trade.' ... ' [3]

The November 12th advertisement repeated the mistakes in slightly different words:

> 'The above definition authorised by the British Board of Trade ... 'The Harris Tweed Association created by special charter of the British Board of Trade ... ' [4]

These statements, of course, went well beyond the bounds of accuracy.

The Board of Trade had made it quite clear to the HTA in 1954 that it had no power to make definitions or to place any definition on a statutory basis. That ruling ought to have been familiar to all agents acting on behalf of the Harris Tweed Association. Before placing the advertisements, Stanley Brown had submitted the copy to Andrew Graham, the Harris Tweed Association's US attorney, for approval. Both these gentlemen were under the impression that because the Harris Tweed Association was a Company limited by guarantee, it had been created by a 'Special Charter'. [5]

Although the meeting with the FTC had been pre-arranged to consider the tariff question, complaints made to the FTC by Roger Diplock of the RTSA about Stanley Brown's advertisement dominated the minds of those present. For the benefit of the FTC officials, Mr Macrae reviewed the background to the amended definition of 1934, the role of the Board of Trade in negotiating an acceptable definition at that time, and finally he explained why it was vital to the Hebridean economy that the terms of the definition should be maintained. It was noted that Mr Diplock's opinions and activities were not representative of the whole of British industry, and indeed, that some members of the RTSA stood to benefit if a watered down version of the definition of Harris Tweed were to be established. [6] Lest anyone who did not know the Rev. Murdoch Macrae should be surprised at the temerity of this minister from a remote island parish venturing to debate with officials of the FTC in Washington, it is worth recalling that Murdoch Macrae belonged to a community in which the close family ties of most people span the Atlantic. The accents of Washington and New York would be no more daunting to him than those of his parishioners in Lochs.

The extent of misunderstandings and partial knowledge in this incident is somewhat surprising. The edict from the HTA that all copy should thereafter be sent to McKenna & Co. in London for review was too late to deflect the repercussions which reverberated from the Retail Trading Standards Association, the Board of Trade, the House of Commons and the Federal Trade Commission in the United States.

Under the heading 'FTC Power to Act on Harris Tweed Ad is Uncertain', the *Daily News Record* described the reaction of the RTSA to the advertisements and the dilemma facing the Federal Trade Commission.

> 'The Federal Trade Commission may not have the authority to do anything about a protest against recent advertisements of Harris Tweed. ... Mr Diplock (of the Retail Trade Standards Association) objected to an ad placed by the Harris Tweed Association Ltd., London in the *Daily News Record,* Nov. 12. Under the heading 'There is Only One Harris Tweed' ... Mr Diplock attacked the exclusiveness of the definition and also questioned the Association's claim that it was 'created by special charter of the British Board of Trade'. He asked the FTC to investigate the ad. ... FTC officials ... explained, ... it was evident that before they can even consider the accuracy of the ad they must first settle a question of jurisdiction. ... '[7]

The initial task facing the FTC was to establish whether the HTA was 'engaged in commerce in the United States'. As a non-profit making organisation, the Association was, in fact, not engaged in trade or commerce. If this was established, then the FTC would be powerless to take action against the Association. The only recourse would be for the FTC to proceed against Stanley Brown in person, as he was an American citizen. The *Daily News Record* report went on to quote a British Embassy spokesman who said that Mr Diplock's group had been trying for some time to extend the definition of Harris Tweed to cover cloth woven outside the Hebrides. The Embassy feared that such broadening of the definition would lead to dilution of the trade mark and 'the sort of muddle we were in when the Harris Tweed label appeared on cloth not made according to the Association definition'. [8] Ominously, the report then pointed out that the FTC had been known to change its mind and that it might decide to reconsider the definition if it could be convinced that changing conditions had made it obsolete. [9]

In early January 1958, Stanley Brown reported to the HTA on the meeting with FTC officials in Washington on 10th December. [10] The report, in which one sentence runs to no less than fourteen typewritten lines, suggests that Stanley Brown was under considerable stress over the affair. Present at the meeting with the FTC in December were the HTA Attorney, Andrew Graham, Rev. Murdoch Macrae and Provost Alasdair Mackenzie from Stornoway who was in attendance as an observer. It is also worth noting the presence at this meeting of an FTC official, one Colonel Jess C. Radnor who was in charge of the FTC's trademark department. Within a very short time, Jess C. Radnor was to be crucially important in determining the attitude of the FTC towards the Harris Tweed Association. As with Mr Diplock, Col. Radnor's impartiality was open to question.

In his memorandum of 3rd January 1958 in which he too reported to the HTA on the December meeting with the FTC, Andrew Graham gave a robust defence of the definition which is worth quoting in part. He rejected the 'fly-specking criticism of the RTSA' and its 'dialectical exercise in hyper-technical semantics'. The memorandum continued:

> 'We are confident that the overwhelming majority of people in this country who have any familiarity at all with Harris Tweed know that it is a product of the Outer Hebrides made in accordance with the definition contained in the Association's certification mark. ... The term means what the definition says it means. If it is not a fabric produced in accordance with the definition then what is it? It is our firm conviction that if the definition of Harris Tweed is allowed to be diluted so that the term loses its primary significance, there will no longer be any justification for the existence of the Harris Tweed industry so far as the American market is concerned. ... Recently we have heard reports to the effect that ... an attempt is being made to create a secondary meaning for 'Harris Tweed'. ... If anyone who chooses can whittle away at the definition in England, we are in a very poor position here should we be forced to complain about some opportunistic mill owner in North Carolina who decided to imitate the general appearance of the fabric ... If steps are not taken in the British Isles to keep the definition intact, we predict without fear of contradiction that the Islanders will lose their American market.' [11]

Andrew Graham was not helped in his dealings with the FTC by the sudden death of Stanley Brown in early 1958. One cannot but wonder if the distress caused by the debacle had been a factor in Stanley Brown's death. Despite the loss of Stanley Brown, Andrew Graham continued to be a staunch and able advocate of the Orb mark in the protracted battle with Colonel Radnor and the FTC which began within the year. As a young attorney, Andrew Graham had been employed by the FTC, before joining Rogers, Roge and Hills, a firm which specialised in trade mark law. When working for the FTC, he had acquired personal knowledge of the history of the Harris Tweed industry and of the steps taken by the FTC to prevent infringement of the definition of Harris Tweed within the United States by the issuing of orders to 'cease and desist'. Defending the HTA against the complaint made by the RTSA to the FTC, Andrew Graham declared:

> 'I believe there is something very important at stake here. It is not whether the Association's charter is 'special' or whether the Board of Trade 'approved' or merely 'adopted' the definition. Underlying the complaint which has been made to the (Federal Trades) Commission is a concerted effort to break down the long accepted definition of Harris Tweed in order that some selfish individuals can make a few dollars at the expense of the welfare of the crofters in the Outer Hebrides. Frankly, I am incensed by what those selfish, commercial-minded people are trying to do.' [12]

From the correspondence between Andrew Graham and Colonel Radnor between 1958 and 1961, in conjunction with the evidence given by Colonel Radnor in January 1963 for the Harris Tweed Case, it becomes clear that the Harris Tweed Association was in serious danger of having to disclaim the words 'Harris Tweed' in their entirety, or have the registration of the Harris Tweed trade mark in the United States cancelled. For all that Colonel Radnor portrayed himself to Andrew Graham in that correspondence as the only person who was staving off an FTC decision to cancel registration of the Harris Tweed trade mark, it became apparent from his correspondence with Edwin T. Stevens, solicitor in Scotland for the IHTP, that his sympathies lay with the IHTP, even to the extent of providing that group with legal advice in the court cases in Britain over the trade mark in the early 1960s. [13]

After the embarrassment caused to the HTA by the inaccurate advertisements in late 1957, and the meeting with the FTC in early 1958, it seemed as if the Commission was disposed to take no further action on the matter of the Harris Tweed trade mark for the time being. For reasons which 'Commission policy did not permit him to divulge', Colonel Radnor began to investigate the validity of the HTA's certification registration just prior to February 1959, in order 'to determine whether a ground for cancellation of the certification registration as provided in Section 14 of the Trademark Act existed'. [14] It emerged later that Colonel Radnor had written in April 1959 to a firm of importers in New York stating that investigations were being made as a result of:

> 'a complaint that the Harris Tweed Association of England has taken action to prevent the importation into the United States of fabrics marked 'Harris Tweed' because they were not inspected and approved by the Harris Tweed Association. The complaints which have reached the Commission contend that the term 'Harris Tweed' is descriptive of a fabric made in the islands off Scotland by weavers who are not members of the Harris Tweed Association and do not subscribe to it but whose products meet the definition of 'Harris Tweed' as it is generically accepted in England and thus their products are entitled to be so labelled even though they have not been approved by the Harris Tweed Association.' [15]

The source of the complaint which led to the investigations is not identified, but the use of the words, 'weavers who are not members of the Harris Tweed Association' is significant. In August 1959, on the instructions of the FTC, Colonel Radnor wrote, informing Andrew Graham that:

> 'As a result of these investigations ... the Commission considers that it might be in the public interest to apply for cancellation of the Association's Certification Registration ... the matter has accordingly been returned to me with instructions to so advise you but to afford the Association an opportunity to voluntarily amend its registration in such a manner that will prevent its being used in the future to control the importation and sale of fabrics marked and described as 'Harris Tweed'.' [16]

Andrew Graham was given 60 days in which to indicate to the FTC whether he would entertain the proposed amendment. Whether Andrew Graham was stalling, or whether it took longer than three months for the HTA to make a decision on amendment, is not clear. Apart from a statement that the HTA did not wish to enter into controversy with the

FTC, no decision on amending the US Certification Mark had been made by the deadline of October 25th 1959. Instead, Andrew Graham offered to communicate with the US Customs authorities to make it clear that the registration of the Certification Mark was not deemed to entitle US Customs to prevent entry of goods bearing the words 'Harris Tweed', but without the (Orb) Certification Mark. [17]

This response was far from satisfactory to Colonel Radnor who had by 25th November reported to the FTC the failure of the HTA to agree to amending the Certification mark. Colonel Radnor replied to Andrew Graham saying:

> 'I have noted what you say regarding a proposal that we jointly discuss the matter with the Bureau of Customs and reach an agreement as to a definition of 'Harris Tweed'. ... The Commission would have no basis to request the Bureau of Customs to ignore a registrant's request such as filed by the Association, or any modification in its manner of administering the Tariff and Trademarks Acts. The Association's certification registration was the basis of Customs action in refusing entry of goods marked 'Harris Tweed'. We believe it was improperly obtained. That registration is capable of being used again to suppress competition and that possibility can be prevented only by cancellation or its amendment to reduce it to the 'orb' which is the only distinctive feature of the Association.' [18]

A number of points in this letter are worthy of note. Colonel Radnor's accusation of the HTA 'improperly obtaining' registration of the Certification trade mark was explained by him in a letter to Edwin Stevens of the IHTP in December 1959. The letter reveals how closely Colonel Radnor had become identified with the cause of the IHTP. Colonel Radnor writes:

> 'the Association's representative (Andrew Graham) avoided the requirement of the Patent Office Examiner that Harris Tweed be disclaimed by contending that it was the only association in the world authorised to certify genuine Harris Tweed. I intend to rely on that as 'fraud in procurement' which is a ground for cancellation of all registrations.' [19]

Radnor's accusation that the HTA avoided having to disclaim the words 'Harris Tweed' by falsely claiming to be 'the only association in the world authorised to certify genuine Harris Tweed' (a statement which was actually perfectly true and which was later shown to be true in the Harris Tweed case) was based on a declaration made to the US Commissioner of Patents in 1947 by W. H. Martin, then Secretary of the HTA, in an application for registration of the Harris Tweed trade mark in the U. S. The relevant parts of that Declaration stated:

> 'William Hubert Martin being duly sworn, deposes and says that he is Secretary of the Harris Tweed Association Limited ... that he believes that said corporation is the owner of the certification mark ... and that to the best of his knowledge and belief, no other person, firm, corporation or association, has the right to authorise the use of such mark, ... either in the identical form, or in such near resemblance thereto as might be calculated to deceive, the drawing and description (i. e. the words 'Harris Tweed') truly represent the certification mark sought to be registered ... and that the applicant itself is not engaged in the production or marketing of goods with which the mark is used ... .' [20]

An attempt was also made by Colonel Radnor to demonstrate that the Association was engaged in the marketing of goods on the basis of its promotion of Orb-stamped Harris Tweed. He informed Edwin Stevens:

> 'Our own investigation in the New York area will show that HTA has busied itself with promoting the sale of 'orb' goods and that should come under the prohibition against marketing the articles certified.' [21]

Colonel Radnor would seem to have been unaware that the objects for which the Harris Tweed Association had been established in 1909 were:

> 'the protection of the interests of manufacturers ... of tweed made in the Islands of Lewis, Harris and Uist in Scotland and to promote the manufacture and sale of such tweed. To protect the trade against offences under the Merchandise Acts and otherwise

to prevent the use of false trade marks and descriptions in respect of tweed made in imitation thereof.' [22]

It is difficult to avoid the impression that Colonel Radnor was seeking grounds for cancellation of the Harris Tweed Certification mark when we find him adding to these serious charges, Stanley Brown's careless use of the phrase 'the definition of Harris Tweed approved by the Board of Trade'. This was taken by Colonel Radnor to show that the HTA had

'represented the Board of Trade's approval as amounting to an official action by the British Government, adopting its definition of 'Harris Tweed' fabric and the HTA as the officially ordained body to decide - not what fabric was entitled to wear the 'orb' but what fabric was entitled to be called 'Harris Tweed'.' [23]

An explanation for Colonel Radnor's conviction that the HTA had been guilty of false procurement of its registration may well lie in his contacts with Roger Diplock and members of the IHTP. He wrote to Edwin Stevens saying:

' ... I am depending on the testimony of Mr Macnaughton, Mr Diplock and Mr Macnaughton of Los Angeles. I intend to introduce as relevant documents the little booklet on the industry in Scotland, the report of the questioning in Parliament, and if possible portions of the judge's opinion in the case against Veitch. I have asked Mr Diplock to see if he could get a letter from the Board of Trade addressed to him by the President of the Board of Trade stating just exactly what it had granted the HTA ... until Mr Diplock's complaint reached us we were not aware that any difference of opinion existed with respect to the place where the yarn was spun and dyed.' [24]

It must have been somewhat uncanny for the HTA to see the old skeletons of the Embargo case and the Scottish Council for Industry Report on Harris Tweed raising their heads again some twenty years later! Having been persuaded by Roger Diplock and members of the IHTP that unstamped Harris Tweed was as 'genuine' as Orb-stamped

Harris Tweed, it was not a huge step for Colonel Radnor to adopt the belief that the HTA and the Orb producers, whom he quite wrongly insisted on calling 'members of the HTA', [25] were a 'combination' or 'Trust', guilty of practices 'in restraint of trade' conduct which was forbidden under US Anti-Trust legislation, initiated by the Sherman Act of 1890.

The demand that the Harris Tweed trade mark should be reduced to no more than the Orb itself without the words 'Harris Tweed' seemed ludicrous to Andrew Graham who had argued all along that their use as part of the trade mark did not imply an exclusive right in the words. He had written to Radnor on this point in October saying:

> 'I can't understand why the Patent Office required the word 'tweed' to be disclaimed. There should have been no disclaimer whatsoever. The whole problem arises from the fact that some people just don't understand the true nature of the certification mark. The generic name of the thing certified is never considered to be part of the mark, but how on earth can you state what it is being certified without using the name of the thing which in our case is Harris Tweed. ... The Harris Tweed Association has never asserted any proprietary right to the words 'Harris Tweed'.' [26]

In essence, Andrew Graham's point was that the purpose of the certification trade mark was to signify that the Harris Tweed Association, the proprietor of the mark, certified that goods sold under it were genuine. This certification was indicated by the Orb (with the Cross). The words 'Harris Tweed' occurring underneath the Orb in the registered mark merely answered the question, 'Certified as genuine what?'. They did not mean that an unauthorised user of the words alone (without the Orb and Cross) could be sued by the HTA for infringement of the certification trade mark. However, this observation was without prejudice to any claim in respect of goods not conforming to the HTA's definition of 'Harris Tweed', provided that the claim was based on the common law of passing off, and not on the law of registered trade marks. [27]

Having rejected Andrew Graham's offer to discuss the trade mark with Customs officials, Colonel Radnor sent, at Andrew Graham's telephoned request, a formal Stipulation and Agreement which he required the Harris Tweed Association to sign on threat of proceeding to trial.[28] In essence the Stipulation and Agreement declared that the HTA was willing 'to take certain corrective actions to prevent further misuse of the Certification Registration'.[29] At this stage in the argument it was clear that the alternatives were for the Harris Tweed Association to fight the FTC in trade mark proceedings, which would probably have been lost, or to submit to the FTC demands. In a letter of 21st January 1960, Andrew Graham reported to Colonel Radnor that all of the actions which the Federal Trades Commission demanded had been taken. He enclosed a copy of the disclaimer of the word 'Harris' which had been filed in the Patent Office and a copy of his letter advising the Commissioner of Customs of the disclaimer. He closed with a postscript, saying that as the action provided for in the Stipulation had already been taken there would be no sense in having the Stipulation executed.[30]

Colonel Radnor was by no means satisfied with this! He replied with an indignant letter informing Andrew Graham that 'the Commissioner of Customs and his staff were completely bewildered' by his letter and did not know what it asked them to do! On checking with the Patent Office, Colonel Radnor had learned 'that an informal paper had been received regarding the Harris Tweed Association's Certification registration, but that it could not be accepted as a petition to amend in that it did not follow the prescribed practice and no amendment fee accompanied the submission'. This 'complete and utter failure of the Harris Tweed Association to take the necessary actions' left him 'without any excuse for postponing the filing of a petition to cancel the offending registration'.[31] The bewilderment of the Customs officials seems to have been caused by the fact that the relevant paragraph announcing the disclaimer of the word 'Harris' comes at the foot of the second page of a three-page letter in which Andrew Graham rehearses the same arguments against the need for a disclaimer which he had used unsuccessfully with Colonel Radnor.

Over the ensuing weeks of early 1960, exchanges between the two lawyers became increasingly tetchy, with Colonel Radnor continuing his threats to file for cancellation and only being restrained from doing so by the expressed wish of the Harris Tweed Association to avoid an adversary proceeding with the FTC. Eventually, on 16th February, a satisfactory version of the amendment of the registration of the Harris Tweed trade mark was lodged with the Patent Office and Colonel Radnor was informed that this would appear in the *Official Gazette* on 22nd March 1960. [32] As a result of the amendment to disclaim the word 'Harris', Customs officials were asked whether this meant that any woollen fabric could now clear Customs, regardless of its country of origin. The reply given was that 'the marking of wool fabrics as 'Harris Tweed' which were not handwoven in the Outer Hebrides of Scotland would constitute a false description under the Trademarks Act of 1946'. [33]

Within twenty-four hours of being advised of the filing of the disclaimer to the word 'Harris', Colonel Radnor wrote Andrew Graham asking whether, in view of the HTA's wish to avoid adversary proceedings, he would be willing to negotiate a Stipulation and Agreement regarding the advertising of Harris Tweed, as this complaint had been held in abeyance while the amendment to the trade mark was in progress. [34] A relatively non-committal reply from Andrew Graham, which expressed the hope that the FTC would offer the HTA an opportunity to negotiate, was copied to John Gwatkin of McKenna & Co. in London, for instructions. [35]

The inhibitions which Colonel Radnor sought to impose on the HTA in April 1960, were comprehensive. His letter portrays him as seeking to stand between the HTA and judicial action by the Federal Trade Commission over the 'misrepresentation' which had allegedly taken place. Colonel Radnor's belief was that the Harris Tweed Association had engaged in 'misrepresentation of its status, misrepresentation of its right to control the common descriptive term 'Harris Tweed', threats to sue others for misuse of a common descriptive term, and restraint of trade'. Some of these activities, he maintained to Andrew Graham, fell into a category which the Federal Trades Commission would not, as 'a matter of policy, dispose of by Stipulation'. Colonel Radnor was willing to attempt to have the Commission consider the matter on the basis of a Stipulation if he could indicate that the HTA had accepted and would execute a Stipulation including those inhibitions necessary to terminate the practices he mentioned in his letter. (See Appendix.) His only excuse for recommending a course which was in direct conflict with the FTC's normal policy was that, in the Trade Mark case, the Commission 'had first offered the Association an opportunity to voluntarily take corrective action before the Patent Office and the Bureau of Customs, instead of immediately petitioning to cancel the certification registration'. He emphasised that the letter was not a Commission offer to accept the attached inhibitions, or to settle the matter by Stipulation. It was simply an essential element in his own attempt to dispose of the case, despite the fact that by its nature a complaint should be issued. Naturally, he wished to be advised immediately if Andrew Graham felt unable to recommend that the HTA accept the inhibitions listed, as he had 'assumed personal responsibility' in preventing the case going to complaint. [36]

When news of Colonel Radnor's proposed inhibitions on all their normal promotion and protection of Harris Tweed reached the HTA in London, they felt that the best course of action was to send their lawyer, John Gwatkin of McKenna & Co., to Washington to discuss the matter with the FTC. Colonel Radnor advised Andrew Graham that unless Mr Gwatkin came with authority to enter into a Stipulation accepting the inhibitions on behalf of the Harris Tweed Association, his visit would not be worthwhile. [37] Clearly, the HTA had to send officials who had authority to act on its behalf and the decision was that the Chairman, George Ellis, and Colonel Macarthur were best fitted to discuss the matter with the FTC.

Judicial proceedings were staved off until Mr Ellis and Colonel Macarthur could visit Washington in the autumn of 1960. With Andrew Graham, they called on the FTC and received a hostile reception from Colonel Radnor. Andrew Graham had been informed that the file on the HTA certification mark had been passed to the Prosecuting Department of the FTC and he had been given to understand that, at that late stage, no discussions between the Investigating Department of the Commission (in which Colonel Radnor worked) and the Association could deter the Prosecuting Department from taking such action as it saw fit. It emerged some weeks after the visit by the HTA representatives that, in fact, the file had been passed back from the Prosecuting Department to the Investigating Department before their visit. This may suggest that the Prosecuting Department had been unsure of its ground in the matter. [38]

When planning the case which he hoped the FTC would take against the Harris Tweed Association, Colonel Radnor wrote to Edwin Stevens saying that he believed that the case would be unique, both procedurally and as a matter of substantive law regarding certification marks. Procedurally it would be unique because the evidence, in his view, would consist almost entirely of proof of the position and capabilities of the Harris Tweed Association in the United Kingdom. As a matter of substantive law, it would be the first decision defining the rights and obligations of a registrant of a certification mark as distinguished from an ordinary trade mark.[39] As it turned out, Colonel Radnor was to be disappointed when the FTC for reasons which are not apparent decided not to proceed against the Harris Tweed Association. In his judgement in the Harris Tweed Case, Lord Hunter dismissed Colonel Radnor's contention that the HTA had made a false statement in 1947 when its Secretary W. H. Martin declared that the HTA 'has functioned and now functions as the sole certifying authority in the entire world respecting the origin of Harris Tweed'.[40] Lord Hunter went on to dismiss all the other grounds on which Colonel Radnor had based his case for cancellation of the Harris Tweed trade mark in the United States.[41]

An apparent postscript to this affair took place towards the end of 1960, when the US Consul-General in Glasgow arrived in Stornoway, unannounced, and expressed a wish to see something of the islands and the Harris Tweed industry. His visit coincided with one from the Association Secretary, W. H. Martin. Apparently the two gentlemen were given VIP treatment by the Island producers, in the hope, no doubt, that, if the Consul-General's visit had been at the behest of the FTC, a favourable report on the industry would prevent further action. It is also possible that the FTC chose not to pursue the Stipulation in view of the action for passing off which had been raised in the High Court, Chancery Division, in England, on 6th July 1960, by a number of Orb-producers against Hepworths Ltd., Independent Harris Tweed Producers Ltd., Argyllshire Weavers Ltd. and Scottish Crofter Weavers Ltd.

Reference - The Problems for the Orb in the USA

1 See Chapter 13, The RTSA and the Board of Trade p.205.
2 Statement to Interdepartmental Committee for Reciprocity: Information submitted by the Harris Tweed Association Ltd. on behalf of the Harris Tweed industry in support of application for relief from the operation of the present Wool Fabric Tariff Quota, 20. 11. 1957. HRA/D190/ 3 (c).
3 *Daily News Record*, 8. 10. 1957.
4 *Daily News Record*, 12. 11. 1957.
5 Gwatkin, Notes on the Historical Development of the Harris Tweed Industry and the Part Played by the Harris Tweed Association Ltd. [hereafter: Gwatkin, 'The Harris Tweed Industry'], 79.
6 Memorandum and Opinion of Andrew J. Graham of Rogers, Roge and Hill of New York relating to the Status of the term 'Harris Tweed' in USA, 3. 1. 1958. HRA/D190/ 3a-d.
7 *Daily News Record*, 9. 12. 1957. HRA/D190/ 3 (c).
8 *ibid*.
9 *ibid*.
10 Review of complaint concerning Harris Tweed Advertising in the USA and the Definition of Harris Tweed, 3. 1. 1958. HRA/D190, 3a-d.
11 Memorandum and Opinion of Andrew J. Graham, Relating to the Status of the term 'Harris Tweed' in USA, 3. 1. 1958. HRA/D190/ 3a-d.
12 Andrew Graham to William Hill, FTC, 7. 3. 1958. HRA/D190/ 1n (i).
13 Jess C. Radnor to Edwin T. Stevens, 1. 3. 1961. HRA/D190/ 1n (i).
14 Interrogatories to be administered to Colonel Jess Covington Radnor by Charles Weigel, USA Commissioner appointed by Interlocutor of 8. 1. 1963 by the Hon. Lord Hunter in *causa Argyllshire Weavers et al. against A. Macaulay (Tweeds) Ltd. et al.* 28. 1. 1963, p. 4. HRA/D190/1aa [ii].
15 Jess C. Radnor, Bureau of Investigation, Office of Chief Project Attorney to E. Y. Stroud, Ltd. 200 Fifth Ave., New York, 9. 4. 1959. HTA Office, Stornoway.
16 Jess C. Radnor to Andrew Graham, 25. 8. 1959. HRA/D190/ 1n (i).
17 Andrew Graham to Jess Radnor, 16. 11. 1959. HRA/D190/1n (i).
18 Jess C. Radnor to Andrew Graham, 25. 11. 1959. HRA/D190/1 n (i).
19 Jess C. Radnor to Edwin Stevens, 29. 12. 1959. HRA/D190/1 n (i).
20 Statement and Declaration to the Commissioner of Patents from Harris Tweed Association, Ltd., 5. 8. 1947. HRA/D190/ 1n (ii).
21 Jess C. Radnor to Edwin Stevens, 29. 12. 1959. HRA/D190/1 n (i).
22 Memorandum and Articles of Association of the Harris Tweed Association Ltd, incorporated 9th December 1909. p.1.
23 Jess C. Radnor to Edwin Stevens, 1. 3. 1961. HRA/D190/1n (i).
24 Jess C. Radnor to Edwin Stevens, 29. 12. 1959. HRA/D190/1n (i).

25 Jess C. Radnor to Edwin Stevens, 1. 3. 1961. HRA/D190/1n (i).
26 Andrew Graham to Jess C. Radnor, 27. 10. 1959. HRA/D190/ 1n (i).
27 James A. McLean, Burness, Solicitors, Edinburgh, 9. 9. 1999.
28 Jess C. Radnor to Andrew Graham, 23. 12. 1959. HRA/D190/ 1n (i).
29 Stipulation as to the Facts and Agreement to Amend a Certificate Registration and Take Other Corrective Action in the Matter of Harris Tweed Association Ltd. FTC File 5910086. HRA/D190/1n (i).
30 Andrew Graham to Jess Radnor, 21. 1. 1960. HRA/D190/1n (i).
31 Jess C. Radnor to Andrew Graham, 5. 2. 1960. HRA/D190/1n (i).
32 Harold S. Carmen, Hervey Barber & McKee to Jess C. Radnor, 12. 2. 1960. HTA Office, Stornoway.
33 D. B. Strubinger, Acting Commissioner of Customs to William P. Flanders, Harris Tweed Association, Ltd., 295 Madison Ave., New York. HRA/D190/1 n (ii).
34 Jess C. Radnor to Andrew Graham, 17. 2. 1960. HRA/D190/1n (i).
35 Andrew Graham to Jess C. Radnor, 19. 2. 1960. HRA/D190/1n (i).
36 Jess C. Radnor to Andrew Graham, 21. 4. 1960. HRA/D190/n (i).
37 Jess C. Radnor to Andrew Graham, 5. 5. 1960. HRA/D190/ 1n (i).
38 Gwatkin, 'The Harris Tweed Industry', 1961, 100-102.
39 Jess C. Radnor to Edwin Stevens, 29. 12. 1959. HRA/D190/ 1n (i).
40 'Harris Tweed Case' [1964] RPC No. 16, 578.
41 *ibid.*, 578-584.

17

In Court at Last

Any possible connection between Champagne and Harris Tweed is not immediately obvious. Yet the decision in the so-called 'Spanish Champagne case' in December 1960 established a new rule of common law in regard to the offence of passing off. This case, properly called *J. Bollinger and others v. The Costa Brava Wine Company Ltd.*, was an action for passing off by the sale of Spanish sparkling wine as 'Spanish Champagne'. When the Costa Brava Wine Company Ltd. produced 'Champagne' in Spain and called it 'Spanish Champagne' they were, in effect, stealing the goodwill of French producers of Champagne.

A number of points relevant to Harris Tweed emerged during the 'Spanish Champagne case'. Firstly, this case established in law the concept of 'collective goodwill', which means that a group of producers could have a 'collective goodwill' in a particular description, in this case in the denomination 'Champagne'. Secondly, it was deemed that, although the informed section of the wine-drinking public might know the meaning of the term 'champagne', uninformed members of the public could be deceived. The fact that the wine trade, or the well-informed public, would not be deceived was irrelevant. Thirdly, if the passing off practised by the Costa Brava Wine Company had been allowed to continue unchecked, eventually the term 'champagne' would have become debased into a mere generic name. An injunction was granted to J. Bollinger and others to restrain the Costa Brava Wine Company Ltd. from passing off their Spanish sparkling wine as 'Champagne'.[1] This case opened the door to the use of the law of passing off to prevent the sale of Harris Tweed that did not conform to the 1934 definition which, as was demonstrated in court some four years later, had established what the public expected to get when they bought Harris Tweed. For this reason, the action raised in England in 1960 by a number of Orb producers of Harris Tweed against Hepworths Ltd., Independent Harris Tweed Producers Ltd., and three member companies of IHTP Ltd., was based on the grounds that the public was not getting what it expected to get.

To the layman, the sequence of legal cases between 1960 and 1965 was, and still is, somewhat difficult to follow. In essence, what happened was that, in the first instance, a number of Harris Tweed producers, A. Macaulay (Tweeds) Ltd., James Macdonald Ltd., Kenneth Mackenzie Ltd., Kenneth MacLeod (Shawbost) Ltd. and S. A. Newall & Sons Ltd., on behalf of themselves and all other Orb producers of Harris Tweed in the Outer Hebrides, raised an action of passing off against Hepworths Ltd., Independent Harris Tweed Producers Ltd., Argyllshire Weavers Ltd., A. & J. Macnaughton Ltd. and Scottish Crofter Weavers Ltd. The Orb producers (A. Macaulay (Tweeds) Ltd. and others) sued Hepworths Ltd. and others, for passing off, by selling, in England, tweed jackets labelled 'Harris Tweed'. The Orb-producers included Independent Harris Tweed Producers Ltd. as a defendant in this action because that company had authorised the use of the labels used by Hepworths Ltd. and had advertised the IHTP label in England. They also included the three IHTP producers, Argyllshire Weavers Ltd., A. & J. Macnaughton Ltd. and Scottish Crofter Weavers Ltd. in the action because these companies were named in the advertisements of the IHTP as suppliers of tweed under that label.[2] This initial action was commenced in England in the Chancery Division of the High Court of Justice. The case was heard before Mr Justice Cross.

While there is some danger in simplifying the sequence of events and in reducing to the absolute minimum the arguments put forward for both sides in the dispute, anyone who wishes to follow the detail of the cases should consult the relevant reports which are cited in the references for this chapter. Counsel for the defendants, that is for Hepworths, the IHTP and the three IHTP producers named above, put forward a number of reasons as to why the action should not proceed. For all practical purposes, the most important of their reasons for arguing that the case should not proceed was concerned with the jurisdiction of an English court over themselves as Scottish defendants. Their Counsel argued that this was 'essentially a Scottish dispute and that it could be tried more cheaply in Scotland'.[3] Mr Justice Cross did not accept the arguments put forward by the IHTP producers on the question of jurisdiction of an English court over themselves as Scottish companies. He held that the Orb producers, A. Macaulay & Others, did have an arguable case upon the passing off, and that therefore the action was properly brought. He also held that all the defendants, whether based in Scotland or in England, were proper parties to the action.[4]

These decisions issued on 1st February 1961 by Mr Justice Cross would simply have enabled the action of passing off to go ahead in the Chancery Division of the High Court of Justice. It is important to realise that Mr Justice Cross did not give a decision on the merits of the action of passing off at this stage. The decisions issued by Mr Justice Cross in February 1961 were given on what Lord Hunter later described as 'the preliminary proceedings in the Chancery Division of the High Court of Justice'. [5] In the hope of preventing that action in the Chancery Division from going any further, and because they reckoned that they had a better chance in Scotland, the three member companies of the IHTP, Argyllshire Weavers Ltd., A. & J. Macnaughton Ltd. and Scottish Crofter Weavers Ltd. plus Macdonald's Tweeds Ltd. of Oban, went on the offensive and raised an action in the Court of Session in Scotland before Lord Hunter against fourteen Orb producers of Harris Tweed, Kemp & Company (Stornoway) Ltd. (a dyeing and finishing company) and the Harris Tweed Association Ltd. (See Appendix.)

While the action commenced in England by the Orb producers had been based on the law of passing off, the case raised in Scotland at the instance of the individual member companies of the IHTP, asked the court to declare (1) that Independent Harris Tweed Producers Ltd. were entitled to describe their product as 'Harris Tweed' and (2) to interdict the Orb producers and the Harris Tweed Association from wrongfully asserting, in Scotland or elsewhere, that IHTP-produced tweed was not properly described as 'Harris Tweed'. The Orb producers, who were the defenders in the Scottish action raised against them by member companies of the IHTP, argued that as the same issue was already pending before the High Court in England, the action raised in Scotland should be dismissed or alternatively, *sisted*, that is, temporarily suspended, to await the decision in the action of passing off raised by themselves in England. [6]

Clearly, before considering the merits of the case, the judge, Lord Hunter, had to decide whether the action should be heard in Scotland or in England. The IHTP companies had contested the jurisdiction of the English court and the Orb producers had contested the jurisdiction of the Scottish court. The point at issue was, should the case being heard in the Court of Session in Scotland go ahead or await the decision in the High Court in England? The decision in the first instance was primarily concerned with points of law, rather than with the dispute between the IHTP companies and the Orb producers over a definition of 'Harris Tweed'.

Most of the reasons given by Lord Hunter for his decision on 17th November 1961, that the case should be heard in Scotland rather than in England, are of interest principally to lawyers. For example, one reason given stated that the Scottish action had 'priority' because it had reached a more advanced stage than the English action 'by a narrow margin of three days'. Another reason given, which was of more interest to the general public, was that the composition of the parties involved in the dispute had changed. [7] Macdonald's Tweeds Ltd. of Oban had not been party to the action in England, but had joined Argyllshire Weavers Ltd., A. & J. Macnaughton Ltd., and Scottish Crofter Weavers Ltd., as one of the pursuers in the Scottish action. Hepworths Ltd., and Independent Harris Tweed Producers Ltd. (as a company) were not parties to the Scottish action. This meant that the dispute was, in fact, between a group of mainland producers (the first named being Argyllshire Weavers Ltd.,) and a group of Orb producers (the first-named being A. Macaulay (Tweeds) Ltd.). For convenience and brevity the parties to the action in Scotland will henceforth be referred to as the mainland producers and the Orb producers. Finally, Lord Hunter held that, although there were issues in common between the Scottish and English actions, the Scottish action was 'designed to have a wider geographical effect' and, if the interdict sought by the pursuers (Argyllshire Weavers and others, the mainland producers) was granted, it 'would provide them with a different remedy from that sought in England'. [8] Therefore the plea by the Orb producers (A. Macaulay (Tweeds) Ltd. and others) that the action raised against them in Scotland by the mainland producers should be dismissed, or alternatively *sisted* (temporarily suspended) to await the decision of the English court, was refused. The mainland producers thus appeared to have won the first round.

As the decision by Lord Hunter that the case should be heard in Scotland had gone against them, the Orb producers appealed against this decision. The appeal was heard by Lord Clyde, Lord Carmont and Lord Guthrie and on 26th May 1962, the decision of the appeal court also went against the Orb producers. While accepting that, in certain circumstances, priority might be the criterion for deciding whether an English or Scottish court was the more appropriate forum in the litigation between these producers of 'Harris Tweed', a more important criterion was that,

> 'the parties concerned in the dispute as to the meaning of Harris Tweed are almost all Scottish companies. The manufacturing operations in issue take place wholly in Scotland. The evidence will, obviously, to quite a substantial extent, be drawn from the remoter areas of Scotland. All these considerations point strongly to the appropriateness of refusing a sist (a temporary suspension) in the present action.' [9]

Lords Carmont and Guthrie agreed with the Lord President, Lord Clyde, that the appeal by the Orb producers to have the action in Scotland dismissed, or alternatively temporarily suspended, should be refused. Thus Lord Hunter's decision that the case should be heard in Scotland was affirmed by the appeal court. The mainland producers seemed to have won the second round!

By May 1962 when the decision on the appeal by the Orb producers was announced, the litigation between the mainland producers and the Orb producers had been underway for the best part of two years. Naturally, it had caused a measure of interest in legal circles as well as in the Highlands and Islands. At that stage of the litigation, nearly all Scottish legal opinion believed that the Harris Tweed Association was an English company taking advantage of the Harris Tweed industry by trying to prevent Scottish companies doing what Scottish companies had been doing for generations. The general perception in Scotland was that the merits of the case were entirely in favour of the mainland producers. This perception was partly a hangover from vague memories of the 1934 dispute over the definition of Harris Tweed, then the Embargo Case and more recently the impression created by the complaints from the RTSA that the Harris Tweed Association had been involved in sharp practice in the American markets. Everybody was very dubious as to the prospects of success for the Orb producers.

Direction of the action on behalf of the Orb producers was in the hands of McKenna & Co. who had been solicitors for the Harris Tweed Association ever since it was first registered in England in 1909. When Argyllshire Weavers Ltd., and the other mainland producers raised an action against the Orb producers in Scotland it became necessary for the Orb producers and the Harris Tweed Association to have legal representation in Scotland. On 20th February 1961, all the defenders, i.e. the Orb producers, signed a document authorising the Harris Tweed Association to instruct W. & J. Burness, W.S., to defend them in the proceedings brought against them by Argyllshire Weavers, Ltd., A. & J. Macnaughton Ltd., Scottish Crofter Weavers Ltd. and Macdonald's Tweeds Ltd. Solicitors for the pursuers, i.e. the mainland producers, were J. Miller Thomson & Co., W.S. Both sets of Scottish solicitors then instructed Counsel to conduct the case on behalf of their clients in the Court of Session. W. R. Grieve Q.C. represented the mainland producers who were the pursuers in the action. The Orb producers, who were the defenders in the action, were represented in the first instance by R. S. Johnston, Q.C., later Lord Kincraig. He was succeeded by W. McIlwraith, Q.C. whose patient advocacy in the face of hostility did much to persuade the court of the Orb producers' cause.

The 'Harris Tweed case' as it came to be known, was, at the time, one of the longest cases in Scottish legal history. Preparation for the case, the defenders' request that the action in Scotland be dismissed or alternatively sisted, the appeal on Lord Hunter's decision that the case should be heard in Scotland, the adjustment of pleadings by both parties, the collecting of evidence and the taking of depositions took many months. When the preliminary procedures had been completed, the case opened in the Court of Session before Lord Hunter on 29th January 1963 and continued until June 1963 when Counsel for both sides began to address the court on the evidence. This stage of the proceedings lasted until July 1963 when the case was taken to *avizandum* (private consideration of a case by a judge before giving judgement). Lord Hunter's judgement was issued in July 1964.

The Report on the Harris Tweed case [10] provides not only a careful analysis of the issues in dispute in the early 1960s, but also a concise history of the Harris Tweed industry from its origins in the mid-nineteenth century up to circa 1961. The information provided in the Report has been of immense value to the writer of this book. The length of the report is such that only a brief summary of the case can be given here.

The main objects sought in the action brought by the mainland producers were:

> (1) 'for declaration that the pursuers (the mainland producers) were entitled to produce, process and market as 'Harris Tweed' cloth made from pure virgin wool produced in Scotland, dyed and spun in the Outer Hebrides or elsewhere in Scotland, handwoven by the islanders in the Outer Hebrides and finished in the Outer Hebrides or elsewhere in Scotland as Harris Tweed and (2) to interdict the defenders, (the Orb producers) or anyone on their behalf, from wrongfully asserting, in Scotland or elsewhere, that the pursuers' (the mainland producers') production, processing, marketing and disposal in Scotland or elsewhere as Harris Tweed of cloth made from pure wool produced in Scotland, dyed and spun in the Outer Hebrides or elsewhere in Scotland, handwoven in the Outer Hebrides and finished in the Outer Hebrides or elsewhere in Scotland, was not the production, processing, marketing and disposal of Harris Tweed.' [11]

In short, the mainland producers were asking the court (1) to declare that the product made in accordance with the definition which had been adopted by the IHTP on its formation in 1958 was entitled to be called 'Harris Tweed' and (2) to forbid any person anywhere from saying that such a product was not entitled to be called Harris Tweed. The IHTP definition differed of course from the 1934 definition of Harris Tweed in maintaining that the processes of dyeing, spinning, and finishing could be carried out in the Outer Hebrides or elsewhere in Scotland. On the other hand:

> 'The defenders (the Orb producers) contended that it was essential for all these processes to be carried out in the Outer Hebrides, as required in the definition of 'Harris Tweed' laid down by the amended Regulations of 1934 governing the use of 'The Harris Tweed Trade Mark' otherwise known as the 'Orb' and that hand weaving should be carried out by the Islanders at their own homes.' [12]

When the judgement was issued in July 1964, it became clear from quite an early stage that the tenor of Lord Hunter's remarks were not what the mainland producers might have hoped for. Comparing the IHTP definition with the Orb definition, he noted that both definitions included the requirement for 'pure virgin wool produced in Scotland'. He went on to point out that until 1959, 'all the pursuers (the mainland producers) to a greater or lesser degree were using non-Scottish wool in the production of cloth which ... reached the eventual purchaser under the name of 'Harris Tweed'.'[13] A little later, commenting on the phrase 'in the Outer Hebrides or elsewhere in Scotland', in the IHTP definition, Lord Hunter described it as being 'nothing more than an elaborate way of saying 'in Scotland',' and again as a 'portmanteau phrase ... (which) might convey the picture of the Long Island stretching romantically from the Butt of Lewis to Barra Head, rather than the more mundane enchantments of Paisley or Galashiels, or even Oban, Pitlochry or Aberdeen'. Lord Hunter clearly felt that the repeated use of the phrase 'in the Outer Hebrides' in conjunction with the words 'or elsewhere in Scotland' had some ulterior purpose and that the mainland producers' explanation of the use of the words was less than convincing and even a little less than candid.[14] Finally, before turning to the history of the industry, he commented on the importance of the phrase 'handwoven by the Islanders at their own homes' in the Orb definition and contrasted this with the IHTP definition which merely said 'handwoven by the Islanders in the Outer Hebrides'. He believed that 'the practical and social consequences of the inclusion' in the Orb definition of the words 'at their own homes' were, or should be, far-reaching.[15] All these pointers may well have been seen at an early stage as indicative of the final outcome of the case.

On finishing his summary of the history of the Harris Tweed industry, Lord Hunter expressed his regret that justice had hardly been done to the huge volume of information with which the court had been provided. It is a sentiment echoed by the writer and, no doubt, by all those who sat through the hearing. Turning to the request made by the pursuers, (the mainland producers), for a declarator that tweed made to the IHTP definition was entitled to be called 'Harris Tweed', Lord Hunter said:

> 'In my opinion a declarator in the form sought by the pursuers cannot be granted in the light of the evidence led. The parties to the present action are agreed that 'Harris Tweed' has not become a purely generic name ... and this is conclusively established by the evidence.'[16]

By careful examination of witnesses from the retail clothing trade and the general public, W. McIlwraith Q.C. had demonstrated the essential point that whatever they did in mainland mills, the public still expected the 1934 definition of Harris Tweed as a bare minimum. In fact they really expected Harris Tweed to be handwoven, handspun and hand-dyed. They certainly expected Harris Tweed to be a complete product of island industry, which the Orb definition required and the IHTP definition did not. While discussing the differences in the respective definitions, Lord Hunter returned to the importance of the use in the Orb definition of the phrase 'handwoven at their own homes', a point made at the beginning of his judgement. He contrasted this phrase with the IHTP formula which had been made sufficiently elastic to accommodate the hand-weaving on concentrations of looms done in sheds, mills or factories, such as was carried out by Macdonald's Tweeds Ltd. in South Uist. [17] The significance attached by Lord Hunter to the phrase 'handwoven at their own homes' encapsulated those features which have made Harris Tweed a distinctive product from its origins in the homes of Lord Dunmore's tenants until the present day. Lord Hunter said:

> 'The evidence satisfies me that part of the reputation which Harris Tweed enjoys and has for long enjoyed with the purchasing public is based on the fact that it is not only a product of the Outer Hebrides, but also the product of a cottage or home industry. This part of the reputation of the material now survives very largely on the strength of the hand-weaving process, but I am satisfied from the evidence that in the mind of the purchasing public, and indeed also in the mind of the trade, it is an important factor and an important selling point that the main surviving hand-process should be carried out, not under factory conditions, but at the home, at the cottage, at the 'croft' ... The conception of a home or cottage product has always in my opinion been a very important selling point of the genuine article. ... the fact remains that one reason why producers and sellers of cloth, including the pursuers, are so anxious to make use of the name is its reputation as a home or cottage product. It is felt, and in my opinion rightly felt, by those who purchase Harris Tweed that they are assisting the inhabitants of remote islands to supplement the bare living which they are able to wrest from the soil or the sea by engaging in their own time in weaving, not necessarily actually inside their home, but in its reasonably close vicinity.' [18]

In the by-going, it is worth mentioning that the weaving sheds at Inaclete Road used by weavers in Local Authority houses in Stornoway had provided Counsel for the mainland producers with grounds for claiming that the Orb stamp had been 'fraudulently' applied to tweeds woven in these sheds. [19] Lord Hunter considered that 'in a very small number of cases' the HTA stampers had interpreted the words 'at their own homes' too widely, but that it would be stretching matters too far to hold that the reputation of Harris Tweed had been built up dishonestly by these few instances. [20] He also said that he was satisfied from the evidence that the 'cottage' or 'home' or 'croft' aspect of the production of genuine Harris Tweed had never been materially departed from in relation to the handweaving process. [21]

Expanding on his reasons for refusing the declarator requested by the mainland producers, Lord Hunter expressed the view that the evidence had established that, to be legitimately described and marketed as Harris Tweed, a tweed must at least conform to the requirements of the 1934 definition, and that the reputation of the genuine article with the purchasing public depended on it being a handwoven tweed wholly made, manufactured and produced in the Outer Hebrides from 100% pure Scottish virgin wool, and that the name 'Harris Tweed' had become distinctive of a tweed so made and manufactured. Despite having been produced in accordance with the IHTP definition, the product of the mainland producers fell short of conforming to those requirements, the cloth produced by Macdonald's Tweeds Ltd., under factory conditions in South Uist, falling furthest short of them. Lord Hunter considered that the wording of the declarator requested by the mainland producers was, like their operations, 'a mere device designed to enable them, by attaching the name 'Harris Tweed' to their product, to use the reputation attaching to the genuine article and to pass off their goods as the goods of other manufacturers and producers'. He concluded this part of the judgement by saying:

> 'I should be sorry to think that the law of Scotland is unable to give protection to a class of producers ... in a locality or region, such as was provided by the English court in *J. Bollinger v. Costa Brava Wine Co. Ltd.* and I should not hesitate to follow the reasoning of that decision if I considered that the description of the present action by Counsel for pursuers as a 'passing off action in reverse' was accurate, rather than merely plausible.' [22]

Having dismissed the request for a declarator that tweed produced in accordance with the IHTP definition was entitled to be called 'Harris Tweed', Lord Hunter moved on to consider the request for interdict. It would seem self-evident to the layman that if the request for declarator had failed the request for interdict would also fail and that is what happened. [23] Nonetheless, Lord Hunter wished to deal with the elaborate arguments presented on both sides. While his comments on these arguments are of considerable interest, particularly as they refute the charges made by the mainland producers of dishonesty by the HTA in the registration of its Certification Mark in the United States, [24] Lord Hunter concluded this section of the judgement by saying:

> '... There is in my opinion, no proof of any admission made by, or on behalf of the HTA, that they made any of the statements complained of in Article 3 of the Condescendence either falsely or maliciously, nor is there in my opinion any evidence from which a fraudulent course of conduct on the part of the HTA can justifiably be inferred.' [25]

The final matter to be dealt with was a claim by the mainland producers that the Orb-producers had intended to cause them 'pecuniary damage' when they had disparaged IHTP cloth by saying that it was not genuine Harris Tweed and as such was an inferior article. The mainland producers asserted that they were entitled to claim damage in respect of 'this slander'. [26] Lord Hunter took the view that the evidence had shown that a statement by the Orb producers that IHTP tweed was not genuine Harris Tweed was in fact true, and that there was no proof of malice on the part of the Orb producers in any such statement made by them or the Harris Tweed Association. [27] Lord Hunter then concluded by saying:

> 'I have accordingly reached the conclusion that none of the specific wrongs said to have been done or threatened to the pursuers (the IHTP producers) by the defenders (the Orb producers) have been established by the evidence, nor in general am I satisfied that the pursuers have established any grounds on which the interdict sought by them ought to be granted. It follows that the conclusion for interdict fails as well as that for the declarator.' [28]

Although Argyllshire Weavers Ltd., Scottish Crofter Weavers Ltd., and Macdonald's Tweeds, Ltd., (these three companies having merged into Grampian Textiles Ltd. circa 1960) [29] and A. & J. Macnaughton Ltd., had decided to appeal when Lord Hunter's judgement went against them, the appeal was abandoned relatively quickly. A press statement issued in November 1964 announced that IHTP Ltd. and its member companies, had agreed to abandon their appeal, and that IHTP would go into voluntary liquidation. The statement added 'The litigation in Scotland between the producers of Harris Tweed in the Outer Hebrides and the mainland producers is thus concluded'. [30]

The action raised in England by A. Macaulay (Tweeds) Ltd., representing all the Orb-producers, had been held in abeyance during the Scottish case. A decision in this action was given by Mr Justice Cross in January 1965 whereby injunctions were granted against the defendants (IHTP and their member companies) restraining them from passing off as Harris Tweed any cloth which did not conform to the Orb definition. [31] Although the Scottish case is the one remembered, it would be fair to say that the English case was, in fact, just as important as the 1964 Harris Tweed case, because it had the effect of stopping anyone from selling as 'Harris Tweed' anything which did not conform to the Orb standards, i.e. it gave the Orb producers a positive weapon. The Harris Tweed case was, in a sense negative, based as it was on the Orb producers being the defendants. A spokesman for the HTA said that the Harris Tweed Association's definition of Harris Tweed had thus been upheld in the Courts of both countries. The name 'Harris Tweed' had been preserved for the Outer Hebrides, to the benefit of the many families whose welfare depended on the Harris Tweed industry. [32]

There were many loose ends to be tied up in the immediate aftermath of Lord Hunter's decision in July 1964. The IHTP companies were required to inform the Retail Trading Standards Association, the National Association of Scottish Woollen Manufacturers, the International Wool Secretariat and the Federal Trades Commission that they accepted the opinion contained in Lord Hunter's judgement that, to be legitimately described as 'Harris Tweed', a tweed had to conform to the Orb definition. They were also required to withdraw all charges of bad faith made against the HTA, to withdraw applications lodged by them with the Registrar of Trade Marks, and to revoke an application by them to the Board of Trade for withdrawal of the HTA Certification Mark. [33]

Partly as a result of the Harris Tweed case and its attendant publicity, or perhaps partly because the market was in one of its cyclical boom periods anyway, sales of Harris Tweed increased between 1964 and 1967 by over one and a half million yards. It is arguable that the most significant legacies of the litigation lay in the recognition by the industry of two fundamental principles. The first of these was the vital importance of the buyer's understanding of what was meant by the name 'Harris Tweed'. The evidence in the Harris Tweed case showed that the buying public understood Harris Tweed to be a wholly island-made product. Their understanding of the term 'Harris Tweed' was a general, but reasonably accurate, awareness of the requirements laid down in the 1934 definition. There can be little doubt that many degrees of deception took place in the marketing of 'unstamped Harris Tweed'. Deception varied from silence, - the less you tell the customer the better [34] - to calculated attempts to mislead the customer, - 'our tweed has been purchased direct from the crofter' - when such a statement was totally untrue. [35] When these machinations were shown by the evidence to be no more than subterfuges to deceive the customer by purloining the reputation of genuine Harris Tweed, the whole basis of the case for the IHTP companies was seen to be untenable. Thus the litigation put an end to attempts to deceive the buying public by passing off something other than the genuine article as 'Harris Tweed'. The second principle which could be seen as a legacy of the litigation was recognition by all those concerned with the industry of the vital importance of maintaining the craft status imparted to Harris Tweed by 'handweaving at the weaver's own home'. [36] Lord Hunter's emphasis on that phrase provided a warning that bringing the craft status of the industry into question would re-open the door to the abuses which had dogged the industry throughout the first half of the twentieth century. It is therefore surprising that by the mid-1970s, the HTA were considering the introduction of power-weaving in community weaving sheds!

While the total outlawing of mainland-spun yarn in the manufacture of Harris Tweed may have been seen by some as a factor in the eventual demise of the small independent producers, the likelihood is that this section of the industry was going to succumb, sooner rather than later, to increasing competition in the textile market. Market conditions over the twenty years after the Harris Tweed case brought about a gradual contraction in the Harris Tweed industry which eventually squeezed out many of the large producers. In the harsh economic climate which lay only a decade ahead, the days of small independent producers in every village making a good living from Harris Tweed were bound to be numbered. Had the HTA not challenged the IHTP when it did, the probability is that the production of Harris Tweed would have disappeared quite quickly from the Islands to the mainland as economies of scale became the only means of survival.

Reference - In Court at Last

1 *J. Bollinger and Others v. The Costa Brava Wine Company Ltd.*, [1961] RPC No. 5, 116 at 117. ('The Spanish Champagne Case').

2 *Macaulay, (A.) (Tweeds) Ltd., & Ors. v. Independent Harris Tweed Producers Ltd., and Others*, [1961] RPC No. 8, 184. (This was the action raised by the Orb Producers against IHTP Ltd. and Hepworths Ltd. in England in the High Court, Chancery Division before Mr Justice Cross).

3 *ibid.*, 186.

4 *ibid.*, 184.

5 *Argyllshire Weavers Ltd. and Others v. A. Macaulay (Tweeds) Ltd., & Others*, Outer House (Lord Hunter), 1962 SLT 25 at 29. [hereafter: 'Harris Tweed Case, 1961'].

6 *ibid.*, 25.

7 *ibid.*, 29-30.

8 *ibid.*, 30.

9 *Argyllshire Weavers Ltd. and Others v. A. Macaulay (Tweeds) Ltd., and Others*, 1962 SLT 310 at 312. (This is the decision by Lord President Clyde, Lords Carmont and Guthrie, on the Appeal by A. Macaulay (Tweeds) Ltd. and Others against Lord Hunter's decision on jurisdiction of the Scottish Court).

10 *Argyllshire Weavers Ltd. and Others v. Macaulay (A.) (Tweeds) Ltd., and Others*, [1964] RPC No. 16, 477 [hereafter: 'Harris Tweed Case'].

11 *ibid.*, 477.

12 *ibid.*, 478.

13 *ibid.*, 482.

14 *ibid.*, 483.

15 *ibid.*, 484.

16 *ibid.*

17 *ibid.*, 566.

18 *ibid.*, 566-67.

19 *ibid.*, 568.

20 *ibid.*

21 *ibid.*, 504.

22 *ibid.*, 569.

23 *ibid.*, 572.

24 *ibid.*, 576-84.

25 *ibid.*, 584.

26 *ibid.*, 590.

27 *ibid.*, 591.

28 *ibid.*

29 Copy of Settlement Document prepared by W. & J. Burness on behalf of the defenders in the Scottish action (the Orb Producers) to Messrs J. Miller

Thomson & Co. acting for the pursuers in the Scottish action, offering to conclude all outstanding matters between the defendants and Grampian Textiles Ltd., as successors to certain of the pursuers in the Scottish action, Independent Harris Tweed Producers Ltd., and Hepworths Ltd., 12. 11. 1964. [hereafter: 'Settlement Document, 12. 11. 1964']. HTA Office, Stornoway.

30 *Stornoway Gazette*, 21. 11. 1964.

31 McKenna & Co. immediately informed all interested parties of the decision given by Mr Justice Cross in the English action which concluded the litigation on 26th January, 1965. These 'interested parties' included Stornoway Pier and Harbour Commission. Letter from McKenna & Co. on 27. 1. 1965 in HTA Office, Stornoway.

32 *Stornoway Gazette*, 6. 2. 1965.

33 'Settlement Document', 12. 11. 1964. HTA Office, Stornoway.

34 'Harris Tweed Case' [1964] RPC No. 16, 477, at 551.

35 *ibid.*, 553.

36 *ibid.*, 504.

18

The Domestic Scene: 1960 to 1970

Although the protracted litigation with IHTP Ltd. was of prime importance to the Harris Tweed industry as a whole, there were other events which must have seemed of more immediate significance to the industry in the islands between 1960 and 1970. Confidence in the future of Harris Tweed was sufficiently high in the late 1950s for three firms to expand. Kenneth MacLeod (Shawbost) had finishing plant under construction which was expected to come into operation in 1960. In 1966 this firm opened the first dyeing, carding and spinning mill outside Stornoway. Stephen Burns Ltd. were about to install carding and spinning plant with a capacity of about 6,000 lbs of yarn per week near their existing premises. This mill was officially opened by the Secretary to the Board of Trade in 1963. A. J. and H. Maclean (Labost) Ltd. had carding, spinning and finishing plant in operation with a spinning capacity of 2000 lbs of yarn per week. [1] Despite the optimism which prevailed among producers at the beginning of the decade, fundamental change in the structure of the mills was on the horizon by 1970. External factors such as tariff discrimination between Britain and EEC countries, an increase in the US tariff from 25% to 38% [2] a period of severe economic restraint in the mid-sixties, a move towards automation in pattern-cutting which put single width tweed at a disadvantage, and the growing popularity of man-made textiles, all forced the Harris Tweed industry to adapt to changing circumstances.

The most pressing problems in the industry were an apparent inability to recruit young men into weaving and dissatisfaction with the methods of distributing tweeds to weavers. The perception was that the mills favoured weavers nearer to Stornoway, leaving weavers at a greater distance short of work when orders were slack. There was also the on-going complaint by Independent Producers that the cost of yarn from the mills was so high that they made little or no profit on their tweeds. Yet this was the decade which saw production reach a peak of over seven and a half million yards in 1966, a figure which had never been seen before and was never to be seen again. In 1966 the Export magazine *Ambassador* recognised the outstanding contribution of the industry to Britain's export drive with one of its annual awards.[3] The ten year average for the decade was close on six million yards, despite a drastic drop in production of 2 million yards in 1967.

Because there is a scarcity of written references to the industry in Harris as opposed to the industry in Lewis, it would be all too easy to forget that Harris was still making a significant contribution to overall production, despite the overwhelming difficulty of poor communication links with its larger neighbour in the north. Through lack of alternative forms of employment, the original important ethos of the 'crofter-weaver' continued to be stronger in Harris than in Lewis. Just after the Second World War, the Harris Crofters' Association was established by Colonel Douglas Walker, who had come to Borve Lodge in south Harris in the mid-1930s. Colonel Walker, himself a veteran of the First World War, had a personal as well as an altruistic motive for setting up the HCA. As both his own sons had died in the war, he wanted to extend his help to those ex-servicemen from Harris who would be coming home. Well aware of the desperate economic conditions in Harris before the outbreak of war, he felt that in forming the Harris Crofters' Association he was helping crofters in Harris to help themselves by supplementing their income from crofting with an income from weaving Harris Tweed.

Approximately 400 shares of £1 each were issued and Colonel Walker arranged an overdraft with his bank to get the HCA started. A selection of traditional patterns woven by a local weaver was sent to potential buyers in Britain and abroad. In due course, orders for particular patterns came in. Hand-spinning had been the norm in Harris before the war and Colonel Walker started by buying carded wool, *rollagan* (slivers or rovings in English), from the carding mill at Lòn na Fèille at Direcleit, just south of Tarbert. This carded wool was sent out to local hand-spinners. When the handspun yarn was returned to the headquarters at Borvemòr, the spinners were paid per pound of yarn returned. This handspun yarn was used for the weft and millspun yarn was bought from the Tarbert mill for the warp, thus producing what was known as a 50-50 tweed. The Harris Tweed Association had first became aware of the existence of 50-50 tweed during the Second World War and approached the Board of Trade about stamping it. At that time, the Board of Trade did not consider that an amendment to the Regulations for stamping would be required. The Association therefore authorised that such tweed should be stamped with the words 'Handspun weft'. [4] Thereafter the Government included tweed in which the weft was handspun and the warp millspun as a category for which the controlled price fell between wholly handspun and wholly millspun tweed. [5]

Local warpers were employed at Borvemòr to warp the millspun yarn and then the warp and weft were distributed on the HCA lorry to weavers. When the greasy tweeds were ready they were collected by the HCA lorry and taken up to Stornoway for finishing in the Stornoway mills. The tweeds were then collected again by the HCA lorry and taken back to Borvemòr where they were stamped and baled ready for dispatch to customers. The decline in hand-spinning eventually forced the HCA to use millspun yarn for both warp and weft. The production of tweed entitled to the handspun weft cachet thus lasted for a relatively short time and thereafter HCA became producers distributing yarn for out-weaving in much the same way as other small producers in Lewis. Over time, a problem with achieving deadlines for delivery became evident. Eventually, much of the weaving was done, firstly in Lochs, and then in other districts of Lewis, where weavers were known to be available. Colonel Walker died in 1954 and the Harris Crofters' Association managed to keep going for a year or so after his death, but it was decided to wind up the HCA in 1956. Shareholders were repaid and the staff at Borvemòr were treated generously in Colonel Walker's will. [6] By providing employment for local people, both at the headquarters at Borvemòr and in the wider island community at a critical time, the benevolence of this ageing gentleman, who came to Harris as a stranger and grew to love the island and its people, was very much in the tradition established a century earlier by Lady Dunmore and Mrs Thomas.

The existence of the Harris Crofters' Association did not preclude individual crofters from making their own tweed and selling it directly to contacts in the south or to the passing tourist trade. It has been said that when the cruise liner *Killarney* came into Tarbert, every house in the village would have a table outside the door with tweed for sale. To a diminishing extent this tradition of selling to the passing tourist trade lingered, particularly in the Bays of Harris, for many years. As the traditional skills of home-dyeing and hand-spinning died out, weavers in Harris came to depend on millspun yarn and mill finishing of their tweeds. In this situation they faced the same problems as small producers in Lewis. The cost of millspun yarn made it difficult to sell their tweeds at a competitive price and yet retain a margin of profit for themselves.

Harris District Council approached the Harris Tweed Association in 1959 asking for reinstatement of the handspun weft cachet which had been withdrawn because of the alleged use of entirely millspun yarn in tweed claiming to be handspun weft. The HTA was told that while there were few people left in Harris who could hand-spin both warp and weft, there were scores who could spin the weft alone and that a number of weavers in Harris were still keen to produce 50-50 tweeds. [7] They were unable to get supplies of carded wool anywhere in the islands as the carding mill at Tarbert had been closed for over two years. The District Council also approached Kenneth Mackenzie Ltd. and that firm was willing to provide carding facilities at the Tarbert mill on condition that it was economic to do so. [8] Although the HTA agreed in June 1960 that the handspun weft cachet should be restored, there was a delay in implementing the decision as the Board of Trade decreed that the Regulations should be amended to include the words 'handspun weft'. The amended Regulations were finally approved in April 1961 and the amendment read as follows

> '... and for the purpose of distinction there shall also be added the word 'Handspun' in the case of Tweeds made entirely from handspun yarn or the words 'Handspun Weft' in the case of Tweeds made as to the weft entirely from handspun yarn.' [9]

Although it formed a relatively small proportion of the total output of Orb-stamped tweed, production in Harris and the Southern Isles rose in the boom of the sixties from just over 36,000 yards in 1958 to 73,386 in the peak year of 1966. Most of the tweed woven in Harris was stamped in Tarbert in 1958, but by 1966 most of the tweed woven in Harris was being stamped in Stornoway (67,512 yards in 1966) It is likely that this tweed stamped in Stornoway had been woven on commission for the Harris Handwoven Tweed Co. in Tarbert. Production in the Southern Isles was seldom more than a few hundred yards, apart from 1966 and strangely 1967, when the yardage stamped in North Uist rose to just over 1000 yards. Weaving in South Uist,

Berneray and Scalpay was intermittent and dropped off as the decade advanced. Stamping at Borvemòr had been over 2000 yards in 1958, but dropped to 177 yards in the peak year of 1966, although, as in North Uist, it went up to 300 yards in the difficult year of 1967. In 1968, production in Harris and North Uist increased to 78,892 yards. By 1970 the boom had passed with production declining year on year throughout the 1970s. Stamping stopped in the Uists and at Borvemòr. Stamping in Harris was confined to Tarbert and Geocrab. [10]

The perception of the HTA in the Islands had long been that, as it was based in London it was too remote to understand the everyday problems experienced by producers. In 1959 (just as the IHTP problem was becoming acute) the Secretary of the HTA, Harry Renfrew, was delegated to visit a number of Independent Producers and all the spinning mills in Lewis. Apart from inquiring about the use of mainland yarn, his remit was:

1. To ascertain the difficulties of the Producers and how the HTA could assist in solving them;
2. to ascertain if the Association had the confidence of the industry; how it could be maintained or improved;
3. to ascertain what had been reported by the Sub-Committee on yarn distribution. [11]

The main problem of Independent Producers was said to be the price of yarn from the local mills. In the early sixties at least, this long-standing complaint was attributed by the Spinners to the increasing use of 'twist' yarn in tweed for the North American market. Twist yarn was 1/- per pound more expensive than ordinary yarn. The result was that Independent Producers felt that they were being squeezed out of the market. On the question of distribution of yarn, the alleged lack of fair treatment by the Island mills was given as the reason for some 100 out of a total of 1500 island weavers being willing to work for IHTP firms. At a meeting between Spinners, (i.e. the mills) Independent Producers and a representative of the HTA, it was suggested that a scheme operated by Kenneth Mackenzie Ltd. offered a solution to the problem. Under this scheme, yarn was delivered to different districts strictly by rotation. If such a scheme were to be adopted it would need co-operation between the mills. It was suggested that the Association could help in setting up such a scheme by giving a quarterly return of weaving by districts. No immediate solution to the problem of equitable distribution of tweeds was found until the early 1970s and charges of alleged bias towards weavers close to Stornoway continued to fester.

On the question of confidence in the HTA, the feeling among both Spinners and Producers was that there was need for more frequent and closer liaison with the industry. [12] The HTA responded by closing its London office and moving its administration to 92 Academy St, Inverness in 1962. As the Association was a company registered in England, it was necessary to keep its Registered Office there and this was transferred to the office of McKenna & Co. at 12 Whitehall in London. [13] Whether because common sense eventually prevailed, or because communications with the Islands gradually improved, or even because representatives of the Hebridean Spinners on one occasion refused to attend a meeting in Inverness as they thought it should have been held in Stornoway, a branch office was opened in Stornoway in 1969 [14] and eventually all the administration was transferred to that office. The fact that John Morrison, a Harris member of the Committee of Management, was unable to attend a meeting in Inverness in May 1962 because he was stormbound was, unfortunately, not seen as a good reason for transferring business meetings to Harris!

Because of the resentment between the Independent Producers (who had almost without exception gone over to Orb production) and the Spinners over yarn supplies, it appeared that it might be difficult to achieve a united front in the litigation against IHTP Ltd. in 1960. A meeting was held between the HTA and representatives of the various sections of the industry to assess support for an action of passing off against IHTP Ltd. A spokesman for the Independent Producers within the islands said that while his Association had considered their attitude to proceedings against IHTP Ltd. present yarn prices and supplies offered them no encouragement to take such a step. The cost of yarn and the uncertainty of supplies made it impossible for them to compete with the Spinners and at the same time show a reasonable margin of profit. The Spinners argued that while there were times when the margin on yarn was good, at other times it was quite uneconomic for the Spinners. Spinners could not be expected to carry unpredictable stocks to meet unknown demands.

Having listened for some time to this jousting between sectional interests, Rev. Murdoch Macrae intervened with all the authority of his calling. He pointed out that however important the problem of yarn might be, it was a domestic issue between Producers and Spinners. The object of the meeting was a matter which affected the livelihood of the whole island, now and in the future, and both sides ought to consider the full effect of what they were trying to do by allowing purely domestic issues to over-ride the major issue of litigation against IHTP. A number of proposed solutions to the problem of the price of yarn were put forward. Eventually it was agreed that all the Spinners would examine their own costings, and, if the Registrar of Restrictive Trade Practices would permit them to make a collective investigation into costings, they would do so. On the basis of this undertaking the Independent Producers agreed to join in the action against IHTP Ltd. [15]

When proposals for an agreement on yarn prices were referred to the Registrar of Restrictive Trade Practices, the Spinners were told that while Spinners could come to an agreed price for exported cloth, an agreed price for the Home market would be examined by the Court, but prices for yarn and finishing could not form part of an agreement. It was suggested to the Spinners that an investigation of their costs by an independent accountant might place them outside the Restrictive Practices Court. [16] Whether any of these attempts to resolve the tensions between Independent Producers and Spinners could be seen as successful would be open to question, as complaints about yarn prices continued to surface from time to time for many years. [17]

Lord Hunter's comment in 1964 that in his view stampers had been too liberal in their interpretation of the rules when they were called on to stamp tweeds made in the weaving sheds in Inaclete Rd, led to a reappraisal of the location of weaving sheds for tenants in Local Authority houses in Stornoway. New 'weavers' colonies' were established, 'within reasonable distance of the weavers' homes', on sites at Rigs Road, between Island Rd and Caberfeidh Rd, on Tolmie Terrace and on Westview Terrace. The existing colony at Cannery Rd was upgraded by draining and installing a water supply. [18] The Harris Tweed Association agreed to bear the costs of the sheds and make them available to weavers free of charge. [19]

By 1965 the Harris Tweed industry was in the middle of an unprecedented boom. Well over 70% of production went to export markets at a time when British industry was being urged to 'export or die'. The mills were working double shifts to meet orders from the continent, America, Australia and New Zealand. 1966 was an even better year with production in excess of seven and a half million yards. In this happy situation the weaver was naturally seen as a key factor in the industry. The age profile of island weavers was in the middle-aged and upwards bracket, a matter of concern when the economy of the Islands was so dependent on Harris Tweed. Recruitment of young weavers became an urgent priority. Negotiations between the Lewis and Harris Youth Employment Committee, the Wool Industry Training Board, the Education Authority and the Harris Tweed industry, led to the establishment of a weavers' training school for boys under eighteen at Lews Castle College. At the official opening Mr Robert Stewart of James Macdonald Ltd. told the first students to graduate in the course that the well-being of the Harris Tweed industry rested largely on their shoulders. Whatever the contribution of the mills to the industry, only weavers could ensure the prompt return of tweeds. He said,

> 'To tell a customer on the 56th floor of the Empire State Building in New York that his goods were going to be late because there was a fank in Balallan, or that the weather in Shawbost was right for peat-cutting simply will not do.' [20]

Classification of weavers as self-employed was thought to be a strong disincentive to recruitment. The Wool Industry Training Board met with representatives of the producers with a view to including weavers in the Board's training schemes. Unfortunately for all concerned, it became clear that as the crofter-weaver was self-employed he did not come within the scope of the Industrial Training Act! The question of reclassification was discussed with the Weavers' Branch of the TGWU and with producers for some time. Eventually the Western Isles Crofters Union produced an informative report on the issues surrounding reclassification of weavers. The Report listed the disadvantages suffered by weavers because of their self-employed classification. They were not entitled to unemployment benefit, holiday pay, graduated pension rights, industrial injuries benefit, redundancy pay, or wage-related supplement during unemployment or illness. Reclassification meant that a weaver would be employed under a contract of service which would give his employer the right to supervise and direct the weaver in the performance of his work. The Report also stated that the number of weavers who would be accepted in the new category would only be such as would reasonably be kept employed in the industry, an estimated 800. [21]

Both weavers and producers eventually decided that the status quo should remain unchanged. Surveys had shown a majority of weavers in favour of reclassification, then a degree of ambivalence and finally a majority against it. Most of the weavers lived in rural crofting communities and when faced with the prospect of being tied to a producer's timetable, preferred to retain their freedom to fit their weaving around the demands of crofting. Producers, under the auspices of the Hebridean Spinners Advisory Committee, sought the opinion of Counsel on the legal implications of weavers being employees of producers, a step which would become necessary if they were to be reclassified as employed persons. Counsel was of the opinion that the proposal that weavers should be thirled to a producer was extremely dangerous. He explained the legal position that 'Harris Tweed' was what the purchasing public thought it was, and emphasised the risk of an action for passing off if the purchasing public was deceived about what it was buying. Emphasising the importance of the 'crofting' element, Lord Hunter had said in 1964:

> 'It is felt and in my opinion rightly felt, by those who purchase Harris Tweed that they are assisting the inhabitants of remote islands to supplement the bare living which they are able to wrest from the soil or from the sea by engaging in their own time in weaving ... ' [22]

In his Opinion, Counsel advised as follows:

> 'the idea of a full-time employee-weaver thirled to and under the control of, one particular mill or producer, is not consistent with the public conception of Harris Tweed as a 'crofter' product ... The independence of the crofter-weaver ... is in my view an essential element in the public perception of what Harris Tweed is. I must therefore advise that, in my opinion, adoption of the present proposal would involve a degree of misrepresentation to the purchasing public which would in turn endanger the distinctiveness of the 'Harris Tweed' mark. ... I would advise even more

strongly against dividing up the Island into 'spheres of influence', moreover, I question whether such an arrangement would be defensible under the Restrictive Trade Practices Acts.' [23]

In making their decision not to become thirled to the producers, the weavers seem to have been guided by an inherent instinct to protect whatever measure of independence they saw themselves having as self-employed persons. As it transpired, had the weavers become employees they would have been better protected when Clansman Ltd. collapsed in 1989. The Hebridean Spinners Advisory Committee, who had sought the opinion of Counsel, called a meeting of producers and representatives of the Harris Tweed Association to discuss Counsel's Opinion and the various alternatives to reclassification, such as a central employment and distributing agency. In the course of the discussion, Counsel suggested that to prevent any possible challenge to the definition of Harris Tweed, the industry should press the Government to give statutory sanction to the 1934 definition. The Hebridean Spinners Advisory Committee decided to pursue this proposal. [24]

When a Report on the meeting with Counsel came before the Harris Tweed Association, members of the Committee of Management felt unanimously that it would be 'unwise' to be seen to be seeking 'special protection for the industry'. It was thought that such a move would invite opposition from the Borders textile industry and provoke adverse publicity. Instead, it was agreed to make a further attempt to get a trade description from the Board of Trade. [25] An application for a Definition Order in respect of Harris Tweed had already been made to the Board of Trade under the Trades Descriptions Act 1968. That application had been rejected, apparently because the Board of Trade felt that there was no need for a Definition Order in view of Lord Hunter's Judgement. [26] Despite the advice of Counsel that a Statutory Definition of Harris Tweed might be advisable, some fifteen years were to pass before the matter was given serious consideration again.

In contrast to the double shifts worked by the mills at the height of the boom, 1967 saw a 10% drop in production. The mills were working one week on and one week off as falling sales hit an island in which unemployment figures ranged from 19% to 27%. Contemporary analysis blamed the drop in production on 'a constriction of markets, mostly foreign markets'. [27] A survey of the Scottish textile industry as a whole maintained that the initial momentum of exports to Europe could not be sustained as long as Britain was excluded from the Common Market. The tariff of 13% on Scottish cloth exported to Germany compared harshly with a 2.5% tariff on Italian cloth. Sooner or later the tariff difference would tell and sales would decline. This situation was exacerbated by the slowing down of economic expansion within the EEC. Recession in Italy led to exports of Scottish cloth being halved in that country. In 1965 and 1966 deliveries to Germany fell sharply. Although 1965 and 1966 had been good years for Harris Tweed, this success had been based on orders placed before recession in Europe began to bite. In 1967 the downward trend in all six EEC member countries continued. [28] The American market, which accounted for half of all tweed exports, had also declined. One school of thought put this down to overbuying in 1965-66. Another theory was that American buyers were exercising restraint because of the war in Vietnam. [29] A spokesman for the HTA said that the record total of 1966 was unusual and that the present cutback was no more than part of the normal cyclical movement in the trade. [30] The HTA spokesman seems to have been correct in the short term: production in 1969 and 1970 rose to over 6.5 million yards each year.

Predictions that a take-over of Kenneth Mackenzie Ltd. by the Scottish, English and European Textiles group, SEET, was imminent were confirmed in August 1969. The existing Board members, including Kenneth Mackenzie and his brother, Ex-Provost Alasdair Mackenzie, retired. Harris Mackenzie, son of Kenneth, and grandson of the founder of the firm, became Managing Director and Chairman of the company. Another member of the family, Rae Mackenzie continued his association with the firm. Explaining the take-over, the new Chairman, Harris Mackenzie said:

> 'The reasons for joining SEET are twofold. Firstly to avoid the possibility of crippling death duties and thereby guaranteeing continuity of employment for our mill-workers and out-weavers. Secondly, there will be a tremendous improvement in our marketing resources which would not have been possible if we had remained a small family concern.' [31]

Kenneth Mackenzie Ltd. was, at the time, the largest single producer of Harris Tweed with a large export market, principally in West Germany.

Chairman of the SEET group, J. H. M. (Jock) Mackenzie was not of the same family, although his research into family history led him to believe that he and the Stornoway Mackenzies had a common origin. [32] When interviewed by the Financial Editor of *The Scotsman*, Jock Mackenzie said:

> 'One of SEET's main interests is investing in well-run family businesses where the family wish to remain in control and at the same time solve their death-duty problems.' [33]

Another firm which caught the headlines at the end of the decade was MacLeod's Tweeds Ltd., Shawbost who announced in February 1970 that they would be undertaking an extension of their premises worth £150,000. This firm of sixteen employees was the only Scottish company to receive an export award for small firms from the British National Export Council in 1969. Their exports, largely to Denmark, had more than doubled over a year, rising from £73,000 in 1968 to £162,000 in 1969. Within a few months of announcing plans for expansion, the market for tweed slumped and MacLeod's Tweed Company were working half-time. A year later, with only six full-time employees left, but with 170 weavers on its books, this enterprising company went into voluntary liquidation. *The People's Journal* commented at the time:

> 'A typical firm of small Harris Tweed producers, MacLeod's didn't produce or process any cloth themselves. They bought yarn from island spinning mills, which, in turn they farmed out to self-employed weavers to make for them.' [34]

When Kenneth Mackenzie Ltd. gave an undertaking to supply carded wool and yarn from the Tarbert mill to weavers in Harris it was on the understanding that this would be done only if it was economically viable. By early 1970, the mill at Tarbert was deemed to be no longer viable. On the closure of this mill, Harris Mackenzie, Chairman and Managing Director of Kenneth Mackenzie Ltd., offered to introduce a new delivery system of yarn from Stornoway and provide those who were to be made redundant with looms on an interest free loan repayable over three years. Any employees who did not wish to accept these offers would be given, in addition to their redundancy pay, a bonus based on their length of service.[35]

Rumours of significant changes at S. A. Newall & Sons Ltd. had been circulating for some months before confirmation of the changes emerged in the *Stornoway Gazette*. Murdo Morrison, Managing Director of Newalls, told the *Gazette* that, at the request of Albany Newall, and with the approval of the shareholders, he had been invited to become Chairman of the company. Before this appointment had been ratified an offer to take over Newalls had been received 'from a mainland group with some interests in Harris Tweed'. The shareholders decided not to sell. Because of the involved way in which family investments were locked up in Trusts, it seemed desirable to release some of these and re-arrange the capital structure of the company. As Chairman, Murdo Morrison then opened discussions with Thomas Smith & Co. (Peterhead) Ltd. to see if their associate company Thomas Smith & Co. (Stornoway) Ltd. and Newalls could achieve 'a degree of integration of their manufacturing processes so as to enable both companies to keep abreast of technical developments and minimise rising costs of production'. Both companies would retain their identities and operate under separate management. Future plans included 'a substantial new investment in plant and machinery and diversification into spinning of specialised yarn for general household textiles'.[36]

It could be argued, in light of these events, that the industry was already experiencing as early as 1970 the first breeze of a wind of change which eventually saw the small Independent Producers going to the wall while the larger firms survived by rationalisation and a series of amalgamations. Although the industry recovered again and again from the cyclical slumps which were the norm, only in 1984 did production reach anything like the peak years between 1960 and 1970.

Reference - The Domestic Scene: 1960 to 1970

1 Report on a visit to Stornoway by HTA Secretary, November 1959. HTA Office, Stornoway.
2 *Stornoway Gazette*, 16. 1. 1965.
3 *ibid.*, 12. 2. 1966.
4 Transcripts of evidence in *Argyllshire Weavers Ltd. and Others v. A. Macaulay (Tweeds) Ltd. and Others* (1964) CSess OH [hereafter: 'Transcripts of Evidence in Harris Tweed Case'], Vol. 1, 4707-08: Evidence from Col. Neil Macarthur. HRA/D190/1a (xxxv).
5 Statutory Rules and Orders, 1947, No. 2639. Goods and Services (Price Control) Apparel and Textiles. The General Apparel and Textile (Manufacturers Maximum Prices and Charges) Order, 1947, Part II of the First Schedule. Sub-paragraph (5) of paragraph 1 was amended to read: (5): 'In respect of goods being tweed (including Harris Tweed) handwoven in the Outer Hebrides and being tweed:- sub-section (ii) made from yarn spun in the Outer Hebrides of which not less than 50 per cent was handspun, to which the certification trade mark has been applied, together with the words 'handspun weft', the sum of 10s 5d per yard.'
6 Based on oral information supplied by Mrs Mary Macdonald, Sgarastamhòr and John Mackay, Horgabost in July, 1999.
7 *Stornoway Gazette*, 23. 12. 1960.
8 HTA Minutes 1. 9. 1959.
9 *ibid.*, 19. 4. 1961.
10 HTA Stamping Records.
11 Report on a visit to Stornoway by HTA Secretary, November 1959. HTA Office, Stornoway.
12 *ibid.*
13 HTA Minutes, 17. 5. 1962. HTA Office, Stornoway.
14 *ibid.*, 8. 12. 1960.
15 Report of a Meeting between HTA Ltd. and representatives of the Hebridean Spinners Advisory Committee and Independent Producers, 21. 4. 1960. HTA Office, Stornoway.
16 HTA Minutes, 8. 12. 1960. HTA Office, Stornoway.
17 Report of a Joint Meeting of HTA, Hebridean Spinners Association and Independent Producers Association, 17. 8. 1962. HTA Office, Stornoway.
18 *Stornoway Gazette*, 27. 3. 1965.
19 HTA Minutes, 28. 9. 1965. HTA Office, Stornoway.
20 *Stornoway Gazette*, 21. 6. 1969.
21 *ibid.*, 28. 10. 1967.
22 *Argyllshire Weavers Ltd. and Others v. Macaulay (A.) (Tweeds) Ltd., and Others* [1964] RPC No. 16, 477 [hereafter: 'Harris Tweed Case'], at 567.

23 Opinion, from D. A. O. Edward to HTA, 16. 10. 1969.
24 Report to the Harris Tweed Association by W. H. Renfrew on Meeting held under the auspices of the Hebridean Spinners Association, 8. 1. 1970. HTA Office, Stornoway.
25 HTA Minutes, 3. 3. 1970.
26 *ibid.*, 25. 6. 1969.
27 Douglas Crawford, 'Harris Tweed: the crucial years' in *Scotland* [hereafter: Crawford, 'Harris Tweed'].
28 *The Scotsman*, 23. 6. 1967, 'Textiles: A decade of change for the woollen cloth industry'.
29 W. G. Lucas, 'Harris Tweed industry's new production record', in *Scotsman*, 23. 6. 1967.
30 Crawford, 'Harris Tweed'.
31 *Stornoway Gazette*, 30. 8. 1969.
32 *Scotsman*, 22. 8. 1969.
33 *ibid.*
34 *People's Journal*, 23. 10. 1971.
35 *Stornoway Gazette*, 25. 4. 1970.
36 *ibid.*, 7. 3. 1970.

19

On the Horns of a Dilemma: 1970 to 1974

A number of features mark the early 1970s as a turning point in the Harris Tweed industry. There was a dramatic decline in production from just over five million yards in 1970 to a low point of two and a half million yards in 1975. This decline was accompanied by an inevitable contraction in the number of producers. Family companies which had survived for generations disappeared to be replaced by conglomerates. Unemployment in the Western Isles was the highest in the UK. The Highlands and Islands Development Board, in consultation with the Harris Tweed Association, tried to alleviate the desperate situation in the islands by embarking on plans to restructure the Harris Tweed industry, principally by introducing double-width looms to meet the market demand for double-width Harris Tweed. These double-width looms were to be situated in weaving units in rural townships. Whether these radical plans would have been the salvation or the death-knell of the industry, or indeed whether the situation of the looms would have offended the 'at their own homes' requirement of the definition, was never put to the test, as island weavers rejected the plans by a 98% majority in 1976, as will be described in Chapter 20. The market for Harris Tweed began to improve slowly from 1977, but never again regained the buoyancy of the mid-1960s.

While the plans for restructuring the industry were certainly a radical departure from the perception of Harris Tweed given in the Hunter judgement of 1964, they were influenced by trends which were becoming all too clear within the textile trade. Firstly, the market for single-width Harris Tweed appeared to be in terminal decline. Secondly, the existing Hattersley looms had scarcely changed in forty years and it was becoming increasingly difficult to get spare parts for them. Weavers were buying up discarded looms simply for the spare parts. Instances of power-weaving to lighten the task were becoming prevalent among individual weavers and within the mills. By definition Harris Tweed was a handwoven product, and therefore weavers who fitted a motor to their looms were breaching the definition of Harris Tweed, yet instances of weavers applying a motor to their Hattersley looms increased alarmingly in the early 1970s. By law, the HTA had to refuse to stamp power-woven tweed with the Orb mark and had to remove the weaver's name from the list until he signed an undertaking to desist from power-weaving. More damaging to the industry than individual instances of power-weaving was the insidious spread of power-weaving of double-width cloth in the mills. Even although manufacturers of this double-width cloth did not pretend (at least as far as could be proved) that it was Harris Tweed, mill-made double-width cloth was thought to be replacing Harris Tweed in some markets.

By the autumn of 1970, the mills were working half-time and weavers were said to be leaving the islands for jobs in Dewsbury, Glasgow and Wales. [1] Despite public optimism among mill spokesmen that this was no more than a seasonal slowing down, there was little apparent prospect of the general recession improving. Stamping figures for the eight months to the end of August 1970 were down by almost three quarters of a million yards (703,387 yards) compared to the corresponding period the previous year. By the end of 1971 stamping was down by almost one and a half million yards. Unemployment in the islands was worse than it had been for twelve years. As the major employer, recession in the Harris Tweed industry naturally affected the prosperity of every other business in the islands.

The island economy, fragile at the best of times, was seen to be approaching crisis point in 1970-71.

When the HIDB was set up in 1965 its remit was to keep under review all matters relating to economic and social development in the Highlands and Islands. Clearly, the HIDB would have been failing in its duty if it had ignored the deteriorating economic situation in the Western Isles in 1971. Unemployment, depopulation, the threat to local fishing if Britain entered the Common Market and of course, the serious decline in the Harris Tweed industry were among the topics discussed by Sir Andrew Gilchrist, the new Chairman of the HIDB, on a visit to Lewis in February 1971. Announcing plans for a 'wide-ranging survey covering every aspect of the Harris Tweed trade', Sir Andrew said,

> 'The study, like our previous examination of the Shetland woollen industry, will be designed to lead to action. We will try to identify ways and means of improving, expanding and diversifying the industry - we want at the end of the day to have a stronger and healthier industry which will bring benefits to the economy of

> Lewis. ... If our studies reveal that there is a marketing potential for double-width handwoven cloth and that a suitable hand-loom can be built, then there are other important matters - re-equipment, training, larger premises for the looms, maintenance and financing of development - to which we would have to give careful and full consideration.' [2]

The Board had discussed their proposed study with the Harris Tweed Association, trade unions, and tweed manufacturers and had been assured of their full co-operation. [3]

Although Sir Andrew's vision of the way ahead may have seemed revolutionary in the press headlines, the vision did not originate with the HIDB: it originated with a number of Hebridean Spinners. At a joint meeting of the Hebridean Spinners Advisory Committee and the HTA in September 1970, representatives of the Spinners had proposed (1) a revision of the existing specification for Harris Tweed; (2) a double-width loom capable of being hand-operated. The rationale for the proposal that the specification for Harris Tweed should be revised was based on the fact that with the increasing demand for lighter weight Harris Tweed and the introduction of new weaves, the existing specification had become unsuitable. That specification, which required a minimum of 18 ends and 18 picks, had been introduced when Harris Tweed was a heavy cloth of 10/11 ozs. per yard. The specification of 18 ends and 18 picks was made just after the 2nd War to prevent deliberately loose weaving. Thus the specification as it stood put a restriction on manufacturers and made no allowance for the lighter weight yarns which the market had come to demand. It could result in an inferior lightweight cloth being stamped by the Association's inspectors. [4]

The rationale for a double-width loom lay in the belief that 'the industry was at a stage where no further expansion was likely if conditions remained as they were'. The representatives of the Hebridean Spinners Advisory Committee suggested that a technical Panel should be set up consisting of the Harris Tweed Association, the Highlands and Islands Development Board and the Hebridean Spinners Advisory Committee. The weavers should be consulted and the whole matter thoroughly investigated to find out if a double-width loom was a feasible proposition. One of the contributory factors which had persuaded the Spinners that it was necessary to produce a double-width Harris Tweed was that mass producers of made-up garments were going off traditional single-width Harris Tweed. Most of the processes in making-up and cutting were automated and geared only to double-width cloth where up to twelve thicknesses were cut by laser, an obviously more efficient cutting method than manual cutting of individual garments. Within this structure it was uneconomic for makers-up to handle a single-width tweed. It was suggested that all moving parts of a new double-width loom should be made from lightweight materials. The loom should have a shuttle that would rest on one side and not return to the box as it did on the Hattersley loom. The cost of developing a prototype double-width loom could be shared by one third from the industry, one third from the HIDB and one third from the loom manufacturers who would benefit if the loom was successful. It was suggested that the HTA should take a lead in these tasks and set a deadline for reports from loom manufacturers, and, if the proposition was feasible, for the production of a prototype double-width loom. [5]

In light of the subsequent criticism which was heaped on the HTA it seems important to record the initial reaction of the Association to the proposals made by the representatives of the Spinners. On the question of the specification, the Chairman agreed that the existing specification had been laid down many years earlier when lighter weight cloths and a variety of weaves had not been envisaged. He said that the HTA were 'anxious to assist producers to develop and increase their trade' and suggested that the Spinners put their recommendations in writing to the Association who would take the matter further. Regarding a double-width loom, the Chairman reminded the meeting that the HIDB had already put a substantial amount of money into developing an improved version of the Hattersley loom. It would be necessary for the Association to get the views of those Spinners and Small Producers who were not represented and, most importantly, of the weavers who would be vitally concerned in the proposals. Arrangements were made to discuss the matter with the Transport and General Workers' Union to which weavers belonged. [6] Thus from the earliest stages of considering a double-width loom, the HTA recognised that the weavers should be consulted and it relied on the TGWU representatives to keep the weavers informed as to what was happening.

The extent to which the Harris Tweed Association was called upon to arbitrate in disputes between different interests in the industry was a measure of the desperation of all sections in the early 1970s. The price paid by Small Producers for yarn had long been a bone of contention between them and the Spinners. The selling price of Harris Tweed was a vexed question which frequently caused ill-feeling between rival manufacturers. During the recession of the early 1970s, both the price of yarn and the selling price of Harris Tweed became a matter of serious concern to the industry at large. The Small Producers Association brought their complaints against the Spinners to the HTA. They maintained that the price of yarn made it impossible for them to compete in the home market and very difficult to get business in the overseas market. They felt that the HTA was not safeguarding the interests of the Small Producer, who was being squeezed out of the industry. The HTA, while agreeing that Small Producers were an integral part of the industry, told the Small Producers' Association that the price of yarn was outwith the Association's jurisdiction. The low price of Harris Tweed on the home market was also causing concern to all sections of the industry. The difference between home and export prices was as much as 3/2d per yard. [7] The HTA made it clear to all concerned that the selling price of tweed was a matter for the manufacturers, not for the Association. [8]

Price-fixing by commercial interests as a way of limiting competition had been the norm before the war. During the war and for a spell just after it, the Government had specified the price at which particular types of Harris Tweed were to be sold. Part of the threat from IHTP tweed in the late 1950s had been that, by using non-Scottish wool for their yarn, IHTP tweed could undercut Orb-stamped Harris Tweed in home and foreign markets. In the UK resale price maintenance (imposed by a supplier on those further down the chain) was outlawed in 1968, but collusion among suppliers about prices had been illegal, unless registered and not objected to by the Registrar (later the Director General of Fair Trading) in the UK since the Restrictive Trade Practices Act of 1956. [9] When clandestine price-fixing was suspected in any branch of industry, the Government referred such cases to the Office of Fair Trading to adjudicate whether there was indeed a case of price-fixing against the public interest. [10]

By the 1970s, as markets contracted, some island manufacturers seem to have been willing to sell Harris Tweed at an uneconomic price for the sake of additional business, regardless of the long term effects this might have on the prestigious cachet of Harris Tweed. When the exceptionally low price of some Harris Tweed was brought to the attention of the HTA by island producers, the Association decided to have their legal advisers ascertain whether proposals for some form of central selling agency would be a contravention of the Restrictive Practices Act. [11] The legal advice received was that none of the proposals for a central selling agency would be approved by the Registrar of Restrictive Practices 'as they were clearly designed to fix the price and abolish competition and this was contrary to the purpose of the Act'. [12]

An intimate picture of the grass-roots of the industry was supplied in 1970 in a survey conducted by pupils of Shawbost School. It threw some interesting light on the weavers' conditions of work. The survey, which was part of the school's 'Highland Village Project', revealed that, on average, looms on the West Side of Lewis were twenty years old, only three were under ten years and the oldest loom was forty years old. A two-year-old loom was found to be no more advanced and required the same physical effort as the oldest loom. The weavers' own suggestions for improvement included (1) new looms at low cost; (2) better distribution of tweeds; (3) a weekly wage with employers paying the normal insurance stamp; (4) a reduction in the price of spare parts (5) payment in cash rather than by cheque, as the travelling bank only came once a fortnight, and (6) availability of spare parts in each district. £80 per annum was considered to be a more realistic figure than the existing Income Tax Allowance of £50 for spares, electricity and clothes. [13] The survey of eighty West Side weavers revealed that the majority of weavers were in the upper age bracket, 82% had weaving as their only source of income, and weaving processes involved help from within the family or paid external help. Despite a recent pay increase, only 5% thought that weavers were well-paid, and a more realistic wage was needed, particularly if weavers were to continue as self-employed persons. Interestingly, 86.5 % of weavers would have preferred to be employed by a mill. Only 44 % were satisfied with the running of the weavers' Union. The establishment in February 1973 of a rota system by which all the mills distributed tweeds to weavers in each district by rotation went some way to settling the question of fair distribution, but dissatisfaction with the Union and employers over wages and distribution of tweeds continued to surface from time to time. [14]

The era of amalgamations began in 1970 with 'a degree of integration' between S. A. Newall & Sons and Thomas Smith (Stornoway) Ltd. 'to enable both companies to ... minimise rising costs of production'. [15] In 1972, in a very small news item in the *Stornoway Gazette* the formation of a 'new Independent Holding Company' was announced. The Company was to be called 'Clansman Holdings Ltd.' The Highlands and Islands Development Board participated in the equity of the venture and the Board of Directors comprised Murdo Morrison and Ian Lawrence from the Newall group, with Bruce Burns and William Burns from Stephen Burns Ltd. [16] The name 'Clansman' had originally belonged to David Tolmie Ltd. and this name had been sold to Stephen Burns Ltd. about 1966 when David Tolmie's successors came out of the industry. Stephen Burns Ltd. had also taken over Crofter Tweeds, another small producer, and somewhat later, Garry Weavers owned by Garry MacLean who had bought the mill at Geocrab from Kenneth Mackenzie Ltd. when they became part of SEET. Thus within a short space of time, the number of individual manufacturers had begun to contract with Small Producers being absorbed within larger conglomerates.

Further rationalisation took place a month later in July 1972, when Kenneth Mackenzie Ltd. and the Harris Tweed Trading Company Ltd. (James MacDonald Ltd.) formed a joint company, Kemp Tod Ltd., to handle dyeing and finishing processes for both firms. A press statement said that although formation of the new company would involve fifteen redundancies in each mill, 'these would be kept to a minimum and the Transport and General Workers' Union had been informed'. Gilbert Archer, Chairman of Kemp Tod Ltd., said that the new company would invest in 'the most modern dyeing and finishing plant to combat the continual rise in costs and cope with the anticipated demand for new double-width cloth'. [17] In December 1974, James MacDonald & Co. closed with the loss of 85 jobs. Kenneth Mackenzie Holdings Ltd., parent company of Kenneth Mackenzie Ltd. made an offer for MacDonald's trading interests. They intended to continue trading under the names James MacDonald & Co., David Tolmie, Scottish Islands Tweed Company and the Harris Tweed Trading Company. [18]

The subsequent recurrence of company names which are thought to have gone out of business is confusing, but the purpose in retaining a company name after the original company has closed is that the goodwill and market outlets of defunct companies form part of that company's trading assets and as such are of value to the Holding company which buys them.

Because orders for single-width Harris Tweed were slow, some manufacturers turned to producing double-width cloth for which there was a ready market. Much to the concern of other manufacturers and of the Harris Tweed Association, double-width cloth was being power-woven in a Stornoway mill and at the mill in Geocrab. [19] The Stornoway company producing the power-woven, double-width cloth explained that if they were to continue in business they had to diversify, as they could not keep going on Harris Tweed alone. Their cloth was not sold as Harris Tweed and could not be mistaken for Harris Tweed, although the Geocrab mill did use Harris yarn and its cloth was similar to Harris Tweed. [20] Concerned as the HTA was at any power-weaving in island mills and that the double-width cloth might supplant Harris Tweed, the Association did not have the authority to stop producers diversifying. The best that the Association could do in the circumstances was to ensure that the Orb mark was being applied only to cloth entitled to carry it, and that no power-woven cloth produced by a manufacturer of Harris Tweed was being passed off as Harris Tweed further down the line. [21] By 1974 production of power-woven double-width tweed was giving even greater cause for concern. Despite the best efforts of HTA stampers, when power-woven 'Harris Tweed' jackets turned up in Germany there were strong suspicions that some island manufacturer was going as far as providing labels to retailers in order to pass off power-woven tweed as Harris Tweed. [22]

By 1974, the Harris Tweed Association was truly on the horns of a dilemma. Stamping returns had been dropping month after month for almost four years. Annual stamping figures dropped each year by approximately half a million yards per year. The psychological effect of hearing these gloomy figures at every meeting must have been extremely alarming for the Committee of Management. Equally alarming was the fact, not known to the general public, that at least two, at times three or four, of the largest manufacturers could not pay their outstanding stamping fees, a classic sign of a company in financial difficulties. The Harris Tweed Association carried a burden of outstanding stamping fees which gradually climbed from under £10,100 in March 1970 to over £30,000 in 1973 and over £40,000 in 1975, at which point the Association was forced to arrange overdraft facilities to carry on its own day to day administration. [23] Critics might say that this situation should never have been allowed to develop, but the only alternative for the HTA was to refuse further stamping facilities to the manufacturers concerned. Such action would have created a vicious circle which might well have led to the liquidation of any or all of these manufacturers, or at the very least, to loss of employment for island people as manufacturers paid off staff. Threats of charging overdraft interest on the outstanding fees had little more effect than eliciting an occasional, relatively small payment to account, if that. [24]

Because of the drop in income from stamping fees, the Association was forced to curtail its advertising budget, thereby adding another twist to the spiral of decline. When in late 1971, the Association had turned to the HIDB for help with advertising, the Board was prepared to make available a special grant of £25,000 on condition that the industry made steady progress towards the formation of a Central Marketing Organisation. The approach to marketing Harris Tweed was generally seen as one of the weaknesses in the industry. Another condition imposed by the HIDB when awarding the grant was that the stamping fee should be increased by 50% as from April 1st 1972 and by a similar amount on 1st October 1972. [25] Both the large manufacturers and the Small Producers complained about the increase, but, in imposing these conditions, the HIDB was not being unduly harsh, simply prudent in its use of public money.

While testing of the prototype loom and discussions with the Department of Trade and Industry about the need for amendment of the definition went ahead, it seems as if consultation with the weavers did not make satisfactory progress. According to the *Stornoway Gazette* of 21 April 1973, 'Stornoway Labour Party' wrote to Gavin Strang, MP, Opposition Spokesman on Highland Affairs, complaining that 'weavers in the Western Isles were concerned about the lack of consultation about the double-width loom which was being developed'. Gavin Strang wrote to the Rt. Hon. George Younger MP, Parliamentary Under Secretary of State for Development at the Scottish Office, who consulted the HIDB before replying. While this roundabout approach seems a strange way of acquiring information which should have been readily available through the Weavers' Branch of the TGWU, George Younger's reply gave a useful review of events between 1970 and 1973. He explained that the work being done by the HIDB was concerned with the Harris Tweed industry as a whole and not simply with the possible introduction of double-width looms. He wrote:

> ' ... late in 1970, because of the generally depressed state of the industry, the Board decide to carry out a wide-ranging review, following discussion with the interests chiefly concerned, including the six main manufacturers, in Lewis, the Hebridean Spinners Advisory Committee, the TGWU, the Federation of Crofters Unions, Lews Castle Technical College and the HTA. As part of that review the Board commissioned three separate studies:-
>
> 1. A survey of the distribution of Harris Tweed in the UK (Inbucon)
> 2. A marketing study of the Harris Tweed industry (AIC Ltd.)
> 3. A technical and organisational study of the industry.
>
> The major aim of the review was to identify ways and means of improving, extending and diversifying the industry, including the feasibility of the use of a double-width loom. Reports on the three studies have been received by the HIDB. While these cannot be made public as they contain information which is confidential to commercial interests, I can tell you that the marketing report revealed that there is considerable room for development, providing advantage is taken of the design capabilities of double-width tweed. Jointly with the Spinners Association, the Board accordingly commissioned Messrs Wilson & Longbottom of Barnsley (who are also meeting part of the cost) to design and build a prototype double-width hand-loom capable of producing double-width cloth without a much increased physical effort on the part of the weaver. A prototype loom has been constructed, but some technical difficulties encountered delayed progress thus making it hard to give an accurate prediction about when a production model will be available. ... The principal interests concerned are those I refer to above; and I understand from the HIDB that the TGWU and its

Weavers Branch have been kept closely informed as work on the prototype loom has proceeded and indeed have been represented on a Technical Committee set up by the Board to guide work on the loom. The other bodies represented on this committee are the Hebridean Spinners Advisory Committee, the HTA and the Board. If individual complaints have been made about lack of consultation, the Board suggest that in the first instance these might be best referred to the weavers' own Union. ... The stage has been reached when arrangements are in hand by the Union to nominate up to eight weavers to travel to Barnsley, where the prototype loom is being built, to inspect and test it in operation. I think the foregoing will demonstrate that the HIDB is very conscious of the fact that the weavers should be fully consulted on matters which have a vital bearing on their livelihood.' [26]

Gavin Strang said that he intended to ask the HIDB for summaries of the reports. His main concern was 'to dispel the persistent rumour that the double-width loom was too heavy to be kept going at an economic rate by an average Western Isles weaver'. [27]

As it turned out the rumours circulating in the islands were not too far off the mark. In August 1974, after meetings with 'various interests in the industry', Rear-Admiral Dunbar-Naismith, Deputy Chairman of the HIDB, and Chairman of the Restructuring Committee, held a press conference 'to give information to the weavers and others in the industry'. He outlined a number of 'suggestions for discussion', not 'cut-and-dried proposals'. He said that while the new double-width Wilson and Longbottom loom could be worked manually with much the same amount of physical effort as the Hattersley, the capital cost was so great that 'its use in this way would not be justified'. The Board believed that if power were applied to the new loom, or a comparable one, the operation could be a commercial success. [28] Abandoning the craft element in production of Harris Tweed was the first fatal flaw in the restructuring plan.

The central feature of the proposals was that the new looms should be grouped in workshops in the rural communities, each workshop containing twelve looms. Envisaging a 'factory' type situation for the looms was the second fatal flaw in the plan. A new holding company would be formed to own the looms. The weavers would have a major say in the running of the holding company and the TGWU would be invited to invest in it. The existence of the weavers' holding company might make it possible for weavers to have a contract of employment, thus removing the obstacles to their eligibility for insurance benefits. He drew attention to problems associated with the transitional period as the new looms were being phased in, particularly the problem of keeping a balance between users of the new loom and those who would continue to produce single-width tweed on the Hattersley. Raymond MacDonald, Scottish Secretary of the TGWU and a member of the HTA, welcomed the practical approach of all concerned in the discussions and felt sure that they would have the full support of all sections of the industry.[29] He congratulated the trade's representatives on the manner in which the workers had been consulted at every level and brought into discussions about the future.[30]

The weavers' reaction to the 'very tentative' proposals for change was guarded. They were willing to listen but wanted to know a good deal more of specific details before committing themselves. One weaver said,

> 'If security of work was guaranteed it would be worth investing in. Paying out perhaps over £1000 towards a new loom and then finding the whole lot going flat because of a drop in market demand was not something to be lightly undertaken. Before engaging in discussions about future plans, what about rectifying some present-day shortcomings? What about holiday pay? It's about time that was seen to. And it is high time weavers were regarded as eligible for National Insurance.'[31]

The obvious sense of insecurity in this statement, the misapprehension about individual weavers paying out £1000, and the sense of grievance so ready to come to the surface, should have been warning enough that much more work had to be done to win the weavers' confidence. Whatever willingness to listen may have existed at the end of 1974, by early the following year, island opinion seems to have turned against the proposals for restructuring the industry. For whatever reasons, and many reasons have been advanced since then, the whole plan began to go seriously wrong for the Restructuring Committee in early 1975.

Reference - On the Horns of a Dilemma: 1970 to 1974

1 *Stornoway Gazette,* 26. 9. 1970.
2 *ibid.*, 6. 2. 1971.
3 *ibid.*
4 Report of a meeting of the HTA Committee of Management with Hebridean Spinners, 25. 9. 1970.
5 *ibid.*
6 HTA Minutes, 25. 9. 1970.
7 *ibid.*, 27. 1. 1971.
8 *ibid.*, 22. 12. 1971.
9 Information supplied by J. A. McLean, Burness, Solicitors.
10 John Stevenson 'Price-Fixing', 616.
11 HTA Minutes, 27. 1. 1971.
12 *ibid.*
13 *Stornoway Gazette,* n.d. 1971.
14 *ibid.*, 10. 3. 1973.
15 *ibid.*, 7. 3. 1970.
16 *ibid.*, 10. 6. 1972.
17 *ibid.*, 22. 7. 1972.
18 *ibid.*, 4. 1. 1975.
19 HTA Minutes, 9. 1. 1973.
20 *ibid.*
21 *ibid.*
22 W. H. Renfrew, Secretary HTA to C. B. Powell-Smith, McKenna & Co., 6. 3. 1974. HTA Office, Stornoway.
23 HTA Minutes, 15. 9. 1975.
24 *ibid.*, 28. 3. 1972.
25 *ibid.*
26 *Stornoway Gazette,* 22. 4. 1973.
27 *ibid.*
28 *ibid.*, 3. 8. 1974.
29 *ibid.*
30 *ibid.*, 10. 8. 1974.
31 *ibid.*

20

The Weavers Say No

1975 was a particularly difficult year for all sections of the industry. Stamping of single-width Harris Tweed declined to just over two and a half million yards, less even than in 1951, the worst year since the end of the war. With no end to the recession in sight, marketing of double-width Harris Tweed was seen as the key to recovery. The proposals for restructuring the industry gained a new momentum as the crisis intensified.

A report for the HIDB by Inbucon/AIC Management Consultants in January stated that double-width machine-woven Harris Tweed would be readily accepted by all markets at the same price per square metre as single-width and it would eclipse single-width in all markets except the USA. The Report laid particular emphasis on central control, if marketing success and a proper return on investment in new looms were to be achieved. [1] The Harris Tweed Association was about to make an application to the Department of Trade and Industry for an amendment of the Orb trade mark. The amendment, if granted, would cover cloth hand-woven by the islanders at their own homes, in which case the cloth would be clearly marked 'hand-woven'. The amendment would also cover double-width cloth, power-woven by the islanders within the crofting townships 'in premises approved by the Harris Tweed Association.' [2] Tests on three 'power-weaving machines', including the Wilson and Longbottom power-driven loom, were about to start. The Restructuring Committee had discussed how a Weavers' Holding Company should be formed and had decided that sites recommended by weavers for sheds should be identified and examined. [3]

The members of the Restructuring Committee represented all sections of the industry and the HIDB. They were Rear-Admiral Dunbar-Naismith and J. A. Macaskill of the HIDB, James Shaw Grant and Harry Renfrew of the HTA, William MacLeod, Shawbost, and W. Bremner of the TGWU, representing the weavers, Ian Lawrence of Clansman Holdings Ltd., A. W. Hay of Kenneth Mackenzie Ltd., Derek Murray of Kenneth MacLeod (Shawbost) representing the Spinning Companies and Kenneth MacLeod of Seaforth Harris Tweeds, (on behalf of the Small Producers.) [4]

The announcement of the HTA's decision to go ahead with an application to the Department of Trade and Industry (DTI) to have the Orb trade mark amended seems to have rung warning bells in Harris. At its AGM in February, the Harris Craft Guild Ltd. agreed to lodge an official objection with the DTI. The grounds of the objection, which were based on the Hunter judgement of 1964, contended that production of Harris Tweed on double-width power-looms did not constitute hand-weaving, and that a factory containing a number of looms did not constitute the Islanders' own homes. Tweed produced in the manner proposed by the HTA would fall into the same category as tweed produced by IHTP in 1964. On behalf of the Guild, its Secretary, Ruaraidh Halford MacLeod, said in an interview with the *Scotsman* in March 1975, that if Orb-stamped tweed was to be produced on power looms in a factory, it would not be very long before the tweed was woven in the mills in Stornoway. That would be against the interests of all crofter-weavers who needed their looms at their homes so that they could carry on both jobs. Once in the mills in Stornoway, there would be no more rural weaving in Harris or even Lewis. The suggestion of including the word 'handwoven' was not sufficient distinction between tweed produced on a hand-loom and a power-loom. [5] Mr MacLeod also said that power-woven tweed would be the impostor and suggested that the new tweed should be called 'Lewis tweed', as it would all be made in Lewis. Then genuine Harris Tweed could be made by the genuine hand-weavers in Harris, rural Lewis and the Southern Isles. [6]

Close on the heels of the Harris Craft Guild, the Western Isles Constituency Labour Party issued a statement saying,

> 'It might be unwise to seek an amendment to the present definition of the Orb mark as this is the best protection the individual hand-weaver can have in the mechanised age into which the local industry appears to be moving. At the same time, the WICLP fully appreciates that there is an increasing demand for double-width cloth and the Party argues that the Isles mill-owners must do everything - and be encouraged to do everything - to satisfy it. Since it is now evident that the double-width man-powered loom is not a feasible proposition, powered looms must be used in the manufacture of the new cloth. And since the new

product will, under the WICLP proposals, be produced outside the limits of the Orb description, the Party proposes that a high-powered sales campaign, financed by mill-owners and the HIDB must be instituted to compensate for this disadvantage. In addition, a local name (possibly 'Lewis Tweed') could be found for the new product. ... The benefits of this proposal are seen by the WICLP as allowing a phased contraction of the Harris Tweed industry to a realistic level - to match the decreased demand for single-width cloth- whilst at the same time allowing island mill weavers to break into the new market which demands double-width cloth.' [7]

As a result of a BBC Current Account documentary on Harris Tweed on 23rd March, sixty Shawbost weavers voiced their opposition to the proposed changes in a statement to the Department of Trade and Industry. As two members of the Restructuring Committee, William MacLeod, the TGWU representative, and Derick Murray of Kenneth MacLeod (Shawbost) Ltd. actually lived in the same village as the sixty weavers, their covering letter with the petition to the DTI does raise the question as to how effective communications between the Shawbost weavers and the two members of the Restructuring Committee really were. The covering letter with the petition said:

'We learned from a recent BBC Scotland television programme (Current Account, 21/3/75) that the Harris Tweed Association has applied for a re-definition of Harris Tweed so that this name and its trade mark, the Orb, can be applied to double-width cloth woven on power looms. The enclosed petition shows that we are completely opposed to such a change in the definition of Harris Tweed. Of the sixty-three weavers in Shawbost who were given the opportunity to sign this petition, all but three were only too willing to do so. We feel certain that the vast majority of weavers throughout Lewis and Harris are of the same opinion as ourselves. We are therefore informing you that the weavers' viewpoint has not been sought or considered in this matter which is so crucial to our livelihood. It would seem that our TGWU representative puts across his personal viewpoint at meetings, rather than the viewpoint of the members which he is there to represent. The weavers were not informed by the Union, nor by the Harris Tweed Association, that they were applying to have the trade mark definition altered to include cloth woven on power looms. At a recent Union meeting in Shawbost after the television programme, not one single member knew what the wording of the new definition would be. At this recent meeting in Shawbost the Union delegate was asked to hold a TGWU general meeting in Stornoway taking in all weavers in Lewis and Harris so that the weavers could discuss and vote on the matter. Such a meeting has not been held to date. Nevertheless, we know that the weavers in areas such as Bragar are virtually unanimously opposed to any change of definition. ... On the television programme, the Chairman of the HTA said that with the power-driven double-width looms they could do with less than half the weavers they have at present. It is with the majority of weavers who are going to be made redundant that we are concerned. The weavers, in losing their jobs through changing the trade mark would not get any redundancy money and they would not be compensated in any way for the looms, winders and loom sheds they would have left lying on their hands.' [8]

Most of the information contained in the progress report published in the press in early February and the BBC television documentary should already have been common knowledge to everyone in the industry and to everyone who had been reading the Scottish press over the previous year. As William MacLeod, Chairman of the Weavers' Branch of the TGWU reminded people, press statements had been issued after meetings on 31st July 1974 and again on 21st January 1975. He also reminded weavers that he had given members a full report at quarterly meetings. He suggested that the poor attendance at Union meetings could account for the weavers' 'current state of ignorance'. [9]

While opposition from the Harris Craft Guild and from the Shawbost weavers dismayed those who were convinced of the need for an amended definition to include double-width tweed, it should not have been entirely surprising. Whatever the intention of a press statement issued by the Hebridean Spinners Advisory Committee on 25th April 1975, opposition would not have been expected from the body which, in September 1970, had been the first to propose an amended definition to include double-width Harris Tweed because 'garment manufacturers had turned against single-width Harris Tweed'. [10] At the very least, the Spinners' statement reflected a change of heart on their part. The statement said:

> 'The Hebridean Spinners Advisory Committee ... has viewed with concern the very serious consequences which might arise in the event of there being any diminution whatsoever in the protection given by the Orb mark in respect of narrow width cloth. It is the firm view of members of this committee that any application for an amendment to the definition must not prejudice in any way the present safeguards in respect of narrow width cloth. The Spinners also wish that the current narrow width hand-woven quality be continued with its own label and stamp. The proposed double-width quality could be given a new label and description. The existing format incorporating the 'Orb' and 'Cross' symbol coupled with the name 'Harris Tweed' should be common to both, but the label for each width should be quite distinctive. ... The Spinners would prefer to have an entirely new trade mark for double-width power-woven cloth, but having gone into the matter from a commercial point of view and having taken advice from various sectors of the market and the trade, the conclusion is that the basic form of the existing trade mark should be retained to obtain maximum sales benefit. ... Protection of this nature is sought so that any failure of the double-width cloth by reason of the definition, or for any other cause, would leave the narrow width Harris Tweed with no less protection and status than it presently commands.' [11]

The Spinners may have thought that by giving the same reassurance three times at the beginning of their statement, each time in slightly different words, they would convince the weavers and Harris Craft Guild of their good intentions and allay any suspicions that they wished to gain absolute control of the industry. The closing sentences suggest that their prime concern was, quite naturally, to achieve the 'maximum sales benefit' associated with sharing in the Orb trade mark. At least the spinners envisaged both single and double-width power-woven tweed coming under the Orb trade mark, in contrast to those who spoke in terms of single-width tweed being replaced by double-width power-woven tweed overnight.

At that point, the Restructuring Committee could have reported back to the HIDB and HTA saying that in light of the opposition encountered it would be a waste of time and money to take the proposals any further. In that they persevered, it must be assumed that they were all convinced that a change to production of power-woven double-width Harris Tweed was the only salvation available to the industry. Perhaps unlike the weavers, who tended to blame the mills for slack periods, they were only too well aware that all the evidence pointed to a continuing decrease in sales of single-width Harris Tweed. Despite the opposition, the committee continued with their plans and kept the island public informed of the progress made. The Committee saw 1975 as a period for general discussion, as final decisions had not yet been made on some details of the plan.

An Interim Report was issued to all weavers in August 1975, informing them about those aspects of the plan which had been decided. These were:

1. that double-width power-weaving of Harris Tweed would take place only in specially built weaving units, (probably constructed by the HIDB) and these would be situated in the weaving communities of the crofting areas of Lewis and Harris. This would preclude the manufacture of double-width cloth within the actual town of Stornoway.
2. that the cost of new looms would not fall on individual weavers.
3. that those weavers who chose to work in the new weaving units would automatically become Class 1 employees with entitlement to unemployment benefit.
4. that there would still be a market for single-width hand-woven cloth, particularly in the United States. [12]

The report also showed that output of Harris Tweed had dropped by more than half in the previous eight years The number of weavers had gone down from 1329 to 630. Even with this decline in the number of weavers, there was not enough full-time employment for the remaining weavers over much of the year. A survey of the main markets showed that, given the availability of double-width Harris Tweed cloth and a vigorous marketing policy, the demand for Harris Tweed could be extended considerably. Without double-width cloth, the chances were that the decline would continue with more short-time working and redundancies among the weavers and in the mills. The loom trials had been completed, although an additional British loom had still to be investigated in Yorkshire. In order to introduce double-width power-weaving the Harris Tweed Association would have to apply for a change in the Orb mark regulations. This step had not yet been taken and would not be taken until the views of the weavers were known.

With the use of power, fewer weavers would be needed to produce a given quantity of cloth, but with an expanding demand for double-width cloth against a declining demand for single-width cloth, the number of weavers employed in five to ten years could be as great, given the use of power, as it would be if the industry continued to decline. The weavers employed would have greatly improved working conditions. The Committee expressed the belief that if no changes took place to allow double-width Harris Tweed to be produced, the pressure of market forces would continue to be uncontrolled so far as weavers were concerned and employment of weavers would diminish without the right to unemployment benefit or redundancy pay. [13]

A substantial part of the double-width power-woven tweed already being produced in island mills was being made at Geocrab by Garry Weavers Ltd. which, by 1970, was 'part of the recently reconstituted Clansman Holdings Ltd. in which the Highlands and Islands Development Board had a minority share-holding'. [14] Because the Geocrab mill produced its own electricity from a water-powered generator, it had been able to continue production during the 'three-day week'. The Geocrab mill was 'working non-stop for three or four years, including overtime, often five nights a week because they could not produce enough of their double-width 'Hebridean Tweed', according to Manager, Garry MacLean in January 1976.' [15] This Hebridean Tweed was being sold at a lower price than Harris Tweed and its output was increasing at a time when the output of Harris Tweed was declining. Naturally, the production of this double-width tweed at Geocrab was seen as adversely affecting sales of genuine Harris Tweed. [16] Kenneth Mackenzie Ltd. decided that they too would have to produce a similar cloth. [17] It would appear that Clansman Holdings Ltd. agreed to cease production at Geocrab about the end of 1975 as a result of pressure.

Bruce Burns, Managing Director of Clansman Ltd., said, 'We were forced into the situation where we had to take this action very much against our better judgement'. He was unwilling to make any further comment except to say that Clansman Ltd. was 'exploring new avenues' which could mean work for Garry Weavers. [18] While the fate of Garry Weavers Ltd., and those in Harris whose jobs at Geocrab had come to an end, aroused public sympathy, this incident was just one part of the long drawn out effort to restructure the Harris Tweed industry in order to meet the demands of a textile market which had largely switched to more economical cutting of double-width low-cost products from Taiwan and South Korea. [19]

When asked to comment in early 1976 on the state of progress achieved towards a final package of proposals, the HIDB said:

> 'Despite the efforts of the HIDB and the HTA during the past year, it has not so far been possible to reach agreement with the weavers and the manufacturing companies on the proposals to introduce double-width power looms in the Harris Tweed industry. The Board are obviously disappointed that mor progress has not been made. They feel that any delays could adversely affect the future of the industry. The sales of Harris Tweed are still falling. They are also conscious that until agreement is reached, no move can be made towards an application for a change in the Orb mark regulations to allow the use of power looms in the production of Harris Tweed and no decision can be taken on the number of weaving units, their location and control.' [20]

A general meeting of the Weavers' Section of the TGWU was held on 26th February 1976. The proposals laid before the meeting were, in essence, the same as those described in the Interim Report of August 1975. Raymond MacDonald, Scottish Secretary of the TGWU and a member of the Harris Tweed Association, described the restructuring package to the sixty weavers present. The proposals were as follows:

'1. Application for an amendment of the regulations governing the Orb would be necessary before double-width power-woven Harris Tweed could be introduced.

2. Production of Hebridean tweed would cease if the proposals were accepted.
3. Specifically built weaving units in which power-woven double-width tweed would be produced would be located in the rural weaving communities and not in the town of Stornoway. Each unit would operate for sixteen hours per day on two shifts over five days a week. Wages would be negotiated.
4. The cost of the new loom would not fall on individual weavers.
5. It was accepted that there would be a continuing market for single-width Harris Tweed and those weavers who made single-width tweed for direct sale would not be affected by the proposals. Special efforts would be made to protect the interests of those weavers.
6. Manufacturers accepted in principle that if they controlled the weaving units a special yardage charge should be levied on double-width Harris Tweed in order to provide a Trust Fund for the benefit of those weavers who were displaced as a direct result of the introduction of double-width Harris Tweed. A redundancy payment, possibly £500, depending on the number of redundancies, would be made to displaced weavers.
7. A Distribution Centre, to be run by the HTA for single-width weavers, would be set up if the proposals were accepted. Weavers employed in the units would be classified as Class 1 employees and be entitled to the relevant benefits.

Therefore the options available to weavers if the restructuring proposals were accepted would be: to work as Class 1 employed weavers if they lived in an area with a weaving unit; to remain self-employed part-time hand-weavers with the benefit of a distribution centre or to retire from the industry and benefit from the Trust Fund. Raymond MacDonald concluded by urging the weavers to take time to think about the proposals.' [21]

To the annoyance of William MacLeod, Chairman of the Weavers' Section of the TGWU, Ruaraidh Halford MacLeod, turned up at the weavers' general meeting without permission from the Union. [22] This 'spokesman' for Harris was neither a weaver nor a Union member. He was simply Secretary of the Harris Craft Guild, a body which included only four weaver members - hardly a representative body! After the meeting, Ruaraidh Halford MacLeod supplied a report on the meeting to the *Stornoway Gazette* [23] which was, according to William MacLeod, 'rather inflammatory' and in which 'the figures quoted were quite incorrect'.[24] Raymond MacDonald of the HTA also repudiated the version of the Weavers' Welfare Fund which Ruaraidh Halford MacLeod issued to the *Stornoway Gazette* after the meeting of 26th February. [25] Whether Ruaraidh Halford MacLeod's participation in the debate exercised undue influence for someone so peripheral to the industry or whether the mood of the weavers was determined without his 'inflammatory' and 'inaccurate' contribution [26] is now difficult to judge. A second meeting was arranged for Tuesday 9th March. James Shaw Grant, Chairman of the HTA, was invited to speak at this second and much larger meeting at which 150 weavers were present. He described the five main criteria which the HTA had applied to the proposals placed before the meeting.

> 'First, the weaving employment had to be as widely distributed through the rural parts of Lewis and Harris as possible. Second, the benefits arising from power-weaving should be shared by the hand-loom weavers as well as by the employers. Third, the work available for hand-loom weavers should be as equitably distributed as possible. Fourth, double-width tweed should contribute to the promotion of single-width tweed to prolong the demand as far as possible and fifth, double-width tweed should be introduced gradually under close control and directed into those markets which did not find single-width acceptable.' [27]

Whether, as all the signs had been indicating, the weavers had already made up their minds to reject the plan, or whether James Shaw Grant's strong rebuttal at this meeting of Ruaraidh Halford MacLeod's interpretation of the proposals did not go down well with them, the result of a postal ballot on 17th April was that the weavers overwhelmingly rejected the proposals for restructuring the Harris Tweed industry. As had been promised by the HTA, that rejection was accepted as a democratic decision by those whose livelihood was at stake.

Probably the strongest motivating force in the weavers' decision was the fear that if the proposals were accepted, single-width Harris Tweed would very quickly be eclipsed by double-width, a reasonable fear in light of the success of double-width power-loomed Hebridean Tweed. If that had happened, then the relatively few weavers left in the industry would have become totally dependent on the mills to keep them in work. By rejecting the restructuring proposals and retaining the Orb mark for single-width cloth, they felt that they were retaining what little independence of action still remained to them. The Small Producers had for long been implacably opposed to the restructuring plan. They saw it as yet another manifestation of the large manufacturers exercising undue influence on the Harris Tweed Association in pursuit of their own interests. In a letter to the *Gazette,* Angus MacLeod, Marybank, articulated what seems to have been the common perception of the plan among weavers and Small Producers. He wrote:

> 'This is not a take-over by the mills, says Mr J. S. Grant. in reply to Halford MacLeod. Would it be more accurate to call it a sell-out to the mills by the HTA in the face of pressure from the Spinners, or more particularly, one Spinner, who introduced power-woven double-width imitation Harris-type tweed in the mid-1960s on the pretence of diversifying his production at a time when the industry was at its busiest period ever? ... It is morally wrong for a Lewis mill which is engaged in the manufacture of Orb-stamped Harris Tweed to undermine the protection afforded to genuine Harris Tweed by manufacturing an imitation power-woven double-width identical to genuine Harris Tweed in all respects, and selling it at a lower price in the same market place in competition with the hand-woven ... the mill concerned was taken to task by the HTA and by every mill and small producer in the industry at the time.' [28]

The most thoughtful and perceptive reaction from the national press came from *The Glasgow Herald*.

> 'Having bravely put tradition before economics, the home weavers of Harris Tweed must concentrate on their future. Demand for their justly famed products has dropped sharply in the past decade and they have rejected one obvious commercial answer, the switch to double-width power-woven cloth and the concentration into bigger industrial units. Probably no other

community in Britain would have rejected that alternative so decisively in the depths of an economic recession. But where do the weavers go from here? They should not retreat into commercially out-dated practices. ... It may be preferable for weavers to keep on working exclusively at home, despite an ever-diminishing market. But this must have an end somewhere - if not for the present working generation then for the next. It would be tragic if the weavers' dedication to their craft and their spirit of sturdy independence paved the way for the disintegration and decline of their industry.' [29]

Faced with what appeared to be terminal decline in sales of traditional single-width Harris Tweed, and receiving advice from manufacturers and the HIDB Inbucon/AIC Reports on the need to produce a double-width cloth, the Harris Tweed Association would have been perverse if they had refused to consider the introduction of double-width Harris Tweed, despite all the problems involved in such a departure from tradition. Looking back at the way the industry had been forced to adapt to market demands over the years, it seemed to them that yet another watershed had been reached at which the industry had either to accept once again the need for change or be left behind. When the HTA accepted the fundamental principle of adapting to meet market demands, the whole affair seems to have gathered a momentum of its own. Members of the Association were persuaded that double-width looms made power necessary. Power and larger looms made weaving units necessary, and so on until the restructuring package became a Frankenstein monster dictating its own pace and direction, sweeping the HTA, the HIDB and the TGWU along in its path. It might be tempting to portray the weavers as the dragon-slayers, but despite the plaudits of the *West Highland Free Press* for their stance, that would be carrying a colourful analogy too far. Crucially, in the discussions on restructuring the industry, members of the HTA seem to have forgotten the advice given by their lawyer in March 1972. The HTA Minutes record that the Committee of Management agreed that it

'should try to find a solution to the problem of double-width looms and their location without breaching the regulations.' [30]

On that occasion, one member of the Committee of Management said that he felt that weavers were not being kept fully informed of the new developments taking place in the industry and that there had to be closer co-operation with them if the plans were to be successful. He said that the weaver had a vital part to play and the crofter-weaver image must be maintained. Responding to these remarks, the Association's lawyer said that he believed that some changes might be necessary, but he advised caution.

> 'Weaving should not be in factories or under the control of another section of the industry, but before any changes affecting the weavers were considered there would have to be a careful study to ensure that the image of Harris Tweed as a cottage industry was not jeopardised.' [31]

With hindsight, it would seem that the fatal mistake was made when those involved in the restructuring plans forgot, or perhaps allowed themselves to be deflected from, one fundamental principle: that is that the name 'Harris Tweed' is the badge of a genuine craft industry with a local connection. If Harris Tweed is not hand-woven, it is not a craft product. It is the status of Harris Tweed as a craft product which makes it possible to protect it from factory-made imitations. If that special status had been relinquished in 1976, Harris Tweed would have become little different from any other factory-made tweed. Critics of the HTA and HIDB have cited the recovery, which started in 1977 and continued until 1984, as proof that the HTA was misguided in even considering the changes proposed by the Restructuring Committee. While the self-perpetuating momentum of the restructuring plan may have taken them down the blind alley of power-weaving and factory-type units, events in the late 1980s and early 1990s may suggest that the principle of accepting market demands was correct.

Once members of the Harris Tweed Association had recovered from the disappointment of the weavers' ballot, they turned their minds to another restructuring proposal first mooted by the then Chairman, James Shaw Grant, in 1975. This was the restructuring of the Association itself. [32] Membership of the Association was increased to twenty-three, of whom seven would be nominated by the producers and seven by the TGWU to represent both weavers and mill-workers.

Members of the Harris Tweed Association at Harris Hotel c.1948.

Back row left to right: Simon MacKenzie, Leverburgh; Col. Neil Macarthur; W. H. Martin, HTA Secretary, Donald M. Morrison, Tarbert; Mr Veitch, TGWU.

Front row left to right: Rev. Murdoch MacRae; George Ellis, HTA Chairman; Norman Robertson, Factor, North Harris Estate.

Members of the Harris Tweed Association c.1960.

Back row left to right: William Scholes, TGWU; Callum Gillies, C.A.; John Morrison, Northton, Harris; W. H. (Harry) Renfrew, HTA Secretary;

Front row left to right: Alasdair MacLeod, Stornoway Town Clerk; Col. Neil Macarthur, HTA Chairman; Roderick MacRae, HTA Stamper.

First AGM of the re-organised membership of the HTA in the Caberfeidh Hotel, Stornoway, 22nd February 1979.

Back row left to right: A. Alliston & Don Smith, Millworkers K. MacKenzie Ltd.; D. A. Stewt, Millworker, Clansman Ltd.; W. MacMonagle, TGWU; A. Hay, Director, K. MacKenzie Ltd.; G. Richardson, Newtec; M. Murray, Secy, Weavers' Union; Mr Harding, Accountant; D. R. Murray, Managing Director, K. MacLeod Ltd.; D. Chisholm, Chairman Weavers' Union; Charles Fraser, Edinburgh, Lawyer for HTA.

Front row left to right: R. MacDonald and D. MacDonald, Directors HTA; B. Burns, Managing Director, Clansman Ltd.; C. J. MacDonald, Chief Inspector HTA; C. Oakley, Director HTA; J. S. Grant, Chairman HTA; W. H. Renfrew, Secy. HTA; M. Macaulay, Inspector HTA.

© Courtesy of J. M. Morrison, Tarbert

Royal visit to Harris, August 1956.

Dr Wood, Tarbert; Rev. Norman MacDonald, Scarista; Mrs A. MacDonald, Drinishader; H.M. Queen Elizabeth; H.R.H. Duke of Edinburgh; Norman Mackillop, Tarbert; T. Cameron, Harris Hotel; Mrs R. W. MacDonald, Drinishader, presenting the Tweed.

(a) Still in use.

(b) Has been superseded by **(2)** on page 318.

HARRIS TWEED
WOVEN IN UIST

(c) Still in use.

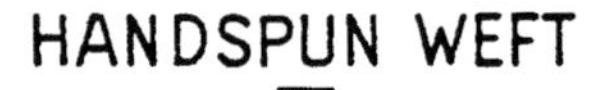

(d) Still in use.

Harris Tweed Association Stamps.

(1) This Orb was the original one registered in many countries.

(2) This version of the Orb is now used in all registrations except USA.

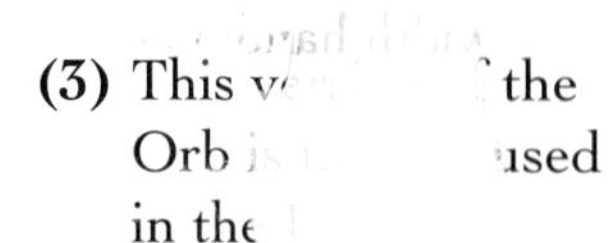

(3) This v the Orb used in the

Versions of weed Trade Mark, commonly known as 'The Orb'.

© Courtesy of Eòlas for HTA

Kenny J[illegible] MacKenzie
on the B[illegible]riffith
double-[illegible]ndloom.

© Courtesy of F. Trotter

Bridal outfit in white Harris Tweed.

The other places were to be taken up by the seven members of the Board of Directors with two other members appointed 'to represent the special interests of Harris and the Southern Isles'.[33] Many years later, Jim Grant, as he was always known to islanders of his generation, described the HTA as it was when he was its Chairman.

> 'Although the HTA rendered great service to the Harris Tweed trade over many years its structure was ramshackle and inefficient. It began life as a privately owned trade organisation and gradually evolved into a non-profit-making body, protecting the industry as a whole from imitations through the Orb trade mark. It still retained the structure of a private limited company and was described by an eminent lawyer as a 'self-perpetuating oligarchy'. Like an oligarchy it could easily have slipped into the wrong hands with disastrous consequences for the islands. I devised a new constitution which secured three important objectives. It entrenched the rule that directors of the HTA received no payment for their services. It established, for the first time, a rule that no one who had any financial stake in the industry could be a director, so no one could have an axe to grind. It also introduced an entirely new rule that everyone appointed a director must be acceptable to both sides of the industry: employers and employees alike. At the time I got this new constitution accepted, the HTA was top heavy with elderly directors. Even the Secretary, on whom everything depended, was well into his seventies with no apparent intention of retiring and no contract which specified a retiral date. Getting rid of the geriatrics (including myself) was one of the most unpleasant tasks I have ever undertaken, but it had to be done in the interests of the industry.'[34]

The closing years of the decade between 1970 and 1980 saw the industry making up lost ground. Production of traditional Harris Tweed increased by over a million yards between 1977 and 1978 and closed the decade approaching a respectable four and a half million yards in 1980. The long-awaited Distribution Centre was established in 1977 as an independent body allocating work impartially throughout the island. A Supervisor was appointed and he was responsible to a Management Committee under an independent chairman. This was seen as a major step towards improving efficiency in matching demand to weaving capacity at a time when the industry could not get enough weavers to fulfil orders. The supply of second-hand looms had dried up and the HIDB made looms available for leasing through a loom bank. What a marked contrast this was to the lean years at the start of the decade when hundreds of weavers and mill-workers were being made redundant and small producers were closing down in despair. When Kenneth Mackenzie Ltd. won the Queen's Award for Export in 1978 everyone assumed that the industry had at long last turned the corner.

Reference - The Weavers Say No

1 Report by Inbucon/AIC Management Consultants, January 1975: Vol. 1, p. 1, Summary of Conclusions and Recommendations.
2 *Stornoway Gazette*, 1. 2. 1975.
3 *ibid.*
4 *ibid.*
5 *Scotsman*, 6. 3. 1975.
6 *Stornoway Gazette*, 8. 3. 1975.
7 *ibid.*
8 M. Gillies and A. Murray, South Shawbost to The Minister, Department of Trade and Industry, House of Commons, 12. 4. 1975, copied to *Stornoway Gazette*, 19. 4. 1975.
9 *Stornoway Gazette*, 26. 4. 1975.
10 Report of meeting of HTA with Hebridean Spinners, 25. 9. 1970.
11 *Stornoway Gazette*, 25. 4. 1975.
12 *ibid.*, 2. 8. 1975.
13 *ibid.*
14 *Press and Journal*, 23.1. 1976.
15 *ibid.*
16 HTA Minutes, 4. 12. 1975.
17 *Stornoway Gazette*, 27. 3. 1976.
18 *Press and Journal*, 26. 1. 1976.
19 W. G. Lucas in *The Scotsman*, 26. 1. 1976, 'Crucial Year for Harris Tweed Industry'.
20 W. G. Lucas in the Press and Journal, 23.1. 1976, 'Crucial Year for Harris Tweed Industry'.
21 *Stornoway Gazette*, 6. 3. 1976.
22 *ibid.*
23 *ibid.*
24 *ibid.*, 27. 3. 1976.
25 *ibid.*, 20. 3. 1976.
26 *ibid.*, 27. 3. 1976.
27 *ibid.*, 20. 3. 1976.
28 *ibid.*, 27. 3. 1976.
29 *Glasgow Herald*, 19. 4. 1976, 'Tangled threads'.
30 HTA Minutes, 28. 3. 1972.
31 *ibid.*
32 *ibid.*, 4. 12. 1975.
33 *Press and Journal*, 23. 12. 1978.
34 James Shaw Grant, 'Democracy or Dictatorship?' in *Stornoway Gazette*, 31. 7. 1997.

21

A Contracting Industry: 1980 to 1990

If the importance of Harris Tweed to the economy of the Outer Hebrides were to be estimated in terms of column inches in the local press between 1980 and 1985, a reader might well assume that it had been replaced by farmed salmon and shellfish as the principal products of these islands. Yet, despite fluctuations from year to year, production of Harris Tweed rose between 1980 and 1985 by almost a million yards per year compared to the five years between 1975 and 1979. 1984 was a boom year with production reaching 5.3 million yards. Output of tweed began to drop in the middle of 1985, while the value of seafood increased. In 1987, Comhairle nan Eilean's Department of Economic Development and Planning confirmed that the combined first sale value of all seafood was well over £17 million, without counting the added value of processing. Sales of Harris Tweed, at just over 3 million yards, contributed about £20 million to the island economy in 1987, [1] which represented a considerable drop from earlier in the decade. By the end of the decade, production had plummeted to levels which had not been seen since the mid-1930s. Yet another manufacturer disappeared from the island scene and the weaving force continued to contract.

Whatever may be said, perhaps with some measure of truth, about the damage done to the industry by internal rivalries between Spinners and Small Producers, or between individual producers, the undeniable fact is that in the late 1980s the vital North American market collapsed before new export markets had reached a comparable level. The desperate situation was certainly exacerbated when large quantities of Harris Tweed were off-loaded onto the lower end of the North American market at a depressed price. This panic reaction by some manufacturers had a severe knock-on effect at the top end of the market. Major retail stores in the United States and Canada were reluctant to display Harris Tweed in 1988 because similar garments of lower quality were being discounted. [2] The prestige of Harris Tweed was so seriously affected that the British Wool Marketing Board expressed reservations about the use of its name alongside that of Harris Tweed, lest the discounting which had had an adverse effect on the image of the Harris Tweed Association might also affect the image of the British Wool Marketing Board. [3]

Yet the 1980s seem to have been a period of considerable achievement in the industry. Kenneth Mackenzie Holdings Ltd. won the Queen's Award for Exports for the third time. New markets were developed in the Far East, particularly in Japan. Despite a steady decline in production between 1985 and 1989, the industry embarked once again on a programme of re-tooling and restructuring. This time the Harris Tweed Association and the Highlands and Islands Development Board took good care to avoid making the mistakes which had taken the industry down a blind alley in the mid-1970s. The lesson that Harris Tweed was a craft industry, and must be protected as such, had been learned. A comprehensive review of the legal status of the Harris Tweed trade mark in Europe and the United States led, after some years of preparation, to the establishment in 1993 of a statutory body, the Harris Tweed Authority, which was legally empowered to safeguard the well-being of the industry, in contrast to the voluntary status of the Harris Tweed Association. In the second half of the decade, modern business management skills were the hallmark of a new and younger HTA Board of Management, employing a Chief Executive rather than a Secretary to handle day-to-day affairs.[4] The Board of Management made much greater use of public relations to dispel the old image of autocracy and secrecy which had been the common perception of the Association in earlier years. A new emphasis was laid on accurate forecasting of anticipated production in order to allow advance planning for advertising. Promotion and public relations campaigns, based to a much greater extent than previously on research and analysis of home and foreign markets, largely replaced press advertisements.[5] Sadly, as it turned out, planned promotions were often curtailed when production failed to meet expectations. In these circumstances, the HIDB made advertising grants available.

A programme of networking which ranged from regular visits to weavers in the Western Isles to entertaining leaders of the textile industry was established. On visits to weavers, the topics discussed included spare parts for looms, apprentice weavers, fathers training their sons to weave, grants for bobbin winders, education and training, legal processes, the optimum numbers of weavers, and stocks of unfinished tweeds. The important message put across was that the HTA was willing to listen and act, as far as possible, on matters of concern to the weavers. The programme of entertaining people like the Chairmen of the Woollen

Industry Research Association, the National Wool Textile Export Corporation, the British Wool Marketing Board and the Confederation of British Textiles established useful links between these bodies, members of the HTA Board of Management and Island producers.

Although weavers may have felt that their interests were ignored by the rest of the industry, the Harris Tweed Association and the mill-owners were very well aware of their importance. When Robert Stewart, Managing Director of James MacDonald Ltd. told the first weaving students to graduate from Lews Castle College in 1969 that whatever the contribution of the mills to the industry, the well-being of the Harris Tweed industry rested largely on their shoulders, [6] he was speaking from many years of experience as a producer of Harris Tweed. The undeniable tensions which have always existed between weavers as self-employed craftsmen and other sections of the industry, no doubt have their roots in the evolution of the weavers' role in the production of Harris Tweed. At the beginning of the century, as crofter-fishermen who turned temporarily to weaving to supplement their incomes, weavers could often market the tweed themselves or sell it through a local independent producer. In this situation weavers had a degree of independence and autonomy which employees in the mills did not have. Gradually over the twentieth century, as production became more commercialised, the weavers' dependence on the mills increased and their original autonomy was eroded, particularly in 1934, and again in 1964, when the importance of observing the regulations pertaining to the Orb stamp were emphasised and re-emphasised.

The fact that external authority, whether in the shape of County Councils based in Dingwall or Inverness, or national government based in London, could all too frequently be accused of having scant regard for the particular needs of the Western Isles, may explain the anti-establishment sentiments which have so often coloured the political history of the area. From at least 1934, the Harris Tweed Association came to be perceived as an external authority enforcing its will on weavers, over the origin of the yarn to be used, over standards of production, in attempting to alter the definition of Harris Tweed to include power-woven double width cloth in the mid-1970s, and in the 1980s, over the use of electric motors on looms. As James Shaw Grant pointed out, the introduction of electricity to the Hebrides was undoubtedly a boon but, paradoxically, the availability of electric power led to conflict between the HTA and those weavers who succumbed to the temptation of attaching an electric motor to their looms - a sensible enough thing to do, it might seem, except that it contravened the definition of handwoven Harris Tweed. Although a small number of 'occasional' weavers were found to have broken the rules from time to time, the solid core of weavers who depended on weaving as their main income knew very well that the penalty for being caught power-weaving was refusal of the Orb stamp for their finished tweeds. [7]

Achieving the right balance between having enough weaving capacity to meet demand when orders were plentiful, and not having too many weavers looking for work when a cyclical slump occurred, was an almost insoluble problem. When the Distribution Centre was established in 1977, weavers registering with the Centre had indicated how many tweeds they could undertake over a certain period. During the slump of the mid-1970s, the number of weavers dropped. When orders began to increase between 1978 and 1981, the mills found that they had to turn away orders and make staff redundant because some weavers had over-estimated their own levels of production. The Chairman of the Weavers' Union admitted that weavers had undertaken to produce an agreed amount of tweed over a given period and that some of them had failed to meet that target. Explaining the failure he said,

> 'Anybody who knows the history of the Harris Tweed industry knows that in the past it worked hand in glove with crofting and peatwork, but now there are many people who depend on it completely for their livelihood. The weaver has been his own Lord and Master for so long and is reluctant to accept that he must produce so many yards of tweed a week.' [8]

The inherent problem lay in reconciling the practices and attitudes of a craft industry providing a supplementary income to its practitioners with the needs of a fully commercialised textile industry competing in world markets.

It was estimated in 1980 that there were only 640 active weavers when the industry needed about 750 weavers to meet production demands. In an effort to attract more weavers into the industry, a loom fund to buy 50 looms and winders was jointly financed by the Hebridean Textile Manufacturers Association, the HIDB, the HTA, Western Isles Islands Council, the TGWU, the Department of Trade and

Industry and the Royal Bank of Scotland. Weavers using the fund were required to repay their loan at the rate of £4 per tweed over 4 years. Because of rising costs and some loss of funding from the HIDB, repayments increased to between £6 and £7 per tweed. [9] All the weavers who received a loom through the loom fund were covered by insurance for sickness, so that they could maintain payments if they were unable to work. [10] Weaving courses which had started at Lews Castle College in 1978 trained thirty weavers per year, a total of 90 weavers between 1978 and June 1981. In the early 1980s there were many more applicants for the weaving course than there were places, partly because this course at Lews Castle College was one of the few such courses in Scotland which guaranteed a job at the end of training.

The normal pattern of work in the industry was that orders were supplied to dealers and agents in the U.S. at the beginning of the year. Depending on the dealers' or agents' ability to sell Harris Tweed to customers, there would be repeat orders which kept weavers in work in the late summer and autumn. A recession in the United States in 1982 led to a lack of orders in the autumn of that year. The weaving course at Lews Castle College was withdrawn and Ian Mackenzie, Secretary of the Weavers' Union, said that they would shortly have to rationalise the number of weavers by natural wastage. [11] Harris Mackenzie of Kenneth Mackenzie Ltd. told the *West Highland Free Press* that whatever problems Harris Tweed might be having, those were as nothing compared to the textile industry on the mainland. Referring to textile workers elsewhere in Britain, he said, 'They think they are lucky if they are working two days a week. Whether the current American recession will be as bad as the papers claim is in the lap of the gods.' [12] The gods must have looked favourably on the Harris Tweed industry when the expected downturn was averted in late 1982 - early 1983, principally because the weakness of the pound against the dollar led to larger orders than had been expected from the US at a time when the West German and home markets were at an all-time low. Despite the concerns at the beginning of the year, production for 1983 reached almost 4.5 million yards.

In 1984 and early 1985, because of the comparative weakness of the pound to the dollar - they were at parity for some time - large quantities of tweed were selling in the US at a quarter of the usual price under 'normal' rates of exchange. [13] This artificial boom was by no means the blessing that it appeared to be. Production for 1984 was a staggering 5.4

million yards. So keen was the industry to recruit weavers, preferably young weavers, that the College restarted its weaving course and also offered a three-day test to weavers who already had some experience. Any weaver under twenty who passed the test was guaranteed automatic entry to the Weavers' Branch of the TGWU. If the applicants for the test were over twenty, they went on the Union's waiting list. [14] With Harris Tweed very much in fashion in the United States and 'the dollar and pound still virtually interchangeable', [15] 1985 looked like being as good as 1984. The imminent problem, if the boom continued, lay in recruiting sufficient skilled weavers to meet demand. The Managing Directors of Kenneth Mackenzie's, Clansman and MacLeods of Shawbost all said that they had had to turn down orders. The manufacturers estimated the optimum number of weavers at between 800 and 900, while the TGWU felt that the existing number of slightly over 700 was about right. With 1500 tweeds a week being returned to the mills, payments to weavers, at an average of £58 per tweed, injected some £90,000 per week into the island economy in 1984-85. [16]

As it transpired, the Weavers' Branch of the TGWU was right to exercise caution in the number of weavers it admitted to the industry. During a boom, it was all too tempting for aspiring weavers to leave other employment and commit themselves to buying a loom only to find that they had come into the industry just as the need for weavers was in decline. In July 1985 the signs were that demand for Harris Tweed was on the wane, at least for the time being. One weaver's complaint that the industry did not ensure that there was an even spread of tweeds throughout the year, rather than 'twenty one month and hardly any the next', suggests that he at least did not realise the extent to which the mills were dependent on fulfilling orders as they came in and could not provide work if orders failed to materialise. Confirming that the industry was 'quieter than usual for the time of year', Willie John MacDonald, Manager of the Harris Tweed Distribution Centre, denied that the market had been flooded. He attributed the drop in orders to the fact that, the 'almighty dollar took a bit of a banging and the pound had improved'. [17]

By November 1985, it was quite clear that the boom was over. The Weavers' Branch of the TGWU closed its books to all but trainee weavers graduating from Lews Castle College. (The Union had given the College a 3-year guarantee that they would accept all trainee weavers completing the course.) Ian Mackenzie, Secretary of the Weavers' Union, described 1984 as 'a freak year' during which the pound had been low against the dollar. This had led to a 'terrific demand' for Harris Tweed. Many of those closely involved with the industry maintain that a fair proportion of the tweed bought in 1984 had been stockpiled and this accounted for the lack of orders in 1985. Commenting on the restrictions imposed on weavers joining the Union, Ian Mackenzie said,

> 'We will not be going over the 700 mark in membership in future because it has been proved that the work is just not there for us. Demand is down about 25% compared to last year. About 1600 tweeds per week were issued last year, and it has been hovering between 1050 and 1250 per week for the past month. Sometimes it was down to 700 or 800 per week. We have had six months without a regular issue.' [18]

By mid-1986 most people in the industry were prepared to admit that the boom of the early 1980s had passed. Demand from foreign markets had slumped and the mills faced the prospect of an indefinite three-day working week. Harris Mackenzie of Kenneth Mackenzie Ltd. said that a peak in production normally lasted for only three years and that it was quite exceptional for a fashion product like Harris Tweed to enjoy a peak lasting as long as the four to five years they had just experienced. [19] The ensuing four years make gloomy reading. Stamping returns at the end of 1986 were the lowest for ten years at approximately 3. 27 million metres. [20] They continued to drop each year until, at 1.38 million metres in 1990, they reached the lowest level recorded since 1935. [21] The HTA and the manufacturers were all agreed on the need to re-establish the position of the industry in North America, the largest export market, but with continued discounting of Harris Tweed in Canada, and a decline in the dollar, prospects of improvement were remote. In descending order of sales, the main markets for Harris Tweed were Canada, the USA, the UK, Japan, France, Germany, Italy, Holland, Spain, Belgium and Switzerland. [22]

Even although island manufacturers, when speaking in public, expressed confidence in an eventual upturn in demand, it was inevitable that external confidence in the industry would begin to falter. When the annual Report of Scottish English and European Textiles showed, in August 1989, that Group profits had slumped from £10.2 million to £9.5 million, Jock Mackenzie, Chairman of the SEET Group, suggested that, because production of Harris Tweed, at 2.2 million yards in 1988, had fallen to the lowest figure for over 40 years, it might be sensible for the three largest island producers to consider a merger or mergers. Speculation in the islands was fuelled still further by his comment that he thought that 'something might be agreed by the end of the year'. [23] Harris Mackenzie of Kenneth Mackenzie Ltd., whose company was a member of the SEET group, said that he knew nothing of any merger or mergers. Mike Ferris, Managing Director of Clansman Holdings Ltd., and Derek Murray of Kenneth MacLeod (Shawbost) Ltd., both denied any knowledge of a proposed merger. Jock Mackenzie's later comment that as 'it was a sensitive area he should say nothing more', [24] did nothing to allay the fears of mill employees and weavers who were concerned about the future of their own jobs. In private, the Board of Management of the Harris Tweed Association expressed their 'concern at the adverse effect on the image of the industry' caused by the statements made by the Chairman of SEET. [25]

It was common knowledge in the islands that the Highlands and Islands Development Board was a major shareholder in Clansman Holdings Ltd. (HIDB held a 40% shareholding in the company. This holding had originated as part of a 'rescue operation' in 1975.) The frequently expressed fear was that, if the HIDB pulled out, Clansman would be ripe for a take-over or merger. Speaking to a reporter for the *Stornoway Gazette*, in September 1989, a spokesman for the HIDB said that the Board had 'a standing instruction from the Scottish Office that they should dispense with shares, if possible, and not hold on to them on a long-term basis'. He went on to explain that because of those instructions, the HIDB would be 'open to offers' in regard to Clansman, although as yet 'there had been no suggestion of any'. [26] Within six weeks of this statement, fears for the viability of Clansman were confirmed with the news that the receiver had been called in. Mike Ferris (who had been Finance Director of Clansman from 1975 to 1988, and had become Managing Director when Bruce Burns took early retirement in 1988 over 'major company policy disagreements') explained why the company had decided to call in the receiver. He gave two main reasons for the collapse: 'the falling away of the

American market and the price war between manufacturers that ensued'. Announcing the receivership he said,

> 'We are losing money at a fairly alarming rate. We feel obliged to ask the Bank to appoint a receiver at a stage when, hopefully, we can still pay all our creditors. It may well be that the receiver can sell the company as a going concern. We have looked at doing deals on the island. That can be pretty well ruled out now.' [27]

Explaining in further detail the background to the company's problems, Mike Ferris said that turnover had dropped over the four years between 1985 and 1989 from more than half their production of Harris Tweed being sold to America to virtually nothing being sold there in 1989. As there was no sign of an upturn in the industry within a short enough time-scale, it was impossible to persuade people to lend them money to rationalise manufacturing processes in one location in order to improve efficiency. [28] (This was a reference to a detailed study of Clansman which had highlighted the fact that the company's operations were less than fully efficient because they were spread over a number of sites on Rigs Rd and Bells Rd in Stornoway.) The rationalisation plan produced by the study would have required a 'substantial investment in new buildings, plant and reorganisation costs'. The costs which would have been incurred in implementing the rationalisation plan proved to be in excess of the anticipated sale proceeds from surplus premises. In the absence of any prospect of either an upturn in sales of Harris Tweed, or a profitable sale of surplus premises, finance for rationalisation could not be raised. In these circumstances, the company recognised that it had no option but to cease trading while there was still some hope of paying its creditors. Despite persistent rumours that the Highlands and Islands Development Board, as a major shareholder in Clansman, had influenced the decision to call in the receiver, Mike Ferris explicitly denied any suggestion that the HIDB had put pressure on them. [29]

Clearly from Mike Ferris' own statement to the press, the option of selling the company as a going concern had been discussed with other island manufacturers when Clansman's precarious financial position demanded urgent action. Preliminary discussions about selling seem to have run into insurmountable difficulties. Mike Ferris explained that 'the selling of Clansman to another business was not as simple as it might seem'. He said that Clansman could not simply make all its employees redundant and allow the new company to select their own employees, without being automatically liable to unfair dismissal proceedings, under the 'transfer of undertakings' legislation. The potential financial liability of this option was such that it had ruled out the possibility of doing a deal with another island manufacturer. [30] The only remaining hope was that the receiver, Murdoch Mackillop of Arthur Anderson and Co., would be able to keep the company trading while a buyer willing to take over the whole Clansman group was found.

Forty-seven Clansman employees were paid off almost immediately. While the remaining employees continued working for a few weeks to fulfil existing orders, the business was offered for sale in the *Financial Times* as a going concern. A number of employees left voluntarily and most of the others were paid off in November and December, leaving a skeleton staff off twenty-six by the end of December 1989. [31] Some forty responses to the advertisement raised a 'glimmer of hope' that a buyer might yet be found. In the event, a 'seamless' take-over of Clansman Holdings by one buyer was not achieved. Kenneth MacLeod (Shawbost) Ltd. bought all Clansman's plant and machinery, and the trading names of the marketing companies, S. A. Newall & Sons Ltd., Smiths of Stornoway Ltd. and Stephen Burns Ltd., all names which were well-known throughout the world. [32] Clansman had continued to use these original mills' names for marketing purposes and they would have been of significant value to Kenneth MacLeod (Shawbost) Ltd. The HIDB, who owned the mill in Bells Rd (previously used by Stephen Burns as a spinning and finishing mill) consented to the assignation of the lease of these premises by the receiver to Kenneth MacLeod (Shawbost) Ltd. [33] and the mill was eventually purchased by that firm. [34]

News, firm news, of what exactly was happening at Clansman was anxiously awaited by the island community and news was scarce. When news did come out, it came out in unsatisfactory dribs and drabs which did not allay the fears of creditors, in particular the fears of weavers whose £98,000 'holiday pay' was held by Clansman. (This 'holiday pay' was composed of a deduction on the rate of payment for tweeds woven. The accumulated money was held over and paid in a lump sum as 'holiday pay'.) When the take-over by Kenneth MacLeod (Shawbost) Ltd. was announced, the press statement gave no details of the arrangements between the receiver and Kenneth MacLeod (Shawbost) nor of the price paid. The receiver had been called in in October 1989, but the first meeting of creditors did not take place until the end of January 1990. The complexity of the structure of Clansman, which included eight separate companies, each with different assets and liabilities, no doubt explains the delay in presenting creditors with an account of the financial situation. Three months was however an excruciatingly long wait for those whose future hung in the balance. The greatest worry for those who wove for Clansman was whether or not they would be granted preferential status, or whether they would be deemed to be ordinary creditors who were expected to receive only 50p in the pound.

At the Creditors' meeting the receiver reported that in August 1987, the company had shown a loss of £84,000. In 1988, losses had increased to £278,000. The unaudited accounts for 1989 showed a loss of £437,000. The company was certainly 'losing money at a fairly alarming rate'. A buyer had not yet been found for South Harris Seafoods Ltd., a fish farm situated in what had been the mill at Geocrab in which Clansman had an 80% holding. It was estimated that preferential creditors would be paid in full, but ordinary, unsecured creditors, including the 550 self-employed weavers, would receive 50p in the pound. Most of the questions asked at the Creditors' meeting were related to the £98,000 'holiday pay' due to the weavers. The receiver explained that as the weavers were not employees they had to be treated like any other ordinary creditors. He felt that it was unfortunate that the agreement between the Weavers' Union and the mill had not stipulated that 'holiday pay' should be set aside in a formal trust. [35] The forecast in January 1990 that ordinary creditors might receive a payment of 50p in the pound proved to have been too cautious as the eventual payment reached 80p in the pound by 1993. [36]

There can be little doubt that the decline in demand for Harris Tweed, particularly the decline in the North American market from 1986, placed an enormous strain on all the island manufacturers. That Clansman was the first to succumb may well have been related to the acknowledged need for rationalisation and increased efficiency of production on a purpose-built site, something which eventually proved to be impossible to achieve in a depressed market. On the other hand, the final crisis had possibly been foreshadowed when an earlier slump in sales exerted similar pressure on Clansman in 1975-76. A series of mergers in the early 1970s led to the formation of Clansman Holdings Ltd. Another merger in 1973 with a Shetland knitwear company, Shetland Fashions Ltd., led to the creation of a company called Gaelspun as a Holding company for Clansman. The rationale behind this merger was that although Clansman had a strong asset base, it was not making much profit, while Shetland Fashions was a very profitable company. The hope was that the merger between Clansman and Shetland Fashions Ltd. would produce a strong Scottish textile group. [37] By late 1974, both Gaelspun and Clansman were in serious financial difficulties with losses amounting to £300,000 and liabilities totalling over £1 million. [38] In 1975, Gaelspun relinquished formal control of Clansman. With the help of the Highlands and Islands Development Board a restructured Clansman Group was formed in which Gaelspun and the HIDB retained a substantial shareholding with a representative nominated by the HIDB as a Director and Chairman of the restructured company. At the time, the reasons for the financial crisis were given as 'high wool prices, major labour cost increases, astronomical interest rates, falling demand and the general recession'. The hope was expressed that 'more modern plant and a new marketing policy would bring eventual salvation for the restructured company'. [39]

Despite attempts to modernise plant and improve efficiency in the subsequent twelve years, resolution of some fundamental problems at Clansman seems to have been postponed during the boom of the early 1980s rather than resolved. It would be fair to concede that Clansman had a fundamental problem in its 'inherited multi-site manufacturing facility' and this problem had undermined the efficiency and competitive capacity of the firm for many years. The full effect of this problem was not appreciated until it became necessary to examine employee numbers and remuneration in the 1980s and compare these figures with those of other companies. Mike Ferris believes that the only realistic solution would have been to build a completely new mill on a 'green field site' with new plant. Such a radical step would have been prohibitively expensive. [40] All less drastic attempts to resolve the problem, such as modernising the finishing department, seem to have been to no avail. When the testing slump of the late 1980s hit the industry, Clansman was ill-equipped to see it through the crisis. Perhaps it was inevitable that a contracting market would seek out the weakest link in the industry, and that would seem to have been Clansman.

Reference - A Contracting Industry: 1980 to 1990

1 *Stornoway Gazette*, 26. 11. 1988.
2 HTA Minutes, 2. 12. 1988.
3 *ibid.*
4 *ibid.*, 9. 7. 1982.
5 *ibid.*, 25. 3. 1983.
6 *Stornoway Gazette*, 21. 6. 1969.
7 James Shaw Grant to the author, July 1999.
8 *Stornoway Gazette*, 30. 8. 1980.
9 *ibid.*, 19. 7. 1980.
10 *ibid.*, 6. 6. 1981.
11 Peter Hetherington, 'Business wears thin for Harris Tweed', in the Guardian, 16. 8. 1982.
12 *West Highland Free Press*, 7. 1. 1983.
13 *Stornoway Gazette*, 9. 2. 1985.
14 *ibid.*
15 *West Highland Free Press*, 1. 3. 1985.
16 *ibid.*
17 *Stornoway Gazette*, 20. 7. 1985.
18 *West Highland Free Press*, 29. 11. 1985.
19 *ibid.*, 4. 7.1986.
20 HTA Minutes, 4. 12. 1986.
21 *ibid.*, 23. 9. 1988. and 13. 3. 1990.
22 *ibid.*, 1. 10. 1987.
23 *West Highland Free Press*, 8. 9. 1989.
24 *Stornoway Gazette*, 9. 9. 1989.
25 HTA Minutes, 5. 10. 1989.
26 *Stornoway Gazette*, 9. 9. 1989.
27 *ibid.*, 28. 10. 1989.
28 *ibid.*
29 *ibid.*
30 *ibid.*
31 *West Highland Free Press*, 15. 12. 1989.
32 Correspondence between M. Ferris (ex-Managing Director Clansman Ltd.) and the author December, 1998.
33 *Stornoway Gazette*, 23. 12. 1989.
34 Correspondence between J. A. MacAskill, (Secretary to HIDB in 1989) and the author, 1. 12. 1998.

35 *West Highland Free Press*, 26. 1 1990.
36 *Stornoway Gazette*, 2. 10. 1993.
37 Interview with M. Ferris (ex-Managing Director Clansman Ltd.) 29. 7. 1997.
38 Neil Munro in the *West Highland Free Press*, 1. 10. 1976.
39 *ibid*.
40 Correspondence between M. Ferris (ex-Managing Director Clansman Ltd.) and the author, 7. 12. 1998.

22

The Harris Tweed Act: The Industry in the 1990s

By 1990 it had become clear that a radical process of modernisation offered the best hope of recovery for Harris Tweed. There were three main areas in which the industry had failed to keep abreast of the changes which had taken place over some twenty years. These were (1) in meeting the demand for a wider, softer light-weight cloth which still retained the quality demanded of the name Harris Tweed; (2) in modernisation of marketing and promotional techniques and (3) in finding an effective means of protecting the Harris Tweed trade mark as Britain moved towards conformity with European trade mark law. These were the tasks to which the Harris Tweed Association turned its attention. Significant progress had been made in two of those areas by 1993 with the development of a new double-width handloom and the creation of a statutory body, the Harris Tweed Authority, in place of the Harris Tweed Association as guardian of the Orb Certification trade mark. A marketing and promotional strategy took longer to implement. Naturally, the change which impinged most closely on the lives of the weavers, the introduction of the double-width loom, was the topic which preoccupied the press. Just as the debate in 1933-34 over the amended definition of Harris Tweed and the use of mainland-spun yarn aroused controversy within the industry at that time, the introduction of the double-width loom divided those who wished to retain the old traditional method of weaving single-width cloth from those who recognised the need to adapt to market demands for a wider cloth.

Unfortunately, the late 1980s and early 1990s also saw the recession in the textile industry biting even deeper. The slump brought further contraction of the Harris Tweed manufacturing base with yet another amalgamation of major manufacturers. The lesson that interest in Harris Tweed expressed at Trade Fairs, such as Premier Vision, did not automatically translate into firm orders was driven home as sales showed no sign of improvement. Equally alarming for the HTA was the 'domino' effect of reduced stamping fees restricting the Association's budget and thus its ability to promote Harris Tweed in much needed foreign markets. In his review of 1990 presented to the Harris Tweed Association in mid-1991, the Chief Executive said,

> 'The metreage stamped for the year was one of the lowest on record at 1.38 million metres and (this) has had a consequent effect on the finances of the Association and impaired its activities to a very high degree. As a result of the downturn, further redundancies were announced by the HTA and by Kenneth Mackenzie Ltd. - and the impact on the island community was severe. However, the rest of the textile industry was going through more traumatic problems with closures, redundancies and lay-offs extending from Aberdeen through all sectors of the industry down to the British Wool Marketing Board itself where the total disbandment of the Projects Division was a major loss for the industry as a whole.' [1]

It is safe to say that without the ongoing financial support given by the HIDB, and its successor HIE, and by Comhairle nan Eilean, the Harris Tweed Association and even the industry itself might well have failed to weather the crisis.

In June 1990, despite the inauspicious commercial climate, Bruce Burns, who had retired in 1988 as Managing Director of Clansman on the grounds of 'major company policy disagreements', [2] opened a new Harris Tweed mill, Lewis and Harris Textiles, in the former Smith's mill which he leased from the then owner, Sardar Mohammed. Brave as it may have seemed, the decision to come out of retirement ended in disappointment for Bruce Burns when Lewis and Harris Textiles went into liquidation after a series of confrontations and disagreements with the HIDB over funding for his new venture, with Comhairle nan Eilean over arrears of non-domestic rates and with the Harris Tweed Authority over a number of points, including eventually the move towards double-width looms. As relations between Bruce Burns and the industry as a whole became more difficult, one of the criticisms he made was based on the fact that double-width tweed would not be eligible for the preferential tariff for single-width tweed won in the USA by the Rev. Murdoch Macrae in 1957. As market surveys had emphasised for quite some time that customers wanted a lighter softer tweed than the traditional heavy, hairy cloth favoured by sportsmen, Bruce Burns specialised in meeting that demand with his 'gossamer-weight' tweed. He was, of course, not alone in moving to meet the demand for a lightweight tweed, as the other manufacturers also produced their own versions described by names such as 'lightweight', 'bantam weight' and 'featherweight' tweed. This was a trend which made it necessary for the HTA to introduce new standards for each weight of tweed, something which was achieved in 1996.

Other veterans of the industry besides Bruce Burns suffered in the on-going recession, when in 1991 Kenneth Mackenzie Ltd. was bought over by Kenneth MacLeod (Shawbost) Ltd. In August 1989, Jock Mackenzie, Chairman of SEET, had hinted at the possibility of a merger between Island manufacturers. [3] Nothing came of this at the time. However, speculation about a merger between the two major island manufacturers came to the fore again in March 1991, when Kenneth Mackenzie Ltd. disclosed losses of £637,000 for the preceding six months. [4] Announcing 47 redundancies, Managing Director Harris Mackenzie said,

> 'For the past few years we have kept everyone on in the hope that the textile recession would end and that the American market would come back. However it is not just a textile recession now - it is a major recession. The Americans are just not buying and we make to order, we do not build up stock.' [5]

Kenneth Mackenzie's parent company SEET, was itself suffering from the recession in the textile trade with an operating loss of £1.25 million in the year to April 1992. [6] In May, 1991 Harris Mackenzie retired from the Board of SEET after twenty years service. Many months went by while SEET considered how best to tackle the problem posed to the Group by the slump in demand for Harris Tweed. Despite a slight improvement in orders which had all the mills working overtime and enabled Kenneth Mackenzie Ltd. to take on an additional 50 employees in the early months of 1992, [7] expectations of a merger between Kenneth Mackenzie Ltd. and Kenneth MacLeod (Shawbost) Ltd. gained ground. By September 1992, negotiations reached a mutually satisfactory outcome and SEET shareholders agreed to the sale of Kenneth Mackenzie Holdings Ltd. to Kenneth MacLeod (Shawbost) Ltd. Harris Mackenzie remained as Managing Director of Kenneth Mackenzie Ltd. and, according to a spokesman for Kenneth MacLeod (Shawbost) Ltd., the two mills, to be known as the KM Group, would 'continue to trade, manufacture and market their cloth independently.' [8]

While fears were expressed by such diverse interests as clothing retailers and political parties at the potentially adverse effects of the merger thus created, it was generally welcomed within the islands. Ian Angus Mackenzie, Secretary of the Weavers' Branch of the TGWU, thought that the merger would 'probably increase job opportunities as well as safeguarding existing jobs'.[9] Donald John MacKay, Chief Executive of the HTA, was pleased to see control of a large sector of the industry returning to the islands and said,

> 'In view of all the other developments taking place in Harris Tweed, an integrated strategy and policy should be to the advantage of the islands community.' [10]

Asked by the *West Highland Free Press* to comment on the merger, a spokesman for HIE replied,

> 'It's something we would generally welcome. We don't want to see any increase in manufacturing capacity: that would not help in the long term. We are trying to re-position Harris Tweed as a niche market and double-width is part of that. HIE would welcome the merger between MacLeod and Mackenzie Holdings because the industry is better focused. With all the companies together it makes sense if we're talking to one or two individuals.' [11]

To the *Stornoway Gazette*, a HIE spokesman said,

> 'In many ways, the merger reinforces the approach we are taking towards re-shaping the industry. We certainly welcome the merger because it means there is going to be less price competition within the industry. Having fewer mills producing cloth for a small market can only be to the long-term benefit of the market. It is also good that it is a local take-over and control of the industry is remaining in the Western Isles.' [12]

If these statements accurately reflected HIE policy for the Harris Tweed industry, the question arises as to whether the increased manufacturing capacity created by Bruce Burns' firm, Lewis and Harris Textiles, was, perhaps, seen as a complicating factor in the discussions between the industry and HIE. When set in an historical context, it is perhaps possible to see a certain irony in the role reversal represented by the take-over of the long-established Stornoway manufacturer by an erstwhile small producer based in rural Lewis. While the clock had not quite come full circle, the balance of power had certainly swung back to the country as opposed to the town, which had dominated the industry for so many years.

The 'integrated strategy' mentioned by the Chief Executive of the HTA and the 're-shaping of the industry' mentioned by the HIE spokesman referred to 'a five-year plan to revitalise the industry' with funding of some £10 million coming from the industry itself, from Western Isles Enterprise and from the EC. [13] Three main areas were identified as the basis of the strategy. These were meeting the market demand for a double-width cloth, finding an effective means of protecting the Harris Tweed trade mark in the European Community and in other world markets, and modernising marketing of Harris Tweed. Some years later, Duncan Martin, who was Chairman of the Development Working Party set up by the HTA to promote the new strategy, described the situation that faced the HTA Board of Management in 1990:

> 'It has to be recognised that the Harris Tweed industry was dying. Radical action had to be taken if the fate of so many other communities built round textiles was to be avoided. Many of the large-scale customers of the glory years such as Hepworths, Burtons and Dunns have gone or have changed beyond recognition. The world is no longer beating a path to our door to buy Harris Tweed. We have to change, adapt, evolve to satisfy the present day marketplace or pay the price ... In the late eighties it became apparent that the industry had severe problems which had to be addressed if there was to be any hope for the future.
>
> (1) The market was declining at an alarming rate - 80% gone in five years. The US market had virtually disappeared in 1985 and has not come back. 90% of the Canadian market went between 1985 and 1995.
>
> (2) The weaving equipment was antiquated - a nineteenth century loom providing cloth for a late 20th-century market. The quality was declining and some patterns, such as large checks, could not be sold because of inconsistency.

(3) The structure of the weaving force was a great concern - 25% over 65 and 60% over fifty. There was no recruitment of young weavers. The work was seen as drudgery and as insecure.

(4) The reputation of the cloth was suffering from the application of old standards to lighter yarns ...

It was agreed to invest in new technology, retraining and marketing. This would result in:

(1) A new double-width loom capable of producing a higher quality cloth to market specifications. The loom would be easier to operate and enable the weaver to earn more money for less effort. This would attract more young people and women into the industry.

(2) A new cloth, lighter, softer and wider which would meet customer needs and provide an opportunity to produce ladies' garments for a market that had not used Harris Tweed for many years.

(3) A retrained workforce capable of operating new looms and mill machinery to a very high standard.

(4) Finance being available for weavers and producers to invest in the new technology.

(5) A Harris Tweed Act giving better protection to the industry and new standards giving better protection to the customer.

(6) A major marketing exercise to inform the world about the new Harris Tweed which offered exciting new opportunities whilst conforming with the traditions of the industry.' [14]

The Development Working Party to promote this strategy consisted of representatives from the HTA, the Weavers' Union, the Producers, Comhairle nan Eilean, Highlands and Islands Enterprise, Western Isles Enterprise and Lews Castle College. Conscious of the problems which had frustrated the move to double-width tweed in the 1970s, the Working Party was emphatic in its commitment to the terms of the existing definition of Harris Tweed, i.e. that it should be handwoven by the weavers at their own homes from 100% new wool and spun, dyed and finished in the islands. The importance of keeping the weavers informed about the strategy was recognised and a series of nine meetings was held at which weavers were given an opportunity to ask questions about the new double-width loom. The loom, which was seen as central to the whole strategy, was expected to cost about £13,000 per loom, with weavers being expected to meet around 30% of the cost. While there was widespread support for the strategy from weavers, some people were concerned as to where they would raise their share of the cost. Donnie MacAulay, Chief Executive of Western Isles Enterprise said,

> 'It is quite understandable that weavers who have endured some lean times over the past few years do not want to be saddled with debts which they cannot repay ... Banks in the Western Isles are aware of the importance of a successful Harris Tweed industry to the islands' economy. We will be going back to discuss further what kind of flexibility would be available to help weavers.' [15]

The Development Working Party had a precedent in an earlier Loom Development Working party which had been established in 1987 to find an alternative to the Hattersley loom when spare parts, particularly axles, became difficult to get and new Hattersley looms prohibitively expensive to buy. In addition to these problems, research undertaken at Leeds University showed that a weaver using a Hattersley loom expended 10% more physical effort than a miner. Eventually, two prototype single-width looms were developed, one by WIRA (Woollen Industry Research Association) and one by John Griffith of Bonas Griffith Ltd., a Sunderland-based textile engineering company. The Bonas Griffith Interloom had several advantages over the WIRA prototype and proved to be less expensive. Besides being clean and quiet to operate, it required much less physical effort than either the Hattersley or the WIRA prototype as it was worked by a pedalling mechanism similar to that on a bicycle. The main difference from the Hattersley loom was that a flexible rapier mechanism replaced the shuttle, thus eliminating the chore of pirn-winding. Because the rapier allowed single-pick weaving, the design capability of the Interloom greatly exceeded that of the Hattersley. [16]

The single-width Bonas Griffith Interloom was going through trials at Lews Castle College in the early 1990s. So encouraging was the response to this loom that the Development Working Party decided to investigate the feasibility of modifying this single-width loom to create a double-width loom operating on the same principles. After some two years spent on development, testing and establishing specification standards, a double-width loom capable of producing a higher quality wider cloth was introduced to the industry. Although the double-width loom cost £13,000, a grant of 70% of the cost was provided, thereby reducing the weaver's financial outlay for the new loom to £3,900. A further grant of 70% was made available for expenditure on a loom shed and any improvements needed to allow access for the lorry delivering the ready-warped beam to be set into the loom. The total outlay for a weaver deciding to switch to the double-width loom was estimated at around £6000. Weavers could also apply for further help in the form of a loan of £3000 over 48 months from the Highland Fund.

While this financial package attracted a substantial number of weavers to the new loom, there were also those who were reluctant to make the change for a variety of reasons. Perhaps, with a predominantly older body of weavers it was inevitable that there would be a measure of resistance. Some weavers, who were nearing the end of their working lives, felt that it was not worth their while taking on the capital commitment. With hindsight, those who were convinced of the need for the double-width loom wonder whether a severance package for older weavers unwilling to invest in the new loom might have made the transition less painful. Among other weavers there was a perception that the double-width loom was being forced on them by the producers. After a cautious welcome for the double-width loom at the trial stages, accusations of lack of information about the new loom and about rates of pay for double-width tweeds led to a split in the ranks of the weavers.

The dissension among the weavers was particularly unfortunate as it involved a splintering of the relatively newly formed Harris Tweed Weavers Association which had been created in 1993 when a large majority of Harris Tweed weavers withdrew from the TGWU. In the late 1980s relations with the TGWU had become increasingly strained over disagreements about collection of dues, local expenses, arrears and differential rates for pensioners. The final disagreement with the TGWU was over the eligibility of weavers for an unemployed level of union fee during times of recession. [17]

Within 18 months of the formation of the HTWA, concerns about the introduction of the new double-width loom led to a meeting of weavers at which they expressed their lack of confidence in the office-bearers of the HTWA. The result of this meeting was the resignation of the HTWA office-bearers and the splintering of the HTWA into those who were whole-heartedly for the new double-width loom and those who had grave concerns about the move to double-width tweed with all its implications for the Hattersley weavers. [18] While the basis of the dispute undoubtedly lay in a quite reasonable fear of committing themselves to the expensive new technology in a cyclical industry, it was marked by all the intensity of feeling to be found in a family row. As so often happens, the intense interest of the media magnified the affair out of all proportion.

While memories of this most recent controversy are still vivid, it is worth remembering that controversy associated with change in the status quo has been a recurrent feature in the history of the Harris Tweed industry throughout its existence. As far back as the 1890s, when it became obvious that a trade mark was needed to protect the small cottage industry from passing off, the Harris merchants resisted the advice to apply for a trade mark. When the need for legal protection was eventually accepted, a number of competing interests lodged applications for a trade mark. The roots of the rivalry between Lewis and Harris as to who should share the trade mark stem from that controversy. In 1933-34, when it became necessary to amend the definition of Harris Tweed to confine all processes of manufacture to the islands, passionate feelings were evoked on all sides and the arguments over imported mainland yarn rumbled on for many years. Probably the only time when radical change evoked unanimity was when the weavers rejected the powered double-width loom in the mid-1970s. Each of these controversies was followed by a period of expansion as new sales records were established. It may well be that the latest controversy over the double-width loom will follow the same pattern of a period of upheaval followed by a period of resurgence as Harris Tweed finds new markets for the new cloth.

'A major marketing exercise' [19] was another aspect of the re-vitalisation strategy. At this point it might be helpful to make a distinction articulated by a major producer between 'promotion' and 'marketing', by describing how producers handled these two aspects of their business. Part of the long-standing problem with promoting Harris Tweed lay in the fact that while the HTA promoted the Orb and Harris Tweed in general, it did not, and legally could not, promote the tweed made by any one producer. It has always been necessary for each producer to advertise his own cloth, in addition to any general advertising of Orb-stamped Harris Tweed done by the HTA. A glance through old magazines, newspapers and Guides to the Western Isles gives a fascinating roll-call of producers, large and small, over the century when we see advertisements such as John Kennedy's *Stamped Harris only of best quality and finish*; Alexander Macaulay Jr.'s *Patterns of Tweed Submitted with Keenest Terms*; Donald MacDonald's *Harris Industries - Direct from the Cradle of the Industry*, or Newalls' *Harris Tweed - Styled with a flair for every market in the world*. It goes without saying that, in contrast to these early examples, modern advertising is highly sophisticated and alarmingly expensive! Kenneth Mackenzie Ltd., for example, employed professional advertising agents to promote their tweed for most of the twentieth century. Sometimes their promotions were mounted in conjunction with a major customer in Europe or the US. Their winning of the Queen's Award for Industry on three occasions testifies to the success of their promotional campaigns.

The way in which Harris Tweed was marketed will be less familiar to most people outside the industry. Large producers had both a Sales Director and a network of agents in all the major markets of the world. These agents were paid on commission and in addition to taking orders for Harris Tweed, their business included taking orders for a wide variety of other textiles. One of the complaints about this system was that agents did not 'push' Harris Tweed sufficiently. The other side of the story is described by Harris Mackenzie. At the start of a season the agent received a set of the producer's new patterns. The agent then took these out into the marketplace. The agent's customers were usually 'makers-up' of garments who in their turn had their own customers who bought the ready-made garments. The Sales Director of a large Harris Tweed firm often went with the agent when he called on his customers, as it was very much in the firm's interests to know exactly what the customer wanted, whether the new patterns were well-received or how they could be improved in choice of colours, weight, 'handle', etc. Vital information emerged from these contacts. Customers wanted a lighter, softer, wider cloth. Customers did not want Harris Tweed when Italian cloth was the latest fashion! This cyclical trend has been in addition to a more recent trend towards materials containing man-made fibres. If customers did not want Harris Tweed for a couple of years because they knew that it would not sell, there was nothing the agent could do to persuade them otherwise. When Harris Tweed was in fashion there was no problem - the cloth virtually sold itself - or as Duncan Martin put it, 'the world beat a path to our door'. This is the point at which we come back to promotion as the means of creating a demand for Harris Tweed! [20]

Recognition of the need for a much more pro-active approach to promotion by producers led to the establishment of the Harris Tweed Promotional Council, through which producers would promote their own cloth. Unfortunately, the HTPC was a short-lived body, mainly because of the imbalance created by the major producers, who were also competitors, having to work with each other and with the few smaller producers who were left in the industry. Although the double-width loom was introduced in the mid-1990s, a major promotional campaign had to wait until enough double-width Harris Tweed was being produced to meet orders. The object of such a campaign would be to extend the season in which orders were placed, extend the customer base by breaking into the women's wear market, and extend the product range with different weights of tweed produced to established standards for each weight. These were the priorities in the last years of the decade. In 1998 applications to Highlands and Islands Enterprise resulted in funding for promotion of double-width Harris Tweed being made available to individual producers and to the HTA.

The major achievement of the 1990s was undoubtedly the establishment of the Harris Tweed Authority. It would be true to say that the majority of the industry, and certainly the majority of the public were, and still are, unaware of the day-to-day activities of the Harris Tweed Association as it was until 1993, and of the Harris Tweed Authority, as it is now. For the very good reason that the Harris Tweed Association was all too well aware of the vulnerability of the definition of Harris Tweed until 1993, and because the activities of one predator could always be copied and surpassed by another, the innumerable instances of infringement of the Orb mark were not publicised. The ingenuity and audacity of predators beggars belief, and, if they were in foreign markets, they were not easily detected. One of the many attempts at counterfeiting successfully tackled by the HTA and its lawyers involved a company in Italy which was marketing 'Harry's Tweed'. When detected, the company applied to register the name 'Harry's Tweed' in Brazil and appealed, unsuccessfully, when the initial application for registration was refused. More often than not, the threat of legal action was enough to make predators desist. If any of them had persisted in passing off their products as Harris Tweed, the Association would have been forced to take legal action which would have incurred expenses running into six figures.

The experience with United States Customs and the Federal Trade Commission in the 1950s where doubts arose as to whether the definition of Harris Tweed was 'legally defined' and whether the words 'Harris Tweed' could be applied to tweed without the use of the Orb, had highlighted the vulnerability of the trade mark. The Hunter judgement in 1964 caused that particular crisis to fizzle out. From 1964 the definition of Harris Tweed rested on the Hunter judgement, i.e. the Harris Tweed case established that the name 'Harris Tweed' meant exactly what the definition said it did. This judgement merely created a precedent. In the opinion of Judge David Edward, who was a member of the HTA when the status of the trade mark in relation to European law came to be re-examined in the mid-1980s, that precedent was not sufficiently strong to provide permanent protection to the trade mark. The situation at the time was that the EC was engaged in the process of harmonising national trade mark laws and in the process of creating a supranational EC wide Community Mark. Anticipating the problems which might arise in relation to trade mark law in Europe, the Association's legal adviser was anxious that it should be placed beyond doubt that the HTA was master of the Orb trade mark with the words 'Harris Tweed' subjoined.

As Harris Tweed is part of a world-wide textile market, it has always been important to register (and regularly renew registrations of) the trade mark in virtually every country in the world. Unfortunately, trade mark law is extremely complex and varies from country to country. Some countries use certification marks which can specify place and/or method of production, i.e. 'origin, material, mode of manufacture of goods or performance of services, quality, accuracy or other characteristics'.[21] Other countries use Collective Marks held by producers, or by legal persons governed by public law. The idea of a mark being held by a public law body is common in Civil Law countries.[22] When presenting itself as the owner of a Certification Mark, the Harris Tweed Association had to stress its independence from the industry, but when presenting itself as the owner of a Collective Mark, it had to present itself as representative of the industry. This dichotomy involved incompatible postures and in certain circumstances could inhibit the Association from taking action against infringement of the trade mark.

By 1990, the UK was reviewing its own trade mark law with the intention of moving towards the single trade mark system for the whole European Community. As we have seen, the HTA Board members and their legal adviser were already considering how best to resolve the dilemma presented by different trade marks laws in different countries. They were also concerned that the HTA should be well-placed for the eventual introduction of collective marks. They recognised that control of the trade mark could pass to the producers if the existing Harris Tweed certification mark were to be replaced by a collective mark. While this might not seem unduly alarming at a superficial glance, Board members were well aware of the economic pressure on producers to erode the craft status of the industry. In addition, they knew that they were custodians of the Orb, not simply on behalf of the producers, but on behalf of the community of the Western Isles as a whole. They came to the conclusion that the best option was to transform the Association into a public law body (i.e. legal persons governed by public law) with statutory functions, one of which would be safeguarding the Orb trade mark.

In early 1990, a delegation consisting of the Chief Executive of the HTA, the Association's legal adviser and a representative of the HIDB met with representatives of the Department of Trade and Industry to discuss renewal of trade mark registrations and a formal appeals procedure for weavers who had been refused stamping because of applying power to their looms. It became all too clear that the DTI officials were quite unfamiliar with the HTA's reasons for believing that control of the trade mark should be retained in the hands of an independent body, rather than it going to the producers. They did not welcome the HTA's preferred option of transforming the Harris Tweed Association into a public law body and put forward a number of objections to the proposal. In order to persuade the DTI of the need for a public law body having responsibility for the trade mark, it was agreed that the HTA would prepare a submission explaining the background to the need for independent ownership of the Harris Tweed trade mark. The HIDB would prepare a submission outlining the fragile economic state of the island economy and its dependence on the Harris Tweed industry. These submissions would then be considered by the DTI. [23]

It is strange that there should be coincidental links between Harris Tweed and alcoholic beverages, Champagne in the 1960s and Scotch Whisky in the 1990s. In response to the DTI's request for a submission on the need for a statutory body to control the use of the trade mark, the HTA consulted parliamentary agents, Dyson Bell Martin and Company. These agents suggested that the Association should be advised by the expert on trade marks, who had advised Counsel on the Scotch Whisky Act, 1988. Having considered various options, the Association and its advisers decided that the best course would be to terminate the Harris Tweed Association and transmute that body into a public body under statute, with Harris Tweed being defined under UK legislation. The new body would take over responsibility for the trade marks which had previously been held by the Association. The Minutes of the Board meeting at which this decision was made, record,

> 'There were two Acts, the Scotch Whisky Act and the Seafish Industry Authority Act which could be used to create an appropriate mechanism for the protection and promotion of a Scottish product. Under this statutory mechanism should be included a statutory definition of Harris Tweed outlining the legal remedies it could undertake, an appeals procedure, provision for the dissolution of the Harris Tweed Association Ltd. and for the new Authority to be the same person, vesting the Trade Marks in the new Body and passing all the assets of the Company (the Harris Tweed Association Ltd.) to the Authority. The intention was that the Act would protect (intellectual) property in the name 'Harris Tweed', a local asset. The arguments were that Harris Tweed was a local resource, there was vested property in it for the

purposes of the legislation, it had a reputation, it had a store of goodwill which was the collective property of the community in the Western Isles ... '[24]

The effect of the submissions seems to have been to render the DTI and the Scottish Office officials more or less neutral in their attitude to the proposed legislation.

Having embarked on the path to the Harris Tweed Act, the HTA hoped that the legislation would move quickly through all the necessary procedural stages of consultation and reading of the Bill. One of the most important decisions made by the Association was to seek financial support from Comhairle nan Eilean and invite them to be joint sponsors of the Bill. The Comhairle agreed and the joint approach by both bodies greatly enhanced the prospect of success. By December 1990, a final draft of the Bill had been circulated. Although it had been hoped that the Secretary of State for Scotland would agree to be responsible for selecting members of the new Authority, the Scottish Office objected to this proposal. Eventually it was agreed that, apart from those nominated by Comhairle nan Eilean as representatives of the Council, appointments to the Authority, would be made by the Sheriff Principal of the Highlands and Islands.[25] It is this feature which makes the Authority not merely a 'legal person' but one governed by public law. At an Extraordinary General Meeting on 12 April 1991, eleven members of the Harris Tweed Association Ltd. unanimously approved the terms of the Bill, 'subject to such alterations as Parliament might think fit to make to it'.

Readings of the Bill took place in the House of Lords in early 1991, and by July, all seemed set for the Bill to have a straight run through the House of Commons by October. Because the DTI believed, wrongly as it happened, that the Bill contained an 'approximation of standards' (details of the definition and specifications for Harris Tweed), to the astonishment, not to say dismay, of the HTA and its advisers, they decreed that, under European law, it would have to be notified to the European Commission. The effect of notification meant a minimum of three months delay, possibly longer if the Commission or another Member State proposed amendments within the initial three months.[26]

Despite all the procedural difficulties encountered between 1990 and 1993, the Harris Tweed Act received the Royal Assent in July of that year. For the Harris Tweed Association, which had been the voluntary guardian of the Orb trade mark for eighty-two years, it was a major achievement to have brought into being a statutory body charged under UK law with safeguarding the industry in the years ahead. Opening the last formal meeting of the Harris Tweed Association, the Chairman, Dr. Calum MacLeod said,

> 'This meeting marks the culmination of many years of hard and devoted effort towards achieving the strategy which the Board devised between 1985 and 1988. On Tuesday, the Queen will give the Royal Assent to the Harris Tweed Act which will establish the Harris Tweed Authority. The new double-width Harris Tweed loom will be undergoing its final tests and there will be major announcements shortly about the funding package of up to £10 million which has been secured for the industry. A rewarding initiative has in major part been completed.' [27]

While the members of the Board of the HTA had reason to feel that they had prepared the ground for a new phase in the history of the industry, they had not found the panacea for all the ills which have afflicted Harris Tweed since the mid-1980s. A future generation must judge the underlying reasons for the recession in sales of Harris Tweed in the 1990s. The reasons which could be cited as having inhibited expansion at this time might include the vagaries of the textile market, trade difficulties with the US, a financial crisis in the far East or, on the domestic front, internal dissension over the double-width loom and resentment of schemes such as the Premier Weavers scheme, whereby the KM Group were accused of trying to bind weavers exclusively to working for them.

Not long before his death in July 1999, James Shaw Grant who had been a close observer of the Harris Tweed industry for over sixty years, stressed a number of features unique to the industry. Throughout its history there has been a non-commercial element, represented initially by the Countess of Dunmore and later patrons, by the Harris Tweed Association for most of the twentieth century and most recently by the Harris Tweed Authority. Those people who contributed to the protection of the industry had no personal stake in it. They gave their services voluntarily to help alleviate the economic problems of the Western Isles. Despite the fact that the Harris Tweed Association was a non-commercial - one might even say an amateur - organisation, it was a pioneer in co-operative advertising. Through its promotion of the Orb trade mark, it enabled a number of firms in competition with each other to share the same promotional advertising. Relations between the HTA and the TGWU were probably unique, and quite certainly innovative, in British industry in the 1930s. The 1934 definition would almost certainly have been destroyed if the Union had not imposed its Embargo on imported mainland yarn. At a later period, it might have been impossible to contain the temptation for weavers to use motors on their looms but for the Union's influence in backing the HTA. On the other hand there was an anomaly in the relationship between the TGWU and the weavers which made it less effective than it might have been. The TGWU was primarily representative of the employees within the mills. When one examines the function of the TGWU in relation to the self-employed weavers, the anomaly becomes quite evident. A widespread lack of understanding of the powers and function of the HTA has been mentioned. It was seen as a regulatory body which ruled the industry. In fact its powers were confined to certifying that the stamped cloth had been made in conformity with the definition, and the promotion of the cloth by advertising. The latter function brought the HTA into close consultation with the mills as producers, thereby creating the false impression that the HTA was 'the spinners' friend'.[28] It must have been difficult for the ordinary island men - and, with the exception of Mrs Mary Stewart-Mackenzie, they were all men until 1993 - who served on the HTA over the generations when they incurred the antipathy of their fellow islanders at times of controversy. The verdict on their service delivered in 1943 in the Lewis Association Report on Harris Tweed is still appropriate: 'It is, indeed, a matter of no small credit to the individuals concerned that the system worked so well'.[29]

While the amount of weaving done in Harris today bears no comparison to what it once was, the situation is perhaps not entirely bleak. A few weavers in North Harris have taken on double-width looms. A few, perhaps half a dozen, still weave single-width tweed for the Lewis mills. The most encouraging picture is to be found in Luskentyre, a small village off the main west coast road. There, a crofter-weaver set up his own business in 1991, weaving light-weight single-width Harris tweed on a Hattersley loom. Donald John Mackay weaves the tweeds on commission for tailoring outlets, and internet customers, using yarn bought from one of the Lewis mills. This business has built up a good reputation with its tartans and brightly coloured tweeds, perhaps the most innovative of these being a white tweed used for a bride's coat and dress at a winter wedding. This unique bridal outfit and an exciting range of children's wear have been designed by Lyndsay Johnson in Glasgow and produced in Harris by Leslie and Fiona Trotter who came to live in Tarbert, specifically to create their range of clothing in Harris Tweed.

Yet the existence of a one-man business in Harris and of the remaining Lewis mills, the KM Group and Donald MacLeod Carloway, can hardly be seen as the new dawn of Harris Tweed which the HTA Development Working Party envisaged. Perhaps it is a miracle that Harris Tweed has survived at all when so many other well-known textile names have disappeared, as British manufacturing industry goes through an industrial revolution that has yet to be resolved. During the 1990s the HTA, Comhairle nan Eilean, HIE and the EC demonstrated their commitment to restructuring the industry for the future. The last link in that restructuring process must surely lie within the industry itself. At the end of the twentieth century, the name 'Harris Tweed' is still known and respected across the world, but that situation will not last indefinitely unless a concerted effort is made, and sustained, by all concerned with the industry to keep the name and reputation of Harris Tweed before those who matter most of all - the customers.

Reference - The Harris Tweed Act: The Industry in the 1990s

1 HTA Minutes, 12. 7. 1991.
2 *West Highland Free Press*, 8. 6. 1990.
3 *ibid.*
4 *ibid.*, 9. 3. 1991.
5 *Stornoway Gazette,* 16. 3. 1991.
6 *West Highland Free Press*, 25. 9. 1992.
7 HTA Minutes, 10. 4. 1992.
8 *West Highland Free Press*, 25. 9. 1992.
9 *ibid.*
10 *ibid.*
11 *ibid.*
12 *Stornoway Gazette,* 26. 9. 1992.
13 *ibid.*, 24. 7. 1993.
14 Report by Duncan Martin, Chairman HTA, to Western Isles 'Economy in Crisis Conference'. [hereafter:' Economy in Crisis Conference'].
15 *West Highland Free Press*, 30. 7. 1993.
16 *Stornoway Gazette,* 9. 3. 1991.
17 From correspondence between Ian A. Mackenzie of the Harris Tweed Weavers' Association and W. Queen of the TGWU, Transport House, Glasgow, 31. 5. 1993.
18 Interview with D. Morrison, Ealigro, Bragar, Isle of Lewis. 1995.
19 Economy in Crisis Conference.
20 Interview with Harris Mackenzie of KM Group, 1995.
21 Current Law Statutes: Trade Marks Act, 1994, 26/49-50.
22 Information from J. A. McLean, Burness, Edinburgh. (HTA Solicitors).
23 HTA Minutes, 30. 3. 1990.
24 *ibid.*, 15. 6. 1990.
25 *ibid.*, 7. 12. 1990.
26 Copy of Supplementary Report of the Secretary of State for Scotland on the Harris Tweed Bill, 12. 7. 1991, included in HTA Minutes of 12. 7. 1991.
27 HTA Minutes, 16. 7. 1993.
28 James Shaw Grant to the author, July 1999.
29 Lewis Association *Report No. 2, The Harris Tweed Industry*, 46.

Appendix

1. The stipulations listed by Colonel Radnor on 21st April 1960 inhibited the Harris Tweed Association from:

    1. Representing that the Association was an impartial certifying organization not connected with any producer of the tweed it certified nor interested in the production or marketing of the fabrics it certified;

    2. Representing that the tweed cloth which the Association certified was the only genuine 'Harris Tweed' cloth and entitled to be described as such;

    3. Representing that the Association had exclusive right to use the term 'Harris Tweed' in connection with woollen fabrics and that use of the term 'Harris Tweed' without its authority was an infringement of any trademark or certification mark which it had registered in the United States Patent Office;

    4. Threatening to sue persons, firms and associations for infringement of its trademark or certification mark because of the use of the term 'Harris Tweed' in connection with woollen fabrics;

    5. Representing that as a British corporation it had been designated as the sole organisation to determine what was genuine 'Harris Tweed' and to certify fabrics as 'Harris Tweed';

    6. Representing that any definition which the Association had established in connection with its symbol trademark or certification mark had been adopted as the definition of the common descriptive term 'Harris Tweed' by the British Board of Trade or any governmental or regulatory agency of the British Government;

    7. Executing licensing or other agreements for the use of its trademark or certification mark, or continuing in effect provisions of existing agreements, which obligated the parties

thereto not to display, advertise or sell as 'Harris Tweed' any fabric which had not been approved or certified or which did not meet the definition which it had adopted as the basis for its certification;

8. Representing that the descriptive term 'Harris Tweed' was an integral part of the Association's trademark.
(Enclosure with letter from Jess C. Radnor to Andrew Graham 21. 4. 1960. HRA/D190/ 1n [i].)

2. The fourteen Orb-producers were: (1) A. Macaulay (Tweeds) Ltd., (2) James Macdonald Ltd., (3) Kenneth Mackenzie Ltd., (4) Kenneth MacLeod (Shawbost) Ltd., (5) S. A. Newall & Sons, Ltd., (6) Harris Handwoven Tweed Co. Ltd., (7) Stephen Burns Ltd., (8) MacLeod's Tweed Co. Ltd., 60 North Shawbost, (9) Angus MacLeod of Park House Marybank, (10) John MacLeod & Co., of 23 New Shawbost, (11) Alexander Morrison of Glenside, Gravir, (12) Angus Nicolson of 39 Inaclete Rd., Stornoway, (13) Seaforth Harris Tweeds Ltd., of 81 Seaforth Rd, Stornoway, (14) David Tolmie & Co. Ltd., of 7 Francis St, Stornoway.)

Bibliography

(i) Manuscript Sources
(ii) Newspapers and Periodicals
(iii) Cases
(iv) Contemporary Printed Sources
(v) Acts of Parliament and Subordinate Legislation

(i) Manuscript Sources

Highland Regional Archive

HRA/D190. Harris Tweed Association Records, 1851-1963.
These records include Court Records, Transcripts of Evidence, Proofs and Interrogatories, Solicitors' and Counsels' papers not part of the Court proceedings, Correspondence Files, Financial Records, Yarn Supply Records, Shipment Records, Publications, Advertising Material, Photograph Albums and Samples and Specimens of yarn and Harris Tweed.

Harris Tweed Association (since 1993, Harris Tweed Authority) papers

Minutes of Meetings of the Committee of Management of the Harris Tweed Association, 1958-1993, which have been used extensively throughout the book.

Memoranda and Articles of Association of the Harris Tweed Association Ltd.

Unclassified Files of correspondence, Stamping records, Minutes of meetings with sections of the Harris Tweed industry, copies of Trade Mark Acts, Reports of Court Cases, Reports from the HTA Secretary, press cuttings, and other miscellaneous documents.

Some of this material is duplicated in the Harris Tweed Association Records, 1851-1963 in Highland Regional Archive.

Among the papers in the possession of the Harris Tweed Association, were four typescript histories of the Harris Tweed Industry prepared by John S. Gwatkin of McKenna & Co. for the Harris Tweed Case. As extensive use has been made of these, in particular of Gwatkin's 'Notes on the Historical Development of the Harris Tweed Industry and the Part Played by the Harris Tweed Association Ltd.', in piecing the story together, the typescripts are listed below in what appears to be chronological order.

1. 'Report on Visit to Lewis and Harris', 8. 9. 1960. The Report is clearly an account of John Gwatkin's first meetings with potential witnesses who might be called on to give evidence on the industry in the High Court proceedings.

2. The Harris Tweed Controversy, 1946-60. This is a summary of the issues surrounding the use of mainland spun-yarn and the controversy as to what was entitled to be called 'Harris Tweed'.

3. 'The Art of Making Harris Tweed'. This undated typescript is a preliminary draft of typescript No. 4 as can be seen from the verbatim use of long sections in both documents. It would appear to have been drafted at the end of 1960 or the beginning of 1961.

4. 'Notes on the Historical Development of the Harris Tweed Industry and the Part Played by the Harris Tweed Association Ltd.'. This typescript was signed 'J. S. G., McKenna & Co., London, 10. 3. 1961'. From the concluding paragraphs the 'memorandum' appears to have been prepared as a briefing for Counsel in the Scottish proceedings. It has been invaluable in supplying an intimate history of events which have not been recorded in such detail elsewhere.

In Private Hands

NRA(S) Survey, No 3253, Dunmore Papers. Rodel Papers, Section II, bundles 7, 31, 32, 33, 37 and 54. (The papers are in the care of Lady Anne Dunmore. Permission to search the papers was given through General Register House, Edinburgh.)

Angus MacLeod, Marybank, Stornoway 'Community Talk: Notes on the Harris Tweed Industry'.

(ii) Newspapers

Bulletin
Bulletin of the RTSA
Daily Mail
Daily News Record (USA Textile Trade Journal)
Daily Record
Glasgow Herald
Highland News
Inverness Advertiser
Overseas Daily Mail
People's Journal
Scotsman
Stornoway Gazette
West Highland Free Press

(iii) Cases

Crofter Hand Woven Harris Tweed Co. Ltd. and Others v. Veitch and Another 1940 SC 140; 1942 SC (HL)1; [1942] AC 435.

J. Bollinger and Others v The Costa Brava Wine Co. Ltd. [1961] RPC No. 5, 116.

Macaulay (A.) (Tweeds) Ltd. & Others v. Independent Harris Tweed Producers Ltd. [1961] RPC No. 8 184.

Argyllshire Weavers Ltd. and Others v. A. Macaulay (Tweeds) Ltd. and Others 1962 SLT 25.

Argyllshire Weavers Ltd. and Others v. A. Macaulay (Tweeds) Ltd. and Others 1962 SLT 310.

Argyllshire Weavers Ltd. and Others v. A. Macaulay (Tweeds) Ltd. and Others 1965 SLT 21.

Argyllshire Weavers Ltd. and Others v. A. Macaulay (Tweeds) Ltd. and Others [1964] RPC No. 16 477-592.

(iv) Contemporary Printed Sources: Reports, Books and Articles

Bremner, David, *The Industries of Scotland: their Rise, Progress and Present Condition,* Edinburgh, 1869.

Cameron, Ewen, *Land for the People? The British Government and the Scottish Highlands, c. 1880-1925,* East Lothian, 1996.

Crawford, Douglas, 'Harris Tweed: the crucial years' in *Scotland,* June, 1967.

Department of Labour and National Service, *Report of Committee of Investigation on the Causes of the Dispute Involving Weavers in the Harris Tweed Industry in the Island of Lewis*, London, May, 1943.

Drysdale, John & Silverleaf, Michael, *Passing off: law and practice*, London, 1995.

Geddes, Arthur, 'Resources and Prospects of the Isles of Lewis and Harris : Harris Tweed 1', Reprinted, from *Stornoway Gazette,* by arrangement with Outlook Tower Association, Castlehill Edinburgh. 1954-55.

Geddes, Arthur, *The Isle of Lewis and Harris: A Study in British Community,* Edinburgh, 1955.

Harris Tweed Authority, Report by Duncan Martin, Chairman Harris Tweed Authority, to Western Isles 'Economy in Crisis' Conference, March 1998.

Harris Tweed Authority, The Harris Tweed Working Party: A strategy for Re-Development, 1993.

Hetherington, Peter, 'Business wears thin for Harris Tweed', in *The Guardian,* 16. 8. 1982.

Highlands and Islands Development Board, Report by David Rigby Associates on 'The Harris Tweed Industry - A marketing Strategy for the Future', February, 1989.

Highlands and Islands Development Board, Report by INBUCON/AIC Management Consultants Ltd. on 'The Implications of Producing Harris Tweed on Double Width Powered Looms', Vol. 1, Summary of Conclusions and Recommendations, 1975.

Hunter, James, (ed.) *For the people's Cause: The Writings of John Murdoch,* Edinburgh, 1986.

Knox, John, *Tour through the Highlands of Scotland, and the Hebride Isles,* 1787.

Lawson, Bill, *Harris Families and how to trace them,* Northton, Isle of Harris, 1990.

Lawson, Bill, *St Clement's Church at Rodel,* 1991, Northton, Isle of Harris.

Lawson, Bill, *The Teampull at Northton and the Church at Scarista,* Northton, Isle of Harris, 1993.

Lewis Association *Report, No. 2: The Harris Tweed Industry,* Stornoway, 1944.

Lucas, W. G., 'Crucial Year for Harris Tweed Industry', in *Press and Journal,* 23. 1. 1976.

Lucas, W. G., 'Harris Tweed industry's new production record', in *Scotsman,* 23. 1. 1976.

MacDonald, Finlay J. *Crowdie and Cream,* London, 1982.

MacKenzie, W.C., *History of the Outer Hebrides,* 1903, Paisley. Reprinted Edinburgh, 1974.

Moisley, H. A., 'Harris Tweed: A Growing Highland Industry', *Economic Geography* 37, No. 4., 1961.

Morrison,. A., 'Harris Estate Papers, 1724-54,' *Transactions of the Gaelic Society of Inverness,* XLV, 1967.

Murray, Norman, *The Scottish Handloom Weavers, 1790-1850: a social history,* Edinburgh, 1978.

Newall, F. J., *The Story of Lewis and Harris Homespuns,* c. 1922.

Nicolson, Nigel, *Lord of the Isles: Lord Leverhulme in the Hebrides,* London, 1960.

Report of the Commission of Inquiry into the Condition of the Crofters and Cottars of the Highlands and Islands of Scotland 1884. (Napier Commission).

Report to the Board of Agriculture for Scotland on Home Industries in the Highlands and Islands, 1914, Edinburgh, HMSO (Scott Report).

Ruskin, John, *The Works of John Ruskin,* 13 vols. London, Chesterfield Society, 1904-1906.

Scottish Council on Industry, *Report of the Committee on the Crofter Woollen Industry,* Edinburgh, 1946.

Scottish Home Industries, *Faladhna Dùthchasach na h-Alba,* c. 1895.

Stevenson, John, 'Price-Fixing', in *The History Today Companion to British History,* (eds.) Juliet Gardiner and Neil Wenborn, London, 1995.

(v) Acts of Parliament and Subordinate Legislation

Statutory Rules and Orders, 1947/No. 2639. Goods and Services (Price Control) Apparel and Textiles. The General Apparel and Textile (Manufacturers Maximum Prices and Charges) Order, 1947.

Harris Tweed Act 1993.

Trade Marks Act 1994.

Index